Bright Stars, Dark Trees, Clear Water

BRIGHT STARS ·
· DARK TREES
CLEAR WATER ·

*Nature Writing from
North of the Border*

SELECTED & EDITED BY
Wayne Grady

NONPAREIL
BOOKS

A Nonpareil Book
David R. Godine, Publisher
BOSTON

A Nonpareil Original

First published in the U.S. in 1999 by
DAVID R. GODINE, PUBLISHER
Box 450
Jaffrey, New Hampshire 03452

Originally published in different form by Douglas & McIntyre,
Vancouver, Canada, in 1992.

Library of Congress Cataloging-in-Publication Data

Bright stars, dark trees, clear water : nature writings from north of
the border / selected and edited by Wayne Grady.
p.   cm. — (A Nonpareil book)
"Originally published in different form by Douglas & McIntyre, Vancouver,
Canada, in 1992"—T.p. verso.
ISBN 1-56792-019-5
1. Natural history—Canada. 2. Nature.   I. Grady, Wayne.
II. Series.
QH106.B75   1995
508.71—dc20   96-10840
                                                              CIP

Design by Barbara Hodgson
Typeset by The Typeworks
Printed on acid-free paper

First U.S. edition
Printed in Canada

FOR MIKE: *A Table of greene fields*

Contents

Introduction

ONE MORNING LAST spring, I watched two muskrats in a shallow pond about thirty feet from the front of our cabin. It was mid-April, the ice had just gone off the pond, and the muskrats seemed to be celebrating the fact: there was a bright clump of lily spears at the edge of the water, and the male would swim over to it, pull up a shoot with his webbed forepaws and feed it straight into his mouth like a pencil into a pencil sharpener, probably the first green food he had had since freeze-up last fall. His mate would swim up to him, touch his nose with hers, then turn abruptly and swim off across the pond, whereupon he would drop his lily shoot and chase off after her, swimming with his own nose close to the base of her smooth, round tail. As I watched, they did this three or four times, then at some point the female stopped to chew on something in shallow water, and the male began vigorously grooming the sleek, wet fur on her back, standing beside her, raising himself on his hind legs and rummaging through her fur as though frantically searching for something valuable he had dropped in it. When he had completed messing up her fur, he smoothed it again: then he climbed up on her back, padded around for a few seconds with all four feet, and then slid head-first down her back into the water and swam away.

Watching this spring ritual, I was aware that I was involved in it on several different levels at the same time. First of all, I *was* involved in it; any time there is an observer and an observed, the two are bound together in a sort of mutual interperformance. Linguistically we've lost this sense in English, but the French still have it: to watch a parade in French is *participer à une parade,* to participate in it, which must make life hell for French anthropologists who have to insist that their presence at the tribal feast did not affect its authenticity. I think that this engagement is especially acute when it is nature that is being engaged, for there is no glass wall, no two-way mirror, between nature and us; we *are* nature. As Roderick Haig-Brown put it, "It may seem strange to write of observation as participation, but no man is solely an observer of the natural world . . . We are all basically hunters or gatherers, gleaners or predators, we all feel the weather in our face at times, and the things that stir and change about us stir within us also."

But I wasn't thinking about that so much while I was watching the muskrats. I was thinking that most of the muskrats I'd seen before had been in the form of pelts hanging from the rafters of a friend's skinning shed, the skins fitted neatly over their wooden stretchers and hung up to dry like so many furry socks, and that if the bottom hadn't fallen out of the fur market a few years ago these two frolicking rodents probably wouldn't have made it through the winter. The thought of rodents made me realize how closely muskrats resemble their near cousins, the beavers; in fact, when I'd first seen them I'd had to wait until they showed their tails before I could be completely sure they weren't juvenile beavers. Then I began to wonder whether the spring run-off would lower their pond (*their* pond?) too much to accommodate their lodge; not being beavers, they wouldn't have built a dam.

I was thus participating in this human-muskrat exchange on at least three different time levels—past, present and future—as well as on several intellectual planes, and not a few emotional ones as well. There have been many attempts to codify these various levels of appreciating nature, as if each level were separate and distinct, and moving from one to another represented some form of advance, a graduation from mere observation to knowledge.

Thus Thomas H. Huxley, the 19th-century biologist (Aldous's grandfather, Darwin's bulldog in England as John Burroughs was in the United States), distinguished three rungs on the ladder to wisdom: Natural History, which he defined as "accurate, but necessarily incomplete and unmethodized knowledge," which is obviously the rung from which I was watching my muskrats (*my* muskrats?); Natural Philosophy, the organizing or systematizing of nature (Linnaeus' passion for order, for example, in which the muskrat is *Ondatra zibethicus*); and Natural Science, "this final stage of knowledge, [in which] the phenomena of nature are regarded as one continuous series of causes and effects," the level on which, I suppose, one would spend a year or two writing a paper with a title like: "Courtship and Mating Behavior Patterns and Semiochemistry in *Ondatra zibethicus.*"

Writing about the same time as Huxley (who died in 1895), John Burroughs pointed out the deficiency in Huxley's cosmology: even advancing to the level of Natural Science gets us only part of the way to nature. "Wordsworth's poet," he wrote in "The Art of Seeing Things," "was contented if he might enjoy the things which others understood. This is generally the atti-tude of the young and of the poetic nature. The man of science, on the other hand, is contented if he may understand the things that others enjoy; that is his enjoyment. Contemplation and absorption for the one; investigation and classification for the other." Either way, he said, "to know is not all; it is only half. To love is the other half." You don't have to be a scientist to participate as I did in a display of muskrat exuberance, or to notice how, at seven o'clock on a late fall evening, the sun suddenly pushes through a bank of heavy clouds to illuminate only the birch trees in a forest. But you do have to love.

At first thought, the love of nature shouldn't differ greatly from any other kind of love, from the romantic to the religious: it is a kind of abnegation of the self, a devotion, and at the same time a yearning for betterment, an uplift-ing of the spirit. "With our sense applied to the surrounding world," Thoreau wrote in his *Journal* on June 21, 1852, "we are reading our own physical and corresponding moral revolutions." He meant that the cycles of nature mirror the changes we ourselves undergo as individuals, as a society, as a species: we are nature. Love of nature is love of ourselves. Emerson thought we couldn't love anything until we learned to love nature. Nature to him was the funda-mental basis of all human activity, including love:

> Nature, uncontainable, flowing, forelooking, in the first sentiment of kindness anticipates already a benevolence which shall lose all particular regards in its general light. The introduction to this felicity is in a private and tender relation of one to one, which is the enchantment of human life; which, like a certain divine rage and enthusiasm, seizes on man at one period and works a revolution in his mind and body; unites him to his race, pledges him to the domestic and civic relations, carries him with new sympathy into nature, enhances the power of the senses, opens the imagination, adds to his character heroic and sacred attri-butes, establishes marriage and gives permanence to human society."

Increased engagement with nature produces not only an increase in knowl-edge; it also produces wonder. The paleontologist Dale Russell once told me that "science is the means by which we proceed from what we think we know to what we think we don't know." We begin in wonder, he said, move through knowledge, and then move back into wonder again. In *Journey Into Wonder*, Canadian scientist N. J. Berrill traces the development of the North American imagination from that of the explorer (*exploiter*) to that of the nat-uralist (*engager*). He quotes the 16th century mariner Richard Hawkins, "lying with a fleet of her majesties ships about the islands of the Azores, al-most six months; the greatest part of the time we were becalmed: with which all the sea became so replenished with several sorts of jellies, and formes of serpents, adders, and snakes, as seemed wonderful; some green, some black, and some there were a yard and a half, and two yards long; which had I not seen, I could hardly have believed."

"With this mind awake," Berrill writes, Hawkins "was lost in wonder." But he was no nature writer. Few of the early exploiters were. The first recorded European sighting of what is now Canada is in Bjarni Harjulfsen's account in the *Greenlandinga Saga* of being blown off-course while trying to reach his fa-ther's farmstead on the west coast of Greenland, in the year 985 or 986. If Bjarni and his crew were lost in wonder as well as in fact, they did not record it. Labrador is described as "a country that was not mountainous, but was well wooded and with low hills." They did not actually go ashore, and to my mind it takes a certain amount of experience to balance the innocence of nature. As Canada's first tourist, Bjarni may have been underwhelmed because he came from Norway, a country whose landscape is very similar to that of Canada's northeast coast. A few years ago, I spent a month flying over Newfoundland and Labrador, doing research into sea-ice composition along the Atlantic coastline, and then later flew to Tromsø, at the northernmost tip of Norway, to join an ice-science research vessel heading, like Bjarni himself, into the Greenland Sea. As the plane passed over Norway's deep fjords and high, glac-ier-scoured mountains, its lichen-covered plateaux and grazing reindeer herds, I had the uncanny feeling that I had been tricked, that the plane had simply taken off from Labrador, circled above the clouds for seven or eight hours, and was now landing again in Labrador.

Five hundred years after Bjarni, John Cabot sailed to Labrador, following the northern Iceland-to-Vinland sea route taken by Bjarni's successor, Thorfinnr Karlsefni. Cabot thought he had found the land belonging to the Great Khan, and claimed to have discovered the route to Cipango, now called Japan. Accounts of his two voyages come to us secondhand, mostly from his son, Sebastian, who claimed to have made the journey himself. Perhaps be-cause Sebastian was lying, there is not much nature writing in his account. The Paris World Map of 1544, however, contains a description of the New World probably derived from Sebastian:

It is a very sterile land. There are in it many white bears, and very large stags like horses, and many other animals; and likewise there is infinite fish, sturgeons, salmon, very large soles a yard long, and many other kinds of fish, and the greater number of them are called baccallaos; and likewise there are in the same land hawks black like crows, eagles, partridges, linnets, and many other birds of different kinds.

But this reads more like a shopping list than nature writing. Thomas Best's narrative of Martin Frobisher's three voyages to the east coast of Canada is no more wonderful. Best accompanied Frobisher on all three voyages, noting on the second (1577) that the seas around North Foreland (Hall Island) were "thickly covered with huge slabs of drifting ice" (Leif Erickson had called this area Slabland). When Frobisher and his men went ashore, they saw "a large dead fish that had apparently been trapped in the ice. In proportion, it was round like a porpoise, about twelve feet long and of a corresponding bulk, having a horn two yards long grown out of its snout or nostril. The horn is wreathed and straight like a wax taper and the beast may truly be looked upon as a sea unicorn." The passage is accompanied by a drawing of what is clearly a narwhal *(Monodon monoceras),* and though Best's description ended Denmark's lucrative sale of narwhal tusks as "unicorn horns" in Europe, which they had been controlling since the Middle Ages, it is not nature writing.

The early explorers were not all that interested in nature except as a commodity to be exploited or a foe to be subdued, or both. Kirkpatrick Sale, in *The Conquest of Paradise,* calls this attitude "ecohubris," the overweening presumption that God gave humankind dominion over the animal kingdom, a classification that included heathens and infidels. Say what you like about Columbus marvelling at the lusciousness of the West Indies, he declined to drop anchor at his first landfall because, as he wrote in his log, the island did not look as though it had gold on it. When he did land, on a more promising-looking island he named San Salvador, the curious natives who wandered down to the shore to watch him and his men erect Europe's first gifts to the New World—a cross and a scaffold—were grabbed by Columbus's men and taken back to Spain as slaves. Gold and profits.

Canada has its own versions of this theme. Martin Frobisher, thwarted in his desire to find gold on his first voyage to the arctic in 1576, but still "very anxious to carry home some token of his having been to a newly discovered land," decided to capture one of the natives who had paddled close to his ship. Using a small ship's bell as a lure, reports Best, Frobisher enticed one of the natives to the ship's side, whereupon "the captain suddenly dropped the bell, grabbed the man, and plucked him out of the sea by main force, boat and all, and into the ship. When he found himself in captivity, the man was so overcome with anger and disdain that he bit his tongue in twain within his mouth." No better symbol comes to mind of the terrible consequences of ecohubris, and the ensuing silence of the native peoples from whom we might have learned how to live in this land.

Samuel de Champlain came to New France (now Quebec) with a similar agenda, capturing natives to use as interpreters, taking them back to Europe as souvenirs. As for the land he was visiting, he assessed everything he saw in terms of its usefulness. On his first voyage (1603), he stopped at a spot about 50 miles up the St. Lawrence river from the present site of Quebec City, and noted there was

> a break in the hills at that point and on either side the land rises sharply. Otherwise the country thereabouts is flat and the soil richer than I had seen elsewhere. It is all densely wooded, though I didn't see much fir or cypress. There are plenty of grapes, pears, hazel-nuts, cherries, currants, and gooseberries. They also have certain small roots, the size of a nut, that taste like truffles and are very good either roasted or boiled. The soil is black and apart from the slate, which is very common, it hasn't many rocks or stones in it. It's easy to turn and if it were properly worked I'm sure it would yield a satisfactory return.

The earliest voyages of discovery did not produce nature writing for the same reason that most corporate board meetings do not produce poetry: it was not their job. The job of Columbus and Frobisher and Cabot and Champlain was to discover the New World and report back to their financial supporters that there was here a "satisfactory return" on their investments. It is true that, given a different European attitude toward nature, which in effect means a different Europe, discovering a New World, a real-life Arcadia, in which man lived un-differentiated from nature, could have been their job. But it wasn't. "Missed in the dynamics of the assumed right of colonialism," writes Sale, "was an ex-traordinary opportunity for a dispirited and melancholy Europe to have learned something about fecundity and regeneration, about social comeliness and amity, about harmony with the natural world."

Harmony with nature can be frightening, if you're not prepared for it. I re-member lying on my back on a south-facing hillside beside the cabin, in the warm spring sunshine, looking up into the sky at a line of Canada geese heading north. They were high up there, who knows how high, but I could hear them honking with every wingbeat, the effort of pushing their wings against the air forcing the breath out of their lungs in a series of involuntary grunts. As the geese passed, I noticed that they did not fly in a V, as everyone inevitably supposes they do, but had rallied into a kind of stylized check-mark formation, five or six on one side of the wedge, and two hundred on the other side, with a second small wedge of five or six at the tail, like the feathered flights at the notched end of a long, noisy arrow. Geese do like pointed letters, though. One earlier morning my daughter, who was four at the time, watching a flight of geese passing overhead, had turned to me and said, "Look, Dad, a perfect double-you!"

These geese flew by very swiftly, and when they were gone their flight path was crossed by a solitary great blue heron, silently cruising the length of the valley in which I was lying. Although flying much lower down, its enormous wings moved in mesmerizing slow motion. Something about the sudden silence and the rhythm of the heron's wings flipped a switch in my brain, and I felt myself being drawn up toward the heron, up into the sky. It was a kind of inverse vertigo, like looking down from a canoe into the reflection of sky; I no longer knew whether I was looking up or down, only that I was about to fall, that I had to press my shoulders into the earth to stop myself from plunging into space. When the heron was gone, my heart was racing, blood roared in my ears, and my shoulders ached.

Much has been made of the differences between American and Canadian literature, and these differences are often attributed to our different experiences of nature. In his contribution to the *Literary History of Canada* (1965), critic Northrop Frye noted that explorers and immigrants to the United States were greeted by a warm, benign, friendly coastline, with luscious deciduous trees and tantalizing grapevines; Canada, by way of contrast, "has, for all practical purposes, no Atlantic seaboard. The traveller from Europe edges into it like a tiny Jonah entering an inconceivably large whale, slipping past the Strait of Belle Isle into the Gulf of St. Lawrence, where five Canadian provinces surround him, for the most part invisible . . . To enter the United States is a matter of crossing an ocean; to enter Canada is a matter of being silently swallowed by an alien continent."

Certainly Frye's image strikes a familiar cord; more than one traveller has been apprehensive about entering the jaws of the St. Lawrence. Louis Hémon, for example, came to Canada in 1911, "in search of easy generalizations," as he wrote in his *Journal*. His first view of North America was of Anticosti Island, several hundred miles inland, "an interminable coast, low, brown, distant, which the fog reveals and conceals, as if playing a game." As his ship felt its way upriver in the fog, Hémon could only "feel the proximity of the two shores of the gulf of St. Lawrence—shores which are always out of sight, but which close in upon us hourly." Hémon compared his experience with that of earlier immigrants approaching the United States, and found it was not so different:

> It is, doubtless, in drawing towards Quebec or Montreal that one recovers most easily and most exactly the state of mind of the *déracinés* who saw New York Bay open before them a hundred years ago. Those who, approaching the city today, watch the Statue of Liberty and the mass of the skyscrapers loom up, can have very different impressions only, because the first aspect offered them by America is that of one city among others, and no longer the primitive, striking aspect of the empty country they are going to reclaim and to fill.

This sense of being swallowed up by a hungry continent, like that of inverse vertigo I felt watching the heron, can produce a fear of nature, can blur the fine line between the awesome and the awful. It can lead to what Frye called a "garrison mentality" to be found in much Canadian literature—a reinforcement of the European idea that nature is sinister, threatening, something to be tamed and exploited rather than embraced. According to Frye, the Canadian imagination developed as a fear-response to nature: just as we built physical fortresses within which we could be safe from nature, so we also developed psychological fortresses against nature. Margaret Atwood extends Frye's thesis in her survey of Canadian literature, *Survival* (1970): "Not surprisingly in a country with such a high ratio of trees, lakes and rocks to people, images from Nature are almost everywhere. Added up, they depict a Nature that is often dead and unanswering or actively hostile to man."

But Frye's fear-of-nature thesis only partly explains the Canadian attitude toward nature, and overemphasizes the difference between the American and Canadian response to wilderness. Perhaps I'm being too literal minded, but many Americans built garrisons (think of those encircled wagon trains, and all those Cavalry stockades), and many Canadians did not. Many Americans feared nature, and some did not find the eastern seaboard as benign as Frye says it was: American nature writer John Hay describes it, for example, as "an almost impenetrable shore line confronting a few men in a wooden ship." And Barry Lopez employs the term "theriophobia," or fear of the beast, to explain why there has been such a determined effort in the United States as well as in Canada to exterminate such predators as wolves, coyotes, grizzlies and cougars. "At the heart of theriophobia," he writes in *Of Wolves and Men,* "is the fear of one's own nature." This sounds very like Frye's comment that our "deep terror in regard to nature . . . is not a terror of the dangers or discomforts or even the mysteries of nature, but a terror of the soul at something that these things manifest."

But there is very little in the way of terror in the journals of David Thompson or Samuel Hearne or Alexander Mackenzie, or some of the later explorers who "opened up" the continent for the fur trade. What there is is a continuous wonder at the vastness and splendor of the Canadian wilderness. Here is Hearne's description of the timber wolf: "They always burrow underground to bring forth their young," he writes, "and though it is natural to suppose them very fierce at those times, yet I have frequently seen the Indians go to their dens, and take of the young ones and play with them. I never knew a Northern Indian to hurt one of them: on the contrary, they always put them carefully into the den again; and I have sometimes seen them paint the faces of the young Wolves with vermillion, or red ochre." Is this theriophobia?

My sense is that in both the United States and Canada, familiarity with nature bred respect. As Hémon suggested in his *Journal,* Canadians and Americans shared a similar experience of nature, only a hundred years apart. Once newcomers to Canada realized they were not sailing up the backside of Asia, they calmed down and took a good look around, and generally liked what they saw. Settlers' diaries and letters home are full of glowing descriptions of the Canadian landscape (though it didn't stop them from changing it irrevocably). Hémon died in 1913, struck from behind by a locomotive while walking along a railroad track in northern Ontario. He was not afraid of the bush; but he would have done better to fear the locomotive. Frye and Atwood point to Susanna Moodie's perpetual battle with the encroaching Ontario woods, but if they had not been so exclusively concerned with fiction and poetry, which they understand to be the sole products of the creative imagination, they might have looked to the nature writers for an alternative paradigm.

If they had, they would not have had to look any farther than to Susanna Moodie's sister, Catharine Parr Traill. Like Moodie, Traill emigrated to Canada and lived with her husband on a farm near Lakefield, Ontario. She is best known for *The Backwoods of Canada* (1836), a collection of letters to her mother back in Suffolk, England: "How often," she writes, "do I wish you were beside me in my rambles among the woods and clearings: you would be so delighted in searching out the floral treasures of the place." But she also wrote *Studies of Plant Life in Canada,* a botanical text that earned her an international reputation as a natural scientist. Her memoir, *Pearls and Pebbles: or, Notes of an Old Naturalist* (1894), published when she was ninety-four years old, is a testament to a lifetime of intimacy with the natural landscape. Traill embraced her new surroundings, strove to understand and describe them, and saw in the riot of nature an invitation to wonder rather than a dark tangle of Jungian turmoil. She engaged nature at its deepest level.

Frye's garrison mentality works fine as long as we look only at poets and novelists, but it breaks down when we begin to consider nature writing as an expression of the creative imagination. Garrisons do not produce much nature writing—you have to get out into nature and give yourself to it. Archibald Lampman's reputation as a nature poet rests on stanzas such as this one, from "An Ode to the Hills," written in 1899:

> The fierce things of the wild
> Find food and shelter in yon tenantless rocks.
> The eagle on whose wings the dawn hath smiled,
> The loon, the wild-cat, and the bright-eyed fox;
> For far away indeed
> Are all the ominous noises of mankind,
> The slaughterer's malice and the trader's greed:
> Your rugged haunts endure no slavery:
> No treacherous hand is there to crush or bind,
> But all are free.

This may sound like nature writing, but it is not. I think of it more as travel poetry, in the sense Frye meant when he wrote that "travellers visit Canada much as they would visit a zoo." No nature writer would have written that "the slaughterer's malice" was "far away indeed" from nature's rugged haunts at the end of a century that had witnessed the reduction of the great bison herds, as Don Gayton writes in "The Grass and the Buffalo," from an estimated 60 million to 1,500. How could Lampman state that the wildcat found food and shelter in the tenantless rocks when, according to the World Wildlife Federation, as a direct result of government bounties and eradication programs, "cougars appear to have virtually disappeared from eastern Canada (where Lampman lived) by the late 1800s"?

Nature writers are not omniscient. Even John Muir could be blind to nature's unnatural enemies. He didn't mind tourism, for example, noting in *Our National Parks* (1901) that "the scenery habit in its most artificial forms, mixed with spectacles, silliness, and kodaks; its devotees arrayed more gorgeously than scarlet tanagers, frightening the wild game with red umbrellas,—even this is encouraging and may well be regarded as a hopeful sign of the times." He thought mining was less harmful to nature than farming (he referred to sheep as "hoofed locusts") and, in a particularly startling passage, tacitly approved of logging because it gave trees, transformed into ships' masts, a chance to travel: "After standing in one place for centuries," he writes, "they thus go around the world like tourists, meeting many a friend from the old home forest; some travelling like themselves, some standing head downward in muddy harbors, holding up the platforms of wharves . . . "

But unlike such "nature" poets as Lampman and Bliss Carman, Muir could not be accused of depicting a nature so sublime that it was at odds with actual experience. Muir never wrote anything quite as silly as Carman did, in *The Kinship of Nature* (1903): "Go into the park or woods any morning now," Carman advises, "and listen until you hear a single rainbird soloing plaintively above the dimmer sounds. At that one touch of the wild wood magic, how uncontemporaneous and primitive we become!" Burroughs enjoyed castigating Ernest Thompson Seton and Charles G. D. Roberts as "nature fakers" (reviewing Seton's *Wild Animals I Have Known* in the *Atlantic Monthly* in 1902, Burroughs remarked that it ought to have been called *Wild Animals Only I Have Known*), but neither of them wrote out of ignorance. Seton's "The Springfield Fox" and Roberts' "The Last Barrier" came after lengthy and meticulous observation of their subjects, written from a scientist's fascination with detail and a writer's passion for getting it down, and from and unabashed love of nature in its true form. Foxes kill chickens. Fish die. Roberts defined the nature story—a genre he invented—as "psychological romance constructed on a framework of natural science," and he and Seton can at least be credited with resisting the delusion that in nature "all are free." They and the Canadian nature writers who followed them, among whom Grey Owl was certainly the best known, devoted themselves to dismantling the walls of Frye's garrison. Nature, for them, was not a zoo; there is no sense that we are here and nature is in there, staring back at us through the bars. Roberts, Seton, and Grey Owl were all working toward a return to a vision of nature in which *Canis lupus* and *Homo sapiens* could coexist in the kind of wonder-filled harmony described by Samuel Hearne before them, and lamented by Barry Lopez and Peter Matthiessen after them.

Grey Owl ushered in what may be called the era of conservation among nature writers. He fought for the establishment of wildlife preserves, particularly for beaver which, like the bison and the timber wolf, had been driven to the edge of extinction since the arrival of the Europeans. Aldo Leopold and Albert Hochbaum both worked to create the Delta Waterfowl and Wetlands Research Station in Manitoba in 1938 (visited and described by Florence Page Jaques in *Canadian Spring* in 1947) for the study of duck migration.

Roger Tory Peterson, best known for his pocket field guides and the RTP "system" of bird identification, is also a tireless worker for wildlife conservation. And Roderick Haig-Brown quit his job as a cougar hunter to become one of Canada's strongest voices calling for preservation. "I believe a chance to see wildlife under natural conditions," he wrote in 1953, "is one of the important rights to man."

Haig-Brown, Fred Bodsworth, and Farley Mowat belong to the long tradition of nonfiction writers who employ fictional techniques to create works of lasting beauty. Nature writers, intent as they are on breaking down the barriers between man and nature, are perhaps also disposed toward breaking down the barriers between literary genres. Nature, as the contributions from both American and Canadian writers attest, knows no political borders, and ought to suffer no artistic ones either. Ironically, Burroughs criticized Seton for exhibiting qualities in his writing that are most admired in nature writers today: "In Mr. Thompson Seton's *Wild Animals I Have Known,*" he wrote, "I am bound to say that the line between fact and fiction is repeatedly crossed, and that a deliberate attempt is made to induce the reader to cross, too, and to work such a spell upon him that he shall not know that he has crossed and is in the land of make-believe." We have now entered an era of free trade, as far as the border between fact and fiction is concerned, and it is in this light that the selections in this collection are most clearly seen. Seán Virgo's "The Falcon" challenges the human impulse "to unriddle—which is to reduce—the monstrous, tormenting stillness" of nature. Nature will not be reduced—we must expand ourselves if we are to fit it. The falcon is "both there and not there," and its eyes are "black brilliant mirrors" in which we see ourselves.

Merilyn Simonds Mohr's story, "Stubborn Particulars of Place," encapsulates in a few pages the entire history of our relationship with nature in North America. At the beginning of the story, as at the beginning of European settlement of the continent, Mohr sees the lady's slipper as something apart from her life, something that belongs to the nature-as-zoo analogue and separate from the everyday affairs of humankind. Throughout the story, as her own marriage falters, Mohr's identification with the flower increases: "I think now that I liked her so well because she survived on so little." In the end, she *is* the flower.

The realization that, in the end, we *are* nature is no mere pastoral convention, no literary but nonliteral return to Arcadia. It is rather a return to an aboriginal North American sense of engagement, a knowledge that as human beings we are simply one of the creatures in the forest, and that which happens to the forest happens to us.

It is in this return to a sense of wholeness and wonder that there is the most hope for the future of the environment, which is our future: this book was put together not to form a record of what we have lost, but as a series of signposts toward what we have to gain.

It is fall now. The evenings come earlier and cooler, and the trees around the lake, reflected in the still water, double the earth. My daughter, who is now ten, is lying in the belly of the canoe. All summer she has been bringing me stories, how she spent half an hour watching a garter snake swallow a frog— "First the snake made a sound like a frog, to attract it"—or how she found a cloud of ants rolling up the side of the cabin. It was a dry summer, and the muskrat pond is gone. I can tell her where the painted turtles went, and the frogs, and the ducks. But I don't know what happened to the muskrats. As our canoe skims over the glassine water, we hear the honking of Canada geese. I look to the horizon above the trees, but don't see them. My daughter looks straight up and points, and there they are, a distant line of tiny specks, like ants leaving a picnic. "Look, Dad," she says; "a perfect I."

WAYNE GRADY

Bright Stars, Dark Trees, Clear Water

PEHR KALM

Travels in North America 1753

PEHR KALM (1716–1779) was born in the Swedish province of
Angermanland and studied natural history under the famous Swedish
naturalist Carl von Linné (Linnaeus) in Uppsala. In 1744, he accompanied
Linnaeus to Russia and Ukraine, received his doctorate in "natural history
and economy," and was elected the following year to the Swedish Academy
of Sciences. From 1747 to 1751, he travelled extensively in North America,
making scientific observations that he later incorporated into his *Travels*,
which was published in Swedish in 1753 and in English in 1770. Kalm travelled through southern Canada in the summer of 1749, and it is from the
notes he made during that trip that the following excerpt is taken.

JULY THE 23RD

THIS MORNING WE set out on our journey to Prairie, whence we intended
to proceed to Montreal. The distance of Prairie from Fort St. John, by land, is
six French miles, and from there to Montreal two and a half, by the St. Lawrence River. At first we kept along the shore, so that we had on our right the
Rivière de St. Jean (St. John's River). This is the name of the mouth of Lake
Champlain, which flows into the St. Lawrence River, and is sometimes called
Rivière de Champlain (Champlain River). After we had travelled about a
French mile, we turned to the left from the shore. The country was always
low, woody, and pretty wet, though it was in the midst of summer; so that we
found it difficult to proceed. But it is to be observed that Fort St. John was
built only last summer, when this road was first made, and consequently it
could not yet have acquired a proper degree of solidity. Two hundred and
sixty men were three months at work in making this road, for which they

were fed at the expense of the government, and each received thirty sols a day. I was told that they would again resume the work next autumn. The country hereabouts is low and woody, and of course the breeding place of millions of gnats and flies, which were very troublesome to us. After we had gone about three French miles we came out of the woods and the ground seemed to have been formerly a marsh which was now dried up. From here we had a pretty good view on all sides. On our right at a great distance we saw two high mountains, rising remarkably above the rest and they were not far from Fort Champlain. We could likewise from here see the high mountain which lies near Montreal, and our road went on nearly in a straight line. Soon after we got again upon wet and low grounds, and after that into a wood which consisted chiefly of the fir with leaves which have a silvery underside (*Abies foliis subtus argenteis*). We found the soil which we passed over today very fine and rich, and when the woods are cleared and the ground culti-vated, it will probably prove very fertile. There are no rocks, and hardly any stones near the road.

About four French miles from Fort St. John, the country had quite another appearance. It was all cultivated, and a continual variety of fields with excel-lent wheat, peas and oats, presented itself to our view; but we saw no other kind of grain. The farms stood scattered, and each of them was surrounded by its cornfields and meadows. The houses were built of wood and were very small. Instead of moss, which cannot be found here, they used clay for stop-ping up the crevices in the walls. The roofs were made at a very steep angle, and covered with straw. The soil was good, flat, and divided by several rivulets, and only in a few places were there any little hills. The view is very fine from this part of the road, and as far as I could see the country it was cultivated. All the fields were covered with grain, and they generally used summer wheat here.—The ground is still very fertile, so that there is no occasion for leaving it fallow. The forests are pretty much cleared, and it is to be feared that there will be a time when wood will become very scarce. Such is the appearance of the country nearly up to Prairie, and to the St. Lawrence River, which at last we now had always in sight. In a word this country was, in my opinion, one of the finest of North America that I had hitherto seen.

About dinner time we arrived at Prairie, which is situated on a little rising ground near the St. Lawrence River. We stayed here today, because I intended to visit the places in this neighborhood before I went on.

Laprairie de la Madeleine is a small village on the eastern side of the St. Law-rence River about two French miles and a half from Montreal, which lies N.W. from here on the other side of the river. All the country round Prairie is quite flat, and has hardly any hills. On all sides are large grainfields, meadows and pastures. On the western side the St. Lawrence River passes by and has here a breadth of a French mile and a half, if not more. To the southwest of this place is a great fall in the St. Lawrence River, and the noise which it causes may be plainly heard here. When the water in spring increases in the river on account of the ice which then begins to dissolve, it sometimes happens to rise so high as to overflow a great part of the fields, and, instead of fertilizing them as the river Nile fertilizes the Egyptian fields by its inundations, it does them much damage by depositing a number of grasses and plants on them, the seeds of which spread the worst kind of weeds and ruin the fields. These inundations oblige the people to take their cattle a great way off, because the water covers a great tract of land, but happily it never stays on it above two or three days. The cause of these inundations is generally the blocking of the water by ice in some part of the river.

The *Zizania aquatica,* or *Folle avoine* [wild rice], grows plentiful in the rivulet or brook, which flows a short distance below Prairie.

JULY THE 25TH

. . . I have been told by some Frenchmen, who had gone beaver hunting with the Indians to the northern parts of Canada, about fifty French miles from Hudson Bay, that the animals whose skins they endeavor to get, and which are there in great abundance, are beavers, wild cats, or lynx, and martens. These animals are the more valued the further they are caught to the north, for their skins have better hair, and look better or worse the further they come from the north or south.

White partridges (Perdrix blanches) is the name which the French in Canada give to a kind of bird abounding during winter near Hudson Bay, and which undoubtedly are our *ptarmigans,* snow-hens *(Tetrao lagopus).* They are very plentiful at the time of a great frost, and when a considerable quantity of snow happens to fall. The greater the cold or snow, the greater the number of birds. They were described to me as having rough white feet, and being white all over, except for three or four black feathers in the tail; and they are considered very fine eating. From Edward's *Natural History of Birds* it appears that the ptarmigans are common about Hudson Bay.

Hares are likewise said to be plentiful near Hudson Bay, and they are abundant even in Canada, where I have often seen and found them, corresponding perfectly with our Swedish hares. In summer they have a brownish gray and in winter a snowy white color, as with us.

JULY THE 27TH

The *common houseflies (Musca domestica)* were observed in this country about one hundred and fifty years ago, as I have been assured by several persons in this town, and in Quebec. All the Indians assert the same thing, and are of the opinion that the common flies first came over here with the Europeans and their ships, which were stranded on this coast. I shall not dispute this; however, I know, that while I was on the frontier between Saratoga and Crown Point, or Fort St. Frédéric, and sat down to rest or to eat, a number of our common flies always came and settled on me. It is therefore dubious whether they have not been longer in America than the term above-mentioned, or whether they have been imported from Europe. On the other hand, it may be urged that the flies were left in that wilderness at the time when Fort Anne was yet in a good condition, and when the English often travelled there and back again; not to mention that several Europeans, both before and after that time, had travelled through those places and carried the flies with them, which had been attracted by their provisions.

Wild cattle were abundant in the southern parts of Canada, and have been there since times immemorial. They were particularly plentiful in those parts where the Illinois Indians lived, which were nearly in the same latitude with Philadelphia; but further to the north they are seldom observed. I saw the skin of a wild ox today; it was as big as one of the largest ox hides in Europe, but had better hair. This was dark brown like that on a brown bearskin. That which was close to the skin is as soft as wool. This hide was not very thick and in general was not considered so valuable (in France) as a bearskin. In winter it is spread on the floor to keep the feet warm. Some of these wild cattle, as I am told, have a long and fine wool, as good if not better than sheep wool. They make stockings, cloth, gloves, and other pieces of worsted work of it, which look as well as if they were made of the best sheep wool. The Indians employ it for several uses. The flesh is as good and fat as the best beef. Sometimes the hides are thick, and may be used as cowhides are in Europe. The wild cattle in general are said to be stronger and bigger than European cattle, and of a brownish red color. Their horns are short, though very thick close to the head. These and several other qualities, which they have in common with and in greater perfection than the domestic cattle, have induced some to endeavor to tame them, by which means they would obtain the advantages arising from their good hair, and, on account of their great strength, could employ them successfully in agriculture. With this view some have repeatedly gotten young wild calves and brought them up in Quebec and other places among the tame cattle, but they have usually died in three or four years' time; and though they have seen people every day, they have always retained a natural ferocity. They have constantly been very shy, pricked up their ears at the sight of man, and have trembled or run about, so that the art of taming them has not hitherto been successful. Some have been of the opinion that these cattle cannot bear the cold well, as they never go north of the place I mentioned, though the summers be very hot, even in those northern parts. They think that when the country about the Illinois is better peopled it will be easier to tame these cattle, and that afterwards they may more easily be accustomed to the northerly climates. The Indians and French in Canada make use of the horns of these creatures to put gunpowder in.

JULY THE 28TH

This morning I accompanied the governor, Baron de Longueuil, and his family to a little island called *Madeleine,* which is his own property. It lies in the St. Lawrence River directly opposite the town on the eastern side. The governor had here a very neat house, though it was not very large, a fine, extensive garden, and a yard. The river passes between the town and this island, and is very rapid. Near the town it is deep enough for large boats, but towards the island it grows more shallow, so that they are obliged to push the boats forward with poles. . . .

Trees and Plants. The smooth sumac, or *Rhus glabra,* grows abundantly here. I have nowhere seen it so tall as in this place, where it had sometimes the height of eight yards and a proportional thickness.

Sassafras is planted here, for it is never found wild in these parts, Fort Anne being the most northerly place where I have found it wild. Those shrubs which were on the island had been planted many years ago; however, they were only small shrubs, from two to three feet high, and scarcely that much. The reason is that the main stem is killed every winter almost down to the very root, and must produce new shoots every spring, as I have found from my own observations here; and so it appeared to be near the forts Anne, Nicholson, and Oswego. It will therefore be useless to attempt to plant sassafras in a very cold climate.

The *Mulberry trees (Morus rubra L.)* are likewise planted here. I saw four or five of them about five yards high, which the governor told me had been twenty years in this place and brought from more southerly parts, since they do not grow wild near Montreal. The most northerly place where I have found it growing wild is about twenty English miles north of Albany. I had this confirmed by the country people who live in that place, and who at the same time informed me that it was very scarce in the woods. When I came to Saratoga I inquired whether any of these mulberry trees had been found in that neighborhood, but everybody told me that they were never seen in those parts, and that the before-mentioned place twenty miles above Albany is the most northern point where they grow. The mulberry trees that were planted on this island succeed very well, though they are placed in poor soil. Their foliage was large and thick, but they did not bear any fruit this year. I was informed that they can bear a considerable degree of cold.

The *waterbeech* had been planted here in a shady place, and had grown to a great height. All the French hereabouts call it *cotonnier*. It is never found wild near the St. Lawrence River, nor north of Fort St. Frédéric, where it is now very scarce.

The *red cedar* is called *cèdre rouge* by the French, and that was also planted in the governor's garden, whither it had been brought from more southern parts, for it is not to be found in the forests hereabouts. However, it grew very well here.

About half an hour after seven in the evening we left this pleasant island, and an hour after our return the Baron de Longueuil received two agreeable pieces of news at once. The first was that his son who had been two years in France, had returned; and the second, that he had brought with him the royal patents for his father, by which he was appointed governor of Montreal and the country belonging to it.

People make use of *fans* here which are made of the tails of wild turkeys. As soon as the birds are shot, their tails are spread like fans, and dried, by which means they keep their shape. The ladies and the men of distinction in town carry these fans, when they walk in the streets during the intense heat.

All the *grass* on the meadows round Montreal consists of a species of meadow grass or the *Poa capillaris L.* This is a very slender grass which grows very close and succeeds even on the driest hills. It is however not rich in foliage; but the slender stalk is used for hay. We have numerous kinds of grasses in Sweden which are much more useful than this.

July the 30th

The *wild plum trees* grow in great abundance on the hills along the rivulets about the town. They were so loaded with fruit that the boughs were bent downwards by the weight. The fruit was not yet ripe, but when it comes to that perfection it has a red color and a fine taste, and preserves are sometimes made of it.

Black currants (Ribes nigrum L.) are plentiful in the same places, and its berries were ripe at this time. They are very small, and not by far so fine as those in Sweden.

Parsnips grow in great abundance on the rising banks of rivers, along the grainfields, and in other places. This led me to think that they were original natives of America, and not first brought over by the Europeans. But on my journey into the country of the Iroquois, where no European ever had a settlement, I never once saw it, though the soil was excellent; and from this it appears plain enough that it was transported hither from Europe, and is not originally an American plant. Therefore it is in vain sought for in any part of this continent except among the European settlements.

SAMUEL HEARNE

A Journey to the Northern Ocean 1792

SAMUEL HEARNE (1745–1792) joined the Royal Navy at the age of eleven, and left it in 1766 to serve with the Hudson's Bay Company as a fur trader in Fort Churchill, in what is now Manitoba. When rumors of a great copper mine to the northwest reached the Company, Hearne, to his great surprise, was ordered to trek across the barren grounds to find it. Each of his three attempts nearly killed him, but he finally reached the mouth of the Copper-mine River on 14 July 1771 and returned to Churchill nearly a year later to report that there were in fact no copper mines in the vicinity. He remained in Churchill until 1787, then returned to London to assist the naturalist Thomas Pennant and to work on his memoirs, *A Journey from Prince of Wales's Fort, in Hudson's Bay, to the Northern Ocean . . . in the Years 1769, 1770, 1771, & 1772,* published posthumously in 1795.

୭୫ • ୫୭

THE WE-WAS-KISH, or as some (though improperly) call it, the Waskesse, is quite a different animal from the moose, being by no means so large in size. The horns of the We-was-kish are something similar to those of the common deer, but are not palmated in any part. They stand more upright, have fewer branches, and want the brow-antler. The hair of this animal is so far from be-ing like that of the Moose, that the nose is sharp, like the nose of a sheep: in-deed, the whole external appearance of the head is not very unlike that of an ass. The hair is usually of a sandy red; and they are frequently called by the En-glish who visit the interior parts of the country, red deer. Their flesh is toler-able eating; but the fat is as hard as tallow, and if eaten as hot as possible, will yet chill in so short a time, that it clogs the teeth, and sticks to the roof of the mouth, in such a manner as to render it very disagreeable. In the Spring of one thousand seven hundred and seventy-five, I had thirteen sledge-loads of this meat brought to Cumberland House in one day, and also two of the heads of this animal unskinned, but the horns were chopped off; a proof of their wearing them the whole Winter. They are the most stupid of all the deer kind, and frequently make a shrill whistling, and quivering noise, not very unlike the braying of an ass, which directs the hunter to the very spot where they are. They generally keep in large herds, and when they find plenty of pasture, remain a long time in one place. Those deer are seldom an object of chase with the Indians bordering on Basquiau, except when moose and other game fail. Their skins, when dressed, very much resemble that of tile moose, though they are much thinner, and have this peculiar quality, that they will wash as well as shamoy leather; whereas all the other leathers and pelts dressed by the Indians, if they get wet, turn quite hard, unless great care be taken to keep constantly rubbing them while drying.

The person who informed Mr. Pennant that the We-was-kish and the moose are the same animal, never saw one of them; and the only reason he had to suppose it, was the great resemblance of their skins: yet it is rather strange, that so indefatigable a collector of Natural History as the late Mr. Andrew Graham, should have omitted making particular enquiry about them: for any foreign Indian, particularly those that reside near Basquiau, could easily have convinced him to the contrary.

WOLVES are frequently met with in the countries West of Hudson Bay, both on the barren grounds and among the woods, but they are not numerous; it is very uncommon to see more than three or four of them in a herd. Those that keep to the Westward, among the woods, are generally of the usual color, but the greatest part of those that are killed by the Esquimaux are perfectly white. All the wolves in Hudson Bay are very shy of the human race, yet when sharp set, they frequently follow the Indians for several days, but always keep at a distance. They are great enemies to the Indian dogs, and frequently kill and eat those that are heavy loaded, and cannot keep up with the main body. The Northern Indians have formed strange ideas of this animal, as they think it does not eat its victuals raw; but by a singular and wonderful sagacity, peculiar to itself, has a method of cooking them without fire. The females are much swifter than the males; for which reason the Indians, both Northern and Southern, are of opinion that they kill the greatest part of the game. This cannot, however, always be the case; for to the North of Churchill they, in general, live a forlorn life all the Winter, and are seldom seen in pairs till the Spring, when they begin to couple; and generally keep in pairs all the Summer. They always burrow underground to bring forth their voting; and though it is natural to suppose them very fierce at those times, yet I have frequently seen the Indians go to their dens, and take out the young ones and play with them. I never knew a Northern Indian hurt one of them: on the contrary, they always put them carefully into the den again; and I have sometimes seen them paint the faces of the young Wolves with vermillion, or red ochre.

The ARCTIC FOXES are in some years remarkably plentiful, but generally most so on the barren ground, near the sea-coast. Notwithstanding what has been said of this animal only visiting the settlements once in five or seven years, I can affirm there is not one year in twenty that they are not caught in greater or less numbers at Churchill; and I have known that for three years running, not less than from two hundred to four hundred have been caught each year within thirty miles of the Fort. They always come from the North along the coast, and generally make their appearance at Churchill about the middle of October, but their skins are seldom in season till November; during that time they are never molested, but permitted to feed round the Fort, till by degrees they become almost domestic. The great numbers of those animals that visit Churchill River in some years do not all come in a body, as it would be impossible for the fourth part of them to find subsistence by the way; but when they come near the Fort, the carcasses of dead whales lying along the shores, and the skin and other offal, after boiling the oil, afford them a plentiful repast, and prove the means of keeping them about the Fort till, by frequent reinforcements from the Northward, their numbers are so far increased as almost to exceed credibility.

When their skins are in season, a number of traps and guns are set, and the greatest part of them are caught in one month, though some few are found during the whole Winter. I have frequently known near forty killed in one night within half a mile of Prince of Wales's Fort; but this seldom happens after the first or second night. When Churchill River is frozen over near the mouth, the greatest part of the surviving white Foxes cross the river, and direct their course to the Southward, and in some years assemble in considerable numbers at York Fort and Severn River. Whether they are all killed, or what becomes of those which escape, is very uncertain; but it is well known that none of them ever migrate again to the Northward. Besides taking a trap so freely, they are otherwise so simple, that I have seen them shot off-hand while feeding, the same as sparrows in a heap of chaff, sometimes two or three at a shot. This sport is always most successful in moon-light nights; for in the daytime they generally keep in their holes among the rocks, and under the hollow ice at high-water-mark.

These animals will prey on each other as readily as on any other animals they find dead in a trap, or wounded by gun; which renders them so destructive, that I have known upwards of one hundred and twenty Foxes of different colors eaten, and destroyed in their traps by their comrades in the course of one Winter, within half a mile of the Fort.

The Naturalists seem still at a loss to know their breeding-places, which are doubtless in every part of the coast they frequent. Several of them breed near Churchill, and I have seen them in considerable numbers all along the West coast of Hudson's Bay, particularly at Cape Esquimaux, Navel's Bay, and Whale Cove, also on Marble Island; so that with some degree of confidence we may affirm, that they breed on every part of the coast they inhabit during the Summer season. They generally have from three to five young at a litter; more I never saw with one old one. When young they are all over almost of a sooty black, but as the fall advances, the belly, sides, and tail turn to a light ash-color; the back, legs, some part of the face, and the tip of the tail, change to a lead color; but when the Winter sets in they become perfectly white: the ridge of the back and the tip of the tail are the last places that change to that color; and there are few of them which have not a few dark hairs at the tip of the tail all the Winter. If taken young, they are easily domesticated in some degree, but I never saw one that was fond of being caressed; and they are always impatient of confinement.

WHITE FOXES, when killed at any considerable distance from the sea coast (where they cannot possibly get any thing to prey upon, except rabbits, mice, and partridges), are far from being disagreeable eating. And on Marble Island I have shot them when they were equal in flavor to a rabbit, probably owing to their feeding entirely on eggs and young birds; but near Churchill River they are as rank as train-oil.

The LYNX, or WILD CAT, is very scarce to the North of Churchill; but is exactly the same as those which are found in great plenty to the South West. I have observed the tracks of this animal at Churchill, and seen them killed, and have eaten of their flesh in the neighborhood of York Fort. The flesh is white, and nearly as good as that of a rabbit. They are, I think, much larger than that which is described in the Arctic Zoology; they never approach near the settlements in Hudson's Bay, and are very destructive to rabbits; they seldom leave a place which is frequented by rabbits till they have nearly killed them all.

The POLAR or WHITE BEAR, though common on the sea coast, is seldom found in its Winter retreats by any of our Northern Indians; except near Churchill River; nor do I suppose that the Esquimaux see or kill any of them more frequently during that season; for in the course of many years residence at Churchill River, I scarcely ever saw a Winter skin brought from the North-ward by the sloop. Probably the Esquimaux, if they kill any, may reserve the skins for their own use; for at that season their hair is very long, with a thick bed of wool at the bottom, and they are remarkably clean and white. The Winter is the only season that so oily a skin as the Bear's can possibly be cleaned and dressed by those people, without greasing the hair, which is very unpleasant to them; for though they eat train-oil, &c. yet they are as careful as possible to keep their clothes from being greased with it. To dress one of those greasy skins in Winter, as soon as taken from the beast, it is stretched out on a smooth patch of snow, and there staked down, where it soon freezes as hard as a board: while in that state, the women scrape off all the fat, till they come to the very roots of the hair. It is sometimes permitted to remain in that position for a considerable time; and when taken from the snow, is hung up in the open air. The more intense the frost, the greater is its drying quality; and by being wafted about by the wind, with a little scraping, it in time becomes per-fectly supple, and both pelt and hair beautifully white. Drying deer, beaver, and otter skins, in this manner renders their pelts very white, but not supple; probably owing to the close texture and thickness of their skins; whereas the skin of the bear, though so large an animal, is remarkably thin and spungy.

BLACK BEARS are not very numerous to the North West of Churchill. Their manner of life is the same as the rest of the species, though the face of the country they inhabit, differs widely from the more mild climates. In Sum-mer they prowl about in search of berries, &c. and as the Winter approaches, retire to their dens, which are always under-ground; and generally, if not al-ways, on the side of a small hillock. The Bears that inhabit the Southern parts of America are said to take up their Winter abode in hollow trees; but I never saw any trees in my Northern travels, that could afford any such shelter.

The places of retreat of those Bears that burrow underground are easily dis-covered in Winter, by the rime that hangs about the mouth of the den; for let the snow be ever so deep, the heat and breath of the animal prevents the mouth of the den from being entirely closed up. They generally retire to their Winter quarters before the snow is of any considerable depth, and never come abroad again (unless disturbed) till the thaws are considerable, which in those high latitudes is seldom till the latter end of March, or the beginning of April; so that the few Black Bears that inhabit those cold regions may be said to sub-sist for four months at least without food. I have been present at the killing [of] two of them in Winter; and the Northern Indian method is similar to that said to be in use among the Kamtschatkans; for they always blocked up the mouth of the den with logs of wood, then broke open the top of it, and killed the an-

imal either with a spear or a gun; but the latter method is reckoned both cow-
ardly and wasteful, as it is not possible for the Bear either to make its escape, or
to do the Indians the least injury. Sometimes they put a snare about the Bear's
neck, and draw up his head close to the hole, and kill him with a hatchet.
Though those animals are but scarce to the North of Churchill, yet they are so
numerous between York Fort and Cumberland House, that in one thousand
seven hundred and seventy-four I saw eleven killed in the course of one day's
journey, but their flesh was abominable. This was in the month of June, long
before any fruit was ripe, for the want of which they then fed entirely on water insects, which in some of the lakes we crossed that day were in astonishing
multitudes. The method by which the Bears catch those insects is by swimming with their mouths open, in the same manner as the whales do, when
feeding on the sea-spider. There was not one of the Bears killed that day, which
had not its stomach as full of those insects (only) as ever a hog's was with
grains, and when cut open, the stench from them was intolerable. I have, however, eaten of some killed at that early season which were very good; but they
were found among the woods, far from the places where those insects haunt,
and had fed on grass and other herbage. After the middle of July, when the berries begin to ripen, they are excellent eating, and so continue till January or
February following; but late in the Spring they are, by long fasting, very poor
and dry eating.

The Southern Indians kill great numbers of those Bears at all seasons of
the year; but no encouragement can prevent them from singeing almost every
one that is in good condition: so that the few skins they do save and bring to
the market, are only of those which are so poor that their flesh is not worth
eating. In fact, the skinning of a Bear spoils the meat thereof, as much as it
would do to skin a young porker, or a roasting pig. The same may be said of
swans (the skins of which the Company have lately made an article of trade);
otherwise thousands of their skins might be brought to market annually, by
the Indians that trade with the Hudson's Bay Company's servants at the
different settlements about the Bay.

BROWN BEARS are, I believe, never found in the North-Indian territories: but I saw the skin of an enormous grizzled Bear at the tents of the
Esquimaux at the Copper River; and many of them are said to breed not very
remote from that part.

The WOLVERINE is common in the Northern regions, as far North as the
Copper River, and perhaps farther. They are equally the inhabitants of woods
and barren grounds; for the Esquimaux to the North of Churchill kill many of
them when their skins are in excellent season: a proof of their being capable of

braving the severest cold. They are very slow in their pace, but their wonderful sagacity, strength, and acute scent, make ample amends for that defect; for they are seldom killed at any season when they do not prove very fat: a great proof of their being excellent providers. With respect to the fierceness of this animal which some assert, I can say little, but I know them to be beasts of great courage and resolution, for I once saw one of them take possession of a deer that an Indian had killed, and though the Indian advanced within twenty yards, he would not relinquish his claim to it, but suffered himself to be shot standing on the deer. I once saw a similar instance of a lynx, or wild cat, which also suffered itself to be killed, before it would relinquish the prize. The Wolverines have also frequently been seen to take a deer from a wolf before the latter had time to begin his repast after killing it. Indeed their amazing strength, and the length and sharpness of their claws, render them capable of making a strong resistance against any other animal in those parts, the Bear not excepted. As a proof of their amazing strength, there was one at Churchill some years since that overset the greatest part of a large pile of wood (containing a whole Winter's firing, that measured upwards of seventy yards round), to get at some provisions that had been hid there by the Company's servants, when going to the Factory to spend the Christmas holidays. The fact was, this animal had been lurking about in the neighborhood of their tent (which was about eight miles from the Factory) for some weeks, and had committed many depredations on the game caught in their traps and snares, as well as eaten many foxes that were killed by guns set for that purpose: but the Wolverine was too cunning to take either trap or gun himself. The people knowing the mischievous disposition of those animals, took (as they thought) the most effectual method to secure the remains of their provisions, which they did not choose to carry home, and accordingly tied it up in bundles and placed it on the top of the woodpile (about two miles from their tent), little thinking the Wolverine would find it out; but to their great surprise, when they returned to their tent after the holidays, they found the pile of wood in the state already mentioned, though some of the trees that composed it were as much as two men could carry. The only reason the people could give for the animal doing so much mischief was, that in his attempting to carry off the booty some of the small parcels of provisions had fallen down into the heart of the pile, and sooner than lose half his prize, he pursued the above method till he had accomplished his ends. The bags of flour, oatmeal, and pease, though of no use to him, he tore all to pieces, and scattered the contents about on the snow; but every bit of animal food, consisting of beef, pork, bacon, venison, salt geese, partridges, &c. to a considerable amount, he carried away. These animals are great enemies to the

Beaver, but the manner of life of the latter prevents them from falling into their clutches so frequently as many other animals; they commit vast depredations on the foxes during the Summer, while the young ones are small; their quick scent directs them to their dens, and if the entrance be too small, their strength enables them to widen it, and go in and kill the mother and all her cubs. In fact, they are the most destructive animals in this country.

OTTERS are pretty plentiful in the rivers to the North of Churchill, as far as latitude 62°; farther North I do not recollect to have seen any. In Winter they generally frequent those parts of rivers where there are falls or rapids, which do not freeze in the coldest Winters; because in such situations they are most likely to find plenty of fish, and the open water gives them a free admission to the shore, where they sometimes go to eat the fish they have caught; but most commonly sit on the ice, or get on a great stone in the river. They are frequently seen in the very depth of Winter at a considerable distance from any known open water, both in woods and on open plains, as well as on the ice of large lakes; but it is not known what has led them to such places: perhaps merely for amusement, for they are not known to kill any game on the land during that season. If pursued when among the woods in Winter (where the snow is always light and deep), they immediately dive, and make considerable way under it, but are easily traced by the motion of the snow above them, and soon overtaken. The Indians kill numbers of them with clubs, by tracking them in the snow; but some of the old ones are so fierce when close pursued, that they turn and fly at their pursuer, and their bite is so severe that it is much dreaded by the Indians. Besides this method of killing them, the Indians have another, which is equally successful; namely, by concealing themselves within a reasonable gun-shot of the Otters usual landing-places; and waiting their coming out of the water. This method is more generally practised in moonlight nights. They also shoot many of them as they are sporting in the water, and some few are caught in traps.

The Otters in this, as well as every other part of the bay, vary in size and color, according to age and season. In Summer, when the hair is very short, they are almost black, but as the Winter advances, they turn to a beautiful dark auburn, except a small spot under the chin, which is of a silver gray. This color they retain all the Winter; but late in the Spring (though long before they shed their coat) they turn to a dull rusty brown; so that a person who is acquainted with those changes can tell to a great nicety, by looking at the skins (when offered for sale), the very time they were killed, and pay for them according to their value. The number of their young is various, from three to five or six. They unite in copulation the same as a dog, and so do every other animal that has a bone in the *penis*. I will here enumerate all of that description that I know of in those parts, *viz.* bears of all sorts, wolves, wolverines, foxes, martins, otters, wejacks, jackashes, skunks, and ermines.

JACKASH.This animal is certainly no other than the lesser Otter of Canada, as its color, size, and manner of life entirely correspond with the description of that animal in Mr. Pennant's Arctic Zoology. They, like the larger Otter, are frequently found in Winter several miles from any water, and are often caught in traps built for martins. They are supposed to prey on mice and partridges, the same as the martin; but when by the side of rivers or creeks, they generally feed on fish. They vary so much in size and color, that it was very easy for Mr. Pennant to have mistaken the specimen sent home for another animal. They are the easiest to tame and domesticate of any animal I know, except a large species of field-mice, called the Hair-tailed Mouse; for in a very short time they are so fond, that it is scarcely possible to keep them from climbing up one's legs and body, and they never feel themselves happier than when sitting on the shoulder; but when angry, or frightened (like the skunk), they emit a very disagreeable smell. They sleep very much in the day, but prowl about and feed in the night; they are very fierce when at their meals, not suffering those to whom they are most attached to take it from them. I have kept several of them, but, their over-fondness made them troublesome, as they were always in the way; and their so frequently emitting a disagreeable smell, rendered them quite disgusting.

Though the WEJACK and SKUNK are never found in the Northern Indian country, yet I cannot help observing that the foetid smell of the latter has not been much exaggerated by any Author. When I was at Cumberland House, in the Fall of one thousand seven hundred and seventy-four, some Indians that were tenting on the plantation killed two of those animals, and made a feast of them; when the spot where they were singed and gutted was so impregnated with that nauseous smell which they emit, that after a whole Winter had elapsed, and the snow had thawed away in the Spring, the smell was still intolerable. I am told, however, that the flesh is by no means tainted with the smell, if care be taken in gutting, and taking out the bag that contains this surprising effluvia, and which they have the power of emitting at pleasure; but I rather doubt their being capable of ejecting their urine so far as is reported; I do not think it is their urine which contains that pestilential effluvia, for if that was the case, all the country where they frequent would be so scented with it, that neither man nor beast could live there with any degree of comfort.

The COMMON PINE MARTIN is found in most parts of this country, and though very scarce in what is absolutely called the Northern Indian territory, yet by the Indians strolling toward the borders of the Southern Indian country, are killed in great numbers, and annually traded for at Churchill Factory.

The ERMINE, or STOTE, is common in those parts, but generally more plentiful on the barren ground, and open plains or marshes, than in the woods; probably owing to the mice being more numerous in the former situations than in the latter. In Summer they are of a tawney brown, but in Winter of a delicate white all over, except the tip of the tail, which is of a glossy black. They are, for their size, the strongest and most courageous animal I know: as they not only kill partridges, but even attack rabbits with great success. They sometimes take up their abode in the out-offices and provision-sheds belonging to the Factories; and though they commit some depredations, make ample amends by killing great numbers of mice, which are very numerous and destructive at most of the settlements in the Bay. I have taken much pains to tame and domesticate this beautiful animal, but never could succeed; for the longer I kept it the more restless and impatient it became.

DAVID THOMPSON

Swan River Country 1813

Born in England of Welsh parents, DAVID THOMPSON (1770–1857) arrived at Churchill, Manitoba, in 1784, when Samuel Hearne was still there and James Cook's famous map of the world had just been published. Thompson set out to fill in the blanks on Cook's map: virtually all of the interior of North America west of the Great Lakes. He joined the North West Company as a fur trader in 1797 and travelled more than 55,000 miles throughout the north and west of the continent, surveying maps and making notes for *David Thompson's Narrative of His Explorations in Western North America, 1784–1812*, from which the following—an account of an expedition from Lake Winnipegosis to the Red Deer River—is taken. He moved to Williamstown, Upper Canada, in 1815, continuing to survey and map the country until he died, in penury, in 1857. His book, edited by J. B. Tyrrell, was not published until 1916, but has since been acknowledged as one of the great books in Canadian literature.

⁊ · ⁊

PREVIOUS TO THE DISCOVERY of Canada (about 320 years ago), this continent from the latitude of forty degrees north to the Arctic Circle, and from the Atlantic to the Pacific Ocean, may be said to have been in the possession of two distinct races of beings, man and the beaver. Man was naked and had to procure clothing from the skins of animals; his only arms were a stake, pointed and hardened in the fire, a bow with arrows, the points hardened with fire, or headed with stone or bone of the legs of the deer, a spear headed in the same manner, and a club of heavy wood, or made of a round stone of four or five pounds weight, inclosed in raw hide, and by the same bound round a handle of wood of about two feet in length, bound firm to the stone.

Such were the weapons man had for self-defence and with which to procure his food and clothing. Against the bones of an animal, his arrows and spear had little effect, [but] the flank of every animal is open, and thither, into the bowels, the Indian directed his fatal and unerring arrows. . . . Besides his weapons, the snare was much in use, and the spear to assist it for large animals, and by all accounts the deer and fur-bearing animals were very numerous, and thus man was lord of the dry land and all that was on it.

The other race was the beaver; they were safe from every animal but man and the wolverine. Every year each pair having from five to seven young which they carefully reared, they became innumerable, and except the great lakes, the waves of which are too turbulent, occupied all the waters of the northern part of the continent. [On] every river where the current was moderate and sufficiently deep, the banks at the water edge were occupied by their houses. To every small lake and all the ponds they builded dams, and enlarged and deepened them to the height of the dams. Even [on] grounds occasionally overflowed by heavy rains, they also made dams, and made them permanent ponds, and as they heightened the dams increased the extent and added to the depth of water. Thus all the low lands were in possession of the beaver, and all the hollows of the higher grounds. Small streams were dammed across and ponds formed; the dry land with the dominions of man contracted; everywhere he was hemmed in by water without the power of preventing it; he could not diminish their numbers half so fast as they multiplied, and their houses were proof against his pointed stake, and his arrows could seldom pierce their skins. (Note. In my travels, several thousands of the natives were not half so well armed.) In this state man and the beaver had been for many centuries, but the discovery of Canada by the French, and their settlements up the St. Lawrence, soon placed the natives far superior to the beaver.

Without iron, man is weak, very weak, but armed with iron he becomes the lord of the earth; no other metal can take its place. For the furs which the natives traded, they procured from the French axes, chisels, knives, spears, and other articles of iron, with which they made good hunts of fur-bearing animals and procured woollen clothing. Thus armed, the houses of the beavers were pierced through, the dams cut through, and the water of the ponds lowered, or wholly run off, and the houses of the beaver and their burrows laid dry, by which means they became an easy prey to the hunter.

The beaver is an animal well known; the average weight of a full grown male is about fifty-five pounds; his meat is agreeable to most although the fat is oily; the tail is a delicacy. They are always in pairs, and work together. Their first business is to insure a sufficient depth and extent of water for the winter, and if nature has not done this for them, they make dams to obtain it. If there are more families than one in a piece of water, they all work together, each appearing to labor on a particular part.

The dam is made of earth [and] pieces of wood laid oblique to the direction of the dam. The wood employed is always of aspen, poplar or large willow and alders; if pine is used it is through necessity, not by choice. The bottom is well laid, and, if small stones are at hand, they make use of them for the bottom of the dam. The earth is brought between their forepaws and throat, laid down, and by several strokes of the tail made compact. The pieces of wood are with their teeth, which are very sharp and formed like small chisels, cut into the lengths they want, brought to the dam, and worked in, and thus the dam is raised to the height required. It is a remark of many that dams erected by the art of man are frequently damaged or wholly carried away by violent freshets, but no power of water has ever carried away a beaver dam.

Having secured a sufficient depth of water each family builds a separate house. This is in the form of a low dome, from the doorway which is a little way in the water, gradually rising, to about thirty inches in height, and about six feet in diameter. The materials are the same as those of the dam, and worked in the same manner, only the pieces of wood are much shorter, and, if at hand, small flat stones are worked in. . . . The coating of the first year may be about four to five inches thick and every year an additional coat is added, until it is a foot or more in thickness. Grass then grows upon it, and it looks like a little knoll.

The next work is to make burrows of retreat; the first year seldom more than one or two can be made, and sometimes none. These are carried on, from a few inches below the surface of the water direct from it, gradually rising about a foot in height by twenty inches in breadth, so that a beaver can turn in them; their length depends on the easiness of digging the ground. The general length is about ten feet, but in good earth they often are of twenty feet or more. The second and third years the number of burrows is augmented to five or six, and where the beaver have been a long time the ponds and small lakes have numerous burrows.

The Indians think the male and female are faithful to each other. They bring up their young for the first year with care and protection until the next spring when the female is about to litter; [then] she drives them all away, and some of them, before they can be made to stay away, receive severe cuts on the back from the teeth of the old ones. The young beavers are very playful, and whimper like children. The beaver is supposed to attain to the age of fifteen years; some think to twenty years.

The beaver hunter is often at a loss what to do, and sometimes passes a whole day without coming to a determination; his shortest and surest way is to stake up the doorway of the house, the stakes he carries with him ready for the purpose, but the beaver are so watchful that his approach is heard and they retire to their burrows. Some prefer first finding the burrows and closing them up with stakes and cutting off all retreat from the house. Whichever method he takes, difficulties and hard labor attend him.

To determine the place of the beavers, for the whole family of seven or nine are seldom all found in the house, the Indian is greatly assisted by a peculiar species of small dog, of a light make, about three feet in height, muzzle sharp and brown, full black eyes, with a round brown spot above each eye; the body black, the belly of a fawn color, its scent very keen and almost unerring. This dog points out by smelling and scratching the weakest part of the beaver house and the part where they lie; the same in the burrows, which are then doubly staked. The Indian with his axe and ice chisel makes a hole over the place shown by the dog; the beaver has changed its place. To find to which end of the burrow it is gone, a crooked stick is employed until it touches the beaver; another hole is made, and the beaver is killed with the ice chisel, which has a heavy handle of about seven feet in length.

When the dog smells and scratches at two or three places on the beaver house, it is a mark that there are several in it. The doorway being doubly staked, the Indian proceeds to make a hole near the centre of it, to give full range to his ice chisel, and not one escapes, but all [this is done] with hard labor. Such was the manner of killing the beaver until the introduction of steel traps, which, baited with castorum, soon brought on the almost total destruction of these numerous and sagacious animals.

From this long digression, I return to my travels in the Nut Hills; on a fine afternoon in October, the leaves beginning to fall with every breeze, a season to me of pleasing melancholy, from the reflections it brings to the mind, my guide informed me that we would have to pass over a long beaver dam. I naturally expected we should be obliged to lead our horses carefully over it; when we came to it, we found it a narrow stripe of apparently old solid ground, with short grass and wide enough for two horses to walk abreast. We passed on; the lower side showed a descent of seven feet, and steep, with a rill of water from beneath it; the side of the dam next to the water was a gentle slope. To the southward was a sheet of water of about one mile and a half square of area, surrounded by moderate low grassy, banks, the forests mostly of aspen and poplar but very numerous stumps of the trees cut down and partly carried away by the beavers. In two places of this pond were clusters of beaver houses, like miniature villages.

When we had proceeded over more than half way of the dam, which was a full mile in length, we came to an aged Indian, his arms folded across his breast, with a pensive countenance, looking at the beavers swimming in the water, and carrying their winter's provisions to their houses. His form tall and erect, his hair almost white, which was almost the only effect that age appeared to have on him, though we concluded he must be about eighty years of age, and in this opinion we were afterwards confirmed by the ease and readiness with which he spoke of times long past. I enquired of him how many beaver houses there were in the pond before us. He said, "There are now fifty-two; we have taken several of their houses; they are difficult to take, and those we have taken were by means of the noise of the water on their houses from a strong wind which enabled us to stake them in; otherwise they would have retired to their burrows, which are very many."

He invited us to pass the night at his tent which was close by; the sun was low, and we accepted the offer. In the tent was an old man almost his equal in age, along with women and children. We preferred the open air, and made a good fire to which both of the old men came, and after smoking awhile, conversation came on, as I had always conversed with the natives as one Indian with another, and been attentive to learn their traditions on the animals, on mankind, and on other matters in ancient times, and the present occasion appeared favorable for this purpose. Setting aside questions and answers which would be tiresome, they said, by ancient tradition of which they did not know the origin, the beavers had been an ancient people, and then lived on the dry land. "They were always beavers, not men; they were wise and powerful, and neither man nor any animal made war on them. They were well clothed as at present, and, as they did not eat meat, they made no use of fire, and did not want it. How long they lived this way we cannot tell, but we must suppose they did not live well, for the Great Spirit became angry with them, and ordered Weesaukejauk [the Flatterer] to drive them all into the water and there let them live, still to be wise, but without power, to be food and clothing for man, and the prey of other animals, against all which his defence shall be his dams, his house, and his burrows. You see how strong he makes his dams; those that we make for fishing weirs are often destroyed by the water, but his always stand. His house is not made of sand, or loose stones, but of strong earth with wood and sometimes small stones, and he makes burrows to escape from his enemies, and he always has his winter stock of provisions secured in good time. When he cuts down a tree, you see how he watches it, and takes care that it shall not fall on him."

"But if so wise, for what purpose does the beaver cut down large trees of which he makes no use whatever?"

"We do not know, perhaps an itching, of his teeth and gums."

There the old Indian paused, became silent, and then in a low tone [they] talked with each other, after which he continued his discourse. "I have told you that we believe that in years long passed away, the Great Spirit was angry with the beaver, and ordered Weesaukejauk to drive them all from the dry land into the water, and they became and continued very numerous, but the Great Spirit has been, and now is, very angry with them, and they are now all to be destroyed. About two winters ago Weesaukejauk showed to our brethren, the Nipissings and Algonquins, the secret of their destruction: that all of them were infatuated with the love of the castorum of their own species and more fond of it than we are of fire water. We are now killing the beaver without any labor, we are now rich, but shall soon be poor, for when the beaver are destroyed we have nothing to depend on to purchase what we want for our families. Strangers now overrun our country with their iron traps, and we and they will soon be poor. . . ."

JOHN JAMES AUDUBON

The Labrador Journal 1833

JOHN JAMES AUDUBON (1785–1851), although he claimed to have been born in Louisiana, the son of Admiral Audubon, was in fact born Jean-Jacques Audubon in Santo Domingo (now Haiti), the illegitimate son of a French sailor and planter. He studied painting in Paris and emigrated to the United States, where, upon completion of his great project, *The Birds of America*, he was recognized as one of the most gifted naturalist painters of all time. French naturalist Georges Cuvier saw in his work "the greatest monument that art has yet erected to science." In the summer of 1833, Audubon sailed on the schooner *Ripley* from Eastport, Maine, to the north shore of the St. Lawrence River, collecting specimens to paint and describe. The following extracts are from the diary he kept during this voyage; though they have been severely edited by his granddaughter, much of the raw power of the landscape, and of the man himself, remains.

🙒 • 🙔

August 1. BRAS D'OR, COAST OF LABRADOR. I have drawn my *Lestris pomarinus* [Pomarine Jaeger], but under difficulties; the weather has quite changed; instead of a hurricane from the east, we have had one all day from the southwest, but no rain. At noon we were visited by an iceberg, which has been drifting within three miles of us, and is now grounded at the entrance of the bay; it looks like a large man-of-war dressed in light green muslin, instead of canvas, and when the sun strikes it, it glitters with intense brilliancy. When these transient monuments of the sea happen to tumble or roll over, the fall is tremendous, and the sound produced resembles that of loud, distant thunder; these icebergs are common here all summer, being wafted south with every gale that blows; as the winds are usually easterly, the coast of Newfoundland is more free from them than that of Labrador.

August 4. Still raining as steadily as ever; the morning was calm, and on shore the mosquitoes were shockingly bad, though the thermometer indicates only 49°. I have been drawing at the *Numenius borcali* [Eskimo Curlew]; I find them difficult birds to represent. The young men went on shore and brought me four more; every one of the lads observed to-day the great tendency these birds have, in squatting to elude the eye, to turn the tail towards their pursuer, and to lay the head flat. This habit is common to many of the *Tringas* [Sandpipers] and some of the *Charadrius* [Plovers]. This species of Curlew, the smallest I ever saw, feeds on the berries it procures, with a rapidity equalled only by that of the Passenger Pigeon; in an instant all the ripe berries on the plant are plucked and swallowed, and the whole country is cleared of these berries as our Western woods are of the mast. In their evolutions they resemble Pigeons also, sweeping over the ground, cutting backward and forward in the most interesting manner, and now and then poising in the air like a Hawk in sight of quarry. There is scarcely any difference in the appearance of the adult and the young. The *Alauda alpestris* [Shore Lark] of this season has now made such progress in its growth that the first moulting is so forward that the small wing-coverts and secondaries are already come, and have assumed the beautiful rosy tints of the adults in patches at these parts; a most interesting state of their plumage, probably never seen by any naturalist before. It is quite surprising to see how quickly the growth is attained of every living thing in this country, either animal or vegetable. In six weeks I have seen the eggs laid, the birds hatched, their first moult half over, their association in flocks, and preparations begun for their leaving the country. That the Creator should have commanded millions of delicate, diminutive, tender creatures to cross immense spaces of country to all appearance a thousand times more congenial to them than this, to cause them to people, as it were, this desolate land for a time, to enliven it by the songs of the sweet feathered musicians for two months at most, and by the same command induce them to abandon it almost suddenly, is as wonderful as it is beautiful. The fruits are now ripe, yet six weeks ago the whole country was a sheet of snow, the bays locked in ice, the air a constant storm. Now the grass is rich in growth, at every step flowers are met with, insects fill the air, the snow-banks are melting; now and then an appearance as of summer does exist, but in thirty days all is over; the dark northern clouds will enwrap the mountain summits; the rivulets, the ponds, the rivers, the bays themselves will begin to freeze; heavy snowfalls will cover all these shores, and nature will resume her sleeping state, nay, more than that, one of desolation and death. Wonderful! Wonderful! But this marvellous country must be left to an abler pen than mine to describe. The *Tringa maritima* and *Tringa pusilla* [Labrador Curlew] were both shot in numbers this day; the young are now as large as the old, and we see little flocks everywhere. We heard the "Gulnare" was at Bonne Esperance, twenty miles west of us; I wish she was here, I should much like to see her officers again.

August 5. This has been a fine day, no hurricane. I have finished two Labrador Curlews, but not the ground. A few Curlews were shot, and a Black-breasted Plover. John shot a Shore Lark that had almost completed its moult; it appears to me that northern birds come to maturity sooner than southern ones, yet the reverse is the case in our own species. Birds of the *Tringa* kind are constantly passing over our heads in small bodies bound westward, some of the same species which I observed in the Floridas in October. The migration of birds is perhaps much more wonderful than that of fishes, almost all of which go feeling their way along the shores and return to the very same river, creek, or even hole to deposit their spawn, as birds do to their former nest; but the latter do not *feel* their way, but launching high in the air go at once and correctly too, across vast tracts of country, yet at once stopping, in portions heretofore their own, and of which they know by previous experiences the comforts and advantages. We have had several arrivals of vessels, some so heavily loaded with fish that the water runs over their decks; others, in ballast, have come to purchase fish.

August 10. I now sit down to post my poor book, while a heavy gale is raging furiously around our vessel. My reason for not writing at night is that I have been drawing so constantly, often seventeen hours a day, that the weariness of my body at night has been unprecedented, by such work at least. At times I felt as if my physical powers would abandon me; my neck, my shoulders, and, more than all, my fingers, were almost useless through actual fatigue at drawing. Who would believe this?—yet nothing is more true. When at the return of dawn my spirits called me out of my berth, my body seemed to beg my mind to suffer it to rest a while longer; and as dark forced me to lay aside my brushes I immediately went to rest as if I had walked sixty-five miles that day, as I have done *a few times* in my stronger days. Yesternight, when I rose from my little seat to contemplate my work and to judge of the effect of it compared with the nature which I had been attempting to copy, it was the affair of a moment; and instead of waiting, as I always like to do, until that hazy darkness which is to me the best time to judge of the strength of light and shade, I went at once to rest as if delivered from the heaviest task I ever performed. The young men think my fatigue is added to by the fact that I often work in wet clothes, but I have done that all my life with no ill effects. No! no! it is that I am no longer young. But I thank God that I did accomplish my task; my drawings are finished to the best of my ability, the skins well prepared by John. We have been to Paroket Island to procure the young of the *Mormon arcticus* [Common Puffin]. As we approached the breeding-place, the air was filled with these birds, and the water around absolutely covered with them, while on the rocks were thousands, like sentinels on the watch. I took a stand, loaded and shot twenty-seven times, and killed twenty-seven birds, singly and on the wing, without missing a shot; as friend Bachman would say, "Pretty fair, Old Jostle!" The young men laughed, and said the birds were so thick no one could miss if he tried; however, none of them did so well. We had more than we wanted, but the young were all too small to draw with effect. Nearly every bird I killed had a fish in its beak, closely held by the head, and the body dangling obliquely in the air. These fish were all of the kind called here *Lint,* a long slender fish now in shoals of millions. How many must the multitude of Mormons inhabiting this island destroy daily? Whilst flying they all issue a rough croak, but none dropped the fish, nor indeed did they let it go when brought to the earth. The *Larus marinus* [Great Black-backed Gull], have now almost all gone south with their young; indeed, very few Gulls of any sort are now to be seen. Whilst on the island we saw a Hawk pounce on a Puffin and carry it off. Curlews have increased in numbers, but during two fair days we had they could not be approached; indeed, they appear to be so intent on their passage south that whenever the weather permits they are seen to strike high in the air across the harbor. The gale is so severe that our anchors have dragged forty or fifty yards, but by letting out still more chain we are now safe. It blows and rains so hard that it is impossible to stand in the bow of our vessel. But this is not all,—who, *now,* will deny the existence of the Labrador Falcon? Yes, my Lucy, one more new species is on the list of the "Birds of America," and may we have the comfort of seeing its beautiful figure multiplied by Havell's engraver. This bird (both male and female) was shot by John whilst on an excursion with all our party, and on the 6th inst., when I sat till after twelve o'clock that night to outline one of them to save daylight the next day to color it, as I have done hundreds of times before. John shot them on the wing, whilst they were in company with their two young ones. The birds, one would be tempted to believe, had never seen a man before, for these affectionate parents dashed towards the gunners with fierce velocity, and almost instantly died from the effects of two well-directed shots. All efforts to procure the young birds were ineffectual; they were full grown, and as well as could be seen, exactly resembled the dead ones. The whole group flew much like the Peregrine Falcon, which indeed resembles them much in form, but neither in size nor color. Sometimes they hover almost high in air like a small Sparrow Hawk when watching some object fit for prey on the ground, and now and then cry much like the latter, but louder in proportion with the difference of size in the two species. Several times they alighted on stakes in the sandbar at the entrance of Bras d'Or River, and stood not as Hawks generally do, uprightly, but horizontally and much like a *Lestris* or a Tern. Beneath their nest we found the remains of *Alca torda* [Razor-billed Auk], *Uria troile* [Foolish Guillemot], and *Mormon arcticus*—all of which are within their reach on an island here called Paroket Island—also the remains of Curlews and Ptarmigans. The nest was so situated that it could not be reached, only seen into. Both birds were brought to me in excellent order. No more is known of this bird, I believe. My evening has been enlivened by the two Italians from the "Wizard," who have been singing many songs to the accompaniment of John's violin.

August 11. At sea, Gulf of St. Lawrence. We are now, seven of the evening, fully fifty miles from the coast of Labrador. We left our harbor at eleven o'clock with a fair breeze; the storm of last night had died away and everything looked promising. The boats were sent ashore for a supply of fresh water; John and Coolidge went after Curlews; the rest of the crew, assisted by that of the "Wizard," raised the anchors, and all was soon in readiness. The bottom of our vessel had been previously scraped and cleaned from the thousands of barnacles, which, with a growth of seaweeds, seemed to feed upon her as they do on the throat of a whale. The two Italians and Captain Wilcomb came on board to bid us adieu; we hoisted sail, and came out of the Labrador harbor. Seldom in my life have I left a country with as little regret as I do this; the next nearest to this was East Florida, after my excursions up the St. John's River. As we sailed away, and I saw, probably for the last time, the high rugged hills partly immersed in masses of the thick fog that usually hovers over them, and knew that now the bow of our truly fine vessel was turned towards the place where thou, my Lucy, art waiting for me, I felt rejoiced, although yet far away. Now we are sailing in full sight of the northwestern coast of Newfoundland, the mountains of which are high, with drifted snow-banks dotted over them, and cut horizontally with floating strata of fogs reaching along the land as far as the eye can see. The sea is quite smooth; at least I think so, or have become a better seaman through habit. John and Lincoln are playing airs on the violin and flute; the other young men are on deck. It is worth saying that during the two months we have been on the coast of Labrador, moving from one harbor to another, or from one rocky isle to another, only three nights have we spent at sea. Twenty-three drawings have been executed, or commenced and nearly completed. Whether this voyage will prove a fruitful one remains to be proved; but I am content, and hope the Creator will permit us to reach our country and find our friends well and happy.

HENRY DAVID THOREAU

A Yankee in Canada 1866

HENRY DAVID THOREAU (1817–1862) was born in Concord, Massachusetts, educated at Harvard, and studied botany under the great naturalist
Louis Agassiz. Under the influence of Ralph Waldo Emerson, who urged
him to keep a diary and who owned the land on which Walden Pond was
located, Thoreau became one of the most influential writers and thinkers of
the Transcendentalist movement. His best-known book is *Walden* (1854).
Thoreau spent a week traveling by foot and by boat from Montreal to
Quebec City. In his little-known account of the trip, from which this
excerpt is taken, Thoreau is as fascinated by the people who live on the
land as he is by the natural splendors that surround them, and in some ways
he denies his own dictum that "it appears to be a law that you cannot have
a deep sympathy with both man and nature."

ST. ANNE.

BY THE MIDDLE of the forenoon, though it was a rainy day, we were once
more on our way down the north bank of the St. Lawrence, in a northeasterly
direction, toward the Falls of St. Anne, which are about thirty miles from
Quebec. The settled, more level, and fertile portion of Canada East may be
described rudely as a triangle, with its apex slanting toward the northeast,
about one hundred miles wide at its base, and from two to three, or even four
hundred miles long, if you reckon its narrow northeastern extremity; it being
the immediate valley of the St. Lawrence and its tributaries, rising by a single
or by successive terraces toward the mountains on either hand. Though the
words Canada East on the map stretch over many rivers and lakes and unexplored wildernesses, the actual Canada, which might be the colored portion

of the map, is but a little clearing on the banks of the river, which one of those syllables would more than cover. The banks of the St. Lawrence are rather low from Montreal to the Richelieu Rapids, about forty miles above Quebec. Thence they rise gradually to Cape Diamond, or Quebec. Where we now were, eight miles northeast of Quebec, the mountains which form the northern side of this triangle were only five or six miles distant from the river, gradually departing farther and farther from it, on the west, till they reach the Ottawa, and making haste to meet it on the east, at Cape Tourmente, now in plain sight about twenty miles distant. So that we were traveling in a very narrow and sharp triangle between the mountains and the river, tilted up toward the mountains on the north, never losing sight of our great fellow-traveler on our right. According to Bouchette's *Topographical Description of the Canadas,* we were in the Seigniory of the Côte de Beaupré, in the county of Montmorenci, and the district of Quebec; in that part of Canada which was the first to be settled, and where the face of the country and the population have undergone the least change from the beginning, where the influence of the States and of Europe is least felt, and the inhabitants see little or nothing of the world over the walls of Quebec. This Seigniory was granted in 1636, and is now the property of the Seminary of Quebec. It is the most mountainous one in the province. There are some half a dozen parishes in it, each containing a church, parsonage-house, grist-mill, and several sawmills. We were now in the most westerly parish called Ange Gardien, or the Guardian Angel, which is bounded on the west by the Montmorenci. The north bank of the St. Lawrence here is formed on a grand scale. It slopes gently, either directly from the shore, or from the edge of an interval, till, at the distance of about a mile, it attains the height of four or five hundred feet. The single road runs along the side of the slope two or three hundred feet above the river at first, and from a quarter of a mile to a mile distant from it, and affords fine views of the north channel, which is about a mile wide, and of the beautiful Isle of Orleans, about twenty miles long by five wide, where grow the best apples and plums in the Quebec District.

Though there was but this single road, it was a continuous village for as far as we walked this day and the next, or about thirty miles down the river, the houses being as near together all the way as in the middle of one of our smallest straggling country villages, and we could never tell by their number when we were on the skirts of a parish, for the road never ran through the fields or woods. We were told that it was just six miles from one parish church to another. I thought that we saw every house in Ange Gardien. Therefore, as it was a muddy day, we never got out of the mud, nor out of the village, unless we got over the fence; then indeed, if it was on the north side, we were out of the civilized world. There were sometimes a few more houses near the church, it is true, but we had only to go a quarter of a mile from the road to the top of the bank to find ourselves on the verge of the uninhabited, and, for the most part, unexplored wilderness stretching toward Hudson Bay. The farms accordingly were extremely long and narrow, each having a frontage on the river. Bouchette accounts for this peculiar manner of laying out a village by referring to "the social character of the Canadian peasant, who is singularly fond of neighborhood," also to the advantage arising from a concentration of strength in Indian times. . . .

We saw peas, and even beans, collected into heaps in the fields. The former are an important crop here, and, I suppose, are not so much infested by the weevil as with us. There were plenty of apples, very fair and sound, by the roadside, but they were so small as to suggest the origin of the apple in the crab. There was also a small red fruit which they called *snells,* and another, also red and very acid, whose name a little boy wrote for me *"pinbéna."* It is probably the same with, or similar to, the *pembina* of the voyageurs, a species of viburnum, which, according to Richardson, has given its name to many of the rivers of Rupert's Land. The forest trees were spruce, arbor-vitae, firs, birches, beeches, two or three kinds of maple, bass-wood, wild-cherry, aspens, &c., but no pitch pines *(Pinus rigida).* I saw very few, if any, trees which had been set out for shade or ornament. The water was commonly running streams or springs in the bank by the roadside, and was excellent. The parishes are commonly separated by a stream, and frequently the farms. I noticed that the fields were furrowed or thrown into beds seven or eight feet wide to dry the soil.

At the *Rivière du Sault à la Puce,* which, I suppose, means the River of the Fall of the Flea, was advertised in English, as the sportsmen are English, "The best Snipe-shooting grounds," over the door of a small public-house. These words being English affected me as if I had been absent now ten years from my country, and for so long had not heard the sound of my native language, and every one of them was as interesting to me as if I had been a snipe-shooter, and they had been snipes. The prunella or self-heal, in the grass here, was an old acquaintance. We frequently saw the inhabitants washing, or cooking for their pigs, and in one place hackling flax by the roadside. It was pleasant to see these usually domestic operations carried on out of doors, even in that cold country.

At twilight we reached a bridge over a little river, the boundary between Chateau Richer and St. Anne, *le premier pont de St. Anne,* and at dark the church of *La Bonne St. Anne.* Formerly vessels from France, when they came in sight of this church, gave "a general discharge of their artillery," as a sign of joy that they had escaped all the dangers of the river. Though all the while we had grand views of the adjacent country far up and down the river, and, for the most part, when we turned about, of Quebec in the horizon behind us, and we never beheld it without new surprise and admiration; yet, throughout our walk, the Great River of Canada on our right hand was the main feature in the landscape, and this expands so rapidly below the Isle of Orleans, and creates such a breadth of level horizon above its waters in that direction, that, looking down the river as we approached the extremity of that island, the St. Lawrence seemed to be opening into the ocean, though we were still about three hundred and twenty-five miles from what can be called its mouth. . . .

The falls, which we were in search of, are three miles up the St. Anne. We followed for a short distance a foot-path up the east bank of this river, through handsome sugar-maple and arbor-vitae groves. Having lost the path which led to a house where we were to get further directions, we dashed at once into the woods, steering by guess and by compass, climbing directly through woods, a steep hill, or mountain, five or six hundred feet high, which was, in fact, only the band of the St. Lawrence. Beyond this we by good luck fell into another path, and following this or a branch of it, at our discretion, through a forest consisting of large white pines,—the first we had seen in our walk,—we at length heard the roar of falling water, and came out at the head of the Falls of St. Anne. We had descended into a ravine or cleft in the mountain, whose walls rose still a hundred feet above us, though we were near its top, and we now stood on a very rocky shore, where the water had lately flowed a dozen feet higher, as appeared by the stones and drift-wood, and large birches twisted and splintered as a farmer twists a withe. Here the river, one or two hundred feet wide, came flowing rapidly over a rocky bed out of that interesting wilderness which stretches toward Hudson Bay and Davis's Straits. Ha-ha Bay, on the Saguenay, was about one hundred miles north of where we stood. Looking on the map, I find that the first country on the north which bears a name is that part of Rupert's Land called East Main. This river, called after the holy Anne, flowing from such a direction, here tumbled over à precipice, at present by three channels, how far down I do not know, but far enough for all our purposes, and to as good a distance as if twice as far. It matters little whether you call it one, or two, or three hundred feet; at any rate, it was a sufficient Water-privilege for us. I crossed the principal channel directly over the verge of the fall, where it was contracted to about fifteen feet in width by a dead tree, which had been dropped across and secured in a cleft of the opposite rock, and a smaller one a few feet higher, which served for a hand-rail. This bridge was rotten as well as small and slippery, being stripped of bark, and I was obliged to seize a moment to pass when the falling water did not surge over it, and midway, though at the expense of wet feet, I looked down probably more than a hundred feet, into the mist and foam below. This gave me the freedom of an island of precipitous rock, by which I descended as by giant steps, the rock being composed of large cubical masses, clothed with delicate close-hugging lichens of various colors, kept fresh and bright by the moisture, till I viewed the first fall from the front, and looked down still deeper to where the second and third channels fell into a remarkably large circular basin worn in by the stone. The falling water seemed to jar the very rocks, and the noise to be ever increasing. The vista down stream was through a narrow and deep cleft in the mountain, all white suds at the bottom; but a sudden angle in this gorge prevented my seeing through to the bottom of the fall. Returning to the shore, I made my way down stream through the forest to see how far the fall extended, and how the river came out of that adventure. It was to clamber along the side of a precipitous mountain of loose mossy rocks, covered with a damp primitive forest, and terminating at the bottom in an abrupt precipice over the stream. This was the east side of the fall. At length, after a quarter of a mile, I got down to still water, and, on looking up through the winding gorge, I could just see to the foot of the fall which I had before examined; while from the opposite side of the stream, here much contracted, rose a perpendicular wall, I will not venture to say how many hundred feet, but only that it was the highest perpendicular wall of bare rock that I ever saw. In front of me tumbled in from the summit of the cliff a tributary stream, making a beautiful cascade, which was a remarkable fall in itself, and there was a cleft in this precipice, apparently four or five feet wide, perfectly straight up and down from top to bottom, which, from its cavernous depth and darkness, appeared merely as *a black streak*. This precipice is not sloped, nor is the material soft and crumbling slate as at Montmorenci, but it rises perfectly perpendicular, like the side of a mountain fortress, and is cracked into vast cubical masses of gray and black rock shining with moisture, as if it were the ruin of an ancient wall built by Titans. Birches, spruces, mountain-ashes with their bright red berries, arbor-vitae, white pines, alders, &c., overhung this chasm on the very verge of the cliff and in the crevices, and here and there were buttresses of rock supporting trees part way down, yet so as to enhance, not injure, the effect of the bare rock. Take it altogether, it was a most wild and rugged and stupendous chasm, so deep and narrow where a river had worn itself a passage through a mountain of rock, and all around was the comparatively untrodden wilderness.

WALT WHITMAN

Diary in Canada 1880

WALT WHITMAN (1819–1892) was born in Brooklyn, New York, the son of a carpenter, and became first a printer and then a teacher (until 1841) before traveling to New Orleans, where he mingled with artists and Bohemians and began to write the poems that eventually appeared in *Leaves of Grass* (1855). Though attacked for his wildness and physicality by most critics, he was supported by Emerson and Thoreau (who wrote that Whitman "occasionally suggests something a little more than human"), and by John Burroughs, who became his closest friend and biographer. As a prose writer, Whitman's strength was in his powers of observation: *Specimen Days* (1882) is full of sharp insights into the ways of birds, insects and their interrelations with humankind. In 1879, Whitman traveled to London, Ontario, to visit his friend Dr. Richard Bucke, and later sailed up the St. Lawrence to the Saguenay River. The following is excerpted from Whitman's diary of the trip.

ey • ga

SUNRISE, THE ST. LAWRENCE near Quebec, Aug. 5–6. Have just seen sunrise (standing on the extreme bow of the boat), the great round dazzling ball straight ahead over the broad waters—a rare view. The shores pleasantly, thickly, dotted with houses, the river here wide and looking beautiful in the golden morning's sheen. As we advance northeast the earth-banks high and sheer, quite thickly wooded; thin dawn-mists quickly resolving; the youthful, strong, warm forenoon over the high green bluffs; little white houses seen along the banks as we steam rapidly through the verdure; occasionally a pretensive mansion, a mill, a two-tower'd church (in burnish'd tin). A pretty shore (miles of it, sitting up high, well-sprinkled with dwellings of habitans—farmers, fishermen, French cottagers, etc.), verdant everywhere (but no big trees) for fifty miles before coming to Quebec. These little rural cluster-towns just back from the bank-bluffs, so happy and peaceful looking. I saw them through my glass, everything quite minutely and fully. In one such town of perhaps two hundred houses on sloping ground, the old church with glistening spire stood in the middle, and quite a large graveyard around it. I could see the white headstones almost plainly enough to count them.

Approaching Quebec, rocks and rocky banks again, the shores lined for many miles with immense rafts and logs and partially hewn timber, the hills more broken and abrupt, the higher shores crowded with many fine dormer-window'd houses. Sail-ships appear in clusters with their weather-beaten spars and furl'd canvas. The river still ample and grand, the banks bold, plenty of round turns and promontories, plenty of gray rock cropping out. Rafts, rafts, of logs everywhere. The high rocky citadel thrusts itself out—altogether perhaps (at any rate as you approach it on the water, the sun two hours high) as picturesque an appearing city as there is on earth.

Aug. 6, Quebec. To the east of Quebec we pass the large fertile island of Orleans—the fields divided in long lateral strips across the island and appearing to be closely cultivated. In one field I notice them getting in the hay, a woman assisting, loading and hauling it. The view and scene continue broad and beautiful under the forenoon sun; around me an expanse of waters stretches fore and aft as far as I can see; outlines of mountains in the distance north and south; of the farthest ones the bulk and the crest lines showing through strong but delicate haze like gray lace.

Aug. 6. Night—we are steaming up the Saguenay.

Ha Ha Bay. I am here nearly 1000 miles slightly east of due north from Philadelphia, by way of Montreal and Quebec—in the strangest country. Had a good night's sleep; cold,—overcoat, but up before sunrise—northern lights every night, as with overcoat on or wrapt in my blanket, I plant myself on the forward deck.

Aug. 6 and 7, Ha Ha Bay. Up the black Saguenay River, a hundred or so miles—a dash of the grimmest, wildest, savagest scenery on the planet, I guess; a strong, deep (always hundreds of feet, sometimes thousands), dark-water'd river, very dark, with high rocky hills, green and gray edged banks in all directions—no flowers, no fruits (plenty of delicious wild blueberries and raspberries up at Chicoutimi, though, and Ha Ha Bay).

Again I steam over the Saguenay. The bronze-black waters, and the thin lines of white curd, and the dazzling sun-dash on the stream, the banks of grim-gray mountains and the rocks—I see the grim and savage scene.

Made a good breakfast of sea-trout, finishing off with wild raspberries. Hotels here; a few fashionables, but they get away soon; it is almost cold, except the middle of a few July and August days.

A more or less aquatic character runs through the people. The two influences of French and British contribute a curious by-play.

Contrasts all the while. At this place, backed by these mountains high and bold, nestled down the hamlet of St. Pierre, apparently below the level of the bay, and very secluded and cosy. Then two or three miles further on I saw a larger town high up on the plateau. At St. Paul's Bay a stronger cast of scenery, many rugged peaks.

On the Saguenay. THE NOTICEABLE ITEMS ON LAND: the long boxes of blueberries (we had over a thousand of them carried on board at Ha Ha Bay one day I was on the pier); the groups of "boarders" (retaining all their most refined toggery); the vehicles, some "calashes," many queer old one-horse top-wagons with an air of faded gentility. On the water: the sail craft and steamers we pass out in the stream; the rolling and turning up of the white-bellied porpoises; some special island or rock (often very picturesque in color or form); all the scenes at the piers as we land to leave or take passengers and freight, especially many of the natives; the changing aspect of the light and the marvellous study from that alone every hour of the day or night; the indescribable sunsets and sunrises (I often see the latter now); the scenes at breakfast and other meal-times (and what an appetite one gets!); the delicious fish (I mean from the cook's fire, hot).

I had a good opera glass, and made constant use of it, sweeping every shore.

Northern lights every night.

Quebec from the River, Aug. 8, '80. Imagine a high rocky hill (the angles each a mile long), flush and bold to the river, with plateau on top, the front handsomely presented to the south and east (we are steaming up the river); on the principal height, still flush with the stream, a vast stone fort, the most conspicuous object in view; the magnificent St. Lawrence itself; many hills and ascents and tall edifices shown at their best—and steeples; the handsome town of Point Levi opposite; a long low sea-steamer just hauling out.

Aug. 9, Quebec. Forenoon. We have driven out six or seven miles to the Montmorenci Falls, and I am writing this as I sit high up on the steps, the cascade immediately before me, the great rocky chasm at my right and an immense lumber depot bordering the river, far, far below, almost under me to the left. It makes a pretty and picturesque show, but not a grand one. The principal fall, 30 or 40 feet wide and 250 high, pours roaring and white down a slant of dark gray rocks, and there are six or seven rivulet falls flanking it.

Since writing the above I have gone down the steps (some 350) to the foot of the Fall, which I recommend every visitor to do: the view is peculiar and fine. The whole scene grows steadily upon one, and I can imagine myself, after many visits, forming a finally first-class estimate, from what I see here of Montmorenci over a part of the scaly, grim, bald-black rock, the water falling downward like strings of snowy-spiritual beautiful tresses.

The road out here from the city is a very good one, lined with moderate-class houses, copious with women and children. Doors and windows wide open, exhibiting many groups to us as we passed. The men appear to be away: I wonder what they work at? Every house for miles is set diagonally with one of its corners to the road, never its gable or front. There seems little farming here, and I see no factories.

Aug. 9 [on the St. Lawrence]. Very pleasant journey of 180 miles this afternoon and to-night; crowds of Catholic priests on board with their long loose black gowns, and the broad brims of their hats turned into a peculiar triangle.

Aug. 10. Again in Montreal. As I write this I am seated aft in the delicious river breeze on the steamboat that is to take me back west some 380 miles from here to Hamilton. Two hours yet before we start; few passengers, as they come east by the boats, and then generally take the railroad back. Montreal has the largest show of sail ships and handsome ocean steamers of any place on the river and lake line, and I am right in full sight of them.

Going on the river westward from Montreal is pretty slow and tedious, taking a long time to get through the canals and many locks, to Lake St. Francis, where the steamer emerges to the river again. These rapids along here—the boats can descend, but cannot go up them. A great inconvenience to the navigator, but they are quite exciting with their whirls and roar and foam, and very picturesque.

Aug. 14, 5½ P.M. Arrived back in London a couple of hours ago, all right. Am writing this in my room, Dr. B.'s house.

Along the way on the journey from Hamilton to London everywhere through the car-windows I saw locust-trees growing and the broad yellow faces of sunflowers, the sumac bushes with their red cones, and the orchard trees loaded with apples.

The waters, the lakes, and the indescribable grandeur of the St. Lawrence are the beauty of Canada through this vast line of two thousand miles and over. In its peculiar advantages, sanities, and charms, I doubt whether the globe for democratic purposes has its equal.

A grand, sane, temperate land, the amplest and most beautiful and stream of water—a river and necklace of vast lakes, pure, sweet, eligible, supplied by the chemistry of millions of square miles of gushing springs and melted snows. No stream this for side *frontier*—stream rather for the great central current, the glorious mid-artery, of the great Free Pluribus Unum of America, the solid Nationality of the present and the future, the home of an improved grand race of men and women; not of some select class only, but of larger, saner, better masses. I should say this vast area was fitted to be their unsurpassed habitat.

I know nothing finer. The European democratic tourist, philanthropist, geographer, or genuine inquirer, will make a fatal mistake who leaves these shores without understanding this.—I know nothing finer, either from the point of view of the sociologist, the traveler, or the artist, than a month's devotion to even the surface of Canada, over the line of the great Lakes and the St. Lawrence, the fertile, populous, and happy province of Ontario, the [province] of Quebec, with another month to the hardy maritime regions of New Brunswick, Nova Scotia, and Newfoundland.

I see, or imagine I see in the future, a race of two million farm-families, ten million people—every farm running down to the water, or at least in sight of it—the best air and drink and sky and scenery of the globe, the sure foundation-nutriment of heroic men and women. The summers, the winters—I have sometimes doubted whether there could be a great race without the hardy influence of winters in due proportion.

Total Dominion, 3,500,000 square miles. Quebec, Ontario, Nova Scotia, New Brunswick, Prince Edward Island, British Columbia, Manitoba, Hudson Bay, and Northwest Territories. (Newfoundland not in Dominion.) Area equal to the whole of Europe. Population, 1880, four to five millions.

Principal timber: white and red pine. The woods are full of white oak, elm, beech, ash, maple (bird's-eye, curled, etc.), walnut, cedar, birch, tamarack, sugar orchards (maple).

The honey-bee everywhere; rural ponds and lakes (often abounding with the great white sweet-smelling water-lily); wild fruits and berries everywhere; in the vast flat grounds the prairie anemone.

The fisheries of Canada are almost unparalleled. . . . Then the furs. . . .

If the most significant trait of modern civilization is benevolence (as a lead-ing statesman has said), it is doubtful whether this is anywhere illustrated to a fuller degree than in the province of Ontario. All the maimed, insane, idiotic, blind, deaf and dumb, needy, sick and old, minor criminals, fallen women, foundlings, have advanced and ample provision of house and care and over-sight, at least fully equal to anything of the kind in any of the United States—probably indeed superior to them. In Ontario for its eighty-eight electoral ridings, each one returning a member of parliament, there are four Insane Asylums, an Idiot Asylum, one Institution for the Blind, one for the Deaf and Dumb, one for Foundlings, a Reformatory for Girls, one for Women, and no end of homes for the old and infirm, for waifs, and for the sick.

Its school system, founded on the Massachusetts plan, is one of the best and most comprehensive in the world.

Some of the good people of Ontario have complained in my hearing of faults and fraudulencies, commissive or omissive, on the part of the govern-ment, but I guess said people have reason to bless their stars for the general fairness, economy, wisdom, and liberality of their officers and administration.

Aug. 21, '80. I rose this morning at four and look'd out on the most pure and refulgent starry show. Right over my head, like a Tree-Universe spreading with its orb-apples,—Aldebaran leading the Hyades; Jupiter of amazing lustre, softness, and volume; and, not far behind, heavy Saturn—both past the merid-ian; the seven sparkling gems of the Pleiades; the full moon, voluptuous and yellow, and full of radiance, an hour to setting in the west. Everything so fresh, so still; the delicious something there is in early youth, in early dawn—the spirit, the spring, the *feel;* the air and light, precursors of the untried sun; love, action, forenoon, noon, life—full-fibred, latent with them all. And is not that Orion the mighty hunter? Are not those the three glittering studs in his belt? And there to the north Capella and his kids.

Aug. 29. At Dr. B's. The robins on the grassy lawn (I sometimes see a dozen at a time, great fat fellows). The little black-and-yellow bird with his billowy flight [the goldfinch]; the flocks of sparrows.

CATHARINE PARR TRAILL

Notes From My Old Diary 1894

CATHARINE PARR TRAILL (1802–1899) was born in Kent, England, one
of the "literary Stricklands"; she wrote several children's books before she
and her husband (and her sister, Susanna Moodie, and her brother, Samuel
Strickland) emigrated to property near Lakefield, Ontario, in 1832. Four
years later she wrote *The Backwoods of Canada*, her famous collection of
sketches meant for prospective immigrants. *Canadian Wild Flowers*, illustrated
by her niece, Agnes (Moodie) Fitzgibbon, appeared in 1868 and established
Traill as a respected naturalist. *Studies of Plant Life in Canada* (1885)—a more
scientific work aimed at the serious botanist—and *Pearls and Pebbles; or, Notes
of an Old Naturalist* (1894), from which this excerpt is taken, confirmed her
reputation as the foremost authority of her day on Canadian botanical lore.
She died in Lakefield, an "old naturalist" at the age of ninety-seven.

ᏂᎧ • ᏻᏗ

ON LOOKING OVER my old diary of a far-off date, 1839, I find notes of
many things that struck me in the first years of my sojourn in my forest
home—objects that then were new and interesting to me, but which now I
seldom or never see.

There is a change in the country: many of the plants and birds and wild
creatures, common once, have disappeared entirely before the march of civilization. As the woods which shelter them are cleared away, they retire to the
lonely forest haunts still left, where they may remain unmolested and unseen
till again driven back by the advance of man upon the scene.

It is rarely now that I catch a passing glimpse of the lovely plumed crossbill,
or the scarlet tanager; seldom do I hear the cry of the bobolink, or watch the
sailing of the bald-headed eagle or the fish-hawk over the lake, as I did for-

merly in fear for the safety of my little goslings. Even the gay, cheerful note of the chickadee is rarely heard, or the sonorous rapping of the red-headed woodpecker, or the plaintive, oft-repeated monosyllable of the wood phoebe.

I think these birds dislike the appearance of the red brick houses of the modern villages and towns, with their green blinds and fancy work in wood and paint. Perhaps they look upon them as possible traps to cage them, and find the old familiar rude shanty or log-house more to their taste in architecture.

Here is one of my old notes made in that long ago time on the great cat-owl:

A very solemn, formidable-looking bird is this big long-eared owl. One was shot and brought into the house for my inspection. It was still living, having only been winged, and evidently was very angry with its captor, ready to avenge itself by a blow with its strong hooked beak and sharp talons. The glassy round eyes were glaring ominously from beneath the swathe of rich brown mottled feathers that half shaded them from the light. The ears, or the tuft of feathers that concealed them, stood up, giving a warrior-like aspect to the grand, proud bird.

Who is there among the early settlers that has not heard in the deep stillness of night, from some old oak in the woods or out-building near the house, the deep sonorous voice of the cat-owl calling to its mate? The hollow notes sound like "Ho—ho—ho—ho," repeated with a pause between each syllable, as if to prolong the echo.

The Indian notes of lamentation over the dead, *"Wo-ho-ha-no-min,"* seem an imitation of the mournful cry of this night bird.

An old Irish settler in the backwoods once gravely assured me that the "Banshee," the warning spirit of death or trouble which, he said, belonged to his family when he lived in Ireland, had followed him and his house to Canada. I looked a little doubtful. The old man grew angry because I asked:

"Did she come out in the ship with you?"

"Shure an' why should she not?" he replied. "Did she not cry all the time me poor wife—God rest her sowl—was in the death thraws? An' did she not cry the night the cow died?"

That indeed was a proof not to be doubted, so I judiciously held my sceptical tongue, though I thought it might well have been the cat-owl crying to her mate from an old hollow tree near the shanty; but it would have been rank heresy to liken a real faithful family "Cry-by-night" or "Banshee" to a cat-owl.

Later the old man in rather an aggrieved tone, questioned my faith in the "little people," or the fairies. When I suggested it was a long way for them to come across the Atlantic, he took great pains to convince me that if they cared for the family when they lived in Ireland, they would not mind how long the voyage or the distance, so that they could watch over them here.

On the borders of the lake I see many beautiful dragon-flies of all colors— red, blue, green, bronze, and some rare large flies with jet-black gauzy wings.

One kind, that I have tried in vain to capture, had a scarlet crescent mark on each lower pair of wings. Another, not less remarkable, was distinguished by azure blue crescents on the wings. These flies led me a chase for some time, I was so much struck with the beauty of the rare insects. They did not resemble the gay dragonflies in form or color, and I wished to obtain a specimen to send home to a friend; but after that summer I saw them no more, they having disappeared with the pine woods.

There is a pretty and curious insect, one of the Sphinx family, that comes out in the cool of the evening, and is very busy on the mignonette and other low growing border plants. It is very much like a bee in appearance, and sings a low humming song as it darts from flower to flower. Its body is longer and narrower than that of the bee, and its colors are black and white in bands. The lower wings of these curious moths are exceedingly small, the upper ones long and narrow. The swiftness of its hovering motions and the noise of its wings remind one of the humming-bird, hence people call it the Humming Moth.

The most beautiful of our native moths, and also the largest, is the exquisite pale green *Attacus luna*. This classical name was given it from the moon-shaped figure on each wing, showing the bright colors of blue and scarlet in the centre of the eye-like spots.

The lower pair of wings are lengthened into long tails like the school-boy's kite, and are beautifully fringed with a pale gold bordering. These long tails are said to be of essential service in aiding the flight of the moth, serving to maintain a proper balance in its passage through the air. Several of our butterflies—as, for example, *Papilio turnus,* the handsome sulphur-colored Swallowtail—have this form in a great degree, while in others it is absent, as in *Danais archippus,* a fine red butterfly, one of our largest and most showy; also in the representative of the Camberwell Beauty and some others.

The body of the beautiful green *Attacus luna* is thickly clothed with soft silky white down. The legs, feet and antennae are of a coppery-red color, the latter short and finely pectinated—that is, having fine tooth-like projections.

The scarlet and blue colors are very effective in contrast to the exquisite tint of pale green which distinguishes this lovely moth from all others. It is very rarely to be seen now, but seems to love the shade among the orchard and forest trees.

It is in the orchard that we find the cocoons of that grand moth, the *Attacus cecropia,* a splendid insect, both in size, form and rich colors; as large, when its wings are fully expanded, as some of our smaller birds, measuring, indeed, nearly seven inches in width.

The heavy thick body of this insect is red, but marked by deep rings, and the surface clothed with soft whitish hairs. The head is large and the antennae strongly pectinated.

The marks on the wings are in the form of half-moons, showing a variety of shadings, with vivid blue and some red in the centre. There are other lines and wavy marks on the wings, besides a deep rich border pattern.

I am afraid my very unscientific mode of description may offend the learned entomologist. If so, I crave pardon and plead limited knowledge as my sufficient excuse.

The common name for this fine moth is the Apple-tree or Orchard Moth, because its brown felted chrysalid cases are found attached to the twigs of orchard trees.

The first really hot days cause the imprisoned insect to burst from its sealed coffin, and its wonderful and mysterious resurrection to light and life is at once effected. It flutters forth a glorious but short-lived creature, perfect in all its beauty, to soar aloft in the sunlight and enjoy the sweet warm summer air for a brief season—a type to man of the promised resurrection of his own body from the dust of the earth, through the perfect work of redeeming love in the Lord Jesus Christ. "O Death! where is thy sting? O Grave! where is thy victory?"

Since the above description of the *Attacus cecropia* was written, some years ago, I have had knowledge of two varieties of this remarkably beautiful moth.

About two years ago a friend sent me from Chicago three cocoons of this species. These cases, attached to slender twigs, were much smaller in size than the apple-tree variety, and were light brown and finely felted.

The moths (two came out all right, one was abortive) were smaller in every way, but beautiful in markings and color. They remained on a sunny window for some days, then one died and the other disappeared.

Last Christmas I was given another cocoon, fixed to a red-barked dogwood spray. It was of large size and very unlike the brown woolly cases I had hitherto seen. It was constructed of dead leaves and a gray papery substance like that of the wasp. There was no opening whatever in it; all was closely sealed up.

One sunny morning (April 21st) I was delighted at the sight of the tenant of the gray house, a magnificent specimen of the *Attacus* moth. It stood opening and closing its wings as if in flight, but remained for hours on the leaf of a scarlet geranium near the window, giving me a good opportunity of noting its beauty. Especially did I admire the rich coloring and markings on the wide wings, which were about six inches in extent and elegantly rounded and lobed.

The general color or ground-work was a rich dark red brown, with two large irregular white circular figures; within the larger circle was another figure semi-circular in form and of several shaded colors. The lower pair of wings were scalloped and smaller than those of the upper wings, and beautifully marked and fringed with a bordering of white, red and gray.

The body of the moth was short and thick, barred with white, and having deep red spots between the lines. The outer surface of the back, seen between the open wings, was deep red. The legs were clothed with a velvety red down.

As soon as the lamp was lighted, the moth spread its wings and, bat-like, flew to the light, and would have been seriously injured had we not come to the rescue—not, however, before the feathery margin of the wings was somewhat scorched. Taken out of the room it flew about, casting a dark bat-like shadow on the ceiling. For some days it hid itself among the window curtains, coming out of this retreat only at night, and for the past few days it has remained fixed to the corner of the what-not in the parlor. Its wings are closed, and it has apparently lost all of its energy; the light no longer attracts it, the fine red pectinated antennae no longer are moved as at first—the beautiful creature is dead, or dying.

On a minute inspection being made of the empty cocoon, it seemed a mystery how the big, bulky insect could have escaped from its prison. There was no visible aperture for its exit save one small pipe terminating in a tiny orifice, through which it seemed impossible that even the head of the creature could have issued. Yet, this must have been its door of egress, for no other was to be seen.

Among the myriad marvels in Nature, there are no greater than those found in the insect world.

I was given two of the large brown cases of Orchard Moth last winter. I laid them aside in the drawing-room and forgot all about them. One warm May day, on going into the room, great was my surprise and delight to see two beautiful creatures on the window panes, enjoying the sunshine, and, I dare say, longing to be out in the warm free air.

By and by they became very restless, as if bewildered by the novelty of their surroundings, flitting about on the gay flowers of the curtains, and finally, after several days had elapsed, one of the two deposited sixteen gold-colored eggs on the chintz. I make a note of the bare fact, and leave it to be pondered over by the experienced naturalist.

Besides the butterflies I have noticed in my old diary, I might have named the Tortoise-shell and the two Admirals, the red-marked one and the white. There are many others, too, which resemble in color and appearance species I was familiar with when in England.

There are the Tiger Moths, bright, gay creatures that come in at night attracted by the light of the lamp; and some large beautiful gray and rose-colored varieties with damasked wings, which shun the glare of the light and retreat to shaded corners of the walls out of sight.

Our beautiful oak trees are often disfigured when in full leaf by branches of brown or withered leaves, as if some scorching blast had fallen upon them.

I was standing on the lawn at my friends, the Haywards, admiring the glossy foliage of a group of handsome scarlet oaks *(Rubra coccinea),* one of the most beautiful of our native oaks, when my attention was drawn to one of the branches of a fine young tree near me which was affected by a quivering motion, while the rest were quite still.

It was an intensely hot July day, not a breath of air stirring the leaves. Suddenly the branch parted from the tree and fell at my feet. I took it up to examine the cause of its fall. The leaves were still green and fresh, but on close inspection of the severed part, which was nearly half an inch in diameter, I found it finely grooved, as if it had been sawed or filed by some sharp toothed instrument.

This was evidently the work of a Sawyer or Borer, one of the numerous species of the destructive *Bupestrioe,* which in the larvae state are so injurious to our forest trees.

I sought diligently on the ground for the little workman, but while I had been examining the branch he had hidden himself away in the grass, there to undergo the last change to the perfect state of his kind as a small beetle.

Being desirous of obtaining some information concerning the creature and its work, I turned to the report of the "Field Naturalists' Society of Ottawa" for 1884 (page 49), and the following description satisfied me that my sawyer must have been the larvae of a Twig-girdler: "*Oncideres cingulatus.* When the female desires to deposit her eggs she makes punctures in the bark of small twigs or branches. She then girdles the branch by gnawing a ring round it, which kills the branch, and in course of time it breaks off from the tree and falls to the ground, and the larvae feed on the dead wood. The beetle is grayish brown with a broad gray band. It is commonly knows as the 'Twig-girdler.' "

In the present instance the leaf of the branch was still fresh and green, but at the same time I noticed the noiseless fall of branches from the oak trees adjoining, and saw that the ground was strewn with dead withered boughs and sprays, while others still hung by tiny shreds of bark, ready to fall, and disfiguring the appearance of the trees.

The entomologists now employed by the Government and attached to the Bureau of Agriculture, have of late years turned their attention to the appearance and habits of this class of tree-destroying insects, which are doing so much injury to the forests and orchards of the country.

The ravages of the various species of *Scaraboei* are not confined to the oak and pine alone, but every species of hardwood tree nurtures one or several kinds peculiar to itself.

The subject is one of considerable importance, and should not be devoid of interest even to the youngest student of natural history. It is a study particularly recommended to the agriculturist, horticulturist and florist, and it would be well if there were text-books written in simple, plain language, that would be instructive and at the same time awaken an interest in it among our young people.

The habit of close observation inculcated and encouraged in children is a continual source of pleasure and profit in after-life, often, indeed, leading to results that are little anticipated, as in the well-known case of Sir Isaac Newton, who had learned to see and think as a child—results so wonderful that the less observant have been disposed to attribute them to actual inspiration from God. True, He implanted the seed thus nurtured in the child, and brought forth the fruits in the man.

But I am wandering away from my subject, the ways of those tiny insects, the twig-borers.

How marvellous and wonderful is their instinct! Note the curious means employed to accomplish an end which could not be foreknown by experience, by teaching or by reasoning, in the creature working for the future preservation of her unseen offspring. The calculating of the exact date when it should come forth, and the corresponding time when the girdled branch should part from the tree, thus providing a nursery for her infant and sufficient nutriment to sustain it, until in its turn it arrives at the perfect state of the mother beetle, to enjoy like her a brief term of life, prepare a cradle for its offspring, and die.

Surely this leaves a lesson for man to ponder over and confess that he knows but little. The wisdom of man must be but foolishness in the sight of God, since he cannot fathom even the ways of one of the most insignificant of the works of the Creator. How then can man by his puny wisdom find out God?

ERNEST THOMPSON SETON

The Springfield Fox 1898

Born in South Shields, England, in 1860, ERNEST EVAN THOMPSON (he
took the name Seton in 1901) moved with his family to Lindsay, Ontario, in
1866, and to Toronto in 1870. He graduated from the Ontario College of
Art in 1879, determined to become a naturalist-artist. He moved to Manitoba, published *The Birds of Manitoba* in 1891, and sailed to Paris, where his
painting *The Sleeping Wolf* was hung at "waist level" at the 1892 Paris Salon.
That same year he was appointed official naturalist for Manitoba, and the
first of his dozens of books of animal stories, *Wild Animals I Have Known*
(which includes "The Springfield Fox") appeared in 1898. It was an instant
success: animal stories had existed since Aesop, but Seton's were among the
first to portray animals realistically, with close attention to scientific accuracy
and detail. Seton spent most of his years after 1896 in the United States, and
died in New Mexico in 1946. His autobiography, *Trail of an Artist-Naturalist,*
was published in 1940.

ఆఫి · ఫ

I

THE HENS HAD been mysteriously disappearing for over a month; and
when I came home to Springfield for the summer holidays it was my duty to
find the cause. This was soon done. The fowls were carried away bodily one at
a time, before going to roost or else after leaving, which put tramps and
neighbors out of court; they were not taken from the high perches, which
cleared all coons and owls; or left partly eaten, so that weasels, skunks, or
minks were not the guilty ones, and the blame, therefore, was surely left at
Reynard's door. The great pine wood of Erindale was on the other bank of

the river, and on looking carefully about the lower ford I saw a few fox-tracks and a barred feather from one of our Plymouth Rock chickens. On climbing the farther bank in search of more clues, I heard a great outcry of crows behind me, and turning, saw a number of these birds darting down at something in the ford. A better view showed that it was the old story, thief catch thief, for there in the middle of the ford was a fox with something in his jaws—he was returning from our barnyard with another hen. The crows, though shameless robbers themselves, are ever first to cry 'Stop thief,' and yet more than ready to take 'hush-money' in the form of a share in the plunder.

And this was their game now. The fox to get back home must cross the river, where he was exposed to the full brunt of the crow mob. He made a dash for it, and would doubtless have gotten across with his booty had I not joined in the attack, whereupon he dropped the hen, scarce dead, and disappeared in the woods.

This large and regular levy of provisions wholly carried off could mean but one thing, a family of little foxes at home; and to find them I now was bound.

That evening I went with Ranger, my hound, across the river into the Erindale woods. As soon as the hound began to circle, we heard the short, sharp bark of a fox from a thickly wooded ravine close by. Ranger dashed in at once, struck a hot scent and went off on a lively straight-away till his voice was lost in the distance away over the upland.

After nearly an hour he came back, panting and warm, for it was baking August weather, and lay down at my feet.

But almost immediately the same foxy 'Yap yurrr' was heard close at hand and off dashed the dog on another chase.

Away he went in the darkness, baying like a foghorn, straight away to the north. And the loud 'Boo, boo,' became a low 'oo, oo,' and that a feeble 'o-o' and then was lost. They must have gone some miles away, for even with ear to the ground I heard nothing of them though a mile was easy distance for Ranger's brazen voice.

As I waited in the black woods I heard a sweet sound of dripping water: 'Tink tank, tenk tink, Ta tink tank tenk tonk.'

I did not know of any spring so near, and in the hot night it was a glad find. But the sound led me to the bough of an oak-tree, where I found its source. Such a soft sweet song; full of delightful suggestion on such a night:

> Tonk tank tenk tink
> Ta tink a tonk a tank a tink a
> Ta ta tink tank ta ta tonk tink
> Drink a tank a drink a drunk.

It was the 'water-dripping' song of the saw-whet owl.

But suddenly a deep raucous breathing and a rustle of leaves showed that Ranger was back. He was completely fagged out. His tongue hung almost to the ground and was dripping with foam, his flanks were heaving and spume-flecks dribbled from his breast and sides. He stopped panting a moment to give my hand a dutiful lick, then flung himself flop on the leaves to drown all other sounds with his noisy panting.

But again that tantalizing '*Yap yurrr*' was heard a few feet away, and the meaning of it all dawned on me. We were close to the den where the little foxes were, and the old ones were taking turns in trying to lead us away.

It was late night now, so we went home feeling sure that the problem was nearly solved.

II

It was well known that there was an old fox with his family living in the neighborhood, but no one supposed them so near.

This fox had been called 'Scarface,' because of a scar reaching from his eye through and back of his ear; this was supposed to have been given him by a barbed-wire fence during a rabbit hunt, and as the hair came in white after it healed, it was always a strong mark. The winter before I had met with him and had had a sample of his craftiness. I was out shooting, after a fall of snow, and had crossed the open fields to the edge of the brushy hollow back of the old mill. As my head rose to a view of the hollow I caught sight of a fox trotting at long range down the other side, in line to cross my course. Instantly I held motionless, and did not even lower or turn my head lest I should catch his eye by moving, until he went on out of sight in the thick cover at the bottom. As soon as he was hidden I bobbed down and ran to head him off where he should leave the cover on the other side, and was there in good time awaiting, but no fox came forth. A careful look showed the fresh track of a fox that had bounded from the cover, and following it with my eye I saw old Scarface himself far out of range behind me, sitting on his haunches and grinning as though much amused.

A study of the trail made all clear. He had seen me at the moment I saw him, but he, also like a true hunter, had concealed the fact, putting on an air of unconcern till out of sight, when he had run for his life around behind me and amused himself by watching my stillborn trick.

In the springtime I had yet another instance of Scarface's cunning. I was walking with a friend along the road over the high pasture. We passed within thirty feet of a ridge on which were several gray and brown boulders. When at the nearest point my friend said:

"Stone number three looks to me very much like a fox curled up."

But I could not see it, and we passed. We had not gone many yards farther when the wind blew on this boulder as on fur.

My friend said, "I am sure that is a fox, lying asleep."

"We'll soon settle that," I replied, and turned back, but as soon as I had taken one step from the road, up jumped Scarface, for it was he, and ran. A fire had swept the middle of the pasture, leaving a broad belt of black; over this he skurried till he came to the unburnt yellow grass again, where he squatted down and was lost to view. He had been watching us all the time, and would not have moved had we kept to the road. The wonderful part of this is, not that he resembled the round stones and dry grass, but that he *knew he did,* and was ready to profit by it.

We soon found that it was Scarface and his wife Vixen that had made our woods their home and our barnyard their base of supplies.

Next morning a search in the pines showed a great bank of earth that had been scratched up within a few months. It must have come from a hole, and yet there was none to be seen. It is well known that a really cute fox, on digging a new den, brings all the earth out at the first hole made, but carries on a tunnel into some distant thicket. Then closing up for good the first made and too well-marked door, uses only the entrance hidden in the thicket.

So after a little search at the other side of a knoll, I found the real entry and good proof that there was a nest of little foxes inside.

Rising above the brush on the hillside was a great hollow basswood. It leaned a good deal and had a large hole at the bottom, and a smaller one at top.

We boys had often used this tree in playing Swiss Family Robinson, and by cutting steps in its soft punky walls had made it easy to go up and down in the hollow. Now it came in handy, for next day when the sun was warm I went there to watch, and from this perch on the roof, I soon saw the interesting family that lived in the cellar nearby. There were four little foxes; they looked curiously like little lambs, with their woolly coats, their long thick legs and innocent expressions, and yet a second glance at their broad, sharp-nosed, sharp-eyed visages showed that each of these innocents was the makings of a crafty old fox.

They played about, basking in the sun, or wrestling with each other till a slight sound made them skurry under ground. But their alarm was needless, for the cause of it was their mother; she stepped from the bushes bringing another hen—number seventeen as I remember. A low call from her and the little fellows came tumbling out. Then began a scene that I thought charming, but which my uncle would not have enjoyed at all.

They rushed on the hen, and tussled and fought with it, and each other, while the mother, keeping a sharp eye for enemies, looked on with fond delight. The expression on her face was remarkable. It was first a grinning of delight, but her usual look of wildness and cunning was there, nor were cruelty and nervousness lacking, but over all was the unmistakable look of the mother's pride and love.

The base of my tree was hidden in bushes and much lower than the knoll where the den was. So I could come and go at will without scaring the foxes.

For many days I went there and saw much of the training of the young ones. They early learned to turn to statuettes at any strange sound, and then on hearing it again or finding other cause for fear, to run for shelter.

Some animals have so much mother-love that it overflows and benefits outsiders. Not so old Vixen it would seem. Her pleasure in the cubs led to most refined cruelty. For she often brought home to them mice and birds alive and with diabolic gentleness would avoid doing them serious hurt so that the cubs might have larger scope to torment them.

There was a woodchuck that lived over in the hill orchard. He was neither handsome nor interesting, but he knew how to take care of himself. He had digged a den between the roots of an old pine stump, so that the foxes could not follow him by digging. But hard work was not their way of life; wits they believed worth more than elbow-grease. This woodchuck usually sunned himself on the stump each morning. If he saw a fox near he went down in the door of his den, or if the enemy was very near he went inside and stayed long enough for the danger to pass.

One morning Vixen and her mate seemed to decide that it was time the children knew something about the broad subject of Woodchucks, and further that this orchard woodchuck would serve nicely for an object-lesson. So they went together to the orchard-fence unseen by old Chuckie on his stump. Scarface then showed himself in the orchard and quietly walked in a line so as to pass by the stump at a distance, but never once turned his head or allowed the ever-watchful woodchuck to think himself seen. When the fox entered the field the woodchuck quietly dropped down to the mouth of his den; here he waited as the fox passed, but concluding that after all wisdom is the better part, went into his hole.

This was what the foxes wanted. Vixen had kept out of sight, but now ran swiftly to the stump and hid behind it. Scarface had kept straight on, going very slowly. The woodchuck had not been frightened, so before long his head popped up between the roots and he looked around. There was that fox still going on, farther and farther away. The woodchuck grew bold as the fox went, and came out farther, and then seeing the coast clear, he scrambled onto the stump, and with one spring Vixen had him and shook him till he lay senseless. Scarface had watched out of the corner of his eye and now came running back. But Vixen took the chuck in her jaws and made for the den, so he saw he wasn't needed.

Back to the den came Vix, and carried the chuck so carefully that he was able to struggle a little when she got there. A low 'woof' at the den brought the little fellows out like schoolboys to play. She threw the wounded animal to them and they set on him like four little furies, uttering little growls and biting little bites with all the strength of their baby jaws, but the woodchuck fought for his life and beating them off slowly hobbled to the shelter of a thicket. The little ones pursued like a pack of hounds and dragged at his tail and flanks, but could not hold him back. So Vix overtook him with a couple of bounds and dragged him again into the open for the children to worry. Again and again this rough sport went on till one of the little ones was badly bitten, and his squeal of pain roused Vix to end the woodchuck's misery and serve him up at once.

Not far from the den was a hollow overgrown with coarse grass, the playground of a colony of field-mice. The earliest lesson in woodcraft that the little ones took, away from the den, was in this hollow. Here they had their first course of mice, the easiest of all game. In teaching, the main thing was example, aided by a deep-set instinct. The old fox, also, had one or two signs meaning "lie still and watch," "come, do as I do," and so on, that were much used.

So the merry lot went to this hollow one calm evening and Mother Fox made them lie still in the grass. Presently a faint squeak showed that the game was astir. Vix rose up and went on tip-toe into the grass—not crouching but as high as she could stand, sometimes on her hind legs so as to get a better view. The runs that the mice follow are hidden under the grass tangle, and the only way to know the whereabouts of a mouse is by seeing the light shaking of the grass, which is the reason why mice are hunted only on calm days.

And the trick is to locate the mouse and seize him first and see him afterward. Vix soon made a spring, and in the middle of the bunch of dead grass that she grabbed was a field-mouse squeaking his last squeak.

He was soon gobbled, and the four awkward little foxes tried to do the same as their mother, and when at length the eldest for the first time in his life caught game, he quivered with excitement and ground his pearly little milk-teeth into the mouse with a rush of inborn savageness that must have surprised even himself.

Another home lesson was on the red-squirrel. One of these noisy, vulgar creatures lived close by and used to waste part of each day scolding the foxes, from some safe perch. The cubs made many vain attempts to catch him as he ran across their glade from one tree to another, or spluttered and scolded at them a foot or so out of reach. But old Vixen was up in natural history—she knew squirrel nature and took the case in hand when the proper time came. She hid the children and lay down flat in the middle of the open glade. The saucy low-minded squirrel came and scolded as usual. But she moved no hair. He came nearer and at last right overhead to chatter: "You brute you, you brute you."

But Vix lay as dead. This was very perplexing, so the squirrel came down the trunk and peeping about made a nervous dash across the grass, to another tree, again to scold from a safe perch.

"You brute you, you useless brute, scarrr–scarrrrr."

But flat and lifeless on the grass lay Vix. This was most tantalizing to the squirrel. He was naturally curious and disposed to be venturesome, so again he came to the ground and skurried across the glade nearer than before.

Still as death lay Vix, "surely she was dead." And the little foxes began to wonder if their mother wasn't asleep.

But the squirrel was working himself into a little craze of foolhardy curiosity. He had dropped a piece of bark on Vix's head, he had used up his list of bad words and he had done it all over again, without getting a sign of life. So after a couple more dashes across the glade he ventured within a few feet of the really watchful Vix who sprang to her feet and pinned him in a twinkling.

"And the little ones picked the bones e-oh."

Thus the rudiments of their education were laid, and afterward as they grew stronger they were taken farther afield to begin the higher branches of trailing and scenting.

For each kind of prey they were taught a way to hunt, for every animal has some great strength or it could not live, and some great weakness or the others could not live. The squirrel's weakness was foolish curiosity; the fox's that he can't climb a tree. And the training of the little foxes was all shaped to take advantage of the weakness of the other creatures and to make up for their own by defter play where they are strong.

From their parents they learned the chief axioms of the fox world. How, is not easy to say. But that they learned this in company with their parents was clear. Here are some that foxes taught me, without saying a word:—

> Never sleep on your straight track.
> Your nose is before your eyes, then trust it first.
> A fool runs down the wind.
> Running rills cure many ills.
> Never take the open if you can keep the cover.
> Never leave a straight trail if a crooked one will do.
> If it's strange, it's hostile.
> Dust and water burn the scent.
> Never hunt mice in a rabbit-woods, or rabbits in a henyard.
> Keep off the grass.

Inklings of the meanings of these were already entering the little ones' minds—thus, 'Never follow what you can't smell,' was wise, they could see, because if you can't smell it, then the wind is so that it must smell you.

One by one they learned the birds and beasts of their home woods, and then as they were able to go abroad with their parents they learned new animals. They were beginning to think they knew the scent of everything that moved. But one night the mother took them to a field where was a strange black flat thing on the ground. She brought them on purpose to smell it, but at the first whiff their every hair stood on end, they trembled, they knew not why—it seemed to tingle through their blood and fill them with instinctive hate and fear. And when she saw its full effect she told them—

"That is man-scent."

III

Meanwhile the hens continued to disappear. I had not betrayed the den of cubs. Indeed, I thought a good deal more of the little rascals than I did of the hens; but uncle was dreadfully wrought up and made most disparaging remarks about my woodcraft. To please him I one day took the hound across to the woods and seating myself on a stump on the open hillside, I bade the dog go on. Within three minutes he sang out in the tongue all hunters know so well, "Fox! fox! fox! straight away down the valley."

After awhile I heard them coming back. There I saw the fox—Scarface—loping lightly across the river-bottom to the stream. In he went and trotted along in the shallow water near the margin for two hundred yards, then came out straight toward me. Though in full view, he saw me not but came up the hill watching over his shoulder for the hound. Within ten feet of me he turned and sat with his back to me while he craned his neck and showed an eager interest in the doings of the hound. Ranger came bawling along the trail till he came to the running water, the killer of scent, and here he was puzzled; but there was only one thing to do; that was by going up and down both banks find where the fox had left the river.

The fox before me shifted his position a little to get a better view and watched with a most human interest all the circling of the hound. He was so close that I saw the hair of his shoulder bristle a little when the dog came in sight. I could see the jumping of his heart on his ribs, and the gleam of his yellow eye. When the dog was wholly baulked by the water trick, it was comical to see:—he could not sit still, but rocked up and down in glee, and reared on his hind feet to get a better view of the slow-plodding hound. With mouth opened nearly to his ears, though not at all winded, he panted noisily for a moment, or rather he laughed gleefully, just as a dog laughs by grinning and panting.

Old Scarface wriggled in huge enjoyment as the hound puzzled over the trail so long that when he did find it, it was so stale he could barely follow it, and did not feel justified in tonguing on it at all.

As soon as the hound was working up the hill the fox quietly went into the woods. I had been sitting in plain view only ten feet away, but I had the wind and kept still and the fox never knew that his life had for twenty minutes been in the power of the foe he most feared. Ranger also would have passed me as near as the fox, but I spoke to him, and with a little nervous start he quit the trail and looking sheepish lay down by my feet.

This little comedy was played with variations for several days, but it was all in plain view from the house across the river. My uncle, impatient at the daily loss of hens, went out himself, sat on the open knoll, and when old Scarface trotted to his lookout to watch the dull hound on the river flat below, my uncle remorselessly shot him in the back, at the very moment when he was grinning over a new triumph.

IV

But still the hens were disappearing. My uncle was wrathy. He determined to conduct the war himself, and sowed the woods with poison baits, trusting to luck that our own dogs would not get them. He indulged in contemptuous remarks on my by-gone woodcraft, and went out evenings with a gun and the two dogs, to see what he could destroy.

Vix knew right well what a poisoned bait was; she passed them by or else treated them with active contempt, but one she dropped down the hole of an old enemy, a skunk, who was never afterward seen. Formerly old Scarface was always ready to take charge of the dogs, and keep them out of mischief. But now that Vix had the whole burden of the brood, she could no longer spend time in breaking every track to the den, and was not always at hand to meet and mislead the foes that might be coming too near.

The end is easily foreseen. Ranger followed a hot trail to the den, and Spot, the fox-terrier, announced that the family was at home, and then did his best to go in after them.

The whole secret was now out, and the whole family doomed. The hired man came around with pick and shovel to dig them out, while we and the dogs stood by. Old Vix soon showed herself in the near woods, and led the dogs away off down the river, where she shook them off when she thought proper, by the simple device of springing on a sheep's back. The frightened animal ran for several hundred yards, then Vix got off, knowing that there was now a hopeless gap in the scent, and returned to the den. But the dogs, baffled by the break in the trail, soon did the same, to find Vix hanging about in despair, vainly trying to decoy us away from her treasures.

Meanwhile Paddy plied both pick and shovel with vigor and effect. The yellow, gravelly sand was heaping on both sides, and the shoulders of the sturdy digger were sinking below the level. After an hour's digging, enlivened by frantic rushes of the dogs after the old fox, who hovered near in the woods, Pat called:

"Here they are, sor!"

It was the den at the end of the burrow, and cowering as far back as they could, were the four little woolly cubs.

Before I could interfere, a murderous blow from the shovel, and a sudden rush from the fierce little terrier, ended the lives of three. The fourth and smallest was barely saved by holding him by his tail high out of reach of the excited dogs.

He gave one short squeal, and his poor mother came at the cry, and circled so near that she would have been shot but for the accidental protection of the dogs, who somehow always seemed to get between, and whom she once more led away on a fruitless chase.

The little one saved alive was dropped into a bag, where he lay quite still. His unfortunate brothers were thrown back into their nursery bed, and buried under a few shovelfuls of earth.

We guilty ones then went back into the house, and the little fox was soon chained in the yard. No one knew just why he was kept alive, but in all a change of feeling had set in, and the idea of killing him was without a supporter.

He was a pretty little fellow, like a cross between a fox and a lamb. His woolly visage and form were strangely lamb-like and innocent, but one could find in his yellow eyes a gleam of cunning and savageness as unlamb-like as it possibly could be.

As long as anyone was near he crouched sullen and cowed in his shelter-box, and it was a full hour after being left alone before he ventured to look out.

My window now took the place of the hollow basswood. A number of hens of the breed he knew so well were about the cub in the yard. Late that afternoon as they strayed near the captive there was a sudden rattle of the chain, and the youngster dashed at the nearest one and would have caught him but for the chain which brought him up with a jerk. He got on his feet and slunk back to his box, and though he afterward made several rushes he so gauged his leap as to win or fail within the length of the chain and never again was brought up by its cruel jerk.

As night came down the little fellow became very uneasy, sneaking out of his box, but going back at each slight alarm, tugging at his chain, or at times biting it in fury while he held it down with his fore paws. Suddenly he paused as though listening, then raising his little black nose he poured out a short quavering cry.

Once or twice this was repeated, the time between being occupied in wor-rying the chain and running about. Then an answer came. The far-away *Yap-yurr* of the old fox. A few minutes later a shadowy form appeared on the wood-pile. The little one slunk into his box, but at once returned and ran to meet his mother with all the gladness that a fox could show. Quick as a flash she seized him and turned to bear him away by the road she came. But the moment the end of the chain was reached the cub was rudely jerked from the old one's mouth, and she, scared by the opening of a window, fled over the wood-pile.

An hour afterward the cub had ceased to run about or cry. I peeped out, and by the light of the moon saw the form of the mother at full length on the ground by the little one, gnawing at something—the clank of iron told what, it was that cruel chain. And Tip, the little one, meanwhile was helping himself to a warm drink.

On my going out she fled into the dark woods, but there by the shelter-box were two little mice, bloody and still warm, food for the cub brought by the devoted mother. And in the morning I found the chain was very bright for a foot or two next the little one's collar.

On walking across the woods to the ruined den, I again found signs of Vixen. The poor heart-broken mother had come and dug out the bedraggled bodies of her little ones.

There lay the three little baby foxes all licked smooth now, and by them were two of our hens fresh killed. The newly heaved earth was printed all over with tell-tale signs—signs that told me that here by the side of her dead she had watched like Rizpah. Here she had brought their usual meal, the spoil of her nightly hunt. Here she had stretched herself beside them and vainly offered them their natural drink and yearned to feed and warm them as of old; but only stiff little bodies under their soft wool she found, and little cold noses still and unresponsive.

A deep impress of elbows, breast, and hocks showed where she had laid in silent grief and watched them for long and mourned as a wild mother can mourn for its young. But from that time she came no more to the ruined den, for now she surely knew that her little ones were dead.

V

Tip the captive, the weakling of the brood, was now the heir to all her love. The dogs were loosed to guard the hens. The hired man had orders to shoot the old fox on sight—so had I, but was resolved never to see her. Chicken-heads, that a fox loves and a dog will not touch, had been poisoned and scattered through the woods and the only way to the yard where Tip was tied, was by climbing the wood-pile after braving all other dangers. And yet each night old Vix was there to nurse her baby and bring it fresh-killed hens and game. Again and again I saw her, although she came now without awaiting the querulous cry of the captive.

The second night of the captivity I heard the rattle of the chain, and then made out that the old fox was there, hard at work digging a hole by the little one's kennel. When it was deep enough to half bury her, she gathered into it all the slack of the chain, and filled it again with earth. Then in triumph thinking she had gotten rid of the chain, she seized little Tip by the neck and turned to dash off up the wood-pile, but alas only to have him jerked roughly from her grasp.

Poor little fellow, he whimpered sadly as he crawled into his box. After half an hour there was a great outcry among the dogs, and by their straight-away tonguing through the far woods I knew they were chasing Vix. Away up north they went in the direction of the railway and their noise faded from hearing. Next morning the hound had not come back. We soon knew why. Foxes long ago learned what a railroad is; they soon devised several ways of turning it to account. One way is when hunted to walk the rails for a long distance just before a train comes. The scent, always poor on iron, is destroyed by the train and there is always a chance of hounds being killed by the engine. But another way more sure, but harder to play, is to lead the hounds straight to a high trestle just ahead of the train, so that the engine overtakes them on it and they are surely dashed to destruction.

This trick was skillfully played, and down below we found the mangled remains of old Ranger and learned that Vix was already wreaking her revenge.

That same night she returned to the yard before Spot's weary limbs could bring him back and killed another hen and brought it to Tip, and stretched her panting length beside him that he might quench his thirst. For she seemed to think he had no food but what she brought.

It was that hen that betrayed to my uncle the nightly visits.

My own sympathies were all turning to Vix, and I would have no hand in planning further murders. Next night my uncle himself watched, gun in hand, for an hour. Then when it became cold and the moon clouded over he remembered other important business elsewhere, and left Paddy in his place.

But Paddy was "onaisy" as the stillness and anxiety of watching worked on his nerves. And the loud bang! bang! an hour later left us sure only that powder had been burned.

In the morning we found Vix had not failed her young one. Again next night found my uncle on guard, for another hen had been taken. Soon after dark a single shot was heard, but Vix dropped the game she was bringing and escaped. Another attempt made that night called forth another gun-shot. Yet next day it was seen by the brightness of the chain that she had come again and vainly tried for hours to cut that hateful bond.

Such courage and stanch fidelity were bound to win respect, if not toleration. At any rate, there was no gunner in wait next night, when all was still. Could it be of any use? Driven off thrice with gun-shots, would she make another try to feed or free her captive young one?

Would she? Hers was a mother's love. There was but one to watch them this time, the fourth night, when the quavering whine of the little one was followed by that shadowy form above the wood-pile.

But carrying no fowl or food that could be seen. Had the keen huntress failed at last? Had she no head of game for this her only charge, or had she learned to trust his captors for his food?

No, far from all this. The wild-wood mother's heart and hate were true. Her only thought had been to set him free. All means she knew she tried, and every danger braved to tend him well and help him to be free. But all had failed.

Like a shadow she came and in a moment was gone, and Tip seized on something dropped, and crunched and chewed with relish what she brought. But even as he ate, a knife-like pang shot through and a scream of pain escaped him. Then there was a momentary struggle and the little fox was dead.

The mother's love was strong in Vix, but a higher thought was stronger. She knew right well the poison's power; she knew the poison bait, and would have taught him had he lived to know and shun it too. But now at last when she must choose for him a wretched prisoner's life or sudden death, she quenched the mother in her breast and freed him by the one remaining door.

It is when the snow is on the ground that we take the census of the woods, and when the winter came it told me that Vix no longer roamed the woods of Erindale. Where she went it never told, but only this, that she was gone.

Gone, perhaps, to some other far-off haunt to leave behind the sad remembrance of her murdered little ones and mate. Or gone, may be, deliberately, from the scene of a sorrowful life, as many a wild-wood mother has gone, by the means that she herself had used to free her young one, the last of all her brood.

The Stickeen River 1904

JOHN MUIR (1838–1914) was born in Dunbar, Scotland, and emigrated to
Wisconsin at the age of eleven. In 1868, he headed west to explore California,
"the wild side of the continent," as he called it, and became a fierce advocate
of the preservation of the High Sierras, founding the Sierra Club in 1892
and writing constantly and wonderfully about the mountains, especially his
beloved Yosemite Valley, which he almost single-handedly preserved as a
national park. As Edward Hoagland has written, "As an advocate Muir was a
johnny-one-note, but, oh, that note!" In 1879, Muir travelled by Coast Guard
steamer to Alaska, and recorded his voyage in *Travels in Alaska* (from which
this excerpt is taken), which, like most of his work, was not published until
much later. Muir's other books include *Our National Parks* (1901), *My First
Summer in the Sierra* (1911), *The Yosemite* (1912), and *The Cruise of the Corwin*
(1917).

THE MOST INTERESTING of the short excursions we made from Fort
Wrangell was the one up the Stickeen River to the head of steam navigation.
From Mt. St. Elias the coast range extends in a broad, lofty chain beyond the
southern boundary of the territory, gashed by stupendous cañons, each of
which carries a lively river, though most of them are comparatively short, as
their highest sources lie in the icy solitudes of the range within forty or fifty
miles of the coast. A few, however, of these foaming, roaring streams—the
Alsek, Chilcat, Chilcoot, Taku, Stickeen, and perhaps others—head beyond
the range with some of the southwest branches of the Mackenzie and Yukon.

The largest side branches of the main-trunk cañons of all these mountain
streams are still occupied by glaciers which descend in showy ranks, their

massy, bulging snouts lying back a little distance in the shadows of the walls, or pushing forward among the cotton-woods that line the banks of the rivers, or even stretching all the way across the main cañons, compelling the rivers to find a channel beneath them.

The Stickeen was, perhaps, the best known of the rivers that cross the Coast Range, because it was the best way to the Mackenzie River Cassiar gold-minds. It is about three hundred and fifty miles long, and is navigable for small steamers a hundred and fifty miles to Glenora, and sometimes to Telegraph Creek, fifteen miles farther. It first pursues a westerly course through grassy plains darkened here and there with groves of spruce and pine; then, curving southward and receiving numerous tributaries from the north, it enters the Coast Range, and sweeps across it through a magnificent cañon three thousand to five thousand feet deep, and more than a hundred miles long. The majestic cliffs and mountains forming the cañon-walls display endless variety of form and sculpture, and are wonderfully adorned and enlivened with glaciers and waterfalls, while throughout almost its whole extent the floor is a flowery landscape garden, like Yosemite. The most striking features are the glaciers, hanging over the cliffs, descending the side cañons and pushing forward to the river, greatly enhancing the wild beauty of all the others.

Gliding along the swift-flowing river, the views change with bewildering rapidity. Wonderful, too, are the changes dependent on the seasons and the weather. In spring, when the snow is melting fast, you enjoy the countless rejoicing waterfalls; the gentle breathing of warm winds; the colors of the young leaves and flowers when the bees are busy and wafts of fragrance are drifting hither and thither from miles of wild roses, clover, and honeysuckle; the swaths of birch and willow on the lower slopes following the melting of the winter avalanche snow-banks; the bossy cumuli swelling in white and purple piles above the highest peaks; gray rain-clouds wreathing the outstanding brows and battlements of the walls; and the breaking-forth of the sun after the rain; the shining of the leaves and streams and crystal architecture of the glaciers; the rising of fresh fragrance; the song of the happy birds; and the serene color-grandeur of the morning and evening sky. In summer you find the groves and gardens in full dress; glaciers melting rapidly under sunshine and rain; waterfalls in all their glory; the river rejoicing in its strength; young birds trying their wings; bears enjoying salmon and berries; all the life of the cañon brimming full like the streams. In autumn comes rest, as if the year's work were done. The rich hazy sunshine streaming over the cliffs calls forth the last of the gentians and goldenrods; the groves and thickets and meadows bloom again as their leaves change to red and yellow petals; the rocks also, and the glaciers, seem to bloom like the plants in the mellow golden light. And so goes the song, change succeeding change in sublime harmony through all the wonderful seasons and weather.

My first trip up the river was made in the spring with the missionary party soon after our arrival at Wrangell. We left Wrangell in the afternoon and anchored for the night above the river delta, and started up the river early next morning when the heights above the "Big Stickeen" Glacier and the smooth domes and copings and arches of solid snow along the tops of the cañon walls were glowing in the early beams. We arrived before noon at the old trading-post called "Buck's" in front of the Stickeen Glacier, and remained long enough to allow the few passengers who wished a nearer view to cross the river to the terminal moraine. The sunbeams streaming through the ice pinnacles along its terminal wall produced a wonderful glory of color, and the broad, sparkling crystal prairie and the distant snowy fountains were wonderfully attractive and made me pray for opportunity to explore them.

Of the many glaciers, a hundred or more, that adorn the walls of the great Stickeen River Cañon, this is the largest. It draws its sources from snowy mountains within fifteen or twenty miles of the coast, pours through a comparatively narrow cañon about two miles in width in a magnificent cascade, and expands in a broad fan five or six miles in width, separated from the Stickeen River by its broad terminal moraine, fringed with spruces and willows. Around the beautifully drawn curve of the moraine the Stickeen River flows, having evidently been shoved by the glacier out of its direct course. On the opposite side of the cañon another somewhat smaller glacier, which now terminates four or five miles from the river, was once united front to front with the greater glacier, though at first both were tributaries of the main Stickeen Glacier which once filled the whole grand cañon. After the main trunk cañon was melted out, its side branches, drawing their sources from a height of three or four to five or six thousand feet, were cut off, and of course became separate glaciers, occupying cirques and branch cañons along the tops and sides of the walls. The Indians have a tradition that the river used to run through a tunnel under the united fronts of the two large tributary glaciers mentioned above, which entered the main cañon from either side; and that on one occasion an Indian, anxious to get rid of his wife, had her sent adrift in a canoe down through the ice tunnel, expecting that she would trouble him no more. But to his surprise she floated through under the ice in safety. All the evidence connected with the present appearance of these two glaciers indicates that they were united and formed a dam across the river after the smaller tributaries had been melted off and had receded to a greater or lesser height above the valley floor.

The big Stickeen Glacier is hardly out of sight ere you come upon another that pours a majestic crystal flood through the evergreens, while almost every hollow and tributary cañon contains a smaller one, the size, of course, varying with the extent of the area drained. Some are like mere snow-banks; others, with the blue ice apparent, depend in massive bulging curves and swells, and graduate into the river-like forms that maze through the lower forested regions and are so striking and beautiful that they are admired even by the passing miners with gold-dust in their eyes.

Thirty-five miles above the Big Stickeen Glacier is the "Dirt Glacier," the second in size. Its outlet is a fine stream, abounding in trout. On the opposite side of the river there is a group of five glaciers, one of them descending to within a hundred feet of the river.

Near Glenora, on the northeastern flank of the main Coast Range, just below a narrow gorge called "The Cañon," terraces first make their appearance, where great quantities of moraine material have been swept through the flood-choked gorge and of course outspread and deposited on the first open levels below. Here, too, occurs a marked change in climate and consequently in forests and general appearance of the face of the country. On account of destructive fires the woods are younger and are composed of smaller trees about a foot to eighteen inches in diameter and seventy-five feet high, mostly two-leaved pines which hold their seeds for several years after they are ripe. The woods here are without a trace of those deep accumulations of mosses, leaves, and decaying trunks which make so damp and unclearable a mass in the coast forests. Whole mountain-sides are covered with gray moss and lichens where the forest has been utterly destroyed. The river-bank cotton-woods are also smaller, and the birch and contorta pines mingle freely with the coast hemlock and spruce. The birch is common on the lower slopes and is very effective, its round, leafy, pale-green head contrasting with the dark, narrow spires of the conifers and giving a striking character to the forest. The "tamarac pine" or black pine, as the variety of *P. contorta* is called here, is yellowish-green, in marked contrast with the dark lichen-draped spruce which grows above the pine at a height of about two thousand feet, in groves and belts where it has escaped fire and snow avalanches. There is another handsome spruce here-abouts, *Picea alba,* very slender and graceful in habit, drooping at the top like a mountain hemlock. I saw fine specimens a hundred and twenty-five feet high on deep bottom land a few miles below Glenora. The tops of some of them were almost covered with dense clusters of yellow and brown cones.

We reached the old Hudson's Bay trading-post at Glenora about one o'clock, and the captain informed me that he would stop here until the next morning, when he would make an early start for Wrangell.

At a distance of about seven or eight miles to the northeastward of the landing, there is an outstanding group of mountains crowning a spur from the main chain of the Coast Range, whose highest point rises about eight thousand feet above the level of the sea; and as Glenora is only a thousand feet above the sea, the height to be overcome in climbing this peak is about seven thousand feet. Though the time was short I determined to climb it, because of the advantageous position it occupied for general views of the peaks and glaciers of the east side of the great range.

Although it was now twenty minutes past three and the days were getting short, I thought that by rapid climbing I could reach the summit before sunset, in time to get a general view and a few pencil sketches, and make my way back to the steamer in the night. Mr. Young, one of the missionaries, asked permission to accompany me, saying that he was a good walker and climber and would not delay me or cause any trouble. I strongly advised him not to go, explaining that it involved a walk, coming and going, of fourteen or sixteen miles, and a climb through brush and boulders of seven thousand feet, a fair day's work for a seasoned mountaineer to be done in less than half a day and part of a night. But he insisted that he was a strong walker, could do a mountaineer's day's work in half a day, and would not hinder me in any way.

"Well, I have warned you," I said, "and will not assume responsibility for any trouble that may arise."

He proved to be a stout walker, and we made rapid progress across a brushy timbered flat and up the mountain slopes, open in some places, and in others thatched with dwarf firs, resting a minute here and there to refresh ourselves with huckleberries, which grew in abundance in open spots. About half an hour before sunset, when we were near a cluster of crumbling pinnacles that formed the summit, I had ceased to feel anxiety about the mountaineering strength and skill of my companion, and pushed rapidly on. In passing around the shoulder of the highest pinnacle, where the rock was rapidly disintegrating and the danger of slipping was great, I shouted in a warning voice, "Be very careful here, this is dangerous."

Mr. Young was perhaps a dozen or two yards behind me, out of sight. I afterwards reproached myself for not stopping and lending him a steadying hand, and showing him the slight footsteps I had made by kicking out little blocks of the crumbling surface, instead of simply warning him to be careful. Only a few seconds after giving this warning, I was startled by a scream for help, and hurrying back, found the missionary face downward, his arms outstretched, clutching little crumbling knobs on the brink of a gully that plunged down a thousand feet or more to a small residual glacier. I managed to get below him, touched one of his feet, and tried to encourage him by saying, "I am below you. You are in no danger. You can't slip past me and I will soon get you out of this."

He then told me that both of his arms were dislocated. It was almost impossible to find available footholds on the treacherous rock, and I was at my wits' end to know how to get him rolled or dragged to a place where I could get about him, find out how much he was hurt, and a way back down the mountain. After narrowly scanning the cliff and making footholds, I managed to roll and lift him a few yards to a place where the slope was less steep, and there I attempted to set his arms. I found, however, that this was impossible in such a place. I therefore tied his arms to his sides with my suspenders and necktie, to prevent as much as possible inflammation from movement. I then left him, telling him to lie still, that I would be back in a few minutes, and that he was now safe from slipping. I hastily examined the ground and saw no way of getting him down except by the steep glacier gully. After scrambling to an outstanding point that commands a view of it from top to bottom, to make sure that it was not interrupted by sheer precipices, I concluded that with great care and the digging of slight footholds he could be slid down to the glacier, where I could lay him on his back and perhaps be able to set his arms. Accordingly, I cheered him up, telling him I had found a way, but that it would require lots of time and patience. Digging a footstep in the sand or crumbling rock five or six feet beneath him, I reached up, took hold of him by one of his feet, and gently slid him down on his back, placed his heels in the step, then descended another five or six feet, dug heel notches, and slid him down to them. Thus the whole distance was made by a succession of narrow steps at very short intervals, and the glacier was reached perhaps about midnight. Here I took off one of my boots, tied a handkerchief around his wrist for a good hold, placed my heel in his arm pit, and succeeded in getting one of his arms into place, but my utmost strength was insufficient to reduce the dislocation of the other. I therefore bound it closely to his side, and asked him if in his exhausted and trembling condition he was still able to walk.

"Yes," he bravely replied.

So, with a steadying arm around him and many stops for rest, I marched him slowly down to the star-light on the comparatively smooth, unfissured surface of the little glacier to the terminal moraine, a distance of perhaps a mile, crossed the moraine, bathed his head at one of the outlet streams, and after many rests reached a dry place and made a brush fire. I then went ahead looking for an open way through the bushes to where larger wood could be had, made a good lasting fire of resiny silver-fir roots, and a leafy bed beside it. I now told him I would run down the mountain, hasten back with help from the boat, and carry him down in comfort. But he would not hear of my leaving him.

"No, no," he said, "I can walk down. Don't leave me."

I reminded him of the roughness of the way, his nerve-shaken condition, and assured him I would not be gone long. But he insisted on trying, saying on no account whatever must I leave him. I therefore concluded to try to get him to the ship by short walks from one fire and resting-place to another. While he was resting I went ahead, looking for the best way through the brush and rocks, then returning, got him on his feet and made him lean on my shoulder while I steadied him to prevent his falling. This slow, staggering struggle from fire to fire lasted until long after sunrise. When at last we reached the ship and stood at the foot of the narrow single plank without side rails that reached from the bank to the deck at a considerable angle, I briefly explained to Mr. Young's companions, who stood looking down at us, that he had been hurt in an accident, and requested one of them to assist me in getting him aboard. But strange to say, instead of coming down to help, they made haste to reproach him for having gone on a "wild-goose chase" with Muir.

"These foolish adventures are well enough for Mr. Muir," they said, "but you, Mr. Young, have work to do; you have a family; you have a church, and you have no right to risk your life on treacherous peaks and precipices."

The captain, Nat Lane, son of Senator Joseph Lane, had been swearing in angry impatience for being compelled to make so late a start and thus encounter a dangerous wind in a narrow gorge, and was threatening to put the missionaries ashore to seek their lost companion, while he went on down the river about his business. But when he heard my call for help, he hastened forward, and elbowed the divines away from the end of the gangplank, shouting in angry irreverence, "Oh, blank! This is no time for preaching! Don't you see the man is hurt?"

He ran down to our help, and while I steadied my trembling companion from behind, the captain kindly led him up the plank into the saloon, and made him drink a large glass of brandy. Then, with a man holding down his shoulders, we succeeded in getting the bone into its socket, notwithstanding the inflammation and contraction of the muscles and ligaments. Mr. Young was then put to bed, and he slept all the way back to Wrangell.

In his mission lectures in the East, Mr. Young oftentimes told this story. I made no record of it in my notebook and never intended to write a word about it; but after a miserable, sensational caricature of the story had appeared in a respectable magazine, I thought it but fair to my brave companion that it should be told just as it happened.

CHARLES G. D. ROBERTS

The Last Barrier 1907

CHARLES GEORGE DOUGLAS ROBERTS (1860–1943) was born in
Douglas, New Brunswick, attended the University of New Brunswick
and published his first book of poems, *Orion*, in 1880. He worked in
Toronto as the editor of *The Week*, then moved to Windsor, Nova Scotia,
taught at King's College and published his first collection of animal stories,
Earth's Enigmas, in 1896. Encouraged by the success of Seton's *Wild Animals
I Have Known*, he wrote sixteen more books of animal stories, including
The Haunters of the Silences (1907), which included this previously published
story. He defined his animal stories, a genre he is credited with inventing,
as "psychological romance constructed on a framework of natural science,"
a neat definition of the nature story itself. Margaret Atwood suggests, in
Survival, that the fact that Canadian animal stories are almost always told
from the animal's, i.e., the victim's, point of view "provides a key to an
important facet of the Canadian psyche."

◦ • ◦

IN A CIRCULAR hollow in the clean, bright gravel of the river-bar the tiny
egg of the great Quahdavic salmon stirred to life. For months it had lain there
among its thousands of fellows, with the clear, cold, unsullied current streaming over it ceaselessly. Through the autumn the wilderness sunshine and the
bracing wilderness air, playing on the unshaded shallows of the wide stream,
had kept the water highly vitalized—though this was hardly necessary in that
pure and spring-fed current. When the savage northern winter closed down
upon the high valley of the Quahdavic it found difficulty in freezing the swift
current that ran rippling over the bar; and when, at last, the frost conquered,
gripping and clutching through the long, windless nights, it was to form only

a thin armour of transparent, steel-strong ice, through which, as through the mantle of snow which made haste to cover it, the light still filtered softly but radiantly at noon, with an ethereal cobalt tinge.

The bar on which the parent salmon had hollowed their round gravel nest was far up the great South Branch of the Quahdavic, not many miles from the little cold spring lake that was its source. The Great South Branch was a stream much loved by the salmon, for its deep pools, its fine gravel spawning-beds, the purity and steady coldness of its current, and the remoteness which protected it from the visits of greedy poachers. In all its course there was but one serious obstruction, namely, the Big Falls, where the stream fell about twelve feet in one pitch, then roared down for a half a mile over a succession of low ledges with deep pools between. The Falls were such that vigorous fish had no real trouble in surmounting them. But they inexorably weeded out the weaklings. No feeble salmon ever got to the top of that straight and thunderous pitch. Therefore, as the spawning-bars were all above the Falls, it was a fine, long-finned, clean swimming breed of salmon that was bred in the Great South Branch.

When the tiny egg in the gravel stirred to life—as the thousands of other tiny eggs about it were doing at the same time—there was no ice sheet imprisoning the current, which ran singing pleasantly under a soft spring sun. The deep hollow in the gravel sheltered the moving atoms, so that they were not swept away by the current streaming over them. But minute as they were, they speedily gathered a strength altogether miraculous for their size, as they absorbed the clinging sacs of egg-substance and assumed the forms of fish, almost microscopic, but perfect. This advance achieved, they began to venture from behind and beneath the sheltering pebbles, to dare the urgent stream, and to work their way shoreward toward shallower waters where the perils which beset young salmon would be fewer and less insistent.

The egg from which he came having been one of the first to hatch, the tiny salmon mentioned in the opening paragraph was one of the first of the host to find his strength and to start the migration shoreward from the nest on the noisy bar. Perhaps a score started with him, trying the current, darting back to shelter, then more boldly venturing again. A passing trout, hungry and fierce-eyed, darted over them, heading up against the current; but being so few and scattered, they escaped his fatal attentions. Terrified, however, by the sudden shadow, they hid in the gravel and for some time made no further trial of the dangerous world.

When again the salmon atom adventured forth, he found himself in a greater company. Hundreds more of the tiny creatures had left the nest and were moving shoreward with him. As the defenseless throng advanced, he saw a couple of what seemed to him gigantic creatures dashing hither and thither among them, snapping them up greedily by twos and threes; and he himself barely escaped those greedy jaws by shooting forward in the nick of time. These seeming monsters were but young redfins, a couple of inches in length, whom he would soon come to despise and chase from his feeding-grounds.

His superior development and speed having so well served him, he was now a foot or more in advance of the throng, and so escaped another and even more wide-ranging peril. A huge shadow, as vast as that of the trout, swept down upon them, and as he shrank beneath a sharp-edged stone he saw a big sucker settle lazily where the thronging fry were thickest. With round, horribly dilating and contracting mouth turned down like an inverted snout, the big fish sucked up the little wrigglers greedily, even drawing them out by his power of suction from their hidings in the gravel. Of the hundreds that had started on the first migration from the nest not more than three score were left to follow their frightened and panting mite of a leader into the shallows where the big sucker could not come.

Among the little stones close to shore, where the water was hardly more than an inch deep, even the greedy young redfins would not venture. Nevertheless there were plenty of enemies waiting eagerly for the coming of the fry, and the little fellow whose one hour of seniority had made him the pioneer of the shoal found all his ability taxed to guard the speck of life which he had so lately achieved. Keeping far enough from shore to avoid being stranded by some whimsical ripple, he nevertheless avoided the depths that were sufficient for the free hunting of the predatory minnows and redfins. Such of his kinsfolk as stayed further out soon served, the greater number of them, as food for the larger river dwellers, while those who went too close inshore got cast up on the sand to die, or were pounced upon, as they lay close to the surface, by ravenous and unerring mosquitoes, which managed to pierce them even through a film of water a sixteenth of an inch or more in thickness. So it came about in a very brief time that of the countless throng emerging from the nest on the bar there remained but a hundred or so of the tiny fry to sustain the fortunes of that particular salmon family.

Even at the safest and most cunningly chosen depth, however, the little pioneer had plenty of perils to guard against. Secure from the suckers and redfins on the one hand, and from the mosquitoes on the other, he had yet for enemies certain predatory larvae and water-beetles, as well as a few inch-long youngsters of the trout family, who were very active and rapacious. There was a water-beetle with hooked, pincer-like jaws and lightning rapidity of movement, which kept him almost ceaselessly on the alert, and filled him with wholesome terror as he saw it capture and devour numbers of his less nimble or less wary kin. And one day, when he had chanced, in the company of his diminished school of fry, to drift into a shallow cove where there was no current at all to disturb the water, he was chased by the terrible larva of a dragon-fly. The strange-looking creature, with what seemed a blank, feature-less mask where its face and jaws ought to be, darted at him under the pro-pulsion of jets of water sucked into its middle and spurted out behind. Hav-ing taken alarm in time, he made good his escape between the stalks of a fine water-weed where the big larva could not penetrate. From this retreat he saw his pursuer turn and pounce upon a small basking minnow. The mask that covered the larva's face shot out as if on a hinge, developed into two power-ful grappling claws, and clutched the victim in the belly. After a brief strug-gle, which terrified all the tiny creatures within a radius of three feet, the minnow was dragged down to a clump of weed and the victor proceeded to make his feast. The little salmon stole in terror from his hiding-place and darted out into the more strenuous but for him far safer waters where a live current stirred among the gravel. To be sure the beetles were there, and the hungry young trout; but he had learned the ways of both these species of foe and knew pretty well how to elude them. Meanwhile, as he was himself con-tinually busy catching and devouring the tiny forms of life which abounded in those fruitful waters—minute shell-fish, and the spawn of the water-snails that clung under the stones, gnats, and other small insects that fell on the wa-ter, and even other fry just from the egg—he was growing at such a rate that presently the fierce water-beetles and the baby trout ceased to have any ter-rors for him. And at last, turning savagely as one of his old tormentors passed by, he caught a small beetle between his jaws and proceeded to make a meal of him. A few days later one of the baby trout was too slow in getting out of his way. He made a rush, caught his former tyrant, and, though the latter was more than an inch long, found no difficulty in swallowing him head first.

By this time the little salmon was between two and three inches long. He was what those learned in matters pertaining to the salmon would have called a "parr." His coloring was very beautiful, in a higher key than the coloring of a trout, and more brilliant, if less showy. There was none of the pink of the trout, but a clear silvery tone on sides and belly, with a shining blue-black along the back. The sides were marked with a row of black dots, set far apart and accentuated by a yellow flush around them, and with an-other row of spots of most vivid scarlet. Along the sides also ran a series of broad, vertical, bluish gray bars, the badge of the young of all the salmon tribe. He was a slender, strong-finned, finely molded little fish, built to have his dwelling in swift currents and to conquer turbulent rapids. His jaws were strong and large, and he had no reason to fear anything of his size that swam the river.

There were now not more than two score of his brothers and sisters left alive, and these scattered far and wide over the shoaling stream. It was high summer in the Quahdavic country, and the Great South Branch was beginning to show its ledges and sandy bars above water. Deep green the full-leaved boughs of elm and ash, poplar and cedar leaned above the current; and along the little wild-meadows which here and there bordered the stream, where the lumbermen had had camps or "landings," the misty pink-purple blossoms of the milkweed poured a wild sweetness upon the air. In a shallow run near the shore, where the sunlight, falling through an overhanging cedar "sweeper," dappled the clear ripples, and the current was about eight inches deep, and there was no pool near to tempt the larger fish, the active and wary little parr took up his home. The same run was chosen by three of his fellows also, and by a couple of small trout of about the same size. But there was room enough, and food enough, in that run for all of them, so the association was harmonious.

Lying with his head up-stream, his long fins and broad tail slowly waving to hold him in his position against the current, the little parr waited and watched while his food was brought down to him by the untiring flow. Sometimes it was a luckless leaf-grub, or a caddis-worm torn from his moorings, that came tumbling and bumping down along the smooth pebbles of the bottom, to be gathered into the young salmon's eager maw. Sometimes it was a fly or moth or bee or beetle that came bobbing with drenched, helpless wings along the tops of the ripples. And once in a while a pink-shelled baby crawfish in its wanderings would come sidling across the run, and be promptly gobbled up in spite of the futile threatenings of its tiny claws. The river was liberal in its providing for its most favored children, these aristocratic and beautiful parr, so the youngster grew apace in his bright run.

Happy though his life was now, in every kind of weather, he was still beset with perils. He had, of course, no longer anything to fear from the journeying suckers, with their small, toothless mouths, but now and then a big-mouthed, red-bellied, savage trout would pass up the run, and in passing make a dash at one of the little occupants. In this way two of the parr, and one of the little trout, disappeared—the trout folk having no prejudice whatever against cannibalism. But our pioneer, ceaselessly on the watch and matchlessly nimble, always succeeded in keeping well out of the way. Once he had a horrible scare, when a seven-pound salmon, astray from the main channel, made his way cautiously up the middle of the run and scraped over the bar. In this case, however, the alarm was groundless. The stranger was not seeking food, but only a way out of the embarrassing shallows.

Another peril that kept the young parr on the alert—an ever imminent and particularly appalling peril—was the foraging of the kingfishers. A pair of these noisy and diligent birds had their nest of six little ones in a hole in the red bluff just above the run, and they took ceaseless tribute from the finny tribes of the river. Like an azure arrow one of them would dart down into the river with a loud splash, and flap up again, usually with a gleaming trout or parr held firmly between the edges of his great beak. If he missed his shot and came up with empty beak, he would fly off up the river with a harsh, clattering, startlingly loud cry of indignation and protest. Several times one or other of these troublesome foragers dropped into the run. The dappling of the shadow and sun, however, from the cedar, was a protection to the dwellers in this run; and only twice was the fishing there successful. The second little trout, and one more of the parr, were carried off. Then the birds forsook that particular bit of ripple and hunted easier waters.

In leaping at the flies which came down the surface of the run the little salmon one day got a severe but invaluable lesson. A large and gaudy fly, unlike anything that he had ever encountered before, appeared on the ripples over his head. Still more unlike those which he had encountered before, it did not hurry downward with the water, but maintained its position in a most mysterious fashion. While the parr eyed it curiously, wondering whether to try it or not, it suddenly moved straight up against the current, and was followed at a short distance by another queer-looking big fly, green and brown like a grasshopper. Excited by the strange behaviour of these two strangers, the parr rose sharply and hit the green fly with his tail, intending to drown it and investigate it at his leisure. To his astonishment both flies instantly disappeared. Chagrined and puzzled, he dropped back to the tail of the run, sulking.

A moment later, however, the two flies reappeared, slipping very slowly down the current, mounting up again directly in the teeth of it, sometimes dancing on the surface, sometimes sinking a little below it, but always remaining the same distance apart, and always behaving in a manner mysteriously independent of the power of the stream. For a few seconds the parr eyed them with distrust. Then growing excited by their strange actions, he dashed forward fiercely and caught the gaudy red fly in his jaws. There was a prick, a

twitch, a frightful jerk—and he found himself dragged forth into the stran-
gling upper air, where he fell flopping on the dry gravel of the shore.

As he lay gasping and struggling on the hot pebbles, which scorched off
the delicate bloom from his tender skin, a tall shape stooped over him, and a
great hand, its fingers as long as his whole body, picked him up. He heard a
vague reverberation, which was the voice of the tall shape saying, "A poor little beggar of a salmon—but not badly hooked! He'll be none the worse, and
perhaps none the wiser!" Then, with what seemed to him terrible and deadly
violence, but what was really the most careful delicacy that the big hand was
capable of, the hook was removed from his jaw, and he was tossed back into
the water. Dizzy and half-stunned, he turned over on his back, head downward, and for a moment or two was at the mercy of the current. Then, recovering from the shock, he righted himself, and swam frantically to the shelter
of an overhanging stone which he knew, where he lay with heaving sides,
sore, aching, and trembling, till little by little his self-possession returned to
him. But afterward, since he was by nature somewhat more wary and alert
than his fellows, he viewed floating flies with suspicion and inspected them
cautiously before seizing them in his jaws.

All through the summer and autumn the little parr was kept very busy,
feeding, and dodging his enemies, and playing in the cheerful, shallow "run"
beneath the cedar. When the early autumn rains swelled the volume of the
Great South Branch, he first realized how numerous were the big salmon in
the stream—fish which had kept carefully clear of the shallow places wherein
he had spent the summer. Though he held himself well aloof from these big
fish—which never paid him any attention—he noticed them playing tempes-
tuously, leaping high out of the pools, and very busy night and morning on
the gravel bars, where they seemed to be digging with their powerful snouts.

Still later, when, instead of flies and beetles, there fell upon the darkening
surface of the river little pale specks which vanished as he snatched at them,
he grew fiercely and inexplicably discontented. What he longed for he did
not know; but he knew it was nowhere in the waters about him, neither
along the edges of the shore, where now the ice was forming in crisp fringes.
All about him he saw the big salmon—their sides lean and flat, their brilliant
colors darkened and faded—swimming down languidly with the strenuous
current. Hitherto their movements had been all up-stream—upward, upward
incessantly and gladly. Now the old energy and joy of life seemed all gone out
of them. Nevertheless, they seemed very anxious to go somewhere, and the
way to that somewhere appeared to be down-stream. Hardly knowing what
he did, and not at all knowing why he did it, the parr found himself slipping

down-stream with them. He had grown vastly in size and strength, while his vivid and varied hues had begun to soften appreciably. In fact, he was now no longer a parr, but a "smelt"; and after the ordained custom of his kind, he was on his way to the sea.

JOHN BURROUGHS

The Halcyon in Canada 1907

JOHN BURROUGHS (1837–1921) was born near Roxbury, New York, and worked as a teacher and later as a clerk in the Treasury Department. In Washington he met Walt Whitman, who became his lifelong friend, and also published his first nature essays in the *Atlantic Monthly*, which continued to publish them for the next sixty-one years. Burroughs was one of the most popular writers of his time and the progenitor of the modern nature essay. According to Bill McKibbon, Burroughs "figured out a language for making others treasure the small spectacles of nature—he articulated the mute delight that people have always taken in their surroundings." In 1875, Burroughs went on a trout-fishing expedition in Quebec, which resulted in "The Halcyon in Canada." "The halcyon or kingfisher is a good guide when you go to the woods," the essay begins; "follow his rattle and you shall see the source of every trout and salmon stream on the continent."

⚓ • ⚓

THE LAKE BECAME my favorite resort, while my companion preferred rather the shore or the long still pool above, where there was a rude makeshift of a boat, made of common box-boards.

Upon the lake you had the wildness and solitude at arm's length, and could better take their look and measure. You became something apart from them; you emerged and had a vantage-ground like that of a mountain peak, and could contemplate them at your ease. Seated upon my raft and slowly carried by the current or drifted by the breeze, I had many a long, silent look into the face of the wilderness, and found the communion good. I was alone with the spirit of the forest-bound lakes, and felt its presence and magnetism. I played hide-and-seek with it about the nooks and corners, and lay in wait for it upon a little island crowned with a clump of trees that was moored just to one side of the current near the head of the lake.

Indeed, there is no depth of solitude that the mind does not endow with some human interest. As in a dead silence the ear is filled with its own murmur, so amid these aboriginal scenes one's feelings and sympathies become external to him, as it were, and he holds converse with them. Then a lake is the ear as well as the eye of a forest. It is the place to go to listen and ascertain what sounds are abroad in the air. They all run quickly thither and report. If any creature had called in the forest for miles about, I should have heard it. At times I could hear the distant roar of water off beyond the outlet of the lake. The sound of the vagrant winds purring here and there in the tops of the spruces reached my ear. A breeze would come slowly down the mountain, then strike the lake, and I could see its footsteps approaching by the changed appearance of the water. How slowly the winds move at times, sauntering like one on a Sunday walk! A breeze always enlivens the fish; a dead calm and all pennants sink, your activity with your fly is ill-timed, and you soon take the hint and stop. Becalmed upon my raft, I observed, as I have often done before, that the life of Nature ebbs and flows, comes and departs, in these wilderness scenes; one moment her stage is thronged and the next quite deserted. Then there is a wonderful unity of movement in the two elements, air and water. When there is much going on in one, there is quite sure to be much going on in the other. You have been casting, perhaps, for an hour with scarcely a jump or any sign of life anywhere about you, when presently the breeze freshens and the trout begin to respond, and then of a sudden all the performers rush in: ducks come sweeping by; loons laugh and wheel overhead, then approach the water on a long, gentle incline, plowing deeper and deeper into its surface, until their momentum is arrested, or converted into foam; the fish hawk screams; the bald eagle goes flapping by, and your eyes and hands are full. Then the tide ebbs, and both fish and fowl are gone.

Patiently whipping the waters of the lake from my rude float, I became an object of great interest to the loons. I had never seen these birds before in their proper habitat, and the interest was mutual. When they had paused on the Hudson during their spring and fall migrations, I had pursued them in my boat to try to get near them. Now the case was reversed; I was the interloper now, and they would come out and study me. Sometimes six or eight of them would be swimming about watching my movements, but they were wary and made a wide circle. One day one of their number volunteered to make a thorough reconnoissance. I saw him leave his comrades and swim straight toward me. He came bringing first one eye to bear upon me, then the other.

When about half the distance was passed over he began to waver and hesitate. To encourage him I stopped casting, and taking off my hat began to wave it slowly to and fro, as in the act of fanning myself. This started him again—this was a new trait in the creature that he must scrutinize more closely. On he came, till all his markings were distinctly seen. With one hand I pulled a little revolver from my hip pocket, and when the loon was about fifty yards distant, and had begun to sidle around me, I fired: at the flash I saw two webbed feet twinkle in the air, and the loon was gone! Lead could not have gone down so quickly. The bullet cut across the circles where he disappeared. In a few moments he reappeared a couple of hundred yards away. "Ha-ha-ha-a-a," said he, "ha-ha-ha-a-a," and "ha-ha-ha-a-a," said his comrades, who had been looking on; and "ha-ha-ha-a-a," said we all, echo included. He approached a second time, but not so closely, and when I began to creep back toward the shore with my heavy craft, pawing the water first upon one side, then the other, he followed, and with ironical laughter witnessed my efforts to stem the current at the head of the lake. I confess it was enough to make a more solemn bird than the loon laugh, but it was no fun for me, and generally required my last pound of steam.

The loons flew back and forth from one lake to the other, and their voices were about the only notable wild sounds to be heard.

One afternoon, quite unexpectedly, I struck my big fish in the head of the lake. I was first advised of his approach by two or three trout jumping clear from the water to get out of his lordship's way. The water was not deep just there, and he swam so near the surface that his enormous back cut through. With a swirl he swept my fly under and turned.

My hook was too near home, and my rod too near a perpendicular to strike well. More than that, my presence of mind came near being unhorsed by the sudden apparition of the fish. If I could have had a moment's notice, or if I had not seen the monster, I should have fared better and the fish worse. I struck, but not with enough decision, and, before I could reel up, my empty hook came back. The trout had carried it in his jaws till the fraud was detected, and then spat it out. He came a second time and made a grand commotion in the water, but not in my nerves, for I was ready then, but failed to take the fly, and so to get his weight and beauty in these pages. As my luck failed me at the last, I will place my loss at the full extent of the law, and claim that nothing less than a ten-pounder was spirited away from my hand that day. I might not have saved him, netless as I was upon my cumbrous raft; but I should at least have had the glory of the fight, and the consolation of the fairly vanquished.

These trout are not properly lake trout, but the common brook trout. The largest ones are taken with live bait through the ice in winter. The Indians and the *habitans* bring them out of the woods from here and from Snow Lake, on their toboggans, from two and half to three feet long. They have kinks and ways of their own. About half a mile above camp we discovered a deep oval bay to one side of the main current of the river, that evidently abounded in big fish. Here they disported themselves. It was a favorite feeding-ground, and late every afternoon the fish rose all about it, making those big ripples the angler delights to see. A trout, when he comes to the surface, starts a ring about his own length in diameter; most of the rings in the pool, when the eye caught them, were like barrel hoops, but the haughty trout ignored all our best efforts; not one rise did we get. We were told of this pool on our return to Quebec, and that other anglers had a similar experience there. But occasionally some old fisherman, like a great advocate who loves a difficult case, would set his wits to work and bring into camp an enormous trout taken there.

I had been told in Quebec that I would not see a bird in the woods, not a feather of any kind. But I knew I should, though they were not numerous. I saw and heard a bird nearly every day, on the tops of the trees about, that I think was one of the cross-bills. The kingfisher was there ahead of us with his loud clicking reel. The osprey was there, too, and I saw him abusing the bald eagle, who had probably just robbed him of a fish. The yellow-rumped warbler I saw, and one of the kinglets was leading its lisping brood about through the spruces. In every opening the white-throated sparrow abounded, striking up his clear sweet whistle, at times so loud and sudden that one's momentary impression was that some farm boy was approaching, or was secreted there behind the logs. Many times, amid those primitive solitudes, I was quite startled by the human tone and quality of this whistle. It is little more than a beginning; the bird never seems to finish the strain suggested. The Canada jay was there also, very busy about some important private matter.

One lowery morning, as I was standing in camp, I saw a lot of ducks borne swiftly down by the current around the bend in the river a few rods above. They saw me at the same instant and turned toward the shore. On hastening up there, I found the old bird rapidly leading her nearly grown brood through the woods, as if to go around our camp. As I pursued them they ran squawking with outstretched stubby wings, scattering right and left, and seeking a hiding-place under the logs and débris. I captured one and carried it into camp. It was just what Joe wanted; it would make a valuable decoy. So he kept it in a box, fed it upon oats, and took it out of the woods with him.

We found the camp we had appropriated was a favorite stopping-place of the carmen who hauled in supplies for the gang of two hundred road-builders. One rainy day near nightfall no less than eight carts drew up at the old stable, and the rain-soaked drivers, after picketing and feeding their horses, came down to our fire. We were away, and Joe met us on our return with the unwelcome news. We kept open house so far as the fire was concerned; but our roof was a narrow one at the best, and one or two leaky spots made it still narrower.

"We shall probably sleep out-of-doors to-night," said my companion, "unless we are a match for this posse of rough teamsters."

But the men proved to be much more peaceably disposed than the same class at home; they apologized for intruding, pleading the inclemency of the weather, and were quite willing, with our permission, to take up with pot-luck about the fire and leave us the shanty. They dried their clothes upon poles and logs, and had their fun and their bantering amid it all. An Irishman among them did about the only growling; he invited himself into our quarters, and before morning had Joe's blanket about him in addition to his own.

On Friday we made an excursion to Great Lake Jacques Cartier, paddling and poling up the river in the rude box-boat. It was a bright, still morning after the rain, and everything had a new, fresh appearance. Expectation was ever on tiptoe as each turn in the river opened a new prospect before us. How wild, and shaggy, and silent it was! What fascinating pools, what tempting stretches of trout-haunted water! Now and then we would catch a glimpse of long black shadows starting away from the boat and shooting through the sunlit depths. But no sound or motion on shore was heard or seen. Near the lake we came to a long, shallow rapid, when we pulled off our shoes and stockings, and, with our trousers rolled above our knees, towed the boat up it, wincing and cringing amid the sharp, slippery stones. With benumbed feet and legs we reached the still water that forms the stem of the lake, and presently saw the arms of the wilderness open and the long deep blue expanse in their embrace. We rested and bathed, and gladdened our eyes with the singularly beautiful prospect. The shadows of summer clouds were slowly creeping up and down the sides of the mountains that hemmed it in. On the far eastern shore, near the head, banks of what was doubtless white sand shone dimly in the sun, and the illusion that there was a town nestled there haunted my mind constantly. It was like a section of the Hudson below the Highlands, except that these waters were bluer and colder, and these shores darker, than even those Sir Hendrik first looked upon; but surely one felt, a steamer will round that point presently, or a sail drift into view! We paddled a mile or more up the east shore, then across to the west, and found such pleasure in simply gazing upon the scene that our rods were quite neglected. We did some casting after a while, but raised no fish of any consequence till we were in the outlet again, when they responded so freely that the "disgust of trout" was soon upon us.

At the rapids, on our return, as I was standing to my knees in the swift, cold current, and casting into a deep hole behind a huge boulder that rose four or five feet above the water amidstream, two trout, one of them a large one, took my flies, and, finding the fish and the current united too strong for my tackle, I sought to gain the top of the boulder, in which attempt I got wet in my middle and lost my fish. After I had gained the rock, I could not get away again with my clothes on without swimming, which, to say nothing of wet garments the rest of the way home, I did not like to do amid those rocks and swift currents; so, after a vain attempt to communicate with my companion above the roar of the water, I removed my clothing, left it together with my tackle upon the rock, and by a strong effort stemmed the current and reached the shore. The boat was a hundred yards above, and when I arrived there my teeth were chattering with the cold, my feet were numb with bruises, and the black flies were making the blood stream down my back. We hastened back with the boat, and, by wading out into the current again and holding it by a long rope, it swung around with my companion aboard, and was held in the eddy behind the rock. I clambered up, got my clothes on, and we were soon shooting down-stream toward home; but the winter of discontent that shrouded one half of me made sad inroads upon the placid feeling of a day well spent that enveloped the other, all the way to camp.

That night something carried off all our fish—doubtless a fisher or lynx, as Joe had seen an animal of some kind about camp that day.

I must not forget the two red squirrels that frequented the camp during our stay, and that were so tame they would approach within a few feet of us and take the pieces of bread or fish tossed to them. When a particularly fine piece of hard-tack was secured, they would spin off to their den with it somewhere near by.

Caribou abound in these woods, but we saw only their tracks; and of bears, which are said to be plentiful, we saw no signs.

Saturday morning we packed up our traps and started on our return, and found that the other side of the spruce-trees and the vista of the lonely road going south were about the same as coming north. But we understood the road better and the buck-board better, and our load was lighter, hence the distance was more easily accomplished.

E. PAULINE JOHNSON

The Deep Waters 1911

PAULINE JOHNSON (1861–1913) was born on the Six Nations Reserve near Brantford, Ontario, the daughter of Mohawk Chief G. H. M. Johnson and his English wife, Emily Howells, who was related to William Dean Howells. She was best known as a poet and, later, as a reciter of her own poems, for which she dressed in Native fashion and took the name Tekahionwake. As a performer she toured Canada, the United States and England, where in 1906, at a reception at Buckingham Palace, she met Joe Capilano, chief of the Squamish tribe of British Columbia. She retired to Vancouver that same year and began work on *Legends of Vancouver* (1911), a recounting of Squamish myths related to her by Chief Capilano, who "frequently remarked," she wrote in her Foreword, "that they had never been revealed to any other English-speaking person save myself." "The Deep Waters," a comparison of Squamish and Iroquois creation legends, is taken from this collection.

છ • ૪ઠ

FAR OVER YOUR left shoulder as your boat leaves the Narrows to thread the beautiful waterways that lead to Vancouver Island, you will see the summit of Mount Baker robed in its everlasting whiteness and always reflecting some wonderful glory from the rising sun, the golden noontide, or the violet and amber sunset. This is the Mount Ararat of the Pacific Coast peoples; for those readers who are familiar with the ways and beliefs and faiths of primitive races will agree that it is difficult to discover anywhere in the world a race that has not some story of the Deluge, which they have chronicled and localized to fit the understanding and the conditions of the nation that composes their own immediate world.

Amongst the red nations of America I doubt if any two tribes have the same ideas regarding the Flood. Some of the traditions concerning this vast whim of Nature are grotesque in the extreme; some are impressive; some even profound; but of all the stories of the Deluge that I have been able to collect I know of not a single one that can even begin to equal in beauty of conception, let alone rival in possible reality and truth, the Squamish legend of "The Deep Waters."

I here quote the legend of "mine own people," the Iroquois tribes of Ontario, regarding the Deluge. I do this to paint the color of contrast in richer shades, for I am bound to admit that we who pride ourselves on ancient intellectuality have but a childish tale of the Flood when compared with the jealously preserved annals of the Squamish, which savor more of history than tradition. With "mine own people," animals always play a much more important part and are endowed with a finer intelligence than humans. I do not find amid my notes a single tradition of the Iroquois wherein animals do not figure, and our story of the Deluge rests entirely with the intelligence of sea-going and river-going creatures. With us, animals in olden times were greater than man; but it is not so with the Coast Indians, except in rare instances.

When a Coast Indian consents to tell you a legend he will, without variation, begin it with, "It was before the white people came."

The natural thing for you then to ask is, "But who were here then?"

He will reply, "Indians, and just the trees, and animals, and fishes, and a few birds."

So you are prepared to accept the animal world as intelligent co-habitants of the Pacific slope, but he will not lead you to think he regards them as equals, much less superiors. But to revert to "mine own people": they hold the intelligence of wild animals far above that of man, for perhaps the one reason that when an animal is sick it effects its own cure; it knows what grasses and herbs to eat, what to avoid, while the sick human calls the medicine man, whose wisdom is not only the result of years of study, but also heredity; consequently any great natural event, such as the Deluge, has much to do with the wisdom of the creatures of the forests and the rivers.

Iroquois tradition tells us that once this earth was entirely submerged in water, and during this period for many days a busy little muskrat swam about vainly looking for a foothold of earth wherein to build his house. In his search he encountered a turtle also leisurely swimming, so they had speech together, and the muskrat complained of weariness; he could find no foothold; he was tired of incessant swimming, and longed for land such as his ancestors enjoyed. The turtle suggested that the muskrat should dive and endeavor to find earth at the bottom of the sea. Acting on this advice the muskrat plunged down, then arose with his two little forepaws grasping some earth he had found beneath the waters.

"Place it on my shell and dive again for more," directed the turtle. The muskrat did so, but when he returned with his paws filled with earth he discovered the small quantity he had first deposited on the turtle's shell had doubled in size. The return from the third trip found the turtle's load again doubled. So the building went on at double compound increase, and the world grew its continents and its islands with great rapidity, and now rests on the shell of a turtle.

If you ask an Iroquois, "And did no men survive this flood?" he will reply, "Why should men survive? The animals are wiser than men; let the wisest live."

How, then, was the earth re-peopled?

The Iroquois will tell you that the otter was a medicine man; that in swimming and diving about he found corpses of men and women; he sang his medicine songs and they came to life, and the otter brought them fish for food until they were strong enough to provide for themselves. Then the Iroquois will conclude his tale with, "You know well that the otter has greater wisdom than a man."

So much for "mine own people" and our profound respect for the superior intelligence of our little brothers of the animal world.

But the Squamish tribe hold other ideas. It was on a February day that I first listened to this beautiful, humane story of the Deluge. My royal old tillicum had come to see me through the rains and mists of late winter days. The gateways of my wigwam always stood open—very widely open—for his feet to enter, and this especial day he came with the worst downpour of the season.

Womanlike, I protested with a thousand contradictions in my voice that he should venture out to see me on such a day. It was "Oh! Chief, I am so glad to see you!" and it was "Oh! Chief, why didn't you stay at home on such a wet day—your poor throat will suffer." But I soon had quantities of hot tea for him, and the huge cup my own father always used was his—as long as the Sagalie Tyee allowed his dear feet to wander my way. The immense cup stands idle and empty now for the second time.

Helping him off with his great-coat, I chatted on about the deluge of rain, and he remarked it was not so very bad, as one could yet walk.

"Fortunately, yes, for I cannot swim," I told him.

He laughed, replying, "Well, it is not so bad as when the Great Deep Waters covered the world."

Immediately I foresaw the coming legend, so crept into the shell of monosyllables. "No?" I questioned.

"No," he replied. "For one time there was no land here at all; everywhere there was just water."

"I can quite believe it," I remarked caustically.

He laughed—that irresistible, though silent, David Warfield laugh of his that always brought a responsive smile from his listeners. Then he plunged directly into the tradition, with no preface save a comprehensive sweep of his wonderful hands towards my wide window, against which the rains were beating.

"It was after a long, long time of this—this rain. The mountain streams were swollen, the rivers choked, the sea began to rise—and yet it rained; for weeks and weeks it rained." He ceased speaking, while the shadows of centuries gone crept into his eyes. Tales of the misty past always inspired him.

"Yes," he continued. "It rained for weeks and weeks, while the mountain torrents roared thunderingly down, and the sea crept silently up. The level lands were first to float in sea water, then to disappear. The slopes were next to slip into the sea. The world was slowly being flooded. Hurriedly the Indian tribes gathered in one spot, a place of safety far above the reach of the on-creeping sea. The spot was the circling shore of Lake Beautiful, up the North Arm. They held a Great Council and decided at once upon a plan of action. A giant canoe should be built, and some means contrived to anchor it in case the waters mounted to the heights. The men undertook the canoe, the women the anchorage.

"A giant tree was felled, and day and night the men toiled over its construction into the most stupendous canoe the world has ever known. Not an hour, not a moment, but many worked, while the toil-wearied ones slept, only to awake to renewed toil. Meanwhile the women also worked at a cable—the largest, the longest, the strongest that Indian hands and teeth had ever made. Scores of them gathered and prepared the cedar fibre; scores of them plaited, rolled and seasoned it; scores of them chewed upon it inch by inch to make it pliable; scores of them oiled and worked, oiled and worked, oiled and worked it into a sea-resisting fabric. And still the sea crept up, and up, and up. It was the last day; hope of life for the tribe, of land for the world, was doomed. Strong hands, self-sacrificing hands, fastened the cable the women had made—one end to the giant canoe, the other about an enormous boulder, a vast immovable rock as firm as the foundations of the world—for might not the canoe with its priceless freight drift out, far out, to sea, and when the water subsided might not this ship of safety be leagues and leagues beyond the sight of land on the storm-driven Pacific?

"Then with the bravest hearts that ever beat, noble hands lifted every child of the tribe into this vast canoe; not one single baby was overlooked. The canoe was stocked with food and fresh water, and lastly, the ancient men and women of the race selected as guardians to these children the bravest, most stalwart, handsomest young man of the tribe, and the mother of the youngest baby in the camp—she was but a girl of sixteen, her child but two weeks old; but she, too, was brave and very beautiful. These two were placed, she at the bow of the canoe to watch, he at the stern to guide, and all the little children crowded between.

"And still the sea crept up, and up, and up. At the crest of the bluffs about Lake Beautiful the doomed tribes crowded. Not a single person attempted to enter the canoe. There was no wailing, no crying out for safety. 'Let the little children, the young mother, and the bravest and best of our young men live,' was all the farewell those in the canoe heard as the waters reached the summit, and—the canoe floated. Last of all to be seen was the top of the tallest tree, then—all was a world of water.

"For days and days there was no land—just the rush of swirling, snarling sea; but the canoe rode safely at anchor, the cable those scores of dead, faithful women had made held true as the hearts that beat behind the toil and labor of it all.

"But one morning at sunrise, far to the south, a speck floated on the breast of the waters; at midday it was larger; at evening it was yet larger. The moon arose, and in its magic light the man at the stern saw it was a patch of land. All night he watched it grow, and at daybreak looked with glad eyes upon the summit of Mount Baker. He cut the cable, grasped his paddle in his strong, young hands, and steered for the south. When they landed, the waters were sunken half down the mountain side. The children were lifted out; the beautiful young mother, the stalwart young brave, turned to each other, clasped hands, looked into each other's eyes—and smiled.

"And down in the vast country that lies between Mount Baker and the Fraser River they made a new camp, built new lodges, where the little children grew and thrived, and lived and loved, and the earth was re-peopled by them.

"The Squamish say that in a gigantic crevice half way to the crest of Mount Baker may yet be seen the outlines of an enormous canoe, but I have never seen it myself."

He ceased speaking with that far-off cadence in his voice with which he always ended a legend, and for a long time we both sat in silence listening to the rains that were still beating against the window.

VILHJALMUR STEFANSSON

Summer Life in Banks Island 1921

VILHJALMUR STEFANSSON (1879–1962) was born in Arnes, Manitoba, and before the age of thirty held the world's record for continuous arctic service. His classic of wilderness travel, *My Life with the Eskimo,* published in 1913, established him as a master of lucid prose and keen scientific observation. Over his long career as an arctic explorer he wrote twenty-five books. *The Friendly Arctic* (1921), from which this chapter is excerpted, is his controversial account of the 1913–18 Canadian Arctic Expedition he commanded. The expedition established that it was possible for white men to live off the "land," or rather off large, drifting ice floes, in the Inuit fashion, for longer periods than they could carry food. Stefansson's lifelong project was to urge the Canadian government to establish firm territorial rights to the Arctic, especially when trans-Arctic air travel threatened Canadian sovereignty. His autobiography, *Discovery,* was published posthumously in 1964.

ex · ba

ON JULY 2ND MY DIARY records a word against the ravens and gulls. We predatory animals do not get along together any too well and are inclined to be jealous of one another. On this occasion I had killed a caribou that had a little fat, and while I was gone after pack dogs to fetch the meat, some gulls and ravens had found the carcass. They did not have time to eat much, but they did have time to eat every speck of fat. We had given up seal hunting because the pursuit of the seal on the summer ice is a very sloppy undertaking. Caribou fat was therefore precious to us and was as yet of limited quantity because the season was too early. Hence my annoyance at the gulls

Next day I killed two bulls that had half an inch of back fat, and from that time on we no longer stinted ourselves on fat, although it was well towards the end of July before we began to give much of it to the dogs. This was not entirely because we were short of it but partly because we were anxious to save it for the winter. It was conceivable that ice conditions might prevent the *Star*'s coming, in which case we should need fat badly, both for food and for winter candlelight. The first part of the winter we would then spend in Banks Island and begin traveling when the light should be abundant in the spring. We talked of going to Victoria Island and thence to the mainland and over to Great Bear Lake, a country thoroughly familiar to me from my second expedition. But secretly I was hoping that when spring came we should even in the absence of ships, find ourselves in such spirits and so equipped that we could make a second ice journey, preferably northwest from Banks Island.

To spend a summer in Banks Island as we did that one was a delight. Storkerson and I knew well the tricks and methods of living in an arctic land and Ole proved an apt pupil. The caribou grew fatter and their skins more sleek and better for clothing. We killed altogether about forty fat bulls and dried over half a ton of back fat, the equivalent of that much bacon. We lived on the most palatable parts, the heads and back bones, and the dogs lived mainly on the internal organs, while we sliced thin, spread out on stones and dried in the sun for future use the hams, shoulders and other fleshy parts. Being sailors, Storkerson and Ole were both good at sewing, and they talked much about the fine clothes they were going to make from the skins for themselves and me if the ships should fail to bring Eskimo families with their incomparable seamstresses from the mainland.

Like many others, I had gathered from reading polar books that fuel is hard to get in arctic lands, at least where driftwood is absent. But during my previous expedition I had learned that on the mainland of northern Canada, at least, there is excellent fuel to be found nearly everywhere, and so it proved on Banks Island. It has always been a marvel to me how the northern Indians who hunt out on the so-called "barren grounds" and the Eskimos of northern Alaska are able to grow up from childhood to maturity and old age without learning, either by accident or by the instruction of some wiser people, how to use certain common plants for fuel.

Readers of Frank Russell, Warburton Pike, Caspar Whitney, and others know how the northern Indians load up their sleds with dry spruce wood for furtive dashes into the dreaded "barren grounds." They use a little for cooking each day, and when in a week or so the supply is gone they expect to be on their way back and almost within reach of the spruce forests again. And if through any circumstance the journey is a little long, there are tales of hardship which seem to be felt no less keenly by the Indian than by the white narrator. It was so with the Eskimos of northern Alaska. When they went inland in days antedating blue-flame kerosene stoves, they used to take with them driftwood from the coast, or seal or whale oil to burn in their stone stoves or lamps. If they ran out of these they used to dig in the snow for willows, being thus a stage in advance of the northern Indian in resourcefulness in the open country. But if no willows were to be found and the seal oil ran out, they hurried back to the coast without a fire. This in spite of the fact that most or all coast tribes in Alaska knew that there were other Eskimo tribes in the interior—the inland Oturkagmiut and their neighbors—who had the art of finding fuel other than willows in the open country wherever they went. The Mackenzie River Eskimos to the eastward are completely ignorant of how to find fuel in the open country even in summer, except willows. But the Eskimos of Coronation Gulf and east all the way to Hudson Bay find no difficulty in securing it in winter or summer, although their country is not nearly so well supplied with fuel plants as is the southerly "barren ground" into which the Dog-ribs and Yellowknives make their furtive dashes, or the northern portion of Alaska where the Point Barrow Eskimos experience fuel scarcity.

The summer of 1910 I was living with three western Eskimo companions among the Eskimos of Coronation Gulf. When after a day's march across the prairie we camped in the evening, my three Eskimos used to scatter and go sometimes a mile in search of small willows which they would gather with great difficulty into bags and bring home on their backs. Before this willow gathering was done our local Eskimo traveling companions would have their own supper cooked and ready to eat, for they used for fuel a sort of "heather," *Cassiope tetragona,* which grew in many places and always in those we selected for camp sites. I pointed out the great advantage of using these plants for fuel, but conservatism is a trait that is always stronger the more ignorant the people, and my Eskimos were unwilling to listen. Their people had always traveled in this kind of country and they had always used willows. It was an application in a field other than religion of the sentiment of the well-known hymn: " 'Twas good enough for father, 'twas good enough for mother." They seemed to feel there was something essentially wrong or degraded about using a "grass" when wood was available. This same conservatism had prevented their ancestors as long as they lived in Alaska from learning the art of "grass" burning from the Oturkagmiut. There they were in their own country and public sentiment was overwhelmingly on their side, but here they were in the minority with everybody laughing at them. They stood pat for a month, but finally gave in; and before fall we were able to cook a meal as quickly as any of the local people.

This is a digression, the point being that the plant *Cassiope tetragona* grows abundantly in most parts of Banks Island, and that usually we were able to pick a camp site where around our camp fire, in an area no larger than the floor space of a bedroom, would be fuel enough to cook a meal. In sunshiny weather with a moderate breeze blowing I would cook with heather even were dry willow at hand, and in my experience dry willow is rare, at least of that type which is most prevalent in the northern part of the North American mainland. There is, however, in Banks Island and the northerly islands and in rare places on the mainland another "willow" which has roots many times as large as that part of the plant which is above ground. The roots are found dead and sticking out on the tops of high hills, so that occasionally in summer and frequently when there was snow on the ground we used them in preference to heather, and especially in calm weather or after a heavy rain. But no matter how soaked with water, *Cassiope* can easily be burned if you know the method and if there is a strong breeze fanning the fire and kindling enough to start the blaze.

Mosquitoes, the one serious drawback of the North—far more serious in the minds of all who know than winter darkness, extreme cold or violent winds—were not very serious in Banks Island. For one thing the drainage is fairly good; for another, the winds blow often enough from the ocean to keep the temperature lower than mosquitoes like. Perhaps the richest hunting country known to me is the region between Great Bear Lake and Coronation Gulf, but it has the disadvantage of a plague of mosquitoes and flies. And so on the whole these months of tenting and wandering in Banks Island are the most delightful of my summer recollections from the North, though they did not come quite up to autumn and early winter just north of the arctic circle on Horton River or on the Coppermine.

I feel like mentioning here that I cannot understand the psychology of northern travelers who employ Eskimos and Indians to do their hunting for them. I would as soon think of engaging a valet to play my golf or of going to the theatre by proxy. Not that I enjoy the killing of animals as such, but I should dislike extremely the feeling of dependence in work or play, of knowing that it hinged on the skill and good will of any one, no matter how competent, whether I should have something to eat to-morrow or whether my plans were to fail for lack of food. I do not see how any one could get much enjoyment out of living in a camp supported by hired hunters. Neither have I at the time nor in retrospect any hesitancy of mind when I compare the pleasures and ease of the city or the summer resort with the northern caribou hunt, whether it be in the soft air and sunshine of summer or in December's keenest wind and snow. The one sort of pleasure is passive, receptive, enervating—you are jaded by it and the keen edge of your enjoyment turns dull. But the open life of him who lives by the hunt keeps indefinitely the thrill of endeavor and achievement, a thing never to be bought or secured by having others carry out for you the most elaborate or ingenious of programs. And all of this becomes even more worth while when the food and clothing of your companions depend upon the hunt, and most when your very lives hang on success.

The first half of July we hunted from our camp on the mainland opposite Bernard Island, but in the latter half Storkerson and I made a trip into the interior, mainly for exploration but partly for hunting, leaving Ole to guard the depot on the coast. As fat is precious above all things in the Arctic and caribou fat good to eat beyond most food of any kind, we chose to kill old bulls, for they were now the fattest. It is the nature of caribou that different ages and sexes are fat at different times of the year. A comparative statement of their fatness is about as follows:

In late November after the rutting season the old bulls are so thin that there is no trace of fat even behind their eyes, and the marrow in their bones is like blood. At this time both the cows and the young bulls are about at their fattest, although the proportion to the total body weight is never as high as in fat old bulls. By Christmas the young bulls have lost most or all of their fat, while the cows have less but are still not thin. About this time or in January the old bulls shed their antlers and from that time take on fat, although none is discernible at first. By February or March, when the budding antlers of old bulls are six or eight inches long, the marrow improves and traces of fat appear behind the eyes, about the kidneys and on the brisket. The young bulls are still lean and the cows carrying their young have become considerably thinner, although they have a little back fat and considerable intestinal fat, especially caribou in the islands north of Canada where they are fatter than in most places on the mainland. By May or June the cows have lost all fat while the oldest bulls have gained enough so that their meat becomes palatable. The young bulls show no perceptible change. In July, when the cows are just beginning to fatten the old bulls have a slab of fat on their backs covering the entire body forward to the neck, and reaching on the haunches a thickness of perhaps half an inch or an inch. By late August or early September this fat has become three inches thick in extreme cases, and will weigh before drying thirty or forty pounds if the animal is large. At this time the intestinal fat is an additional ten or fifteen pounds besides the great amount on the brisket, ribs, pelvis and elsewhere; so that you have from sixty to eighty pounds of fat on an animal the dressed weight of which when head and hoofs have been re-moved, is probably between 250 and 300 pounds. The cows are moderately fat, and gain a little for the next month or two, as do the young bulls.

From this statement the fatness of caribou is seen to depend not, as is com-monly supposed, upon food and climate primarily but rather on the age and sex of the animal. Neither can it be the fact as set forth by certain writers that in midsummer, which would be July or August, caribou are poor simply be-cause of their persecution by insect pests, chiefly mosquitoes and botflies. The bulls at this season are approaching their fattest, even though the cows, upon which exclusively some authorities apparently base their reasoning, happen to be very poor. Since all caribou are greatly annoyed by mosquitoes and flies, it is reasonable to assume that they would be fatter if these pests were absent, but fat they are in spite of them if age and sex are right.

Another point of evidence that the thinness of caribou in summer is not primarily dependent on mosquitoes is that the cycle of fatness and leanness is about the same in the most mosquito-infested parts of the mainland as in the more northerly islands of the Canadian Archipelago where mosquitoes are so rare that in one island, Lougheed Island, we saw only one mosquito all sum-mer. But in these northerly islands the caribou fatten a few days earlier and become a little fatter in proportion to the total body weight. That a caribou may be as fat in Lougheed Island on the first of August as it would be at Great Bear Lake the middle of August is probably due to the absence of mosquitoes in Lougheed Island; for the feed, although good, does not appear to be any better in the more northerly lands.

The hunting and exploring trip into the interior of Banks Island was an in-teresting and delightful one for Storkerson and me. Here was a beautiful country of valleys everywhere gold and white with flowers or green with grass or mingled greens and brown with grass and lichens, except some of the hill tops which were rocky and barren. These hills differed in coloring, espe-cially as seen from a distance, not so much because of the colors of the rock as because different vegetation prevails in different kinds of soil and different lichens on different rocks. There were sparkling brooks that united into rivers of crystal clearness, flowing over gravel bottoms. When we came to a stream we usually followed along, whether for a few hundred yards or several miles, until we came to a place where the river either split into branches or widened out. Here we took the packs off our dogs, for their short legs unfitted them for keeping a pack dry while fording, and with our good Eskimo boots keep-ing our feet dry we would wade across, the dogs swimming behind us.

Heather was most abundant, and so were bull caribou, so that the meat we lived on and the fuel for cooking it were of the best.

When we are on a hunt proper we pitch our camps on the tops of the highest and most commanding hills, for caribou are such mobile animals that one is likely to see almost as many while favorably encamped as while traveling from place to place. But this time we were not hunting primarily, so we used to camp in sheltered, sunny places beside brooks that had their banks thickly covered with heather, giving both water and fuel right at hand.

I have just mentioned that the animals we were killing for fat were the oldest bull caribou we could find. People who do not know caribou and who think of them by analogy with cattle, imagine that the meat of a bull would not be especially palatable. All experienced hunters, however, Indian, Eskimo or white, know that the bulls are better eating than the cows or the calves, and the more palatable the older they are. To me the main consideration about meat is its flavor. The recommendation that meat is tender is the praise of a toothless generation and one addicted to such artificial cooking that we seldom get in our foods their native flavors, but rather flavors conferred on them by sauces and condiments. I prefer the terminology of our meat-eating ancestors whose various idioms, which we still keep though we hardly understand them, show that they knew meat flavors and appreciated them as hunters do. Having good teeth it is of little concern to me whether a piece of meat is tough or tender; what is important is the taste.

Besides, a caribou can never be tough. No one familiar with their typical life history can believe that the meat will get tough through age, the factor which causes toughness among domestic chickens and cattle. These last under the artificial protection of domesticity may grow to any age, and polar bears and ovibos may live on the reason of their strength and habits. But caribou never live long after they are full grown. Northern wolves in books prey on fawns and yearlings, and doubtless it happens occasionally that a wolf kills a calf, but this is likely to be within twenty-four hours of the calf's birth. A calf is certainly not many days old when he is able to run faster than his mother and faster than any other member of the herd unless possibly the yearlings. The young cows can run faster than the old cows and the young bulls faster than the old bulls that bring up the rear. Observers who enjoy reading chivalry into the actions of animals doubtless find instances where their deductions are correct. I am not in a position to say whether an old bull would by choice bring up the rear so as to expose himself to being first victim of the wolves. But I do say that he has no option, especially at the beginning of the breeding season when he is additionally handicapped by the weight of his huge antlers and his fat. When you see a caribou that has been singled out for pursuit by wolves, it is in the first probability an old bull and in the second an old cow. Skeletons of wolf-killed animals are nearly always found to be the skeletons of these two. In any caribou country the fewness of the old bulls is surprising unless these points are understood. Even the "old" few are never old enough to be tough.

Since that trip which gave me my first familiarity with the interior of Banks Island, I have crossed it in almost every direction, winter and summer, so that were all those routes plotted on the map it would be as if the island were covered with a spider web. We have thus made conclusive our inference on this journey, that cattle, although once numerous in Banks Island, are now either extinct or at the most represented by a few dozen animals near the north or south end, the parts we have least carefully examined.

FREDERICK PHILIP GROVE

Snow 1922

FREDERICK PHILIP GROVE (1879–1948) was born Felix Paul Greve in Radomno, Germany. After leaving university in Bonn, he became a translator, novelist and poet. However, his debts piled up, and in 1909, leaving a false suicide note, he emigrated to Canada and turned up in Winnipeg as Frederick Philip Grove. He worked as a rural schoolteacher until 1929. *Over Prairie Trails* (1922), from which "Snow" is taken, was his first book in English: a collection of nature essays, it describes the change of seasons in the open Manitoba countryside he crossed daily on his way to and from the schoolhouse. He went on to write many novels, including *Settlers of the Marsh* (1925), *A Search for America* (1927) and *Fruits of the Earth* (1933); he died in Simcoe, Ontario. His "autobiography," *In Search of Myself* (1946), which won the Governor General's Award for nonfiction, was accepted as such until Douglas Spettigue unearthed Grove's true origins in 1973.

◦ • ◦

THE BLIZZARD STARTED on Wednesday morning. It was that rather common, truly western combination of a heavy snowstorm with a blinding northern gale—such as piles the snow in hills and mountains and makes walking next to impossible.

I cannot exactly say that I viewed it with unmingled joy. There were special reasons for that. It was the second week in January; when I had left "home" the Sunday before, I had been feeling rather bad; so my wife would worry a good deal, especially if I did not come at all. I knew there was such a thing as its becoming quite impossible to make the drive. I had been lost in a blizzard once or twice before in my lifetime. And yet, as long as there was the least chance that horse-power and human will-power combined might pull me through at all, I was determined to make or anyway to try it.

At noon I heard the first dismal warning. For some reason or other I had to go down into the basement of the school. The janitor, a highly efficient but exceedingly bad-humoured cockney, who was dissatisfied with all things Canadian because "in the old country we do things differently"—whose sharp tongue was feared by many, and who once remarked to a lady teacher in the most casual way, "If you was a lidy, I'd wipe my boots on you!"—this selfsame janitor, standing by the furnace, turned slowly around, showed his pale and hollow-eyed face, and smiled a withering and commiserating smile. "Ye won't go north this week," he remarked—not without sympathy, for somehow he had taken a liking to me, which even prompted him off and on to favor me with caustic expressions of what he thought of the school board and the leading citizens of the town. I, of course, never encouraged him in his communicativeness which seemed to be just what he would expect, and no rebuff ever goaded him into the slightest show of resentment. "We'll see," I said briefly. "Well, Sir," he repeated apodictically, "ye won't." I smiled and went out.

But in my classroom I looked from the window across the street. Not even in broad daylight could you see the opposite houses or trees. And I knew that, once a storm like that sets in, it is apt to continue for days at a stretch. It was one of those orgies in which Titan Wind indulges every so often on our western prairies. I certainly needed something to encourage me, and so, before leaving the building I went upstairs to the third story and looked through a window which faced north. But, though I was now above the drifting layer, I could not see very far here either; the snowflakes were small and like little round granules, hitting the panes of the windows with little sounds of "ping-ping"; and they came, driven by a relentless gale, in such numbers that they blotted out whatever was more than two or three hundred yards away.

The inhabitant of the middle latitudes of this continent has no data to picture to himself what a snowstorm in the north may be. To him snow is something benign that comes soft-footedly over night, and on the most silent wings like an owl, something that suggests the sleep of Nature rather than its battles. The further south you go, the more, of course, snow loses of its aggressive character.

At the dinner-table in the hotel I heard a few more disheartening words. But after four I defiantly got my tarpaulin out and carried it to the stable. If I had to run the risk of getting lost, at least I was going to prepare for it. I had once stayed out, snow-bound, for a day and a half, nearly without food and altogether without shelter; and I was not going to get thus caught again. I also carefully overhauled my cutter. Not a bolt but I tested it with a wrench; and before the stores were closed, I bought myself enough canned goods to feed me for a week should through any untoward accident the need arise. I always carried a little alcohol stove, and with my tarpaulin I could convert my cutter within three minutes into a windproof tent. Cramped quarters, to be sure, but better than being given over to the wind at thirty below!

More than any remark on the part of friends or acquaintances one fact depressed me when I went home. There was not a team in town which had come in from the country. The streets were deserted: the stores were empty. The north wind and the snow had the town to themselves.

On Thursday the weather was unchanged. On the way to the school I had to scale a snowdrift thrown up to a height of nearly six feet, and, though it was beginning to harden, from its own weight and the pressure of the wind, I still broke in at every step and found the task tiring in the extreme. I did my work, of course, as if nothing oppressed me, but in my heart I was beginning to face the possibility that, even if I tried, I might fail to reach my goal. The day passed by. At noon the schoolchildren, the teachers, and a few people hurrying to the post-office for their mail lent a fleeting appearance of life to the streets. It nearly cheered me; but soon after four the whole town again took on that deserted look which reminded me of an abandoned mining camp. The lights in the store windows had something artificial about them, as if they were merely painted on the canvas wings of a stage setting. Not a team came in all day.

On Friday morning the same. Burroughs would have said that the weather had gone into a rut. Still the wind whistled and howled through the bleak, dark, hollow dawn; the snow kept coming down and piling up, as if it could not be any otherwise. And as if to give notice of its intentions, the drift had completely closed up my front door. I fought my way to the school and thought things over. My wife and I had agreed, if ever the weather should be so bad that there was danger in going at night, I was to wait till Saturday morning and go by daylight. Neither one of us ever mentioned the possibility of giving the attempt up altogether. My wife probably understood that I would not bind myself by any such promise. Now even on this Friday I should have liked to go by night, if for no other reason, then for the experience's sake; but I reflected that I might get lost and not reach home at all. The horses knew the road—so long as there was any road; but there was none now. I felt it would not be fair to wife and child. So, reluctantly and with much hesitation, but definitely at last, I made up my mind that I was going to wait till morning. My cutter was ready—I had seen to that on Wednesday. As soon as the storm had set in, I had instinctively started to work in order to frustrate its designs.

At noon I met in front of the post-office a charming lady who with her husband and a young Anglican curate constituted about the only circle of real friends I had in town. "Why!" I exclaimed, "what takes you out into this storm, Mrs.——?" "The desire," she gasped against the wind and yet in her inimitable way, as if she were asking a favor, "to have you come to our house for tea, my friend. You surely are not going this week?" "I am going to go to-morrow morning at seven," I said. "But I shall be delighted to have tea with you and Mr.——." I read her at a glance. She knew that in not going out at night I should suffer—she wished to help me over the evening, so I should not feel too much thwarted, too helpless, and too lonesome. She smiled. "You really want to go? But I must not keep you. At six, if you please." And we went our ways without a salute, for none was possible at this gale-swept corner.

After four o'clock I took word to the stable to have my horses fed and harnessed by seven in the morning. The hostler had a tale to tell. "You going out north?" he enquired although he knew perfectly well I was. "Of course," I replied. "Well," he went on, "a man came in from ten miles out; he was half dead; come, look at his horses! He says, in places the snow is over the telephone posts." "I'll try it anyway," I said. "Just have the team ready. I know what I can ask my horses to do. If it cannot be done, I shall turn back, that is all."

When I stepped outside again, the wind seemed bent upon shaking the strongest faith. I went home to my house across the bridge and dressed. As soon as I was ready, I allowed myself to be swept past stable, past hotel and post-office till I reached the side street which led to the house where I was to be the guest.

How sheltered, homelike and protected everything looked inside. The hostess, as usual, was radiantly amiable. The host settled back after supper to talk, old country. The Channel Islands, the French Coast, Kent and London —those were from common knowledge our most frequently recurring topics. Both host and hostess, that was easy to see, were bent upon beguiling the hours of their rather dark-humoured guest. But the howling gale outside was stronger than their good intentions. It was not very long before the conversation got around—reverted, so it seemed—to stories of storms, of being lost, of nearly freezing. The boys were sitting with wide and eager eyes, afraid they might be sent to bed before the feast of yarns was over. I told one or two of my most thrilling escapes, the host contributed a few more, and even the hostess had had an experience, driving on top of a railroad track for several miles, I believe, with a train, snowbound, behind her. I leaned over. "Mrs. ——," I said, "do not try to dissuade me. I am sorry to say it, but it is use-less. I am bound to go." "Well," she said, "I wish you would not." "Thanks," I replied and looked at my watch. It was ten o'clock. "There is only one thing wrong with coming to have tea in this home," I continued and smiled; "it is so hard to say good-bye."

I carefully lighted my lantern and got into my wraps. The wind was howling dismally outside. For a moment we stood in the hall, shaking hands and paying the usual compliments; then one of the boys opened the door for me; and in stepping out I had one of the greatest surprises. Not far from the western edge of the world there stood the setting half-moon in a cloudless sky; myriads of stars were dusted over the vast, dark blue expanse, twinkling and blazing at their liveliest. And though the wind still whistled and shrieked and rattled, no snow came down, and not much seemed to drift. I pointed to the sky, smiled, nodded and closed the door. As far as the drifting of the snow went, I was mistaken, as I found out when I turned to the north, into the less sheltered street, past the post-office, hotel and stable. In front of a store I stopped to read a thermometer which I had found halfways reliable the year before. It read minus thirty-two degrees. . . .

It was still dark, of course, when I left the house on Saturday morning to be on my way. Also, it was cold, bitterly cold, but there was very little wind. In crossing the bridge which was swept nearly clean of snow I noticed a small, but somehow ominous-looking drift at the southern end. It had such a disturbed, lashed-up appearance. The snow was still loose, yet packed just hard enough to have a certain degree of toughness. You could no longer swing your foot through it: had you run into it at any great speed, you would have fallen; but as yet it was not hard enough to carry you. I knew that kind of a drift; it is treacherous. On a later drive one just like it, only built on a vastly larger scale, was to lead to the first of a series of little accidents which finally shattered my nerve. That was the only time that my temerity failed me. I shall tell you about that drive later on.

At the stable I went about my preparations in a leisurely way. I knew that a supreme test was ahead of myself and the horses, and I meant to have daylight for tackling it. Once more I went over the most important bolts; once more I felt and pulled at every strap in the harness. I had a Clark footwarmer and made sure that it functioned properly. I pulled the flaps of my military fur cap down over neck, ears and cheeks. I tucked a pillow under the sweater over my chest and made sure that my leggings clasped my fur-lined moccasins well. Then, to prevent my coat from opening even under the stress of motion, just before I got into the cutter, I tied a rope around my waist.

The hostler brought the horses into the shed. They pawed the floor and snorted with impatience. While I rolled my robes about my legs and drew the canvas curtain over the front part of the box, I weighed Dan with my eyes. I had no fear for Peter, but Dan would have to show to-day that he deserved the way I had fed and nursed him. Like a chain, the strength of which is measured by the strength of its weakest link, my team was measured by Dan's pulling power and endurance. But he looked good to me as he danced across the pole and threw his head, biting back at Peter who was teasing him.

The hostler was morose and in a biting mood. Every motion of his seemed to say, "What is the use of all this? No teamster would go out on a long drive in this weather, till the snow has settled down; and here a schoolmaster wants to try it."

At last he pushed the slide-doors aside, and we swung out. I held the horses tight and drove them into that little drift at the bridge to slow them down right from the start.

The dawn was white, but with a strictly localized angry glow where the sun was still hidden below the horizon. In a very few minutes he would be up, and I counted on making that first mile just before he appeared.

This mile is a wide, well-levelled road, but every so often, at intervals of maybe fifty to sixty yards, steep and long promontories of snow had been flung across—some of them five to six feet high. They started at the edge of the field to the left where a rank growth of shrubby weeds gave shelter for the snow to pile in. Their base, alongside the fence, was broad, and they tapered across the road, with a perfectly flat top, and with concave sides of a most delicate, smooth, and finished-looking curve till at last they ran out into a sharp point, mostly beyond the road on the field to the right.

The wind plays strange pranks with snow; snow is the most plastic medium it has to mold into images and symbols of its moods. Here one of these promontories would slope down, and the very next one would slope upward as it advanced across the open space. In every case there had been two walls, as it were, of furious blow, and between the two a lane of comparative calm, caused by the shelter of a clump of brush or weeds, in which the snow had taken refuge from the wind's rough and savage play. Between these capes of snow there was an occasional bare patch of clean swept ground. Altogether there was an impression of barren, wild, bitter-cold windiness about the aspect that did not fail to awe my mind; it looked inhospitable, merciless, and cruelly playful.

As yet the horses seemed to take only delight in dashing through the drifts, so that the powdery crystals flew aloft and dusted me all over. I peered across the field to the left, and a curious sight struck me. There was apparently no steady wind at all, but here and there, and every now and then, a little whirl of snow would rise and fall again. Every one of them looked for all the world like a rabbit reconnoitring in deep grass. It jumps up on its hindlegs, while running, peers out, and settles down again. It was as if the snow meant to have a look at me, the interloper at such an early morning hour. The snow was so utterly dry that it obeyed the lightest breath, and whatever there was of motion in the air, could not amount to more than a cat's-paw's sudden reach.

At the exact moment when the snow where it stood up highest became suffused with a rose-red tint from the rising sun, I arrived at the turn to the correction line. Had I been a novice at the work I was engaged in, the sight that met my eye might well have daunted me. Such drifts as I saw here should be broken by drivers who have short hauls to make before the long-distance traveler attempts them. From the fence on the north side of the road a smoothly curved expanse covered the whole of the road allowance and gently sloped down into the field at my left. Its north edge stood like a cliff, the exact height of the fence, four feet I should say. In the centre it rose to probably six feet and then fell very gradually, whaleback fashion, to the south. Not one of the fence posts to the left was visible. The slow emergence of the tops of these fence posts became during the following week, when I drove out here daily, a measure for me of the settling down of the drift. I believe I can say from my observations that if no new snow falls or drifts in, and if no very considerable evaporation takes place, a newly piled snowdrift, undisturbed except by wind-pressure, will finally settle down to about from one-third to one-half of its original height, according to the pressure of the wind that was behind the snow when it first was thrown down. After it has, in this contracting process, reached two-thirds of its first height, it can usually be relied upon to carry horse and man.

The surface of this drift, which covered a ditch besides the grade and its grassy flanks, showed that curious appearance that we also find in the glaciated surfaces of granite rock and which, in them, geologists call exfoliation. In the case of rock it is the consequence of extreme changes in temperature. The surface sheet in expanding under sudden heat detaches itself in large leaflike layers. In front of my wife's cottage up north there lay an exfoliated rock in which I watched the process for a number of years. In snow, of course, the origin of this appearance is entirely different; snow is laid down in layers by the waves in the wind. "Adfoliation" would be a more nearly correct appellation of the process. But from the analogy of the appearance I shall retain the more common word and call it exfoliation. Layers upon layers of paperlike sheets are superimposed upon each other, their edges often "cropping out" on sloping surfaces; and since these edges, according to the curvatures of the surfaces, run in wavy lines, the total aspect is very often that of "moire" silk.

I knew the road as well as I had ever known a road. In summer there was a grassy expanse some thirty feet wide to the north; then followed the grade, flanked to the south by a ditch; and the tangle of weeds and small brush beyond reached right up to the other fence. I had to stay on or rather above the grade so I stood up and selected the exact spot where to tackle it. Later, I knew, this drift would be harmless enough; there was sufficient local traffic here to establish a well-packed trail. At present, however, it still seemed a formidable task for a team that was to pull me over thirty-three miles more. Besides it was a first test for my horses; I did not know yet how they would behave in snow.

But we went at it. For a moment things happened too fast for me to watch details. The horses plunged wildly and reared on their hind feet in a panic, straining against each other, pulling apart, going down underneath the pole, trying to turn and retrace their steps. And meanwhile the cutter went sharply up at first, as if on the crest of a wave, then toppled over into a hole made by Dan, and altogether behaved like a boat tossed on a stormy sea. Then order returned into the chaos. I had the lines short, wrapped double and treble around my wrists; my feet stood braced in the corner of the box, knees touching the dashboard; my robes slipped down. I spoke to the horses in a soft, quiet, purring voice; and at last I pulled in. Peter hated to stand. I held him. Then I looked back. This first wild plunge had taken us a matter of two hundred yards into the drift. Peter pulled and champed at the bit; the horses were sinking nearly out of sight. But I knew that many and many a time in the future I should have to go through just this, and that from the beginning I must train the horses to tackle it right. So, in spite of my aching wrists I kept them standing till I thought that they were fully breathed. Then I relaxed my pull the slightest bit and clicked my tongue. "Good," I thought, "they are pulling together!" And I managed to hold them in line. They reared and plunged again like drowning things in their last agony, but they no longer clashed against nor pulled away from each other. I measured the distance with my eye. Another two hundred yards or thereabout, and I pulled them in again. Thus we stopped altogether four times. The horses were steaming when we got through this drift which was exactly half a mile long; my cutter was packed level full with slabs and clods of snow; and I was pretty well exhausted myself.

"If there is very much of this," I thought for the moment, "I may not be able to make it." But then I knew that a north-south road will drift in badly only under exceptional circumstances. It is the east-west grades that are most apt to give trouble. Not that I minded my part of it, but I did not mean to kill my horses. I had sized them up in their behaviour towards snow. Peter, as I had expected, was excitable. It was hard to recognize in him just now, as he walked quietly along, the uproar of playing muscle and rearing limbs that he had been when we first struck the snow. That was well and good for a short, supreme effort; but not even for Peter would it do in the long, endless drifts which I had to expect. Dan was quieter, but he did not have Peter's staying power; in fact, he was not really a horse for the road. Strange, in spite of his usual keenness on the level road, he seemed to show more snow sense in the drift. This was to be amply confirmed in the future. Whenever an accident happened, it was Peter's fault. As you will see if you read on, Dan once lay quiet when Peter stood right on top of him.

On this road north I found the same "promontories" that had been such a feature of the first one, flung across from the northwest to the southeast. Since the clumps of shrubs to the left were larger here, and more numerous, too, the drifts occasionally also were larger and higher; but not one of them was such that the horses could not clear it with one or two leaps. The sun was climbing, the air was winter-clear and still. None of the farms which I passed showed the slightest sign of life. I had wrapped up again and sat in comparative comfort and at ease, enjoying the clear sparkle and glitter of the virgin snow. It was not till considerably later that the real significance of the landscape dawned upon my consciousness. Still there was even now in my thoughts a speculative undertone. Subconsciously I wondered what might be ahead of me.

We made Bell's corner in good time. The mile to the west proved easy. There were drifts, it is true, and the going was heavy, but at no place did the snow for any length of time reach higher than the horses' hocks. We turned to the north again, and here, for a while, the road was very good indeed; the underbrush to the left, on those expanses of wild land, had fettered, as it were, the feet of the wind. The snow was held everywhere, and very little of it had drifted. Only one spot I remember where a clump of Russian willow close to the trail had offered shelter enough to allow the wind to fill in the narrow road-gap to a depth of maybe eight or nine feet; but here it was easy to go around to the west. Without any further incident we reached the point where the useless, supernumerary fencepost had caught my eye on my first trip out. I had made nearly eight miles now.

But right here I was to get my first inkling of sights that might shatter my nerve. You may remember that a grove of tall poplars ran to the east, skirted along its southern edge by a road and a long line of telephone posts. Now here, in this shelter of the poplars, the snow from the more or less level and unsheltered spaces to the northwest had piled in indeed. It sloped up to the east; and never shall I forget what I beheld.

The first of the posts stood a foot in snow; at the second one the drift reached six or seven feet up; the next one looked only half as long as the first one, and you might have imagined, standing as it did on a sloping hillside, that it had intentionally been made so much shorter than the others; but at the bottom of the visible part the wind, in sweeping around the pole, had scooped out a funnel-shaped crater which seemed to open into the very earth like a sinkhole. The next pole stood like a giant buried up to his chest and looked singularly helpless and footbound; and the last one I saw showed just its crossbar with three glassy, green insulators above the mountain of snow. The whole surface of this gigantic drift showed again that "exfoliated" appearance which I have described. Strange to say, this very exfoliation gave it something of a quite peculiarly desolate aspect. It looked so harsh, so millennial-old, so antediluvian and pre-Adamic! I still remember with particular distinctness the slight dizziness that overcame me, the sinking feeling in my heart, the awe, and the foreboding that I had challenged a force in Nature which might defy all tireless effort and the most fearless heart.

So the hostler had not been fibbing after all!

But not for a moment did I think of turning back. I am fatalistic in temperament. What is to be, is to be, that is not my outlook. If at last we should get bound up in a drift, well and good, I should then see what the next move would have to be. While the wind blows, snow drifts; while my horses could walk and I was not disabled, my road led north, not south. Like the snow I obeyed the laws of my nature. So far the road was good, and we swung along.

Somewhere around here a field presented a curious view. Its crop had not been harvested; it still stood in stooks. But from my side I saw nothing of the sheaves—it seemed to be flax, for here and there a flag of loose heads showed at the top. The snow had been blown up from all directions, so it looked, by the counter-currents that set up in the lee of every obstacle. These mounds presented one and all the appearance of cones or pyramids of butter patted into shape by upward strokes made with a spoon. There were the sharp ridges, irregular and erratic, and there were the hollows running up their flanks—exactly as such a cone of butter will show them. And the whole field was dotted with them, as if there were so many fresh graves.

I made the twelve-mile bridge—passing, through the cottonwood gate—reached the "hovel," and dropped into the wilderness again. Here the bigger trees stood strangely bare. Winter reveals the bark and the "habit" of trees. All ornaments and unessentials have been dropped. The naked skeletons show. I remember how I was more than ever struck by that dappled appearance of the bark of the balm: an olive-green, yellowish hue, ridged and spotted with the black of ancient, overgrown leaf-scars; there was actually something gay about it; these poplars are certainly beautiful winter trees. The aspens were different. Although their stems stood white on white in the snow, that greenish tinge in their white gave them a curious look. From the picture that I carry about in my memory of this morning I cannot help the impression that they looked as if their white were not natural at all; they looked whitewashed! I have often since confirmed this impression when there was snow on the ground.

In the copses of saplings the zigzagging of the boles from twig to twig showed very distinctly, more so, I believe, than to me it had ever done before. How slender and straight they look in their summer garb—now they were stripped, and bone and sinew appeared.

We came to the "half-way farms," and the marsh lay ahead. I watered the horses, and I do not know what made me rest them for a little while, but I did. On the yard of the farm where I had turned in there was not a soul to be seen. Barns and stables were closed—and I noticed that the back door of the dwelling was buried tight by the snow. No doubt everybody preferred the neighborhood of the fire to the cold outside. While stopping, I faced for the first time the sun. He was high in the sky by now—it was half past ten—and it suddenly came home to me that there was something relentless, inexorable, cruel, yes, something of a sneer in the pitiless way in which he looked down on the infertile waste around. Unaccountably two Greek words formed on my lips: Homer's *pontos atrygetos*—the barren sea. Half an hour later I was to realize the significance of it.

I turned back to the road and north again. For another half mile the fields continued on either side; but somehow they seemed to take on a sinister look. There was more snow on them than I had found on the level land further south; the snow lay more smoothly, again under those "exfoliated" surface sheets which here, too, gave it an inhuman, primeval look; in the higher sun the vast expanse looked, I suppose, more blindingly white; and nowhere did buildings or thickets seem to emerge. Yet, so long as the grade continued, the going was fair enough.

Then I came to the corner which marked half the distance, and there I stopped. Right in front, where the trail had been and where a ditch had divided off the marsh, a fortress of snow lay now: a seemingly impregnable bulwark, six or seven feet high, with rounded top, fitting descriptions which I had read of the underground bomb-proofs around Belgian strongholds—those forts which were hammered to pieces by the Germans in their first, heart-breaking forward surge in 1914. There was not a wrinkle in this inverted bowl. There it lay, smooth and slick—curled up in security, as it were, some twenty, thirty feet across; and behind it others, and more of them to the right and to the left. This had been a stretch covered with brush and bush, willow and poplar thickets; but my eye saw nothing except a mammiferous waste, cruelly white, glittering in the heatless, chuckling sun, and scoffing at me, the intruder. I stood up again and peered out. To the east it seemed as if these buttes of snow were a trifle lower; but maybe the ground underneath also sloped down. I wished I had travelled here more often by daytime, so I might know. As it was, there was nothing for it; I had to tackle the task. And we plunged in.

I had learned something from my first experience in the drift one mile north of town, and I kept my horses well under control. Still, it was a wild enough dash. Peter lost his footing two or three times and worked himself into a mild panic. But Dan—I could not help admiring the way in which, buried over his back in snow, he would slowly and deliberately rear on his hindfeet and take his bound. For fully five minutes I never saw anything of the horses except their heads. I inferred their motions from the dusting snow-cloud that rose above their bodies and settled on myself. And then somehow we emerged. We reached a stretch of ground where the snow was just high enough to cover the hocks of the horses. It was a hollow scooped out by some freak of the wind. I pulled in, and the horses stood panting. Peter no longer showed any desire to fret and to jump. Both horses apparently felt the wisdom of sparing their strength. They were all white with the frost of their sweat and the spray of the snow.

While I gave them their time, I looked around, and here a lesson came home to me. In the hollow where we stood, the snow did not lie smoothly. A huge obstacle to the northwest, probably a buried clump of brush, had made the wind turn back upon itself, first downward, then, at the bottom of the pit, in a direction opposite to that of the main current above, and finally slantways upward again to the summit of the obstacle, where it rejoined the parent blow. The floor of the hollow was cleanly scooped out and chiselled in low ridges; and these ridges came from the southeast, running their points to the northwest. I learned to look out for this sign, and I verily believe that, had I not learned that lesson right now, I should never have reached the creek which was still four or five miles distant.

The huge mound in the lee of which I was stopping was a matter of two hundred yards away; nearer to it the snow was considerably deeper; and since it presented an appearance very characteristic of prairie bush-drifts, I shall describe it in some detail. Apparently the winds had first bent over all the stems of the clump; for whenever I saw one of them from the north, it showed a smooth, clean upward sweep. On the south side the snow first fell in a sheer cliff; then there was a hollow which was partly filled by a talus-shaped drift thrown in by the counter currents from the southern pit in which we were stopping; the sides of this talus again showed the marks that reminded of those left by the spoon when butter is roughly stroked into the shape of a pyramid. The interesting parts of the structure consisted in the beetling brow of the cliff and the roof of the cavity underneath. The brow had a honeycombed appearance; the snow had been laid down in layers of varying density (I shall discuss this more fully in the next chapter when we are going to look in on the snow while it is actually at work); and the counter currents that here swept upward in a slanting direction had bitten out the softer layers, leaving a fine network of little ridges which reminded strangely of the delicate fretwork-tracery in wind-sculptured rock—as I had seen it in the Black Hills in South Dakota. This piece of work of the wind is exceedingly short-lived in snow, and it must not be confounded with the honeycombed appearance of those faces of snow cliffs which are "rotting" by reason of their exposure to the heat of the noonday sun. These latter are coarse, often dirty, and nearly always have something bristling about them which is entirely absent in the sculptures of the wind. The under side of the roof in the cavity looked very much as a very stiff or viscid treacle would look when spread over a meshy surface, as, for instance, over a closely woven netting of wire. The stems and the branches of the brush took the place of the wire, and in their meshes the snow had been pressed through by its own weight, but held together by its curious ductility or tensile strength of which I was to find further evidence soon enough. It thus formed innumerable, blunted little stalactites, but without the corresponding stalagmites which you find in limestone caves or on the north side of buildings when the snow from the roof thaws and forms icicles and slender cones of ice growing up to meet them from the ground where the trickling drops fall and freeze again.

By the help of these various tokens I had picked my next resting place before we started up again. It was on this second dash that I understood why those Homeric words had come to my lips a while ago. This was indeed like nothing so much as like being out on rough waters and in a troubled sea, with nothing to brace the storm with but a wind-tossed nutshell of a one-man sailing craft. I knew that experience for having outridden many a gale in the mouth of the mighty St. Lawrence River. When the snow reached its extreme in depth, it gave you the feeling which a drowning man may have when fighting his desperate fight with the salty waves. But more impressive than that was the frequent outer resemblance. The waves of the ocean rise up and reach out and batter against the rocks and battlements of the shore, retreating again and ever returning to the assault, covering the obstacles thrown in the way of their progress with thin sheets of licking tongues at least. And if such a high crest wave had suddenly been frozen into solidity, its outline would have mimicked to perfection many a one of the snow shapes that I saw around.

Once the horses had really learned to pull exactly together—and they learned it thoroughly here—our progress was not too bad. Of course, it was not like going on a grade, be it ever so badly drifted in. Here the ground underneath, too, was uneven and overgrown with a veritable entanglement of brush in which often the horses' feet would get caught. As for the road, there was none left, nothing that even by the boldest stretch of imagination could have been considered even as the slightest indication of one. And worst of all, I knew positively that there would be no trail at any time during the winter. I was well aware of the fact that, after it once snowed up, nobody ever crossed this waste between the "half-way farms" and the "White Range Line House." This morning it took me two and a half solid hours to make four miles.

But the ordeal had its reward. Here where the fact that there was snow on the ground, and plenty of it, did no longer need to be sunk into my brain—as soon as it had lost its value as a piece of news and a lesson—I began to enjoy it just as the hunter in India will enjoy the battle of wits when he is pitted against a yellow-black tiger. I began to catch on to the ways of this snow; I began, as it were, to study the mentality of my enemy. Though I never kill, I am after all something of a sportsman. And still another thing gave me back that mental equilibrium which you need in order to see things and to reason calmly about them. Every dash of two hundred yards or so brought me that much nearer to my goal. Up to the "half-way farms" I had, as it were, been working uphill: there was more ahead than behind. This was now reversed: there was more behind than ahead, and as yet I did not worry about the return trip.

Now I have already said that snow is the only really plastic element in which the wind can carve the vagaries of its mood and leave a record of at least some permanency. The surface of the sea is a wonderful book to be read with a lightning-quick eye; I do not know anything better to do as a cure for ragged nerves—provided you are a good sailor. But the forms are too fleeting, they change too quickly—so quickly, indeed, that I have never succeeded in so fixing their record upon my memory as to be able to develop one form from the other in descriptive notes. It is that very fact, I believe, upon which hinges the curative value of the sight: you are so completely absorbed by the moment, and all other things fall away. Many and many a day have I lain in my deck chair on board a liner and watched the play of the waves; but the pleasure, which was very great indeed, was momentary; and sometimes, when in an unsympathetic mood, I have since impatiently wondered in what that fascination may have consisted. It was different here. Snow is very nearly as yielding as water and, once it fully responds in its surface to the carving forces of the wind, it stays—as if frozen into the glittering marble image of its motion. I know few things that are as truly fascinating as the sculptures of the wind in snow; for here you have time and opportunity a-plenty to probe not only into the what, but also into the why. Maybe that one day I shall write down a fuller account of my observations. In this report I shall have to restrict myself to a few indications, for this is not the record of the whims of the wind, but merely the narrative of my drives.

In places, for instance, the rounded, "bomb-proof" aspect of the expanses would be changed into the distinct contour of gigantic waves with a very fine, very sharp crest-line. The upsweep from the northwest would be ever so slightly convex, and the downward sweep into the trough was always very distinctly concave. This was not the ripple which we find in beach sand. That ripple was there, too, and in places it covered the wide backs of these huge waves all over; but never was it found on the concave side. Occasionally, but rarely, one of these great waves would resemble a large breaker with a curly crest. Here the onward sweep from the northwest had built the snow out, beyond the supporting base, into a thick overhanging ledge which here and there had sagged but by virtue of that tensile strength and cohesion in snow which I have mentioned already, it still held together and now looked convoluted and ruffled in the most deceiving way. I believe I actually listened for the muffled roar which the breaker makes when its subaqueous part begins to sweep the upward-sloping beach. To make this illusion complete, or to break it by the very absurdity and exaggeration of a comparison drawn out too far—I do not know which—there would, every now and then, from the crest of one of these waves, jut out something which closely resembled the wide back of a large fish diving down into the concave side towards the trough. This looked very much like porpoises or dolphins jumping in a heaving sea; only that in my memory picture the real dolphins always jump in the opposite direction, against the run of the waves, bridging the trough.

In other places a fine, exceedingly delicate crest-line would spring up from the high point of some buried obstacle and sweep along, in the most graceful curve as far as the eye would carry. I particularly remember one of them, and I could discover no earthly reason for the curvature in it.

Again there would be a triangular—or should I say "tetrahedral"?—upsweep from the direction of the wind, ending in a sharp, perfectly plane down-sweep on the south side; and the point of this three-sided but oblique pyramid would hang over like the flap of a tam. There was something of the consistency of very thick cloth about this overhanging flap.

Or an up-slope from the north would end in a long, nearly perpendicular cliff-line facing south. And the talus formation which I have mentioned would be perfectly smooth; but it did not reach quite to the top of the cliff, maybe to within a foot of it. The upsloping layer from the north would hang out again, with an even brow; but between this smooth cornice and the upper edge of the talus the snow looked as if it had been squeezed out by tremendous pressure from above, like an exceedingly viscid liquid—cooling glue, for instance, which is being squeezed out from between the core and the veneer in a veneering press.

Once I passed close to, and south of, two thickets which were completely buried by the snow. Between them a ditch had been scooped out in a very curious fashion. It resembled exactly a winding river bed with its water drained off; it was two or three feet deep, and wherever it turned, its banks were undermined on the "throw" side by the "wash" of the furious blow. The analogy between the work of the wind and the work of flowing water constantly obtrudes, especially where this work is one of "erosion."

But as flowing water will swing up and down in the most surprising forms where the bed of the river is rough with rocks and throws it into choppy waves which do not seem to move, so the snow was thrown up into the most curious forms where the frozen swamp ground underneath had bubbled, as it were, into phantastic shapes. I remember several places where a perfect circle was formed by a sharp crest-line that bounded a hemispherical, crater-like hollow. When steam bubbles up through thick porridge, in its leisurely and impeded way, and the bubble bursts with a clucking sound, then for a moment a crater is formed just like these circular holes; only here in the snow they were on a much larger scale, of course, some of them six to ten feet in diameter.

And again the snow was thrown up into a bulwark, twenty and more feet high, with that always repeating cliff-face to the south, resembling a miniature Gibraltar, with many smaller ones of most curiously similar form on its back: bulwarks upon bulwarks, all lowering to the south. In these the aggressive nature of storm-flung snow was most apparent. They were formidable structures; formidable and intimidating, more through the suggestiveness of their shape than through mere size.

I came to places where the wind had had its moments of frolicsome humour, where it had made grim fun of its own massive and cumbersome and yet so pliable and elastic majesty. It had turned around and around, running with breathless speed, with its tongue lolling out, as it were, and probably yapping and snapping in mocking mimicry of a pup trying to catch its tail; and it had scooped out a spiral trough with overhanging rim. I felt sorry that I had not been there to watch it, because after all, what I saw was only the dead record of something that had been very much alive and vociferatingly noisy. And in another place it had reared and raised its head like a boa constrictor, ready to strike at its prey; up to the flashing, forked tongue it was there. But one spot I remember, where it looked exactly as if quite consciously it had attempted the outright ludicrous: it had thrown up the snow into the semblance of some formidable animal—more like a gorilla than anything else it looked, a gorilla that stands on its four hands and raises every hair on its back and snarls in order to frighten that which it is afraid of itself—a leopard maybe.

And then I reached the "White Range Line House." Curiously enough there it stood, sheltered by its majestic bluff to the north, as peaceful looking as if there were no such a thing as that record, which I had crossed, of the uproar and fury of one of the forces of Nature engaged in an orgy. And it looked so empty, too, and so deserted, with never a wisp of smoke curling from its flue-pipe, that for a moment I was tempted to turn in and see whether maybe the lonely dweller was ill. But then I felt as if I could not be burdened with any stranger's worries that day.

The effective shelter of the poplar forest along the creek made itself felt. The last mile to the northeast was peaceful driving. I felt quite cheered, though I walked the horses over the whole of the mile since both began to show signs of wear. The last four miles had been a test to try any living creature's mettle. To me it had been one of the culminating points in that glorious winter, but the horses had lacked the mental stimulus, and even I felt rather exhausted.

On the bridge I stopped, threw the blankets over the horses, and fed. Somehow this seemed to be the best place to do it. There was no snow to speak of, and I did not know yet what might follow. The horses were drooping, and I gave them an additional ten minutes' rest. Then I slowly made ready. I did not really expect any serious trouble.

We turned at a walk, and the chasm of the bush road opened up. Instantly I pulled the horses in. What I saw, baffled me for a moment so completely that I just sat there and gasped. There was no road. The trees to both sides were not so overly high, but the snow had piled in level with their tops; the drift looked like a gigantic barricade. It was that fleeting sight of the telephone posts over again, though on a slightly smaller scale; but this time it was in front. Slowly I started to whistle and then looked around. I remembered now. There was a newly cut-out road running north past the school which lay embedded in the bush. It had offered a lane to the wind; and the wind, going there, in cramped space, at a doubly furious stride, had picked up and carried along all the loose snow from the grassy glades in its path. The road ended abruptly just north of the drift, where the east-west grade sprang up. When the wind had reached this end of the lane, where the bush ran at right angles to its direction, it had found itself in something like a blind alley, and, sweeping upward, to clear the obstacle, it had dropped every bit of its load into the shelter of the brush, gradually, in the course of three long days, building up a ridge that buried underbrush and trees. I might have known it, of course. I knew enough about snow; all the conditions for an exceptionally large drift were provided for here. But it had not occurred to me, especially after I had found the northern fringe of the marsh so well sheltered. Here I felt for a moment as if all the snow of the universe had piled in. As I said, I was so completely baffled that I could have turned the horses then and there.

But after a minute or two my eyes began to cast about. I turned to the south, right into the dense underbrush and towards the creek which here swept south in a long, flat curve. Peter was always intolerant of anything that moved underfoot. He started to bolt when the dry and hard-frozen stems snapped and broke with reports resembling pistol shots. But since Dan kept quiet, I held Peter well in hand. I went along the drift for maybe three to four hundred yards, reconnoitring. Then the trees began to stand too dense for me to proceed without endangering my cutter. Just beyond I saw the big trough of the creek bed, and though I could not make out how conditions were at its bottom, the drift continued on its southern bank, and in any case it was impossible to cross the hollow. So I turned; I had made up my mind to try the drift.

About a hundred and fifty yards from the point where I had turned off the road there was something like a fold in the flank of the drift. At its foot I stopped. For a moment I tried to explain that fold to myself. This is what I arrived at. North of the drift, just about where the new cut-out joined the east-west grade, there was a small clearing caused by a bush fire which a few years ago had penetrated thus far into this otherwise virgin corner of the forest. Unfortunately it stood so full of charred stumps that it was impossible to get through there. But the main currents of the wind would have free play in this opening, and I knew that when the blizzard began, it had been blowing from a more northerly quarter than later on, when it veered to the northwest. And though the snow came careering along the lane of the cut-out, that is, from due north, its "throw" and therefore the direction of the drift would be determined by the direction of the wind that took charge of it on this clearing. Probably, then, a first, provisional drift whose long axis lay nearly in a north-south line, had been piled up by the first, northerly gale. Later a second, larger drift had been superimposed upon it at an angle, with its main axis running from the northwest to the southeast. The fold marked the point where the first, smaller drift still emerged from the second larger one. This reasoning was confirmed by a study of the clearing itself which I came to make two or three weeks after.

Before I called on the horses to give me their very last ounce of strength, I got out of my cutter once more and made sure that my lines were still sound. I trusted my ability to guide the horses even in this crucial test, but I dreaded nothing so much as that the lines might break; and I wanted to guard against any accident. I should mention that, of course, the top of my cutter was down, that the traces of the harness were new, and that the cutter itself during its previous trials had shown an exceptional stability. Once more I thus rested my horses for five minutes; and they seemed to realize what was coming. Their heads were up, their ears were cocked. When I got back into my cutter, I carefully brushed the snow from moccasins and trousers, laid the robe around my feet, adjusted my knees against the dashboard, and tied two big loops into the lines to hold them by.

Then I clicked my tongue. The horses bounded upward in unison. For a moment it looked as if they intended to work through, instead of over, the drift. A wild shower of angular snow-slabs swept in upon me. The cutter reared up and plunged and reared again—and then the view cleared. The snow proved harder than I had anticipated—which bespoke the fury of the blow that had piled it. It did not carry the horses, but neither—once we had reached a height of five or six feet—did they sink beyond their bellies and out of sight. I had no eye for anything except them. What lay to right or left, seemed not to concern me. I watched them work. They went in bounds, working beautifully together. Rhythmically they reared, and rhythmically they plunged. I had dropped back to the seat, holding them with a firm hand, feet braced against the dashboard; and whenever they got ready to rear, I called to them in a low and quiet voice, "Peter—Dan—now!" And their muscles played with the effort of desperation. It probably did not take more than five minutes, maybe considerably less, before we had reached the top, but to me it seemed like hours of nearly fruitless endeavor. I did not realize at first that we were high. I shall never forget the weird kind of astonishment when the fact came home to me that what snapped and crackled in the snow under the horses' hoofs, were the tops of trees. Nor shall the feeling of estrangement, as it were—as if I were not myself, but looking on from the outside at the adventure of somebody who yet was I—the feeling of other-worldliness, if you will pardon the word, ever fade from my memory—a feeling of having been carried beyond my depth where I could not swim—which came over me when with two quick glances to right and left I took in the fact that there were no longer any trees to either side, that I was above that forest world which had so often engulfed me.

Then I drew my lines in. The horses fought against it, did not want to stand. But I had to find my way, and while they were going, I could not take my eyes from them. It took a supreme effort on my part to make them obey. At last they stood, but I had to hold them with all my strength, and with not a second's respite. Now that I was on top of the drift, the problem of how to get down loomed larger than that of getting up had seemed before. I knew I did not have half a minute in which to decide upon my course; for it became increasingly difficult to hold the horses back, and they were fast sinking away.

During this short breathing spell I took in the situation. We had come up in a northeast direction, slanting along the slope. Once on top, I had instinctively turned to the north. Here the drift was about twenty feet wide, perfectly level and with an exfoliated surface layer. To the east the drift fell steeply, with a clean, smooth cliffline marking off the beginning of the descent; this line seemed particularly disconcerting, for it betrayed the concave curvature of the down-sweep. A few yards to the north I saw below, at the foot of the cliff, the old logging-trail, and I noticed that the snow on it lay as it had fallen, smooth and sheer, without a ripple of a drift. It looked like mockery. And yet that was where I had to get down.

The next few minutes are rather a maze in my memory. But two pictures were photographed with great distinctness. The one is of the moment when we went over the edge. For a second Peter reared up, pawing the air with his forefeet; Dan tried to back away from the empty fall. I had at this excruciating point no purchase whatever on the lines. Then apparently Peter sat or fell down, I do not know which, on his haunches and began to slide. The cutter lurched to the left as if it were going to spill all it held. Dan was knocked off his hind feet by the drawbar—and we plunged. . . . We came to with a terrific jolt that sent me in a heap against the dashboard. One jump, and I stood on the ground. The cutter—and this is the second picture which is etched clearly on the plate of my memory—stood on its pole, leaning at an angle of forty-five degrees against the drift. The horses were as if stunned. "Dan, Peter!" I shouted, and they struggled to their feet. They were badly winded, but otherwise everything seemed all right. I looked wistfully back and up at the gully which we had torn into the flank of the drift.

I should gladly have breathed the horses again, but they were hot, the air was at zero or colder, the rays of the sun had begun to slant. I walked for a while alongside the team. They were drooping sadly. Then I got in again, driving them slowly till we came to the crossing of the ditch. I had no eye for the grade ahead. On the bush road the going was good—now and then a small drift, but nothing alarming anywhere. The anti-climax had set in. Again the speckled trunks of the balm poplars struck my eye, now interspersed with the scarlet stems of the red osier dogwood. But they failed to cheer me—they were mere facts, unable to stir moods. . . .

I began to think. A few weeks ago I had met that American settler with the French-sounding name who lived alongside the angling dam further north. We had talked snow, and he had said, "Oh, up here it never is bad except along this grade";—We were stopping on the last east-west grade, the one I was coming to—"there you cannot get through. You'd kill your horses. Level with the tree-tops." Well, I had had just that a little while ago—I could not afford any more of it. So I made up my mind to try a new trail, across a section which was fenced. It meant getting out of my robes twice more, to open the gates, but I preferred that to another tree-high drift. To spare my horses was now my only consideration. I should not have liked to take the new trail by night, for fear of missing the gates; but that objection did not hold just now. Horses and I were pretty well spent. So, instead of forking off the main trail to the north we went straight ahead.

In due time I came to the bridge which I had to cross in order to get up on the dam. Here I saw—in an absent-minded, half unconscious, and uninterested way—one more structure built by architect wind. The deep master ditch from the north emptied here, to the left of the bridge, into the grade ditch which ran east and west. And at the corner the snow had very nearly bridged it—so nearly that you could easily have stepped across the remaining gap. But below it was hollow—nothing supported the bridge—it was a mere arch, with a vault underneath that looked temptingly sheltered and cosy to wearied eyes.

The dam was bare, and I had to pull off to the east, on to the swampy plain. I gave my horses the lines, and slowly, slowly they took me home! Even had I not always lost interest here, to-day I should have leaned back and rested. Although the horses had done all the actual work, the strain of it had been largely on me. It was the after-effect that set in now.

I thought of my wife, and of how she would have felt had she been able to follow the scenes in some magical mirror through every single vicissitude of my drive. And once more I saw with the eye of recent memory the horses in that long, endless plunge through the corner of the marsh. Once more I felt my muscles a-quiver with the strain of that last wild struggle over that last, in-human drift. And slowly I made up my mind that the next time, the very next day, on my return trip, I was going to add another eleven miles to my already long drive and to take a different road. I knew the trail over which I had been coming so far was closed for the rest of the winter—there was no traffic there—no trail would be kept open. That other road of which I was thinking and which lay further west was the main cordwood trail to the towns in the south. It was out of my way, to be sure, but I felt convinced that I could spare my horses and even save time by making the detour.

Being on the east side of the dam, I could not see school or cottage till I turned up on the correction line. But when at last I saw it, I felt somewhat as I had felt coming home from my first big trip overseas. It seemed a lifetime since I had started out. I seemed to be a different man.

Here, in the timber land, the snow had not drifted to any extent. There were signs of the gale, but its record was written in fallen tree trunks, broken branches, a litter of twigs—not in drifts of snow. My wife would not surmise what I had gone through.

She came out with a smile on her face when I pulled in on the yard. It was characteristic of her that she did not ask why I came so late; she accepted the fact as something for which there were no doubt compelling reasons. "I was giving our girl a bath," she said; "she cannot come." And then she looked wistfully at my face and at the horses. Silently I slipped the harness off their backs. I used to let them have their freedom for a while on reaching home. And never yet but Peter at least had had a kick and a caper and a roll before they sought their mangers. To-day they stood for a moment knock-kneed, without moving, then shook themselves in a weak, half-hearted way and went with drooping heads and weary limbs straight to the stable.

"You had a hard trip?" asked my wife; and I replied with as much cheer as I could muster, "I have seen sights to-day that I did not expect to see before my dying day." And taking her arm, I looked at the westering sun and turned towards the house.

A Winter of Hardship 1923

CHIEF THUNDERCHILD (1849–1927) was chief of the River People of the Plains Cree, one of the followers of Big Bear who refused to sign the infamous Treaty Six (1876), which consigned Canada's Native peoples to designated reserves. Thunderchild and his band of thirty families followed the dwindling buffalo herds for three more years until, destitute and starving after the severe winter described in this story, he finally signed the treaty at Fort Carlton, Saskatchewan, in 1879. This story was told to Edward Ahenakew (1885–1961), an ordained minister at the Onion Lake Reserve in Saskatchewan and the nephew of Star Blanket, chief of the House People. The English manuscript of this and other stories, found among Ahenakew's papers after his death, was edited by his friend Ruth Buck and published in 1973 as *Voices of the Plains Cree*.

⁂ • ⁂

WHEN I WAS still young and my father was alive, we came through a winter of great hardship. My brother took me with him on many long hunts, but the buffalo were scarce that year, and there was hardly any food. Everyone looked for old bones to make grease, but it was rancid.

At first there were plenty of foxes. We caught many in deadfall traps, and traded their skins for tobacco, shot, tea, and sugar, when traders came to our camps; but when we tried to buy pemmican, they would not sell us any.

We had travelled far out onto the plains, and there were no more trees to make traps. We were told that there was food at Fort Pitt, and we started in hope towards that post. We still had five horses and many dogs, but wolves followed us, and when we camped our dogs would chase them. Sometimes the dogs killed a wolf, but every day wolves killed some of our dogs. We had to kill dogs too, for we had nothing else to eat; then, we had to kill our horses for food.

One day *Na-pa-ke-kun* (Night Scout) came to our camp. He told us that the people we had left at the encampment had also tried to reach Fort Pitt when they learned that there was food there, and had died along the way. He and his wives were the only ones left. They had five horses, and they killed one for food, but would give us none. We took the skin, and we boiled that and ate it, but we were too weak to follow *Na-pa-ke-kun* north when he went on with his wives and the other horses. We could go no farther.

The winter was ending. Our women seemed to be stronger than the men. Though they were not eating, they kept moving, if it was only to make fires to keep us warm. The three children with us were only skin and bones, and their mothers cried over them. We found it hard even to breathe.

One night I dreamed that someone came to me and said, "You can save yourself. Look to the south!" And looking south, I saw that the country was green, but to the north there was only darkness. I tried to flee to the south. The dream was vivid, and when I awoke it was almost morning. I lay thinking about the dream, and then I told it to my father. "Maybe it is only hunger that made me dream," I said. But my father told me, "Dreams count, my son. Try to go south, all of you; and if I cannot follow, leave me. I will do my best."

The thaw had begun. The women went ahead of us, carrying all they could. I had a gun and I tried to hunt, but I had to rest often. Gophers were appearing, and we killed some and made fires with buffalo chips to cook them. We camped four times before we came to any bush. Then early one morning, my aunt suddenly cried out that she had seen an "old man buffalo." We thought that she had gone crazy but we looked where she pointed and there stood a buffalo, about two hundred yards away. "*A-a-hay-a-ay.* It is going to be hard. Who can go?"

My brother took his loaded gun and moved slowly down the valley, resting often, for he was very weak. We stayed and watched. Sometimes he was out of sight, and then we would see him again, crawling towards where the buffalo had been, but it had moved on and we could not see it.

After a long time, we heard the sound of my brother's gun, and I went to meet him. He told me that he had hit the buffalo, and it would surely die, but we would have to move our camp and follow its trail. It took us a long time to pull down the tent and move slowly after the buffalo. It was not far, but we were weak. My aunt took the gun. "I will follow the trail," she said, "and I will kill the buffalo if it is still alive." The other women went with her, all except my mother.

Night came, and it was bright moonlight when we heard the women returning dragging great loads of meat. They were able to bring most of it back to where we had camped. The buffalo was old and its meat was tough. The women boiled it to make soup, and that was easier for us to eat, but after long hunger my mother and my brother almost died. *A-a-hay,* we were poor, but now we could fatten ourselves a bit, and we began to feel life in our bones once more.

When I was stronger, I wandered through the bushes where we had pitched our tent, and I saw an old camp, with the tracks of foxes and wolves around it. There was a mound of melting snow, and when I kicked it I saw a corpse, a man dead from hunger. I went back to our camp and we moved to the river, hoping that we might meet some Stoneys, my aunt's people.

Each day, we were able to walk a little more, and the snow was almost gone when we reached the river. Away to the west, we could see people moving in single file. We knew they might be Blackfoot and so we loaded our guns in readiness, but when they saw us they turned towards us, moving slowly, for they had no horses and were carrying heavy loads. They were Stoneys, and they greeted my aunt affectionately as a daughter.

There were eleven families, and everything they had was in the loads on their backs, for they had killed and eaten their horses. But they had buffalo meat, and they fed us grease and dried meat. When we had eaten they wanted to go on, though my father asked them to camp with us by the river, at the old Sun Dance place. We gave them tobacco and tea, and they gave us meat; but the next day they crossed the river. We were sorry to see them go.

We camped at the old Sun Dance place, where there was plenty of wood. The women found a buffalo head and neck in the snow, and they made a fire to boil it. I climbed the bank of the river, and as I sat there I saw something that moved and disappeared again with the wind. I went to find out what it was, and I came to a big snowdrift with a pole at the top, from which a bit of cloth blew in the wind. It marked a cache.

I took off my coat and began to dig through the hard crust of snow. Down inside the drift I found hides that covered the meat of two buffalo, cut in pieces. I had to sit down then, for I remembered my dream and was overcome with feeling and with thankfulness to the spirits who had guided us.

I tied the meat into one of the hides and pulled it down the bank as far as I could, and then I left it and went on to our camp. I found the others eating the head that the women had boiled, and my sister-in-law called to me to come and eat. I ate, and when I was finished I said to my father, "We will have another meal, a good one," and I told him what I had found. "Dreams count, my son," he said to me. "The spirits have pitied us and guided us."

The women hurried to bring the meat to our camp, and we stayed at the Sun Dance place until they had dried much of it and made pemmican, and had scraped and tanned the hides. When all that was done, we moved on. It was spring, and we went to where there were maple trees, and made sugar. Truly a change had come, for now we had sugar; and the hunting was good, with a kill every day. It was pleasant in that valley, just to be alive and well, all of us; and yet we felt ashamed to be so poor, without any horses. It was lonely too.

I had begun to feel that I must have things of my own, and I was restless. I said that I would go to see if I could find some of our people, and I had not gone far when I saw a rider, a Stoney whose name was *Chō-ka-se*. I told him all that had happened to us, and he said, "Come with me and I will lend you horses and carts." He came back to our camp with me. My father was surprised that I had come back so soon, and he was pleased that *Chō-ka-se* would lend us horses and carts; but that is the Indian way.

Then *Chō-ka-se* took us to his camp and he gave us what we needed to travel. Scouts who had gone ahead had found the women who had been with *Na-pa-ke-kun*. He had died of starvation and yet they still had the horses that they had refused to share with us. The scouts came on Big Bear's band too, those with horses helping to carry the others. All through the country north of the Saskatchewan River there had been many deaths from starvation, and the Crees were moving west along the river, hoping to make a truce with the Blackfoot. The scouts said that the Blackfoot had not starved, for they had many horses and could follow the buffalo herds.

We travelled west until we came to a Blackfoot camp. They knew of the hardship we had suffered and we were invited into a big tent. At first we could use only signs, and then one of the Crees came who could interpret. My brother made the Blackfoot his namesake; the old man give him a fine horse and cart. He gave me a two-year-old to ride, but I made up my mind after all the troubles of that winter that I would never again be dependent upon others.

ALDO LEOPOLD

Canada, 1924 1924

ALDO LEOPOLD (1887–1948) was born in Iowa. In 1909, he joined the
U. S. Forest Service, and in 1924—the year of the fishing trip into Quetico
National Park recounted in this excerpt from his diaries—he became associate director of the Forest Products Laboratory in Madison, Wisconsin, bought
a "sand farm" in the area and remained there for the rest of his life. He was
also an advisor on conservation to the United Nations. The publication of
A Sand County Almanac in 1949, the year after he died fighting a grass fire on
a neighbor's farm, marked Leopold as not only an important conservationist,
but also one of the best nature writers of his era. His essay "Thinking Like a
Mountain" has become the foundation of the "deep ecology" movement. He
was awarded the John Burroughs medal in 1978, and his notes and diaries,
edited by his son Luna B. Leopold, were first published in 1953 under the
title *Round River.*

⁂

11 June, 1924

'TWAS WEDNESDAY NOON when we set sail from Winton, Minnesota, going up Fall Lake in an old launch, thence by truck over an old logging grade
four miles into the SW arm of Basswood Lake. Here we loaded up our two
16-foot Racine canoes and struck NE for the international boundary. About
5:00 P.M. we got to the Canadian Ranger Station (Quetico Provincial Park),
bought our licenses from Ranger Seeley, headed north about a mile, and
pitched camp. Starker's fishing fever was running high, so we paddled out to a
little island and caught two pickerel for supper.

Our camp was under a fine stand of Norway pine, where hermit thrushes
were singing. It is already apparent that the pine timber on the Canadian side is

all uncut and not much burned, while on the American side there is not a pine left. Fortunately the numerous islands are all covered with fine mature pines.

Roast pickerel for supper. When we went to bed at nine it wasn't yet dark.

12 June

About 4:30 A.M. gave up trying to stay in bed. While eating breakfast saw a black mallard and several small mergansers pass by. Headed north toward Canadian Point, where in a wide part of the lake we found a big bunch of loons, the banks of pine timber echoing their calls. Starker trolled and caught a big pickerel with a parasitic worm projecting from his side. In spite of this he was fat. Put him back, of course. About 10 A.M. reached the Basswood River and soon got to the first falls, portaging around them and finding our outfit good to carry but not quite to the point where we could make it in one trip. Had some lunch, and Carl and Fritz caught two fine wall-eyed pike, in addition to pickerel which we let go. Several red-breasted mergansers passed over. Then we portaged the lower falls, at the foot of which Fritz added another wall-eye and Starker caught a pickerel. About 3 P.M. we camped on the portage of still another very pretty waterfall which is probably the end of the river and the beginning of Crooked Lake. There is considerable style to this camp, which is on a grassy knoll overlooking the falls, with an International Boundary Monument for a tent peg.

13 June

Got under way about 7:00. Rounding a point near the painted cliffs Fritz and Starker saw two does. Carl and I came up and tried to photograph one of them which broke and ran at 40 yards. The scenery is extraordinary. Went up a blind bay by mistake and found a muskeg with moose tracks. They had evidently come down for the lily which has a rosette of red leaves on the bottom. Moose tracks were visible in the lake bottom as well as on the shore.

Soon we came to a narrows with a current literally full of big pike—we caught several and let them go.

No sooner had we started on than I sighted two deer on a grassy shore. Carl and I made the sneak. They seemed to see us at a quarter mile but resumed feeding and playing like a pair of puppies, striking with their front feet and dodging side-ways. They, too, were after the red lilies, fragments of which were floating in the water. We had both the wind and the light in our favor and got up to not more than 30 yards, snapping two films.

We nooned on a fine point of solid rock, open to the breeze, with deep pitchoffs full of big pike, and big shiners along the shoreline. Fritz caught a 7¾ pounder, and Starker a smaller one and a wall-eye. Many grouse were drumming here. A pair of tree swallows had a nest in a woodpecker hole in an old jack pine. The hole was alive with big red ants. How the young would survive the ants I can't imagine.

Continuing through Crooked Lake I caught a big wall-eye of 5¼ pounds, which we kept for supper. Camped on a little rock island with only half a dozen trees and no mosquitoes. Tried a fish mulligan consisting of the planked wall-eye cut into big boneless cubes, ham, potatoes, mixed dehydrated vegetables, rice, and noodles. It was a huge success. We had the broth first (thus avoiding any need for a hot drink) and the rest afterward. It was so good we christened it "Island Mulligan," and the camp, "Mulligan Island."

After supper Fritz and Starker went back to a narrows with a strong current where we had seen many wall-eyes, while Carl and I went trolling for trout. We were soon diverted, however, by a persistent bawling across the lake, which we took to be either a bear cub (which bawls very much like a calf) or a calf moose. We landed and found a lake with a little muskeg full of moose tracks, beds, trails, and piles of sign. By this time the bawling had stopped, as the wind was quartering against us. We lifted the canoe over and found we were on an arm connecting with the channel where the boys were fishing. They had landed a huge pike and were playing another one at a place where the pike had run a school of shiners up into the shore rocks and had them surrounded. The minnows were dashing frantically while the pike slashed right and left in the shallows. One could hook a pike at nearly every cast. Fritz had de-barbed a spoon in order to facilitate getting them off for release. Everybody caught pike (and a few wall-eyes) till the mosquitoes and approaching dark sent us to camp, towing the two big ones to have their pictures taken tomorrow.

We distinctly heard grouse drumming at 9:30 P.M. after dark. The moon was nearly full. Hermit thrushes were also singing.

14 June

Up a little later this morning and got started about 7:00. Trolled for trout a while but caught nothing but small pickerel. Continued west through the channels of Crooked Lake. A party of Indians, headed for La Croix, passed us. Arrived at Curtain Falls for lunch. Two miles before we got there we could hear the roar, and a quarter mile away one could feel the moist cool air full of spray vapor. The falls are really quite a show.

A pileated woodpecker flew across the channel near the falls. We had heard them previously drumming in the woods.

At the falls we had a pow-wow and decided to strike off north into the wilder country rather than continue along the Indian route near Shortess Island. We went down the first bay, where we mistakenly supposed the portage to be, and discovered a little hidden lake on which was an eagle. Moose, deer, and bear tracks, all fresh, were seen on the sand beach at its outlet.

On a bare rock in this bay we found a nest of three young herring gulls. The old ones flew overhead and tried to lead us away. The young took to the water as we approached. We ran one down and caught it—a pretty downy chick, white with black dots. It did not dive, but swam well; however, the down plumage soaked up water rather rapidly.

We now tried the second bay and found the portage. A big buck, whose fresh tracks we found in the sand, snorted and stampeded up the hill as we landed. Saw two grouse and the tracks of both moose and deer on the portage. Crossed an unnamed lake and then portaged into Roland Lake. It was immediately apparent that we had here the green water of the real north country, rather than the brown water of Crooked and Basswood Lakes. We camped on a beautiful rock point full of reindeer moss and backed by pines. Hermit thrushes serenaded us at supper, and a loon called from a far bay. Starker, as usual, started to fish, and from the canoe landing hooked what we supposed (from his spots) to be a small pickerel, but he fought as no pickerel ever did. On landing him we found him to be a beautifully spotted lake trout. This was a barbless spoon—which we shall use hereafter. Starker got two more trout. We have had two big ambitions—seeing moose and catching trout, and have now solved the trout problem.

After supper Fritz stumbled upon a hen mallard setting eight eggs right in the pine forest. The number of adventures awaiting us in this blessed country seems without end. Watching the gray twilight settling upon our lake we could truly say that "all our ways are pleasantness and all our paths are peace."

15 June

A fine chorus of white-throated sparrows when the sun came up. Their note sounds like "Ah, poor Canada!" Thank the Lord for country as poor as this.

We had a laundering and sewing bee around camp. Then explored the lake and found tomorrow's portage into Trout Lake. Trolled to the sand beach, where we found fresh moose tracks and had a fine but brief swim, the water being cold. Coming back to camp we photographed the mallard nest. The nest consisted of a hollow pushed into the dry litter under the overhanging branches of a little spruce. It had a perfect circle of a rim consisting of the gray down of the hen. The behavior of the hen was entirely different when ap-

proached from the water instead of the land—from the land she played cripple, whereas from the water she sprang directly into the air and hardly
quacked. Only eight eggs and nest full.

While we were boiling tea for lunch. Starker caught another trout. After a
nap all round we engaged in the very serious occupation of catching perch
minnows to be used as bait for the evening fishing. Later I made Starker a
bow of white cedar. In the evening we caught a few trout, one of which we
had for supper. It was a female and had pink flesh, whereas the previous ones
had white flesh. Only small fish were caught on first casts, indicating that big
ones get used to a spoon and no longer get excited about it. The first three
minnows also drew bites, but later minnows wouldn't work.

Carl and I learned something while casting in a bay behind camp. The
water was covered with willow cotton, which gummed up the line and the
ferrules so as to make casting nearly impossible.

At dark a solitary loon serenaded us with his lonesome call, which Fritz
imitates very well. This call seems to prevail at night, while the laughing call is
used during the day. Carl remembers the laughing call at night, however, on
the trip we made to Drummond Island with Dad about 1905.

The Lord did well when he put the loon and his music into this lonesome
land.

16 June

Under way by 7:00 and over the portage into Trout Lake. A stiff SW wind
gave us a little tussle getting across into the islands. From here we skirted the
lee shores on an exploration trip into the SW arm, where in a fine sand-
beach bay we noticed all the cedars were defoliated up to a six-foot "high-
water mark." We landed to investigate and decided it was undoubtedly a
winter "deer yard," the occasional spruces not being trimmed up. The cedars
overhanging the water along the shoreline had undoubtedly been browsed-
off from the ice.

Lunched on a little dream of an island consisting of a single tree on a single
rock. Looked like rain, so we decided not to push on to Darkey Lake. Got up
the tent and hustled in some wood from across the channel just in time before
she came down in sheets, whereupon we holed up and made some stew.

A new leech—first seen in Roland Lake. Olive green with orange lines on
each side and a row of orange dots along the dorsal line.

Lichens—our rock island is covered with gray lichens, which in dry
weather flatten out and expose only their "rubberized" upper surfaces, thus
allowing a minimum of evaporation. The minute a drop of water strikes

them, this surface turns olive green and the outer edges curl up, exposing the rough absorptive under-surface to the rain. The individual plants must attain great age, since we have passed numerous places where initials have persisted for years by being scraped into the lichen covers of rocks.

17 June

Packed up and under way by a little after seven. It was a clear sparkling day with a stiff north breeze. We found the portage into Darkey Lake very steep and full of fallen fire-killed pine. On the second trip we bumped right into a pair of partridges with at least ten or a dozen chicks, of which we caught two to take a photo. The old hen had a number of calls, one a hiss like a bull snake, to defy the enemy; another a cluck like a hen to reassure the brood to sit tight; another a meow like a cat-bird, evidently meaning alarm; also an alarm chirp like a Gambel quail. I'm not sure the hen gave all these calls—both she and the cock were on deck all the time, trying to save the day. The chicks had a peep just like any chick. They were in the down—I should guess less than a week old.

Looked for the Indian paintings supposed to be found on the cliffs in the lower part of Darkey Lake but couldn't find them. The water we find is inter-mediate—not so green as Trout Lake and not so brown as Crooked Lake. It has an outlet, and we found later that it contains pike, perch, wall-eyes, trout, and, unfortunately, carp.

Explored the northwest arm down to the outlet, hoping to find bass. We are sure we saw some small ones. At the outlet we found big three- and four-pound carp in great numbers. Had a lot of fun gigging or snagging them with a spoon. I also tried a bow and arrow and later a spear with a nail lashed to the point. The spear worked right now—with the very first shot I got a big one right through the back. These carp were active, hard, and nicely colored, and were spawning. When the spawn dropped from hooked fish, great numbers of minnows gathered to eat it.

Coming back up the arm Fritz and I saw a doe and snapped her, and I caught a huge pike with the tail of a one-pound fish projecting from his throat. We had hooked no bass, so we all set out to catch some supper, using the fine minnows Starker had caught at the outlet. Rigged a bobber and fished off our rock point by camp, where I caught a big trout for supper. After supper we caught a big pike and some wall-eyes, all of which we turned back.

18 June

We were all lazy this morning and slept until about 6:30. The last hour in bed was spent slaughtering large blood-filled mosquitoes that in one way or another had found their way under our netting. Our camp on Darkey was a beautiful one on a high promontory with exceptionally deep water on three sides. Left camp about 8:00 with a strong head wind from the east. The first of five portages to Bunt Lake turned out to be a lining proposition but the other four were bona fide portages—the roughest we have struck to date.

Launched our canoes in a rough bit of water and paddled out to a small Norway-pine island where we had lunch.

After lunch we continued on east to the northeast end of the channel connecting the main east and west sections of the lake; a particularly attractive spot because there is less evidence of fire than in any of the country we have struck so far.

Made camp on the westernmost of a string of four small islands. Camp is made up in apple-pie order because we expect to spend two days here.

In the way of miscellaneous information, the deer we saw yesterday was feeding on young horse-tail just coming up out of the water.

Found beaver lodges both in dead water in narrow inland channels and on the open lakeshore with a mile or more of open water offshore.

In exploring the details of our island I heard a continued peep-peeping and on investigating found a laughing loon's nest containing one chick and one partly hatched egg with a live chick peeping inside. The egg is very large—about the size of a goose egg; color a dull brown with a few black flecks scattered irregularly. The chick is slate gray in color with black feet and bill and whitish belly.

During supper the old loons watched us from a distance of sixty yards. But after supper when we all disappeared into the tent where we kept very quiet, the hen loon took courage and came right up to within thirty feet of our white tent and just now she has the chick out in the water with her. The rooster is off about forty yards making reassuring small talk to the hen while she takes the chances.

20 June

Up bright and early, packed up, and under way about 6:30. Eastward along Brent Lake, which has much spruce shore and many high bold islands. Saw a blue-wing teal and another pair of loons with two tiny chicks trailing them. Down the SE arm of Brent and over a beautiful portage into a little unnamed lake, where we bumped into another pair of loons, one with the young on her back. Another portage put us into McIntyre Lake. We got as far as the narrows when the heavy sea in the SW arm led us to try to portage out of the SE arm, which was calm. We found an old trail about half a mile long into Sarah Lake. On the trail we found some lovely pink lady's-slipper in a swamp, and a mother partridge with a bunch of chicks even smaller than the ones we saw a few days ago. The old hen whined exactly like a puppy dog when we approached the chicks, and played the cripple act to perfection when we started away. She kept ahead of us, leading us almost to the lake.

This portage is through beautiful birch timber with an undergrowth of maple brush and hazel. It has never been cleared but has been used at odd times. On it we found some wolf or bear sign with a big gathering of tiger-swallowtail butterflies on it.

Before leaving McIntyre we saw a big, light-red deer on a rocky point. The water in McIntyre was very high. Could raise no fish.

Cooked lunch near a beaver lodge in the foot of the NE arm of Sarah Lake. More fresh cuttings on the shores (mostly aspen and alder) than any place we have yet seen. In several places recently we have seen old dead pine logs gnawed by beaver—evidently just to exercise their teeth.

All of these waters are now covered with a film of jack-pine pollen, which also makes a line on all the rocks in protected places. It does not seem to gum a fishline as the willow cotton does.

Went south on Sarah to just about the narrows, where we made camp on a fine pine island with bold shores and little underbrush. We thought we had got away from our nursery duties but soon found we had camped in a regular kindergarten. Carl found a loon's nest with one hatched egg and a pipped one, while Starker found a nest full of little juncos right where we were pitching our tent. We moved into another place, but the young were soon hopping all through the camp, while the old birds scolded us constantly and our new hen loon complained in the channel behind us.

During the evening we heard a tree crash across the channel—doubtless the work of beavers. Very few mosquitoes during the night so we all slept fine.

21 June

While we were breakfasting three beautiful loons swam up to within 60 yards several times to look us over. Their motive was evidently curiosity. We have noticed that the trill of the laughing call is produced by vibrating the lower mandible, and not by a mechanism of the throat alone. Also that the "laugh" seems to prevail as a note of alarm or fear, the lonesome call seldom being used when the loon is worried or alarmed.

Packed a lunch and started out on the trail of the big bass. Tried a little bottlenecked bay just across from camp but could raise nothing on spoons. Then tried the pike-minnow plug and got results forthwith, removing two gangs of hooks to give the fish a chance. Also caught them on a pork-rind spinner.

Those caught on a single hook jumped as many as four times; those on a plug never more than once. No plugs for us if we can help it. Carl also caught two huge pike, one on a barbless spoon and the other on a pork rind. Each took forty minutes to land—they were so heavy that the light rod acted exactly as if it were trying to lift a railroad tie. Both pike had scars, and the smaller one a healed nick in his back. Both were the same length but the first one was deeper and heavier. It is impossible to squeeze in the gill covers on these huge fish—they can be lifted only by getting the fingers behind the gills. Even then one's hand would not reach around a much bigger one. Weighed them by using Starker's bow on a paddle, giving the scales three times the leverage of the fish, and multiplying the scale reading by three. Thus we stayed within the capacity of the scales.

We named this Battleship Bay after the huge proportions of the big pike. In it was a large beaver lodge recently extended many feet into the lake by adding sticks of peeled aspen and alder and unpeeled birch. Evidently the birch is not eaten but just cut as building material. The older section of the lodge on the shore end was plastered with gravel and mud—this was evidently the part used last winter.

23 June

Got under way about 8:00 after taking a picture of Starker's big bass and turning him loose. Had the wind behind us, so hoisted our shirt-tail sails and kited down Sarah in a hurry. Starker caught a fine trout trolling and we kept him for dinner. Tried the bass but couldn't raise any. Over a very steep portage into a little lake full of fresh beaver workings. Tried the bass here and saw many little ones but none big enough to strike. Then into another little lake with much fresh beaver work and several lodges, and a fine little lily-padded bay in one end, with muskeg shores. This lake was remarkably deep with a mud bottom and deep, clear, blue water. Raised no fish. Then over a very short portage into a lake so flooded by old beaver work that all the shore timber was killed. We were so hungry that we ate lunch on a shelving rock. There were many old lodges in this lake but no recent signs of beaver and all the aspen within reach of shore had been cut. It was evidently abandoned. Fritz saw a snowshoe rabbit come down to the lakeshore for a drink. Raised no fish here.

P.S. Mistaken about the fish. After lunch Starker saw a trout pass our point and I soon caught a beauty on a small spoon with a piece of skin off the trout caught in Sarah. This fish had only the faintest suggestion of spots and was of a beautiful brown mottled color. We kept him for supper. Now set about to find our portage but couldn't locate it. Spent the whole afternoon cruising around, locating two lakes to the west and one to the south, which we finally concluded was our lake. Meanwhile we had made camp as it was too late to go on. It proved to be one of our prettiest and most interesting camps. A bunch of loons kept inspecting us and providing the music for the evening. After supper I caught another of the beautiful mottled trout. The feeling of not knowing quite where we were, also a fine bunch of rootless alder wood, made this an exceptionally nice camp.

24 June

Under way about 7 o'clock after an extra-fine breakfast of fried trout, applesauce, and cornbread. Decided to chance it down the beaver dam and soon identified the next lake (Brown Lake) as the one we were looking for. Fredrico Lake, with the beaver dam and duck pond, runs into it from the west. Portaged on into what we called Blue Lake, from the blue water. Fish here and Starker had a strike that seemed to be trout but he caught none. Thence over the forked portage into what we thought was the Ranger Station bay but where we soon found we had another long portage to make. Ate lunch here and called it Basswood Jr., from the brown water.

The forked portage was a long one and we rested halfway. There were very big moose tracks on it. The Blue Lake end has been flooded by beaver and we sank up to our knees in places. We observed that a boggy portage was not necessarily a soft one.

At Basswood Jr. we entered the big burn that devastated the "civilized" end of our route about 15 years ago. There is an osprey nest on this lake, and old beaver lodges on its shores.

At lunch today Carl looked wise and trotted out three tailor-made cigarettes, which he, with great forbearance, had been carrying in his pocket these two weeks.

We had a fair breeze quartering against us all afternoon, except for a two-mile stretch at the mouth of Pipestem Bay, which we sailed in no time at all. Going up Pipestem we saw a porcupine drinking. After a long drag got over the lower portage just before sunset. Here we saw several canoes—the first human beings we had seen since 14 June, ten days ago. Noticed basswood growing near the falls—evidently it goes this far north only near water that is open the year long and hence modifies the temperature sufficiently to enable the basswood to survive.

Camped on a pretty little island within sound of the falls. We were lucky to have such a nice place for our last camp. Had been paddling and portaging 16 hours so we cooked a big dinner and turned in early.

25 June

Up at 4:30 and found a big loon inspecting our camp. Also saw a black mal-lard and what seemed to be a bluebill. This country has more marshy bays than do the rock-bound shores where we have been and hence is better adapted to nesting ducks. After a fine breakfast of bacon and fried noodles we sorted our duffel and started out. Soon reached our last portage, where Fritz remarked that there was sign not only of moose but also of elk and knights of Columbus. Even so, we saw a deer in it, in spite of the landing docks, tin cans, and old papers.

Now had a long pull up Fall Lake in the teeth of a very stiff wind. It was quite a tussle, in which Starker had to take a hand to make any progress at all. He did splendidly and we pulled into Winton about 9:30. Peterson came over with the truck and we warmed up in Ely and caught the 12:45 train back to work.

It has been a memorable trip—maybe the best we ever made—and we have made some that are hard to beat. It is the first trip we have made to-gether since we went to Drummond Island with Dad about 1906 or 1907. How Dad would have loved it! I am reminded of Izaak Walton's terse but lov-ing tribute—"an excellent angler, now with God."

All Things Both Great and Small 1936

GREY OWL (1888–1938) was born Archibald Stansfeld Belaney in Hastings, England. As a child, he read and dreamed about North American Indians. He emigrated to Canada in 1906, worked as a guide and trapper in northern Ontario, joined an Ojibwa band, married an Ojibwa, Angele Eguana, and assumed the name Wa-Sha-Quon-Asin, or Grey Owl. After leaving northern Ontario in 1912, he met Anahareo, an Iroquois woman who convinced him that it was nobler to save the beaver than to trap them; with her he moved to Cabano in northern Quebec and created the beaver sanctuary described in *Pilgrims of the Wild* (1935), the book that established his fame as a naturalist: the London *Times* called him "a Canadian Thoreau." *Tales of an Empty Cabin*, from which this essay is taken, appeared in 1936. By the time of his death at the age of fifty, he was the best-known Canadian writer of the period.

THE SUN HAS SET on Ajawaan. The moon shines palely down upon the still surface of the water, and in the lonely forest the shadows of the great trees fall big and dark.

And all around is Silence, the Silence of ten thousand years of waiting, the mighty Hush of a timeless, changeless Purpose.

Ajawaan; a small, deep lake that, like a splash of quicksilver, lies gleaming in its setting of the wooded hills that stretch in long, heaving undulations into the North, to the Arctic Sea. Its waters day by day reflect its countless moods, and the ever-changing colors of the sky; to-day a perfect shadowgraph of the surrounding woods, unruffled, lucent and jade green; to-night, silver in a flood of moonlight, and at the end of every day, crimson with the glory of the sunset.

At its edge there stands a small log cabin, Beaver Lodge, my home. An unpretentious place, built just as I designed it, to be more or less a replica of the House of McGinnis, that faraway Winter camp in Temiscouata which was the beginning of all things, the Empty Cabin of the Tales I lately told you. This Beaver Lodge is not only my home; it is the home, too, of my Beaver People and is the gathering place of many other creatures, denizens of the forest that encircles it on every side. They are of all shapes and sizes, these shy, elusive Dwellers among the Leaves who have broken the rules of all the furtive folk, and have come from out the dark circle of the woods to stay with me, some permanently and others from time to time. They range all the way from the small, black, woolly beaver-mouse who goes hopefully around wondering when I am going to leave the lid off the butter-dish, to the great moose, as big as a horse and having, in the proper season, antlers three feet and a half across, who, an intermittent but fairly regular visitor, does some of his heavier thinking while standing outside my window.

Though living quite alone, and far from the haunts of my fellow-men, I am seldom lonely; for I have but to step outside, and it is not long before some little beast, bedight with gay caparison of flaunting tail, or smart display of tuft or colored stripe, goes racing by and seeing me, or hearing my low call, comes to see what I may have for him. For it has not taken them very long, these smaller fry, to discover where I live, and to find that no one ever leaves here empty-handed. The bigger beasts are not much influenced by offerings of food, as theirs is usually abundant and easily come by, but pay their visits more, apparently, for the companionship they find here; as does a woodsman who goes occasionally to town to share in the small excitements of the place.

But some of the bird population are more practical, being swayed by considerations of an economic nature; and they make no bones about it either, especially the whiskey-jacks, those companionable, impertinent gray brigands who appear, soundlessly like ghosts from nowhere, at the first stroke of an axe or first wisp of smoke from a camp fire. Chiselers and gold-diggers of the first water, they contrive to make themselves welcome by an ingratiating amiability that may, or may not, be counterfeit. Their antics are amusing and they provide considerable light entertainment at times that might otherwise be dull. A man feels that their companionship at a lonely camp fire is worth a few scraps of bannock or meat, until he discovers that they want, not part of his lunch, but all of it. But these lads are pertinacious to a degree that is unbelievable, and if they do not get as much as they expected they will sit around on branches with a kind of sad, reproachful, half-starved look about them that causes the inexperienced traveler to make further and handsome contributions for very shame.

The two original whiskey-jacks who were attached to this spot when first I came here, have called in off the endless, empty streets of the forest, all of their kin who resided within a reasonable distance, say about five miles, judging by the number of them. This assembly of mendicants follows me around closely on my frequent tours of inspection, wholly, I fear, on account of what there is in it for them, and my exit from the cabin with something in my hands, supposing it is only an axe or an empty pot, anything at all, is the signal for piercing outcries from watchful sentinels who have been waiting patiently for hours for my appearance, they calling loudly to their fellows the bird-equivalent of "Here he is, boys!" When I stop, they gather on branches on all sides, regarding me alertly, solemnly, or wheedlingly, according to the disposition of the individual, whispering meanwhile confidentially among themselves. And as they sit in mock decorum, dispersed among their various vantage points, a direct and steady glance nearly always discomposes them, causing some to turn their heads away—whether as a disclaimer of any ulterior motive (they would steal the eyes out of a brass monkey), or from a hypocritical desire to appear not too eager, I cannot attempt to divine. Perhaps they have the grace to simulate some slight feeling of shame at the means, little short of bare-faced robbery, that they are adopting to satisfy an insatiable and very undiscriminating appetite; in which case this assumed diffidence does not prevent them from keeping a keen weather-eye on every move I make, and they readily observe morsels thrown to the ground behind them, or otherwise supposedly out of sight, and are able to detect a single crumb that would be invisible to the eyes of more honest folk. Most of them have learned to alight on my extended hands, and will sit there picking daintily at their portions, while others will dive at me like attacking planes and seize their share in passing. Gourmands and thieves they undoubtedly are, but they are cheerful, good-natured pirates and good company withal, and these engaging rascals have a pleasant, plaintive little ditty that they sing, as if to please the hearer, but which I gravely suspect is but a siren song used only to charm contributions from reluctant prospects.

They will go to almost any lengths to gain their ends, and I once saw one of them, dislodged from a frozen meat-bone by a woodpecker (a far stronger bird), waiting with commendable patience until the red-head should be through. However, the woodpecker was far from expert, and using the same tactics on the bone that he would have employed on a tree, he pecked away with great gusto, throwing little chips of meat in all directions, thinking them to be wood, only to find, when he got to the heart of the matter, that he was the possesser of a clean, well-burnished, uneatable bone. This pleased the whiskey-jack mightily, for at once appreciating his opportunities, he hopped around among the flying scraps of meat and had a very good lunch, while the unfortunate woodpecker, who had done all the work, got nothing.

Birds of bright plumage are not common in the North, and the woodpecker, with his bold, chequered patterns and crimson-tufted head, provides a welcome note of brilliance on his short, darting flights from tree to tree. And he dearly loves a noise. To keep the beaver from cutting down some of the best trees near the cabin, I have been obliged to put high, tin collars around the bases of them, and these are a godsend to the woodpeckers from all over the country, who amuse themselves by rapping out tinny concerts on them with their beaks. It has long been my custom to be up and around all night, going to bed at daylight, but no sooner am I settled when, at the screech of dawn, the woodpeckers commence a rattling tattoo on the tin. The result is a clangorous uproar to which salvos of machine-gun fire would be a welcome surcease, and in the midst of this unholy pandemonium I am expected to sleep—sometimes succeeding, and sometimes not. This diabolical racket takes me somewhat back to my earlier trapping days, when I had no clock, and in order to ensure my early rising, I used to freeze a piece of meat solidly into a tin dish and set it on the low roof of the shack, directly above my head. At the first streak of daylight the whiskey-jacks would hammer on the frozen meat, creating a clatter in the tin dish that would wake the dead. I believe I can claim to be the sole inventor of this very serviceable alarum; and it had one great advantage not shared by alarm clocks in general, that when the weather was bad it remained quiet, as the birds didn't show up, or if it was snowing heavily the sound was deadened, and I knew then that I didn't have to get up.

Near the cabin there lives a mama woodpecker. In a hollow tree she has a nest, with young ones in it, who keep up a continual monotonous chattering which is going on just as stridently when I get up as it was when I went to bed, and I think never ceases. They have very penetrating voices which never seem to tire, and if at any time there is a public demand for bird voices that are guaranteed never to wear out, they would have an excellent future on the radio. The jetty black-birds, very black indeed, with bright carmine patches on their wings, give another note of color, but the most resplendent of all my bird guests is a humming bird. He is a tiny, lustrous little creature, and his feathers are so very miniature that they seem like tiny scales, and in his tightly-fitting iridescent sheath of opal, emerald and ruby red, he seems more like some priceless, delicate work of Chinese artistry, than a living thing. For a short time only he stays, hovering among the wild rose bushes, his wings winnowing at an incredible speed, so as to be a nearly invisible blur until he darts away with almost bullet-like velocity, a brilliant streak of fabulous coloration.

For several years now a brood of partridges has appeared here in the Spring. The owls get a few, but most of them survive, greatly owing to the militant defence tactics of their mother. Ducks and snipes and other water-fowl and even singing birds with nests upon the ground, will feign disability, and retreat as though badly injured, and so appear an easy prey, hoping, with pathetic optimism, to draw an intruder away from young or nest. The par-tridge (or if you want to be meticulous, the ruffed grouse) will do this too, but far more frequently will attack even a man with reckless bravery, flying in his face with shrill battle-cries or rushing at him with outspread wings, hiss-ing like a snake-truly, an exhibition of determined courage that should win the little bird a meed of admiration from even the most callous. In the Win-ter, her brood long gone to parts unknown, she stays around, sleeping warmly in a tunnel in the snow at night, and in the daytime, if it is not too cold, step-ping daintily about the yard. If the weather is cool, she alternately puffs out and flattens down her feathers, so that she looks to be inflating and deflating as she walks, appearing to be first a bird, all sleek and smooth, and then a feathered football going forward on spindling, inadequate legs. She had a habit of feeding up in a good-sized poplar near the house, year after year eat-ing the buds from it all Winter. She always picked on the same tree, until at last the tree gave up, and now is dead.

Today an eagle swept majestically above the camp, flying very low, the beat of his great wings loud and portentous in the still air. He checked a little in his flight as though minded to stay awhile; but he changed his mind and kept going on his way. I had not seen him for two years, though his nest is not over a mile from here. An eagle is the only bird that I have so far noticed who turns his head from side to side and looks around him as he flies, and this one looked back and gave me a look of keen appraisement as he passed.

And now, of a sudden, I hear behind me a light, but furious trampling, and a squirrel hurls himself through the air and lands on my back, and clambering to my shoulder he snatches from my fingers the pea-nut I always have for him. Precipitating himself onto a shelf arranged for his accommodation on the wall of the cabin, he expertly shells his pea-nut and there eats it. He some-times does this for a visitor, if in the mood, and whilst on his shelf keeps one very bright eye keenly on the donor. Most of his kin that visit me are content to hull the nuts, but he is more fastidious, and skins them too. Like all his kind he lives at the rate of about a hundred miles an hour, and when seen is always in a state of delirious activity. This is Shapawee, The Jumper. Vastly different in disposition and unusually sedate, is my little friend Subconscious, so named because, when quite young he would enter the camp and roam around without apparent object, like one in a dream, or under the influence of his subconscious mind, meandering aimlessly around. He was the only squirrel I have ever met who walked, most all of the others moving at nothing less than a round gallop. Subconscious is more leisurely, and very gentle in his ways, one of the very few who have permitted me to handle them. He used to spend most of his day around my feet, monopolizing my time, and when I cut wood he stuck around and different times narrowly escaped being chopped or cut in two. He was on a fair way to becoming a nuisance, when one day he ran across the top of a hot stove. Then he came no more. I mourned him for dead, and missed my merry little companion who had become almost like a familiar spirit. The yard looked a little empty without him, and his familiar trails and vantage points became snowed under, or were used by other and less interesting specimens of his kind. But this Summer he has returned, and is as gentle and friendly as ever, though he has evidently learned something of the ways of the world during his wanderings, as the appearance of another squirrel, regardless of sex or size, transforms him immediately into a little termagant.

During the absence of Subconscious, I undertook to tame another of these flying acrobats and succeeded up to a certain point. Then a third offered himself voluntarily as a candidate (with reservations), so that I now find my footsteps dogged by three of the, to each other, most unsociable, irascible and pugnacious bundles of dynamic energy ever forgathered together in any one place—three minds with but a single thought—to do unto others as they would be done by, but to do it first! Each considers the environs of the camp as his personal property and will fight at the drop of the hat, or less, any of his breed who dare set foot on, or even breathe, in his chosen territory. The squirrel is not a gregarious beast, and these territorial rights are pretty generally respected. But I am afraid that I have somewhat upset the regular balance of things by my well-meant attempts to arrange that a good time is had by all. This difficulty I have endeavored to adjust by feeding each one in his own small district, but have failed signally. Most of what they get is not eaten, but is hidden away in tree tops, crotches of limbs and such places, and on each cache being made the owner issues a long, quivering screech of defiance to all the world. This challenge, instead of driving away possible robbers, under present circumstances only serves as an advertisement, and attracts the attention of the other two of this militant triumvirate, who both know what it is all about. Their appearance on the scene precipitates immediate battle, the aggrieved party being always the aggressor and launching himself at his opponent as though to annihilate him on the spot. But the prospective victim is not there when his assailant lands, being already well on his way, and a lively chase ensues, carried on with shrill skirrings and chatterings of rage, and at a devastating speed. The intruder, however big, seems to feel the weakness of his case, always giving way before the onslaught of the proprietor, irrespective of size. I notice that the pursuer is always careful not to run any faster than the fleeing enemy, so that they keep always the same distance apart, and the duel is never brought to an issue; showing that they possess not only valor, but also the discretion that is said to be the better part of it.

One day Shapawee and Subconscious appeared simultaneously, one on each side of me. With some misgivings I gave them a pea-nut apiece, keeping them as far apart as possible—but they saw one another! Each at once assumed a most ferocious aspect and glared at the other with manifest evil intent. And of a sudden both turned and ran in opposite directions as fast as they possibly could, each thinking the other was behind him. It is all very harmless and entertaining; no blood is spilled and it is doubtless good exercise. And meanwhile the remaining squirrel, the whiskey-jacks, and other non-combatants, make a Roman Holiday with the caches that are being so valiantly defended. Whilst not gifted to the extent that some other creatures are, squirrels are by no means unintelligent. They have good memories too, recognizing me immediately among strangers, even after an absence of a year. It is to be noticed, too, that they will test all cones dropped by themselves from the tree tops, to see if they are good, before laying them away for Winter provision, and will bury the duds separately, out of the way, to avoid mistakes. Their strength is quite disproportionate to their size; I have seen a squirrel with half of a large apple in his mouth, jump without noticeable effort up and onto a root projecting out from a fallen tree, twenty inches above his head—equivalent to a man leaping ten feet into the air with a bushel of potatoes in his arms.

Once a family of muskrats lived under the flooring in one corner of the camp, having reproduced an almost perfect replica in miniature, of the domestic arrangements of the beaver. They were docile little fellows, and they learned to come to my call precisely as the beaver did, and frequented the cabin with the same freedom and lack of fear, save that they were not strong enough to open the door themselves. However, they would pull at a loose board until it rattled loudly, and stand chittering outside, with the greatest impatience, until admitted. One of them, when I fed the beaver tidbits, would sit humbly by waiting for his share until the bigger folk were done, and whenever I called the Mah-wees (young beaver), he thought he was Mah-wee too, and would come helter-skelter through the water along with them. Unlike his fellows he associated with the beaver, except with Jelly Roll, who was jealous of him, and if noticed by her, he would make himself, if not invisible, at least as inconspicuous as possible; though when the young muskrats first appeared out in the open, and were sometimes abroad under the guardianship of this one (as with beaver, muskrats of both sexes help take care of the young), Jelly Roll would swim beside them, exhibiting great interest, and make no hostile demonstration towards him. But if he was alone she would chivvy him around as often as not. These interesting and intelligent little rodents should not be called "muskrats," as they are not rats at all, but are first cousin to the beaver, whom they much resemble in appearance, habits and disposition. I had good company with them for several years, but much to my sorrow, a periodical epidemic, which they, like the rabbits in the woods are subject to, killed every one of them. And I often wonder if their little ghosts do not sometimes swim on Ajawaan, and haunt the small, well-kept home they had, where they had been so happy while they lived.

There was a wood-chuck, a special chum of mine, who year after year made her home under the upper cabin, where she had every Spring a brood of wood-chucklets, or whatever they are called. She was an amiable old lady, who used often to watch me at my work and allowed me a number of privileges, including the rare one of handling her young ones. But if a stranger came, she would spread herself out so as to quite fill the entrance to her domicile, to keep the youngsters in, and when the stranger left she would emit shrill whistling sounds at his retreating back, very sure that she had frightened him away. She too has gone, her time fulfilled, and another has taken over her old home; a well-built, very trim young matron who stands up straight and very soldierly before her doorway, and tries to look in windows.

I must meet these losses with what equanimity I can muster, without vain regrets. Yet I miss these old-time friends of so long-time standing, each a small, humble presence that has entered, for a little time, my life and then passed on.

People having the dim, distorted ideas that are held by so many concerning animals, can gain very little insight into their true natures. Each animal has his separate personality, easily distinguishable to one who knows him. Among the more highly intelligent species no two individuals seem to be alike, each having an individuality all his own. Their ways are often so extraordinarily human, and this is especially true of the rodents. They seem at times so rational, their movements are often so much to the purpose, and their actions, and their manner of expressing their emotions sometimes so childlike—the little

side-glances, the quaint and aimless gestures, their petulance if unduly annoyed, their artlessness and lack of guile, their distress when in some small
trouble, their so-evident affection for each other—I have never ceased to regret the thousands of them I destroyed in earlier days. Even then I never enjoyed killing them, preferring to find them dead, refusing to visualize the
hopeless struggle, the agony, the long hours of awful misery. And today I feel
that however great the inconvenience they may put me to, it can never pay
the half of what I owe them. Only those who have suffered similar tortures
can have any conception of what trapping by present methods really means to
the animal population of the woods.

Perhaps you, whom I am trying to entertain, find these thoughts a little serious. But this life I lead lends itself not only to watchfulness, but also to heed-
ful observation and deep thinking. Remember, reader, that those who live
within the portals of the Temple of Nature, see far into things that are outside
the scope of ordinary existence. There is a kind of sanctity in these forests of
great trees that makes me think of dim cloisters in old, vast cathedrals in England, and causes the ceremonious pomp and the sonorous insincerities of not
a few theosophies to seem cheap and tawdry in comparison.

Owing greatly to the ignorance, thoughtlessness or intolerance of many
who come in contact with them, some really harmless creatures have been
saddled with a reputation for evil that they do not deserve, and are penalized
accordingly. All that most of them need is a little sympathy, and most of all to
be let alone to mind their own business. Though I must admit that sometimes
this "business" is a little ill-judged, as in the case of the skunk who took refuge
in my store-tent, sleeping there regularly, and who repaid my hospitality by
having, in amongst my provisions, a family of kittens, or pups, or skunklings—
or is it skunklets? This was no doubt an oversight and no harm was intended, I
am sure, and everything turned out all right, and no one was a bit the worse off
for it. The skunk is really a natural gentleman (or lady), but unfortunately is not
a mind reader, so he cannot always gauge with accuracy your intentions towards him when you bump into him suddenly in the dark. Usually they (your
intentions) are hostile, and he acts accordingly, but he is slow to anger and of
monumental patience; and his feelings must be badly outraged before he will
turn his battery on you. Meeting him in the moonlight is sometimes startling,
for then his long, white horizontal markings and white cap are accentuated
and, the rest of his coat being black, are all that can be seen; so that as he turns
quickly this way and that with supple movements, he looks at first like some
darting white snake with a venomous head. But he is an inoffensive, happy-
go-lucky beast with a fixed idea that human beings like to find him in tents,

camps, and out-houses, and under the flooring of summer cottages. Even so, finding a skunk in the store-house is not nearly as inconvenient as discovering a moose in a canoe; and I once had this interesting experience, although I hasten to add that I was *not* in the canoe at the time. It was on shore, drawn up, awaiting my early departure that day for Waskesieu, thirty miles away and all by water. As I was making my preparations I heard, outside, a sort of light crackling, crushing sound, and looking through the window saw my friend the moose (previously mentioned) walking slowly, steadily, and very thoroughly, through and along my canoe. I rushed out of the cabin at him, shouting, and this seemed to remind him of something, so he extricated his feet from the various holes, where they must have felt most uncomfortable, and stood aside, surveying the wreckage with an air of rather thoughtful detachment. Now this was nothing but rank carelessness on his part, and I remember having a distinct feeling of annoyance about it. Granted that he was a youngish moose, and perhaps didn't know much, the fact still remains that a canoe is a very handy thing to have when you have a thirty mile trip to make, entirely by water. A moose is rather a terrific object to have around, being about the size of an overgrown horse, and it is as well, if your visiting list includes one, not to leave any breakables around where he can walk on them. So in all fairness I must take some of the blame for this affair, for not having carried the canoe up a tree in the first place and secured it there. So, forgiving the moose, I placed the injured craft up on a rack, intending to mend it, where, in this unusual position, it became an object of intense interest to the beaver. One night these enterprising animals, with the high intelligence for which they are celebrated, carefully felled a large tree across the long-suffering canoe, reducing it to the very best of matchwood.

None of these guests of mine stand in any need of gifts from me. With the exception of the beaver, who came with me, they fended for themselves before I arrived on the scene and if I were to suddenly disappear, though they might disperse, no one would be a whit the worse; though I like to think that some of them would miss me. But it makes me happy to put out treats for them, and to take note of the so very different way in which each one takes his daily portion from my hand; to observe his manner of approach, and his reactions afterwards. It is great fun in the morning (or at noon in my case) to wake up and find everything gone, and to know that small forest people—and sometimes big ones—have been busy whilst I slept, running back and forth with all they can possibly carry with them of my bounty. It pleases me immensely to hear some hungry worker who has been absent for hours on a working party, mumbling his satisfaction as he eats a well-earned meal of dry bread, or an apple, or steps into a dish of rice with both hands at about a mile a minute; and in Winter I view with the deepest satisfaction a hole in the snow beneath an old root, maybe, with a telltale ring of rime around its rim, revealing the home of some happy little beast who has a full belly and is fast asleep.

Every one of these so-busy dwellers in the Wild Lands presents intriguing possibilities, and has a life history well worth a little patience in the studying. Even those that live in the water, or on it, and are therefore more difficult to cultivate, have an interest that is easily discovered by a little investigation; all the way from the water beetles, that leave their natural element and climb on rocks to sun themselves, to the proud, white-throated loons, greatest and most accomplished of all the diving birds, who run races round and round the lake with the most inordinate splashing and other uproar, and play a kind of water-leapfrog, driving the beaver to distraction with their weird, half-human laughter. These royal birds, however, cannot walk, but are strong fliers and real artists in the water. When they take their young ones out for exercise—there are usually only one or two—the wee, jet black chicks sit upon their mother's back, getting a free ride while they look around in the most complacent manner at the scenery. Though they receive visitors, and I have seen as many as eight of them swimming before the cabin together, these stay only a short time, and each lake, unless a large one, provides a home for only two. And here they play and fish all Summer, winging South in early Autumn and returning every year for a period of their lives, which some say to be a hundred years. It seems probable that, like eagles and wild geese, they mate for life, and in support of this supposition is the fact that the same pair has lived on this lake every Summer since I came here, and I do not know how long before. These two know me very well, though the female is not so intimate with me as the male, who always visits near the cabin very punctually, soon after daylight every morning, and holds a conversation with me at a distance of a hundred feet or so, very noisy on his part, and quite unintelligible to me, and he hails me with a not unmusical fanfare of recognition when he sees me pass in the canoe. He is a splendid bird, and besides being highly ornamental he is very useful too, giving out a loud, unusual call should anything uncommon, or a stranger, appear upon the lake or in the timber near the shore.

Every one of these creatures has his proper function, and each, however apparently useless, serves well the purpose for which he was created. Even diminutive birds, negligible appearing denizens of these wide solitudes, have their own appointed place to fill. Seemingly quite superfluous in the vastness of the mighty scheme about them, yet as they hop happily in little groups among the fallen leaves, seeking the wherewithal to maintain their tiny lives, competent, wise, and bright-eyed and very much at home, who that watches them will question their right to be, or doubt but what they also do their part?

Animals quickly know a sanctuary when they find one. How, I cannot tell; something in the atmosphere of the place perhaps, or some kind of telepathic divination all wild creatures seem to be possessed of, may account for this; nor is this sixth faculty of sensing the presence or absence of danger confined to animals alone. While some need time in which to figure out the situation, others will respond almost immediately to my advances, depending on the disposition or intelligence of the individual. Take an instance of the latter case; the time is evening, on a day in Autumn, two years ago. I look out of my window and see a deer feeding in the glade upon a knoll beside the camp. I open the door without sound, unhurriedly; with quiet, easy movements I step out, smoothly, but without any suggestion of stealth. The deer tenses in every muscle, raises his head and stares at me—almost an unseeing stare, you would think. But a squirrel passes swiftly, and inaudibly because the leaves are wet, and with a sudden shift of his eyes (but not his ears) the deer acknowledges the slight, momentary flicker of the tiny beast's passage—he is watching all right; he sees very well indeed. He swings his eyes back into line with his ears, to me. I speak softly, soothingly. Now he flicks his tail—that is the sign; his mind is made up—either he will bound with high, rocking leaps out of sight, or he has decided to accept the situation and stay—which? I speak again, advance a little towards him, talking to him. Then, he relaxes; the stare becomes a gaze and, supreme gesture of confidence, he turns his back on me. He reaches down for some jack-pine shoots a squirrel has obligingly dropped there from the tree-tops, and nibbles at them, looking at me casually from time to time. He is satisfied. I have made another friend.

Seldom am I without one or another of my dependents, even though they are not always visible. The crash of a new-fallen tree, or a shrill outcry of adolescent beaver voices from the lake, may disturb the sleeping echoes. The door is thrown open and a load of mud and sticks comes in, borne in furry arms and intended as materials for the earthen lodge that stands inside my cabin; then a light pitter-patter across the floor, as a muskrat calls in for his nightly apple; comes the rattle of antlers among the willows—these sounds, familiar to me as are street noises to a town-dweller, tell me that I am not, after all, alone.

This region, like any other wilderness, has its population of predatory animals, and I must be for ever on the watch to safeguard my fellow-citizens from harm. Wolves, coyotes, bears, owls and mink and weasels are all potential and very active enemies; nocturnal creatures who can operate in the daytime with the same facility that they do at night, furtive, sly and ever-hungry, could slip silently in to deal out death in a moment of time, and be quickly gone. So I have not spent a night in bed in years, and during all the hours of darkness I travel back and forth through the velvet blackness of the sombre, whispering forest. And as I traverse these imponderable halls of Silence, there comes not a sound that is even faintly audible, but my ears will register it. For these are all the sounds there are to hear. Each has its meaning, which I must determine swiftly and with unerring accuracy; for on the acuteness of my senses and the precision of my findings, may depend the lives of those who look to me; for as I heed their danger signals, so do they mine.

So that my life has become something like that of a scout of ancient days of forest warfare, and even if asleep, any unusual sound from the surrounding woods, an unwonted commotion in the beaver house, or even the abrupt cessation of some familiar noise, brings instant wakefulness. Danger lies hidden in the lurking shadows, waiting for the day when the high-tuned senses of my retainers, or my less perfect ones shall be at fault; yet not without due warning can it ever strike. The wood-chuck who haunts my wood-pile, and who should be sleeping, whistles sharply, for no apparent reason, into the night; comes the discordant warning cry of a whiskey-jack, the sudden alarmed scurry and subsequent shrill defiance from a safe retreat of a squirrel—then, softly, the muffled hoot of an owl who, in his downy, sanctimonious robe of white, like the robber-priest of some false religion fattening on the community about him, broods rapaciously above them like an evil spirit—or, a breath of sound, a flicker that is quick as a flame, the sinuous, reptilian slither of a weasel, small but deadly, swift, lithe and ruthless—gangster and cut-throat par excellence of all the Wilderness. Either one I must destroy at once; there will be no second opportunity.

Later, perhaps, as I listen, the precise, dainty stepping of a deer ceases for a moment, to break into a series of startling leaps; a nearby moose, visible to me by the light of the moon, pauses suddenly in his browsing to catch some seemingly non-existent sound, or to sniff a warning from a vagrant current of air; from the lake the cry of a loon, pitched at an uncommon note, off-key a little, weird and alarming, strikes a jarring note of discord. And then, most portentous of all, shattering the night like a rifle shot, there crashes out the appalling detonation of a beaver's tail-slap on the water—and then falls silence, ominous and nerve-racking, surcharged with menace, as every living creature within earshot stops motionless in its tracks, crouched, or in an attitude of suddenly arrested motion, its senses keyed to an excruciating pitch of sensitivity, waiting for someone to make the first move. And then I see shifting, wavering like a disembodied spirit through the shadows, unsubstantial as a phantom, the ghoul of all the forest lands—a wolf!

And then, if the moon is right and I line my sights quickly enough, and above all, if my calculations are cool and accurate, the smashing report of my rifle will end the incident and save many a day of anxious uncertainty.

And all these things that may be seen and heard, and other things that may not be even heard, but are a kind of feeling, advise me more positively than the spoken word, are as clear to me as lines of print, telling me how it fares with my Little People, and the big ones too, reminding me, sleeping and waking, of my responsibilities towards all things both great and small that within, without, and all about, dwell here under my protection.

HENRY BESTON

Small Birds to the North 1942

HENRY BESTON (1888–1968) was born in Quincy, Massachusetts, the son of a physician. His mother was from France, and throughout his life Beston spoke French as well as English. After graduating from Harvard, he taught English at the University of Lyons, and returned to join the U.S. Navy during the First World War. In 1926, he built a dune cottage, the Fo'castle, on Cape Cod, and wrote his first book, the imperishable nature classic *The Outermost House* (1928), about a year on the Great Beach. He later moved to Maine with his wife, the writer Elizabeth Coatsworth. His other books include *Herbs and the Earth, American Memory,* and *Northern Farm* (1948). "Small Birds to the North" is excerpted from Beston's book about French Canada, *The St. Lawrence* (1942).

I

TO THE NORTH of the great current and the tides, in that region of the Laurentian wall which borders the river from Murray Bay to Tadoussac, a kind of secret country lies between the farming uplands and the stream. It is the brim of the great Laurentian chasm, the region where the terraces and slopes above plunge in a forest chaos of rock, in a greenery of wild and picturesque descents, down to the remote and solitary shore. Sometimes old wood roads manage an almost headlong course to a retired cove but such byways are for the most part overgrown and have become tangles of wild grass and upstart trees. It is a country to know on foot for there are everywhere old and mysterious paths going about their ways with an almost Red Indian naturalness and secrecy. The plunge is deep, and the glens tumble four and five hundred feet to the hidden tides. Some aspects are of a real wilderness savagery. Others romantic and sylvan—it is here that the hardwoods flourish, the oaks and maples sharing with the spruce the shelter from the north—and there is always a haunting sound of brooks, a fountain splashing of cascades falling over succeeding shelves of rock down to the final levels of the beach. In this country of the St. Lawrence to the north, these solitudes and glens enclose the kingdom of the smaller birds.

Who writes of birds must begin at once with saying whence he writes and I am setting down these lines in the pleasant village of Cap à l'Aigle, just to the east of Murray Bay. The village stands on a plateau above the glens, its cleared lands sweeping up behind it to a ridge against the sky beyond whose spruce is nothing—only the north. East and west along the river civilization is still one parish wide. Save for the dividing gash of the Saguenay with its power lines and isolated villages, all the back country is but the forest rolling in the cold wind over the mountains to the fog of Hudson Bay. Of the birds who live on this frontier of cleared land and the forest and of the farming country birds below, I shall write on another page. Too little known to students of bird life, the St. Lawrence has its own particular miracle of birds, a drama vast in scale yet secret in quality and closely related to the country of the glens. It is the northward passing of the river by the migrant warblers who nest on this shore and in the northern and far northern forests of the Hudsonian zone. Considered a family of birds, the wood warblers are distinctively American; they breed, most of them, in the coniferous forest, and all must cross the river to reach their other country towards the pole.

II

As the warblers move north, swept up together in successive waves of the migrational unrest, and forming, as it were, one dispersed army with its vanguard, its center, and its stragglers, species and individuals fall away by every mile. The Maryland yellowthroat will find the blue Cape Cod pond he so often comes to choose, the myrtle warbler his Connecticut glen, and the magnolia his lakeside farm in Maine. Meanwhile the invisible vanguard presses on, seeking the far north as faithfully as the compass needle. The species who are creatures of the evergreens, follow, I think, the evergreen forests of the east. Maine falls behind, and the skies above the mountains, and now is the St. Lawrence seen, and the other sky beyond, and the other and colder light which is the north.

The flights begin with the end of May, and continue till about the tenth of June, the birds arriving on these coasts when the new leaves are small. It is through an awakening world that the warblers pass, arriving every day of good weather from across the miles of river. June has come; in the high country there is still ice under trees growing densely together, but in the farming land below the maple syrup stands in its noble miscellany of bottles, and the dauntless rhubarb of every French-Canadian kitchen garden has been carefully enriched and hoed. Summer is near and the plough is busy, but the Laurentian sun has still something of the quality of spring. Now is the time to visit the lower woods. Not a trace of ice remains on the cold tranquillity of the St. Lawrence. The spring wind is light and coolly-warm, and in the cove opened among the rocks the tiny, flattened waves make scarce a sound. Only the deep-pitched and watery roar of a small cataract tells of the snow that once has been. Now, if you are patient and fortune is with you—for nature is in no showman's mood—you will see your birds. It may be a sound that you will hear first, some pretty note of summer practiced ahead of time in the solitude of the glens, it may be something seen—a fidgetiness and a poise of inquiry on a twig suddenly made to sway above a stream. For miles along the coast, the whole glen country is delicately alive with its facets of living color, seen, lost and seen again in a sunlight and shade delicately tinged with green. The birds are resting in the wood, and will presently be off towards the mountains and the north. Tomorrow you may have neither the smallest sound nor sign. The birds are crossing, I imagine, almost everywhere, some individuals and species preferring an island stepping stone; others taking boldly to the wider air. Some have come early, others will be late, some will nest in these very woods, others will be off at the unknown moment towards the Hudsonian immensities.

It is possible that here at Cap à l'Aigle local migrants follow northwards the beautiful valley of the Murray, that valley whose distant mountains are as blue as those in some nostalgic fairy tale. I offer no dogmatic list of the warblers who cross the St. Lawrence at this spot: lists are often a kind of folly. Be prepared for the Canada, the Black-and-White, the Cape May, the Myrtle, the Magnolia, the Black-throated Green, the Yellow, the Yellow Palm, and the Northern yellowthroat, this last an interesting subspecies of the more familiar Maryland. There are, of course, a number of others: such a migration is always a living cloud-drift of the customary, the possible, and the entirely inexplicable. Last summer, a hundred miles farther to the east and near the mouth of a tributary stream, I chanced to see the Tennessee but I have never seen him here. Wilson's, too, is a bird reported from shores nearer the Gulf. Whatever the year may bring, the interest and beauty of the glens remain. The region has its nesting birds as well as its passers-by. All through the earlier and warmer summers and all a pleasant day long—especially in the later afternoons—the glens can be full of a music you must go quietly down to hear. It is no choir of birds, no music box in the trees, but a music lovely, fugitive and capricious, an earth melodiousness of small and poignant phrases beginning in silence and in this silence ending. The small singer may be near, perhaps in the very arch of leaves above the path; he may be far away and higher up the hill, the song falling through this secrecy of space down to the opening and greater light beside the shore. Sometimes as I walk it is the song of the northern water thrush I hear, or the brisk, independent assertion of the yellow warbler, and often, very often, the "Trees, Trees, murmuring Trees" of the black-throated green.

It is not, however, the drowsy phrase of the black-throated green that I shall call to mind when I remember the glens of the St. Lawrence. The song I shall recall when I am far from the river is the song of the white-throated sparrow, that rustic arrangement in bird music of an opening call followed by three identical notes trilled as by a boy who can whistle with both a natural skill and a good ear. It is a pretty phrase, a kind of folk song of the woods. Indeed, it is because of its simplicity that it has been so loved, for though many things are admired, it is the simple thing which is loved of many. To us in New England the singer is the "Peabody bird" saying "Old Sam Peabody, Peabody, Peabody," but on the St. Lawrence he says "Beautiful Canada, Canada, Canada," or in French "Je t'ai vu Frédéric, Frédéric, Frédéric"—his English, to my mind, being better than his French. The white-throat is one of the good creatures who sing at night, and because of this the French of Canada call him le rossignol, the nightingale.

There are few adventures more characteristically and poignantly of this country than a walk in the glens when night is at hand and the bird is singing. There was a cataract in the glen country to which I used to walk in the early evening, coming to it across the fields and through the woods, discovering at last a huge and sudden amphitheater ringed with trees, and a vast plunging of water faced into the full and rising moon. It was the North America of the imagination of the eighteenth century, a place of the "noble savage" and the romantic grandeur of the earth. The thunder of the fall reverberated back from its encirclement of cliff and forest, seizing upon the spirit's awareness, and haunting and deserting the porches of the ears. It was there I was sure to hear the rossignol, the nightingale of the habitant, singing his folk-song of the river. Now I would hear him from the trees a little back from the fall, now from the very bush in the amphitheater, and now and then as an echo and an answer from the direction of the fields.

As the night deepened, and the beautiful, the orbed moon swam higher in the noble and eighteenth century heaven, the birds came to an end of their singing: one would wait for a last music and hear no more, the last, poor, small, foolish head asleep now under its wing. Only the cataract remained to thunder in the wood, tumbling down in its moon-pale wreaths and veils and roaring away out of space and one's bemused consciousness like some audible overflowing of the stream of earthly time.

III

The skies have cleared this morning after a down-pour of Laurentian rain which began in the very middle of the night, a small sigh of beginning rain abruptly turning into a pattering crepitation which deepened as suddenly into one immense and vehement roar. The first dawn was still gray but now the cloud mass is opening, and a bright midsummer day has the whole village in its keeping. On such a morning the farm country seems as mild and rustic as some small "pays" of the Île de France or Normandy. It is a French "cocorico!" which chanticleer here sounds from his pen—"Cocorico!" the boldest sound we ever hear, I think, of life self-justified and resolute, domestic yet cosmically undaunted. The village world has been quiet and at its breakfast, but now a wagon passes, scaring up a rats' nest of English sparrows from the puddles of the road, and past the window flies an iridescent tree swallow, a civil and pleasant bird and one of the first to return to this country in the spring.

In this advanced region of the north, plants must grow with a will once they are out of the ground, thrusting themselves, as it were, out of the furrow towards a sun who will not stay. The gardens grow fast, various plants taking on a new habit of growth, and towering up into stalks which are weedlike in their energy of life. It is now full midsummer on the river, the gardens are thriving, and in the fields by the road, as one goes through the village, a gay flowering of yellow buttercups, white daisies and purple vetch have made a Laurentian carpet of the grass. What of the birds of this open country between the spruce on the sky line and the hidden quiet of the glens? At first glance, the region does not seem a particularly rewarding field. Its birds are the birds of the higher but not extreme northeast and the birds you will see about a farm in northern Maine, you will—for the most part—see here. The same familiar kingbird crouches on these Canadian wires, the same pretty goldfinch perches on the seeding thistle and has therefrom his French name "le chardonneret," and the same black crows rise cawing from the fields and fly to cover before the darkening wind and rain. Only yesterday while far up the hillside of cleared land, a bobolink, la Goglu, went over the fence rails and down the slopes towards the farms. The northern birds are here, but to this one must add a note that such birds are present in noticeably smaller numbers than they are with us, and that various species familiar to New England are here infrequent or unknown. The bluebird is one of these. He is known; he has his French name—le rouge-gorge bleu—but he is a chance and lovely apparition on these roads.

I note, in particular, a definite lack of orchard birds. Apples grow here, and there is scarce an old farm without a few embattled trees doing their best— but it is not orchard country. I find myself wondering as to the robin we see. The bird is not what he is with us. Across the frontier, the robin is a household bird, a builder on piazzas and in trees near the house, and his song is a part of the life of early morning and the lengthening peace of the midsummer afternoon. In this region, I do not see robins near the houses, and I seldom hear their song. Indeed, there are times when there seem no robins at all. (It has been said that the bird is noticeably less of a household creature in the northern part of his range.) Perhaps it is a matter of two different strains. A number of ornithologists have long suspected that there are two robins in the northeast, or to be more definite, two habitat groups, one a northern bird of the north forest and the farm frontier—such a bird as must have been known to the Indians, and a second bird, more southern in its range—which has adapted itself to the white man's way of life. According to this theory, it is the Canadian robin we see in our New England winters, the bird having come down to us from the Canadian forest, whilst the bird we see in summer, the household retainer and plump piazza-builder, is his southern kinsman come north to raise a family. Is it, then, the northern bird one sees on the Côte Nord a hundred and fifty and two hundred miles down the river from the Saguenay? The bird is there, and in wilderness country. And is it the Canadian robin some have seen in Maine, in the later depth of winter, living in small flocks in the coastal woods? Be the local bird what it is, I miss the morning song, the comic stride across the shadows under the elms, and the cocked head listening for the worm.

The hummingbird—le colibir—is entirely at home, visiting these Laurentian gardens with entire familiarity. An intrepid seafarer, he goes even farther, and crossing the Gulf of St. Lawrence, reaches the remote fishing villages of Newfoundland.

One land bird is the very spirit of the river. All up and down the St. Lawrence from Montreal to the gulf, swallows haunt the borders of the stream. As the valley darkens, and the summer sun vanishes in the clouds of the northwest, the birds come from all their cliffs and habitations, filling the evening light with their darting and skimming wings. They have a great liking for these old half-deserted wharves, perhaps because the loading of pulpwood attracts or releases insect life, and about them they gather in their twilight eagerness and haste, adding their living ecstasy to the eternal onrush of the darkening tides. Such birds are cliff swallows for the most part, and their colonies nest in the glacial fans of clay and gravel which occur along the stream.

To compensate for this lesser number of birds and birds by species, certain birds of the evergreen forest may be seen about the farms. There are always stands of native spruce about the grounds of older dwellings (kept there to act as barriers against the wind and snow) and it is to such trees that the kinglet comes, the tiny roitelet whom Dominion poets both French and English have celebrated as a bold Canadian. Both the ruby-crowned and the golden-crowned are residents, the first being locally the most familiar, and both nest in the farm spruces of the agricultural plateau. (I cannot recall ever having encountered the birds in the wilder country of the upland ridge.) There was a certain pleasant morning long ago, a part of a remembered autumn on the river, when I went walking in a wood of spruce to the south of the coastal road, losing myself half a dozen times on a path which had ceased to be a path, and coming suddenly to a glade in the wood beside a wilderness ravine. On one side, the spruce shone in the full silence and the sun, to the other lay the descent and a chilliness of shade. At the far end of the sunlit wall, there was a picture of bird life such as I had never hoped to see. One tree was astir with kinglets; the tiny, lovely creatures climbing in and out of the spruce branchlets with an incessant and busy eagerness. Had the pretty ornaments on some great, old-fashioned Christmas tree suddenly become alive, and darted about among the candles, the effect could not have been more surprising, so similar was the scale of the flocklet and the sunlit branch thrust from its inner core of shade into the glisten of the sun. There was no singing, but the conversation of small "ksis" or "tsips" was like the chatter of a gathering in a room, a general social sound which had its own being apart from individual noise. Both species were at hand, in this instance the golden-crowned predominating. Friends tell me that this species sometimes winters in sheltered country near Quebec.

It was a charming sight to see such a stir of little hardy birds, and I had plenty of time to watch them on the tree. But, alas, somehow or other they presently became aware of me, and with a concerted rush were off into some hideaway of the deeper glens, leaving their Christmas tree only a spruce by the St. Lawrence standing with others in a wood.

IV

The country which stands above, hiding its distance behind the eternal spruce, is a kind of no man's land as it advances towards the farm. One ought to see and hear various small birds in that upland wood, but I have seen little and heard less. It is a various region, now wild and picturesque and threaded by streams which have each their nameless cataract, now little more than a tract of bush growing where the pulp exploitation has passed like a corrupt storm. I am told that old clearings are woodpecker regions, and that the red-breasted grosbeak—le gros-bec à poitrine rose—is a familiar of the bush country a little farther back into the north. To the casual wanderer, the most familiar of its birds is the ruffed grouse, la gelinotte de Canada. Here in the north the bird one sees appears to represent a geographical race, for the plumage is far more gray than anything I have ever seen over the border. So wild is the back country that the bird has maintained itself well in spite of heavy gunning, and there is scarce a pilgrimage in the spruce without a sudden crash of wings exploding in one's ears, and a feathery, diminuendo rush across the fragrant green and the region sense of nonhuman loneliness.

So much for the coast and the transitional Canadian life-zone of which it is a part: what of the Hudsonian zone which lies behind? Beyond the "height of land," the vast subarctic wilderness of mountain and lonely forest has its own population. It is there you will see the Canada jay as a common sight, and hear at night the hunting owls. In the legends of the bush it is always the great horned owl who is the genius and demon of the forest, falling through the dusk as noiselessly as a snowflake to clutch the fur hat of a returning lumber-jack, and give poor Jean Baptiste the fright of his life. What yells have been heard through a darkening wood! I doubt if there is much relation—during summer—between the two life-zones, though Hudsonian types occasionally are to be seen on the Saguenay and about the Lac St. Jean. (Only a year or two ago a young polar bear wandering far out of his range and away from the sea was shot in the St. Jean country.) Returning to birds, the Laurentian National Park likewise has its northerners, the Canada jay being one of the commonest sights about its camps. A northerner surely, for the bird—to quote Mr. Taverner—has been known to set about incubating its eggs at a temperature thirty below zero Fahrenheit.

It is out of this northern forest, out of these miles of silence and advancing cold that the little, hardy winter birds come south to the open country and the river. The returning warblers will pass almost unseen, trailing a paler sun to warmer earth and longer days: even the snow buntings will press on, blowing like autumn leaves over the great shining slopes to their favorite winter country on the sunlit side of "Chalore" bay. The various grosbeaks, too, will pass and perhaps the strange crossbills whom the habitant believes to be prophets of some black intensity of cold. More and more snow, more and more sleigh bells and red mufflers, and the tiny red poll will be seen, perched on some branch out-thrust from a drift and tearing at the frozen seed. And some farmer walking by the shore will see a hunched, white shape keeping watch on the broken, grinding, churching mass of empty ice, the white owl come south in winter through the arctic air and the icicle brightness of the sun.

V

Far across the steely miles of the river, an earth land and a cloud land of darkened blue, the south shore of the widening estuary stands in a life-zone of quite another kind. From Ontario to the transitional wilderness beyond the Saguenay the north of the river is, as I have said, a part of the Canadian zone; to the south the coast is transitional austral bounded in its own back country by the reappearing Canadian zone of the high forests of New Brunswick and New England. It is geographically a northeastern province, but the influence of the west, of the lakes and the prairies, is concealed in the milder scene, the earth tensions and currents of the great central valley flowing eastward along these southern reaches towards the sea. Now and then, as if to point the moral, birds of the Gulf coast, adventuring north along the Mississippi, turn seaward and find themselves in the St. Lawrence east of Montreal. (An ibis from Louisiana was a recent visitor to the southern marshes of the Lac St. Pierre.) Quite apart from this western and continental influence, the river is in itself a most formidable biological barrier between southern and northern kingdoms, halting all kinds of plants and creatures at each shore. So be not deceived by appearances and similarities; until the Canadian zone leaps the river at the approaches to Gaspé, the whole south region is another world.

It is the south shore, and here are the birds one has been missing just across the river. Here they are, the robins and the brown thrashers, as one might see them on the Merrimac or the Piscataqua. The country, moreover, has lost its northern and mountain shadow, and miles of the actual bank have become as earthy and rural as any little slope overhanging a small New England stream. It is with a musing question that from such a place one's eye escapes to the huge St. Lawrence. In this strange rusticity there is water everywhere, brooks and rills seeping out of the earth bank towards the blue immensity below. The naturalist will now find himself again in shore-bird country, for these flats and tidal meadows have been prepared for those searching beaks and hurrying swift feet. (The hostile, tumbled rocks of the northern coves are not for such wanderers.) Walking through the meadows, I often scare up a flight of greater yellowlegs—le grand chevalier à pieds jaunes—and the wind brings me the sweet tremolo whistle of their call as they fall off into the dusk. Perhaps the most familiar of the shore-bird tribe is the spotted sandpiper—la maubêche tachetée. I find the birds on the open beach; I come upon them in the field country above. Only the other day, I remember, I startled a bird in the fields above, and instead of taking to its wings, it scurried into the shelter of the bush quite like a sort of marine bobwhite. It is a pretty creature, and the line of white through its eye is unusually clear.

I was once on this shore in such a country as I have described, and near a pretty spring overflowing from its pool below the bank. There was a village and a road somewhere above, but the beach was unvisited and still, no distant voice or footfall troubling its solitariness or the mild south wind. Behind me the earth bank was overgrown with hardwood bush in full midsummer leaf, and as it followed the coast it wavered and turned like an old city wall, making its little regions invisible one from the other: only the great river moving direct and free into the east. I remember that it was early in the morning, somewhere between six and seven o'clock, and the sun was in the sky south of the wall. Far across, the Laurentians faced the morning, so far away that houses and villages were lost in the mountain slopes, the heights returning from an association with man back to the elemental earth and their stupendous continents of mist. The place had so lovely a mood of earth and was so pleasant and withdrawn that I lingered awhile beside the spring. Becoming thus myself a part of the quiet and the mood, I presently saw that the small birds of the region had long ago discovered the overflowing rill. A sparrow had flown away as I approached, and presently to the water came a male chewink who fluttered in out of nowhere, drank, and hid again. Much later came a pair of yellow warblers who monopolized the pool with entire fearlessness, hopping about and fluttering, to be gone, too, in their time.

It was a pleasant experience thus to see small birds at their own spring and in their own world, to see the characteristic gestures and gaits, the suspicions and alerts, and the completely natural, the pretty attitudes. I kept at some distance from the scene, not wishing to intrude myself within the borders of its awareness, and was glad to see how untroubled the visitors bent their small heads to the living water. When the yellow warblers had flown, I went nearer, and saw how the marge of the pool was all overprinted with a cross-hatching of many tiny feet. When I returned later in the morning, the beach was still empty and the sun had risen above the bank. There were no birds at the pool, but as I watched I heard stirrings above me in the leaves, and from beyond, some small and half-remembered song.

FLORENCE PAGE JAQUES

Wild Swans in April 1947

FLORENCE PAGE JAQUES (1890–1972) was born in Decatur, Illinois, educated at Millikin University, and in 1927 married wildlife artist Francis Lee Jaques. She wrote exuberantly and knowledgeably about nature and travel in the north, in books illustrated by her husband: *Canoe Country* (1938), *The Geese Fly High* (1939), *Birds Across the Sky* (1939), *Snowshoe Country* (awarded the John Burroughs Medal in 1946), and *Canadian Spring* (1947)—an account of a visit she and her husband made to the Delta Waterfowl Research Station, in Manitoba—from which this excerpt is taken Her tribute to her husband, *Francis Lee Jaques: Artist of the Wilderness World,* appeared a year after her death in New York.

WE PASSED PETER on the path to the inlet. "Spring is really here," he said. "The yellow-headed blackbirds came in this morning."

"There they are now," Al exclaimed. "Don't they look like a flock of dandelions!" Up from the canes rose scores of the birds, their orange-gold heads and breasts such a brilliant contrast to their black plumage that they made the marsh grass almost colorless.

My spirits were as light as flying dandelions, too, for this first morning was April at her fairest, and we were to go out in a canoe, which I prefer to any means of travel in this world or above it.

Out into the sharp light of the morning we slipped through the ripples of Cadham Bay, and I was hard put to be the quiet luggage (which sounds better than baggage) in the center of the canoe. Once more afloat, on blue water with golden cane around us and ducks flying in the wind—that is all we need for complete happiness.

But though the marsh looked like a haven of peace, it soon began to sound like a rehearsal for a witches' Sabbath. Wild yells that made me jump and a weird hilarity mixed with wails and howls were the grebes, Al said. Clucks, gulps, and deep *pump-a-chunks* came from bitterns, or thunder-pumps, as they are sometimes called. The coots gave such an assortment of croaks, squawks, and cries that I never came to the end of them; blackbirds, besides a musical *o-kee-lee,* produced rusty wheezes; rails were railing and rat-tling. These hidden birds were as mad with spring as March hares are sup-posed to be.

In fact, the whole nineteen miles of marsh was one delirious turmoil; the April sun had gone to everyone's head. All around us the wildfowl were in an ecstasy of motion. I have always loved them for their vitality, but now in the midst of the courtship season their fervor was heightened to intoxication.

The place was filled with the gayest carnival spirit. These birds were alert, but not with fear or precaution as they are in the hunting season. On the wa-ter the drakes, in gorgeous nuptial plumage, performed their courtship antics and challenged their rivals. And the air was full of courting parties, flying in the wind. Al's canvasbacks streaked by like rust-tipped arrows, mallard pairs flushed from the reeds and stubby scaups floated off before us. I did not know where to look first.

"See those pintails?" Lee exclaimed. "Did you see him fly in front of her, just to display his wing pattern?" But I had my eye on shovelers courting in the water, lifting their peculiar bills and raising and lowering their heads. They courted in a placid way; they did not seem as excitable as most of the ducks.

"A pair of redheads getting up!" Al said. "Watch this—he'll try to catch her tail feathers. Canvasbacks do this too. There—did you see him?" No, I didn't but at least Lee hadn't either.

"Canvasbacks near the point," Lee muttered. "There's the performance Al wrote up—" As I turned, they took to the air in a furious pursuit flight, the female in front, half a dozen males close after her. However she twisted and wheeled, they were just behind. Down she went again and without the least slackening of speed, dove under the water, the drakes still following.

When she came up she began to preen and the drakes gave her a short re-spite. Then I saw one throw back his head till its top touched his back, and snap it forward. This seemed to start the others off. They stretched their necks high, threw back their heads, and their eyes brightened to ruby. One took the sneak position with his head and neck flat on the water, threatening a rival. We could just hear the low courting notes.

In a sheltered nook the small blue-winged teal were having a reception, all bowing together like little diplomats. Occasionally they took a swift erratic flight together and then landed to resume their bowing. Near by, a pair of gadwall circled side by side, touching bills now and then, in a contented blissful state. I felt slightly disillusioned, however, when they went ashore and the female was forced to defend herself against the advances of two bachelors, while her male, quite oblivious, went on quacking in low and tender tones.

Small buffleheads appeared, and their black and white plumage was very striking. The male's head was iridescent black with a large and flashy triangle of white; it was easy to see, as he puffed it out to twice its size, why his name is a corruption of buffalo-headed.

Though they looked heavy for their small size they rose swiftly and easily from the water. Sometimes they came up from under the surface of the bay, shooting up into the air at full speed. During their courtship antics, the males flew up and then lit standing, to make a long glide as if they were sliding on ice, before they splashed into the water. Then they swam about among the hens, raising their bills, shaking out their crests, and generally showing off like small boys.

"Teal coming in," Lee greeted his small favorites, just as Al mentioned that mergansers were out in front, with the drakes all jockeying for position. I saw neither—I was watching redheads.

The hen redhead seemed to be an aggressive and modern damsel. She was displaying in much the same way that drakes do, jerking her head up and down until a male returned the gesture. She was fickle in her attentions, biting gently at one or another of her swains, teasing them, and generally acting in a most reprehensible manner, though Al said that after mating she settles down into the demure behavior that the other female ducks assume.

The flock suddenly rose into the air. "Oh!" I cried loudly, "I saw him! That redhead—he caught her tail-feathers!"

"Good for you," said Al. "Lots of people never do see that trick—it happens so quickly."

Leaving the wide waters of the bay we pushed through narrow channels out into the marsh. A bittern was making the queer noise which is called stake driving, and then we caught sight of him, standing on bent cattails. Except for his grass-green legs he looked exactly like a broken stick, and I wondered why he didn't choose to resemble a post as long as he could make a sound like driving one.

But he was not immobile. He began to creep forward, in slow motion, putting down his feet very carefully, as if he were in a spy story. When he saw us he felt all was discovered, and made a clumsy escape into the air, flying off with a croak, his feet dangling and his wings beating in a frustrated fashion. A teal came along behind him, shadowing him.

"The ducks are three weeks early at least. I'm sorry you missed the main migration flight," Al said regretfully. "But it was not as spectacular as usual. This is a bad duck year."

Heavens, I thought, what would a good duck year be like? This was dizzy enough for me.

Somewhere in front of us we heard a babble of high-pitched cries, half-trumpeted, half-yelled. Ahead of us in the marsh were wild swans! We heard the spatter of their feet along the surface of the lake; and then three whistling swans, their snowy wings beating slowly, rose above the reeds and vanished to the north.

"Hear that low moan?" Al asked us. "That means more of them are about to fly. They moan like that a minute or thirty seconds before they take off."

We came out of the channel into open water and saw a great flock of floating birds, as dazzling white as if they had been carved from snowdrifts. They glided along by the sunlit canes, holding their slender necks straight or at a slight angle, not curved as the domesticated mute swans do.

They looked slim and graceful, although they rank among the largest of our birds and may weigh up to twenty pounds. Some of them were tipping up to feed, heads down and tails up, which seemed an ungainly attitude for birds of such dignity. Ringnecks were swimming about with them, looking very childish, and snatching at the food their great companions brought up from the depths.

"What are the swans feeding on?" Lee asked.

"Sago pondweed," Al said. "They gouge great holes in the under-water beds and pull up tons—really tons—of the plant. Sago is also a favorite food of the ducks, and all my life I've heard hunters complain that swans should be killed off so there would be more food for ducks. But we've found that the beds the swans do not touch may thrive for a few years, and then they disappear or are crowded out by some less desirable plant—milfoil, for instance—while the finest, healthiest, most thriving beds of sago are where the swans feed. We've come to believe that the annual working over the sago beds get each year from the swans is a sort of cultivation and is the reason for their good condition."

Five of the snowy birds lifted their great wings and ran along the water against the wind before rising into the air. In flight their necks stretched out for more than half their total length, so that the long white triangular wings looked curiously far back. More and more flew over us, and the lifting shimmering birds made me feel as if I were afloat in the wind too; it was hardly a vicarious experience.

Now another group came in from the lake and alighted without the slightest splash, as if they were made of thistledown. The whole flock kept up a constant discussion, murmuring, giving laughterlike hoots and soft calls, or loud single notes in various keys.

Closer to us, a group of swans rose from the water, and their wings sounded like great blankets flapping in the wind. Four came past in a courtship flight, and one made a sudden angry dive at another, who escaped by a quick sideslip which was remarkable in so big a bird.

Al said afterwards that he had seen this mentioned only once in descriptions of the bird, when Seton wrote, in *The Arctic Prairies,* "Flocks of swans flew overhead. . . . 12 were the most in one flock. In this large flock I saw a quarrel. No. 2 turned back and struck No. 3, his long neck bent and curled like a snake. Both dropped several feet, then 3, 4, and 5 left that flock. I suspect they were of another family."

I never saw a swan angry except on this single occasion, but Al said he had seen swans "haul off and give each other real honest-to-goodness knockout blows." He thought the two swans they had found with broken wings were injured in the fights the birds have during courtship, for if they had been shot in the fall hunting season they could not have wintered over, and there is not much chance of hunters wounding them in spring.

I had read an account of a fight between Canada geese in the courtship season, when two males buffeted each other for half an hour or more with their powerful wings, making each other reel under the lashing blows; finally the victor caught his enemy's head in his bill and shook it so ferociously that the victim fled in confused dismay when at last he managed to escape. But to have the swans' serenity lost in such fisticuffs was more entertaining, somehow.

These whistling swans are now increasing in America, but slowly, since they do not breed until their third year. The birds mate for life and seem to have a strong marital devotion. In the research station pond, for instance, there was a wing-clipped female; and her mate, though free, did not go north with the rest of the flock, but stayed all season in the near-by bay.

"We won't go in there and put the swans up," Al said. "I'm afraid if they all fly they might take off for the Arctic. They're due to leave any day now." We crossed the bay and entered the wide curve of a creek.

Bulrushes and cattails were repeated, in wavering zigzags, in the clear water, and pairs of redheads flushed from the reeds or swam before us. The redhead was a duck I had rarely seen, but I had no trouble in distinguishing it from the canvasback it is supposed to resemble, for its crimson head is round and innocent looking, not the sharp sagacious profile of the canvasback.

This creek was a favorite haunt of the redheads. It was to be the favorite haunt of the Jaques too; of the whole marsh we came to love it best. But at the time we were distracted from its beauty by the coots.

Coots always seem like half-witted Pierrots to me, with chalk-white masks plastered to their silly black heads. But they outdid themselves this morning, splattering before the canoe on their big clownlike feet, their faces rigid with a comic dismay, falling down, picking themselves up and falling down again as they tried to escape us by running among the broken cattails.

We had our lunch here. The creek was a pale gold place; the tall fluffed tops of the phragmites swayed above us, and geometry problems done in gilt bulrushes were all around us. Faint waves gurgled and plopped through the stems that walled us in. We could hear the high voices of the swans and little gusts of air brought a chill April sweetness. Although it was the middle of the day, the duck courting parties still dipped above us, with none of the wariness of other seasons.

After lunch we took our way to Windy Landing, four or five miles east of the research station. As we went along Al was telling us of the many people who had loved this marsh, and we were excited to hear that Lord Grey, who had shown us English birds, once visited here. He, and King George (then the Duke of York) had stayed at the lodge. We asked about Flee Island, which our map had shown to be south of the marsh, and Al said that Sitting Bull had retreated there when his warriors were finally defeated, after Custer's last stand.

Peter met us at the Landing with the car, and we left the canoe on the bank. A rough road led us through the marsh to the ridge where the Manitoba maples (we know them as box elders), twisted and bent from the lake winds, and deeply rosy with their tasselled flowers, made decorative arches above the road. They looked almost like autumn trees except for their extreme fragility. Enormous silver pussy willows prowled up and down willow stems and spangles of orange catkins danced before our eyes.

On the way back we saw many groundhogs; one black one had climbed into a treetop, like a porcupine. Snowshoe rabbits were on the ridge, and jack rabbits in the marsh. And there was a maddeningly self-confident skunk who wandered leisurely down the road ahead of us.

He might be the same one, Pete said, who had haunted the road last fall. An Englishman, garbed in tweeds and a grouse cap pulled down front and back, was driving furiously down the road one day, accompanied by his handsome and taciturn Indian guide, when this skunk appeared in his path. It was too late to stop, so on the driver sped. "My God, Jim," he cried to the Indian, "did that skunk hit us?" "No, Mr. Howell," said the guide; "he didn't lead you enough."

We stopped the car at a curve and walked over to Lake Manitoba to see if the geese were still there. The mid afternoon was warm and a queer light pervaded it. All day there had been smoke in the air from the burning stubble fields (why can't Canada learn from our mistakes and not burn the precious substance of her soil, I wailed to myself) but that wouldn't account wholly for this peculiar atmosphere. "I know," said Pete, "the radio last night told about tremendous dust storms in Alberta; they are just getting to us."

Coming out from the dark shadowed ridge through dense and broken reeds to the shore, we saw swans floating on water of forget-me-not blue. The ice floes had vanished; instead a hundred or more swans made snowy rafts against the blue mist. Blue mist so pervasive that you could not tell where the lake ended and the sky began, so that the birds might have been swimming in the sky or flying under water.

For some atmospheric reason the proud wild things looked gigantic as they drifted along, their slim necks erect, their small heads with the ebony bills very regal; and their faint reflections might have been white clouds floating low in the sky. It seemed the vision of some mystic; it had an ethereal, another-world look, all the more so because it was early afternoon.

One swan drank from the lake, with his neck curled into a circlet. Five or six, one with a darker head, came floating past in a row, each swimming dreamily with one foot, their wake a taut silver line behind them. They cried out continually in high single notes, bittersweet.

I wondered if these high clear notes had been the source of the ancient swan song legend. But they were far from a lament—they bore out, rather, Socrates' noble words before he drank the cup of hemlock: "Men, through their own fear of death, belie the swans too, and say that they, lamenting their death, sing their last song through grief, and they do not consider that no bird sings when it is hungry or cold or is afflicted with any other pain, not even the nightingale, or swallow, or the hoopoes, which they say sing lamenting through grief. But neither do these birds appear to me to sing through sorrow, nor yet do swans; but in my opinion, belonging to Apollo, they are prophetic, and fore-seeing the blessings of Hades, they sing and rejoice on that day more excellently than at any preceding time. But I too consider myself to be a fellow-servant of the swans and sacred to the same god, and that I have received the power of divination from our common master no less than they, and that I do not depart from this life with less spirits than they."

There were other birds about that afternoon. A line of red-breasted mergansers flew swiftly down the lake, very white and black. A loon came in, sailing down until it hit the surface with its feet still trailing behind it as if it were in a foggy quandary. Down the shore some Canada geese, in shallows of peacock blue, were having a hilarious time turning backward somersaults. They really were. Heads down, heels (if geese have heels) over, they had forgotten their dignified demeanor and were romping like a gang of schoolboys.

I had always thought that Canada geese were almost too serious-minded, they had such a reputation for wariness and sagacity to maintain. It was a joy to see them frolicking about. We watched them for a long time.

But when I think of that afternoon it is always the floating dream-like quality that I remember.

Voluble Singer of the Tree-Tops 1954

LOUISE DE KIRILINE LAWRENCE was born in Sweden in 1894; her father, Sixten Flach, was a naturalist who helped create the Karlso Islands wildlife sanctuary. In 1918, as a Red Cross nurse in Denmark, she married Gleb Kirilin, a Russian soldier who disappeared in 1924. Louise emigrated to Canada in 1927 and became the nurse for the Dionne quintuplets. In 1935, she retired to a one-room cabin on the banks of the Mattawa River in northern Ontario, married Len Lawrence, and began the intensive study of birds and bird behavior that occupied the rest of her life. She has described thirteen species and banded 25,000 individual birds. Her first book, *The Loghouse Nest*, appeared in 1945, and since then she has written seven others, including *The Lovely and the Wild* (1969), which won the John Burroughs Medal for distinguished writing in natural history, and numerous articles: "Voluble Singer of the Treetops" appeared in *Audubon* magazine in May 1954, and is included in *To Whom the Wilderness Speaks* (1980). She died in North Bay, Ontario, in 1993.

ॐ • ॐ

ONE OF MY favorites among birds is the red-eyed vireo. I know him well and he appeals to me particularly because in looks and comportment he is such a smooth and elegant bird. Slow motion is his specialty, but sometimes he is brimming with nervous energy and moves faster than an arrow in a streamlined fashion all his own. I do not think that the epithet "sluggish," so often used about him, fits him particularly well. It seems to me that we shall need to find another and a better word, one that contains the elements of sobriety and fluidity.

About his singing, terms have been used that are not altogether complimentary—monotonous, repetitious, preacher-like—and I was always inclined to question the aptness of these descriptions. Was he as tireless as his reputation would have him? When in the day did he start singing, when did he stop? Was there any relation between his manner of singing and his character which, if known, would dispel the impression of what might seem monotonous and repetitious? Were his moods, needs, and temperament reflected in the nuances of tone, in the speed and the manner of the delivery of his songs? What I hitherto knew of the red-eyed vireo's singing gave only part of the answer to these questions.

When the call came from the British ornithologist, Noble Rollin, to make an all-day study of some special bird activity, I thought this was a fine opportunity to devote to the red-eye. Everything fitted in very well, too, because the day I was able to do the survey was May 27, 1952, a few days after Male "A" had taken up territory in my study area. At this time my bird was still without a mate and there would, presumably, be few claims upon his attention other than singing and feeding.

Pre-dawn, the most enchanting and mysterious moment in the 24 hours, reigned when I came out at 3:00 A.M. A soft, misty light prevailed, the delicate luminosity of the night, not enough to see but enough to surmise the outlines of the trees and the opening in the woods through which a trail led. A whip-poorwill called at close quarters, a loud song, passionate of tempo, for he was in the midst of his love-making. I counted 37 *whip-poor-wills;* then silence. Then he began again.

I walked into the vireo territory, armed with notebook and flashlight and wearing a warm sweater. It was chilly, the temperature was only 43° F, and the wind light from the west. A faint streak of dawn appeared at the eastern horizon, stealing the light from the stars.

Across my path, two veeries began calling, soft interrogative notes that never waited for an answer. Then, muted like a heavenly whisper, the thrushes began to sing. Penetrating the dusk and hanging deliciously upon the air, these whisperings seemed unearthly, but they represented the most potent reality of these birds' lives. For this was the time when competition between the males was strong, when pairing took place and nesting locations were chosen, when the blood within them ran fast and their sensations were acute.

A purple finch flew over, *tuck*ed, and gave a burst of song sweeter than honey. His season was a little ahead of the veeries', beyond the culmination of passions, and his song, therefore, was like an afterthought, a reminiscence of what had stirred in him before the nest-building and the laying of the first eggs.

As the light increased, the singing of the veeries became louder and intermingled with the weirdest discordant notes and exclamations, suggesting an excitement which intensified with the approach of the day. Startling and strange was this conversation between the thrushes, as it emanated explosively from the depths of the underbrush close to the path where I stood, now here, now over there. Then, all of a sudden, the swish of rapid flight low through the bushes from one place to another. Since their beginning, these rituals and displays, these unanswered and unanswerable queries from one tawny thrush to the other, evolved into the charming game I just now witnessed.

But no vireo was yet awake.

Beyond the valley of the spring, the rose-breasted grosbeak began to sing, songs so deliciously lyrical that the bird itself seemed loath to end such a fine performance and took to its wings, the better to enact an accomplished finale. In the top of a green birch, the robin caught the theme of the grosbeak's utterance, but geared it down to a song modulated to reach the ear of a mate sitting quietly on well-incubated eggs. For at this moment, the robin's song was not one of territorial announcement or self-assertion but symbolized the bond between two closely attached creatures.

Light came at 4:00 A.M. I could see to write without the flashlight. During the next 22 minutes, the number of birds that had testified their awakening rose to 20. A pair of yellow-bellied sapsuckers breakfasted on the sap of a white birch before resuming work on their nest-hole. A crow flew over, welcomed by no one, but busy on its own nest and eggs. A porcupine, climbing an aspen for a feed of green bark, sounded to me like a black bear, and a great blue heron flew over my head and croaked so loudly that, weak-kneed, I nearly sat down on the spot.

By this time, had I not known that my vireo was somewhere on this piece of land whereupon I stood, I would have despaired of his intention ever to sing again. But then, surprisingly (because I had waited so long) exactly nine minutes before sunrise, the red-eyed vireo serenely began dropping phrase upon phrase of song into the confusion of all the other bird voices. With such casual dreaminess did this long-awaited awakening happen that it required some seconds to penetrate into my consciousness, and forced me to start counting his inaugural sets of two or three notes at 4:22 A.M.

I found him high in the crown of a trembling aspen. There he wandered about, hopping from twig to twig, looking around, up and down, from side to side. His bill opened and shut, his throat bubbled, and his crest rose lightly and fell with the rhythm of his melody. He sang, phrase following upon phrase, with just enough interval to mark a disconnection between them. He sang with an aloof intensity and confluence that seemed to divorce his performance totally from any special objectives and reasons. This bird sang simply because self-expression in song was as much a part of his being as his red eye.

In the next 100 minutes, when the birds filled the woods with the greatest volume of music, our vireo achieved all his vocal records of the day. Thus, from 5:00 to 6:00 A.M., he sang the greatest number of songs in any hour— 2,155 phrases. From 4:22 A.M., just as he began singing, to 5:00 A.M., he attained his highest speed of delivery, an average of nearly 44 songs per minute; from 6:05 to 6:10 A.M., he sang the most songs in any five-minute period of the day, an average of 70 songs per minute.

Yet, breathless would not properly describe the performance of this bird. He continued to sing for the next three hours with a perfectly calm and casual continuance that at the end amassed him a total of 6,063 songs, delivered at a speed of 40 songs per minute. During this time, he allowed himself six pauses from one to six minutes each, which he divided equally among the three hours. While he sang, he wandered leisurely from one part of his territory, an area less than three acres, to the other, selecting his way through the foliated crowns of the tallest aspens and birches. Had his trail not been so clearly marked by song, it would have been a problem to follow this bird, which moved at such heights and blended so well with his surroundings. Although my vireo often fed while he sang, and sang with his mouth full, more concentrated feeding called for silence, and the important business of preening claimed all his attention. Once a trespassing vireo, a stranger, interrupted him. Abruptly he stopped singing and, like an arrow released from a taut bow, he shot down from his tall perch directly in pursuit of the intruder. With that the incident closed. With his only red-eyed neighbor settled on an adjacent territory to the north, my vireo had no altercations. On one occasion during the afternoon, the two happened to come close to their common border at the same time; but from this nothing more serious resulted than that the birds for about a quarter of an hour indulged in competitive singing.

A little before 9:00 in the morning, the vireo stopped singing. Up to this time he had spent almost four out of four and a half hours singing continuously.

This was a remarkable record as, apart from the need of advertising himself and his territory, nothing had occurred to call forth extraordinary vocal efforts on his part. Red-eyed vireos do not always sing as persistently as this bird did, especially during the first days after arrival from the south, when leisurely feeding is often the keynote of existence to many of them. Nor do all individuals possess the same capacity for vocal expression. I have known at least one other red-eyed vireo whose total number of songs in a day, even at the most exciting period, probably never reached four figures. (As to the pursuit of the strange vireo, I surmised that this was a passing female, because the male *stopped singing* and dashed off, chasing it, instead of challenging it by voice and gesture. That nothing came of it only suggests that, for the female, the moment was not auspicious.) The next half-hour my bird spent feeding and preening. He descended from the heights of the tree crowns to the middle strata of the woods, where, one may presume, he found more privacy in the secluded leafy niches. Then, once again, he resumed singing. While he still attained a speed of 38 songs when he sang, his average from 9:00 to 10:00 A.M. was only six songs per minute for the whole hour. This proved to be an interesting fact, because regardless of his hourly averages, his speed of singing consistently and gradually declined throughout the day—in other words, he sang more and more slowly as the day advanced.

After his hour of rest, the vireo achieved a forenoon peak of singing that lacked only 13 songs in reaching as high a total as that obtained from 5:00 to 6:00 A.M. He worked up to this peak in the hour before noon, but would, I think have reached it earlier had he not wandered into a grove of trees heavily infested with the forest tent caterpillar. Here he distracted himself with a great deal of flycatching on the wing. If his objective was the eating of the tachinia flies, which prey upon the tent caterpillars, this activity from a human viewpoint may not have been useful. But, of course, I could not be sure these actually were the insects he caught. As to the caterpillars, my vireo tramped lightly over the mass of them. Few birds relish these hairy worms. But, as I watched the shadow of a wriggling caterpillar on a translucent leaf, the vireo snapped it up, dashed it to pulp on a twig at his feet and ate it.

From dawn till noon, the vireo had reached a grand total of 14,027 songs, but after this his singing diminished notably. The interruptions between groups of songs became longer and more frequent, even as he sang more and more slowly. From noon until going to roost, he gave only a little more than half as many songs as during the early part of the day. But even this was a remarkable number. And his voice continued to be heard when most of the other birds sang but little, or were altogether silent. Moreover, compared with the all-day record of 6,140 songs of an unmated European blackbird, made by Noble Rollin on April 5, 1948, my vireo's performance during the afternoon alone exceeded this total by 2,030 songs.

The lower peak of singing, which occurred during the afternoon, may have been due to the encounter at the territorial border with the neighboring red-eye to the north. For quite a while, certainly, this stimulated both birds to greater vocal effort. But the time of afternoon rest came in the next two hours, when my vireo wandered about within a small area, or fed, or sat on a twig trimming and polishing every feather in his plumage, and sang only a little.

The last hour of his day the vireo spent in the top of a quaking aspen. Here he moved from perch to perch. I saw the easy opening and closing of his bill and heard his notes drop, one by one, upon the calm air.

All day I had heard him singing thousands of songs of two to four, seldom five, notes. Monotonous, repetitious, preacher-like? His singing was all of this—if a recitation that was so intrinsic a phase of a creature's character, so innate an expression of self, could be any of these attributes.

Lovely and clear, simple and eloquent, his songs and intonations continued to reach me from the top of the aspen. Hitherto his voice had been un-affected by his day-long singing. But now, as if he had reached the end and only with reluctance gave in, his songs shortened and were often just softly whispered. Then the sun hid behind alto-cumulus and it grew dusky in the vireo territory while out yonder, at the edge of the forest, the sun still threw its gold upon the trees and the hillsides.

Between 6:00 and 6:13 P.M. my vireo sang 44 songs. Two minutes later, with wings closed, he dropped from the crown of the aspen into a thick stand of young evergreens. From there, like an echo of his day's performance, he gave six more songs. Then he fell silent and was heard no more. Officially, the sun set one hour and 39 minutes later.

Fourteen hours, less six minutes, my red-eyed vireo had been awake. Of this time he spent nearly 10 hours singing a total of 22,197 songs. This was his record. But the most important is not the record, but my introduction to an individual bird and the glimpse he gave me of his true character.

At the end of the nesting period, when the young are being fledged or have already left the nest, a curiously relevant resurgence of courtship behavior occurs between the parent birds—nature's reminder of its unyielding continu-ity. Song, this meaningful part of a bird's reproductive period, is also revived. So, at this time, the thrushes' vocal performances come into their own as never before. At dawn, and sometimes also in the evening, in the fullness of summer these birds fill the twilight intervals between day and night with their most in-spired music, full-toned and lingering. Other birds already off tone, induced by the thrushes' example, may suddenly provide an accompaniment of sorts. This late-season singing by the thrushes and others sometimes lasts to the end of July, even into August, producing dawn concerts only the early riser will hear—never to forget.

FRED BODSWORTH

The Last of the Curlews 1954

FRED BODSWORTH was born in 1918 in Port Burwell, Ontario, and worked as a reporter on the *St. Thomas Times-Journal* before joining the *Toronto Star* in 1943, and *Maclean's* magazine, where he worked until 1955. *The Last of the Curlews* (1954), his first novel, follows the migration of a male Eskimo curlew from its breeding grounds in the Canadian Arctic to its summer range in Patagonia, and back along the Pacific coast to the Arctic. His theme is the disastrous effect of man's interference with nature's rhythms, a tragedy further explored in his later novels, including *The Strange One* (1959; published in the U.S. as *The Mating Call*), about the tangled fortunes of a wildlife biologist and a mating pair of geese, and *The Sparrow's Fall* (1967), which explores the ethical implications of imposing Christian concepts of nature on Native people who depend for their livelihood on hunting and trapping.

ॐ • ॐ

THE ARRIVAL OF the female was a strangely drab and undramatic climax to a lifetime of waiting. One second the curlew was feeding busily at the edge of the breakers, surrounded by dozens of plovers, yet alone; the next second the female curlew was there, not three feet away, so close that when she held her wings extended in the moment after landing even the individual feathers were sharply distinguishable. She had come in with a new flock of nine plovers. They had dropped down silently, unnoticed except by the sentinel plover that stood hawk watch while the others fed. She lowered her wings slowly and deliberately, a movement much more graceful than the alighting pattern of the plovers. Her long, downward-sweeping bill turned toward him.

The female bobbed up and down jerkily on her long greenish legs and a low, muffled *quirking* came deep from within her throat. The male bobbed and answered softly.

There was little mental reasoning involved in the process of recognition. It was instantaneous and intuitive. The male knew that he had been mistaken many times before. He knew that the puzzlingly similar Hudsonian curlews were far to the north, wintering on the shores of the Caribbean, and that only another Eskimo curlew could be this far south. He knew this new curlew was smaller and slightly browner, like himself, than the others had been. But these thoughts were fleeting, barely formed. It was a combination of voice, posture, the movements of the other bird, and not her appearance, which signalled instantly that the mate had come.

He had never seen a member of his own species before. Probably the female had not either. Both had searched two continents without consciously knowing what to look for. Yet when chance at last threw them together, the instinct of generations past when the Eskimo curlew was one of the Americas' most abundant birds made the recognition sure and immediate.

For a minute they stood almost motionless, eyeing each other, bobbing occasionally. The male seethed with the sudden release of a mating urge that had waxed and waned without fulfilment for a lifetime. A small sea snail crept through a shallow film of tidewater at his feet and the curlew snapped it up quickly, crushing the shell with his bill. But he didn't eat it himself. With his neck extended, throat feathers jutting out jaggedly and legs stiff, the male strutted in an awkward sideways movement to the female's side and handed her the snail with his bill. The female hunched forward, her wings partly extended and quivering vigorously. She took the snail, swallowing it quickly.

In this simple demonstration of courtship feeding, the male had offered himself as a mate and been accepted. The love-making had begun. There had been no outward show of excitement, no glad display, simply a snail proffered and accepted, and the mating was sealed.

Now they resumed feeding individually, ignoring each other, but never straying far apart. And the cobble bar by the S-twist of the distant tundra river called the male as never before.

At dusk he took wing and circled over the female, whistling to her softly. She sprang into the air beside him and together they flew inland over the coastal hills. They landed on a grassy hillside when darkness fell and they slept close together, their necks almost touching. The male felt as if he had been reborn and was starting another life.

They returned to the beaches at dawn and began to move northward more rapidly, alternating flights of ten miles or so at a time with stops for feeding. The call of the tundra grew more powerful and each day they moved faster than the day before, flying more and eating less. By early February they were a thousand miles north of where they had started, still following the seacoast tideflats, and the springtime turgescence of the sex glands with their out-pouring of hormones began filling them with a growing excitement. Now the male would frequently stop suddenly while feeding and strut like a game cock before the female with his throat puffed out and tail feathers expanded into a great fan over his back. The female would respond to the love-making by crouching, her wings aquiver, and beg for food like a young bird. Then the male would offer her a food tidbit and their bills would touch and the love display suddenly end.

One dusk when the westerly wind was strong off the coastal highlands, they flew inland as they had done every evening, but this time the male led her high above the browning pampas and darkness came and they continued flying. The short daytime flights were not carrying them northward fast enough to appease the growing migratory urge. They left the seacoast far be-hind and headed inland northwesterly toward the distant peaks of the Andes. Now the male felt a sudden release of the tension within him, for with the first night flight there was recognition that the migration had really begun.

They flew six hours and their wings were tired. It was still dark when they landed, to rest till the dawn. Now they moved little during the day, but at sun-set the curlew led his mate high into the air and turned northwestward again. Each night their wings strengthened and in a week they were flying from dusk to dawn without alighting.

They flew close together, the male always leading, the female a foot or two behind and slightly aside riding the air vortex of one of his wingtips. They talked constantly in the darkness, soft lisping notes that rose faintly above the whistle of air past their wings, and the male began to forget that he had ever known the torture of being alone. They encountered numerous plovers but their own companionship was so complete and satisfying that they made no attempt to join and stay with a larger flock. Usually they flew alone.

The northward route through South America was different from the southward flight. When they left the belt of the prevailing westerlies and passed over the pampas into the forested region of northern Argentina, feed-ing places became more difficult to find. Five hundred miles to the west were the beaches of the Pacific but the towering cordillera of the Andes lay be-tween. They were entering the region of the southeast trades and to keep the wind abeam they could fly northeastward into the endless equatorial jungles of Brazil where food and even landing places would be scarce for fifteen hun-dred miles, or they could swing westward to challenge the high, thin, stormy air of the Andes which had the coastal beaches of the Pacific just beyond. The curlew instinctively turned westward.

For a whole night they flew into foothills which sloped upward interminably, climbing steadily hour after hour until their wings throbbed with the fatigue. And at dawn, when they landed on a thickly-grassed plateau, the rolling land ahead still sloped upward endlessly as far as sight could reach, to disappear eventually in a saw-toothed horizon where white clouds and snow peaks merged indistinguishably.

When the sun set, silhouetting the Andean peaks against a golden sky, the curlews flew again. Flight was slow and labored for the angle of climb grew constantly steeper. The air grew thin, providing less support for their wings and less oxygen for their rapidly working lungs. They were birds of the sea level regions and they didn't possess the huge lungs which made life possible here three miles above the sea for the shaggy-haired llamas and their Indian herders. The curlews tired quickly and hours before dawn they dropped exhausted to a steep rocky slope where a thin covering of moss and lichen clung precariously. For the remainder of the night they stood close together resting, braced against the cold gusty winds.

Daylight illuminated a harsh barren world, a vertical landscape of gray rock across which wisps of foggy cloud scudded like white wings of the unending wind. And the top of this world was still far above them. The peaks that they yet had to cross were hidden in a dense ceiling of boiling cloud. Nowhere else in the world outside the Himalayas of India did mountain peaks rear upward so high.

Even here, though, there were insects and the curlews fed. It was slow and difficult feeding, not because food was scanty, but because every movement was a tiring effort, using up oxygen that the blood regained slowly and painfully. At dusk the air cooled suddenly and the fog scud changed to snow. They didn't fly. The turbulent air currents of the great barrier of rock and glacier ahead demanded daylight for the crossing.

There was no sleep, even little rest, that night. The wind screeched up the mountain face, driving hard particles of snow before it, until at times the birds could hardly stand against it. Then a heavy blast lifted them off their feet and catapulted them twisting and helpless into dark and eerie space. The male fought against it, regained flight control and landed again. But the female was gone.

He called frantically above the whine of the storm, but his calls were flung back unanswered by the wind. When the wind eased, he rose into the air and flew in tight, low circles, searching and calling, in vain. The wind rose, became too strong for flight, and he clung to the moss of the steep rock face and waited breathlessly. When it died momentarily, he flew again, but his endurance waned quickly and he couldn't go on. He found a hollow where he could be sheltered from the storm and crouched in it, panting with open bill for the oxygen his body craved. When strength returned he flew out into the wild dark night another time, circling, calling, the agony of loneliness torturing him again.

In an hour he found her, crouched in the drifting snow beneath a shelf of shale, as breathless and distraught as he was. They clung together neck to neck and the heat of their bodies melted a small oval in the hard granular snow.

The wind slackened at dawn and the male knew they had to fly, for there could be no lingering here. When the snow changed to fog again and the sun pierced it feebly in a faint yellow glow, they took off and spiralled upward into the flat cloud layer that hid the peaks above. In a minute they were entombed in a ghostly world of white mist which pressed in damp and heavy upon them. They spiralled tightly, climbing straight upward into air so thin that their wings seemed to be beating in a vacuum and their lungs when filled still strained for breath.

In the cloud layer the air was turbulent. Occasionally there were pockets where the air was hard, and their wings bit into it firmly and they climbed rapidly, then the air would thin out again, and for several minutes they would barely hold their own. Once the light brightened and the curlew knew they were close to the clear air above, but before they could struggle free of the cloud a sudden down-draught caught them, they plunged downward uncontrollably and lost in a few seconds the altitude that had taken many minutes to gain.

They broke free of the swirling cloud mass finally and came into a calm, clear sky. It was a weird, bizarre world of intense cold and dazzling light which seemed disconnected from all things of earth. The cloud layer just below them stretched from horizon to horizon in a great white rolling plain that looked firm enough to alight upon. The sun glared off it with the brilliance of a mirror. A mile away a mountain peak lifted its cap of perpetual snow through the cloud, its rock-ribbed summit not far above. In the distance were other peaks rising like rocky islands out of a white sea.

The curlews levelled off close to the cloud layer and flew toward the peak. Flight was painful and slow. They flew with bills open, gasping the thin air. Their bodies ached.

As they approached the mountain top, the wind freshened again. Stinging blasts of snow swirled off the peak into their path of flight. They struggled through and landed for rest on a turret of grey rock swept bare of snow by the wind. Now a new torment racked their aching bodies, for the dry rarefied air had quickly exhausted body moisture, and their hot throats burned with thirst.

Fifty miles away there were orchids and cacti blooming vividly in the late South American summer, but here on the rooftop of the Americas four miles above the level of the sea was winter that never ended. Not far below their resting place was an eerie zone of billowing white in which it was difficult to distinguish where the snow of the mountainside ended and the clouds began. Yet even here where no living thing could long endure, life had left its mark, for the very rock of the mountain itself was composed largely of the fossilized skeletons of sea animals that had lived millions of years ago, in a lost aeon when continents were unborn and even mountain peaks were the ooze of the ocean floors.

The pain drained from their bodies and the curlews flew westward again past the wind-sculptured snow ridges and out into the strangely unattached and empty world of dazzling sunlight and cloud beyond. They flew a long time, afraid to drop down through the cloud again until there was some clue as to what lay below it, and far behind them the peak grew indistinct and fuzzy beneath its halo of mist and snow. The cloud layer over which they flew loosened, its smooth, firm top breaking up into a tumbling series of deep valleys and high white hills. The valleys deepened, then one of them dropped precipitously without a bottom so that it wasn't a valley but a hole that went completely through a cloud. Through the hole, the birds could see a sandy, desert-like plateau strewn with green cacti clumps and brown ridges of sandstone. It was two to three miles below them, for the Andes' western face drops steeply to the Pacific.

They had been silent all day, for the high-altitude flight took all the energy their bodies could produce, but now the male called excitedly as he led the female sharply downward between the walls of cloud. The narrow hole far below grew larger. The air whistled past them and they zigzagged erratically to check the speed of the descent. At first the air was too thin to give their wings much braking power and they plunged earthward with little control, then the air grew firmer, it pressed hard against their wing feathers and they dropped more slowly. Their ears pained with the change in pressure and when they came out below the cloud layer they levelled off again and headed toward the faint blue line of the Pacific visible at the horizon.

Their brief two or three minutes of descent had brought them with dramatic suddenness into a region greatly different from the cold, brilliant void they had left. They were still so high that features below were indistinct, but they were nevertheless a definite part of the earth again. Now there was land and rock and vegetation below them, not an ethereal nothingness of cloud. Here the day was dull and sunless, not glaring with light, but the air was warm. And the air now had a substance that could be felt. It gave power and lift to their wings again and it filled their lungs without leaving an aching breathless torment when exhaled.

They flew swiftly now, for the land sloped steeply and their plane of flight followed the contour of the land downward. Late that afternoon they alighted on a narrow beach of the Pacific. They drank hurriedly of the salt water for a couple of minutes. Then they fed steadily until the dusk.

With twilight the sky cleared and the great volcanic cones of the Andes, now etched sharply against the greying east, assumed a frightening massiveness. Every year the male curlew's migratory instinct had led him across this towering barrier of limestone, storm, and snow. And every year before the memory of it dimmed, the curlew looked back and even his slow-working brain could marvel at the endurance of his own wings.

H. ALBERT HOCHBAUM

Patterns of Local Movement 1955

Called "Canada's greatest naturalist since Ernest Thompson Seton," HANS
ALBERT HOCHBAUM (1911–1988) was born in Colorado, studied ornithol-
ogy at Cornell University and wildlife management at Wisconsin State Uni-
versity, then moved to Canada in 1938 on the advice of conservationist Aldo
Leopold to establish the Delta Waterfowl and Wetlands Research Station in
Canada's largest wild marsh, the shores of Lake Manitoba. Over the next forty
years, Hochbaum banded and studied seventeen species of wildfowl, wrote
Canvasback on a Prairie Marsh (1944), now a classical ornithological study,
Travels and Traditions of Waterfowl, from which this excerpt is taken, and painted
numerous waterfowl and arctic landscapes: an exhibition of 180 of his water-
colors at the Agassiz Gallery in Winnipeg sold out in a single day. He died leaving behind three unfinished manuscripts, which his son, George, intends to
collect under the title *Autumn Thoughts of a Prairie Naturalist*.

᪣ • ᪢

For, lo! the winter is past.—Song of Solomon

LISTEN! . . . no, it's only the wind.

"*But listen!* Quiet, Tim, you fool hound-dog." No, it is only the children at
their game.

"*Listen!* . . . No, it is nothing at all." A heavy black cloud hangs in the west;
through a rift the sun bathes the marsh in gold. The evening flight has begun;
small parties of ducks lift from the bay, flying into the northwest. The tall poplar by the channel is dark with a thousand blackbirds creaking and tinkling.

"*Listen, listen!* . . . Yes, it *is* the swan! *The Whistling Swans are back!*"

Our eyes scan the purple east. There they are: fourteen great white birds halfway across the bay, coming straight toward us, their high-pitched voices yodeling loud and clear. They swerve, moving north to the lake. They turn again, swinging, wide; now they are coming back, the south wind on their breasts. Now they are overhead. What a sight to behold! They are dropping, dropping. A dozen yards above the water their necks arch, they set their wings, spreading feet wide like Canvasback. Then softly they alight near Archie's Point. Another leg of their northward journey is completed.

A band of Whistling Swan seen in the evening light of the first day of spring stirs the heart and soul of a man so that, for a moment, his communion with the wilderness is complete. Yet tonight I feel more than the beauty of the scene itself. Here, mind you, in the fading day when you or I might lose ourselves in the maze of marshland, this band of swan has come from far beyond the horizon to a place they have not visited since last spring. There was no faltering; they came unerringly to this small corner of marsh that has been the April rendezvous of Whistling Swans for at least forty years. Tomorrow there will be more, and more again on following days, until the chorus of their multitudes will not let us sleep. Then, sometime in mid-May, they will be on with their journey and Archie's Point will be swanless until next April. . . .

Saturday night! For those who live in the country, this is the big event of the week: early supper, hurry with the dishes, change to best clothes, and off to town for three hours of shopping and small talk. Last evening Joan and I crossed the marsh at sunset on our way to Portage la Prairie. We had just slipped past Slack's Bluff when Joan touched my arm and I brought the car to a stop. *"There, over toward Portage Creek.* What are they, ducks or geese?" Far to the southeast there hung a thin line above the horizon, a frail wisp of thread, barely visible. We watched in silence as it grew until finally we could make out its components. *"Geese!"* Then, of a sudden, their voices drifted to us on the south wind. *"Wavies!"* We stepped from the car to stand in the gathering dusk as the birds passed. Most were Blue Geese, but their lines were punctuated here and there by Lesser Snow Geese. They flew in a wide line from which sprouted small branches, the whole forming a great blunt "V." As the mass moved it rose and fell as if riding a rolling swell, the individuals within the flock ever shifting position so that the pattern changed constantly. The geese were in full and constant voice, a guttural gabbling accented by high, nasal shouts, by no means as rousing as the whoop of swans or the bark of Canada Geese, but sweet music, nevertheless, over the April prairie.

The flock held steady course; then at a point near Slack's Bluff it turned sharply toward the annual lakeshore stopping place at the mouth of the Whitemud River. As their voices faded, there came a louder clangor from the southeast. As far as we could see came the geese, one broad "V" after another. It was a great moment in my life, and I removed my hat in unconscious response to some inner urge of respect as they passed.

Each flock followed the same route as the first, and as the second group approached Slack's Bluff it turned sharply to the west. Every successive band held a steady course until it reached the turning place where the bend west was made. Not only were these birds moving toward a destination, but their trailway was marked by some special pattern which they followed. Maybe it was Slack's Bluff. Maybe it was the arrangement of the fields or the plan of the marsh and lake beyond or some other features of the landscape near or far. Whatever it was, these geese moving in the boundless prairie skies followed some cue that held them to their route.

The sun has dropped into the lake. It is an April evening, not of one day or of one year, but of at least three hundred April days of sixteen years. I am standing at the bayside. Before me is the vast expanse of marshland still frozen except at the edges, where a black moat of water separates ice from tules. Behind, to the north, is the narrow ridge of woodland that marks the south shore of Lake Manitoba. Beyond that, far past the northern horizon, are the marshes of Winnipegosis, of the Saskatchewan, of the MacKenzie.

The setting sun is the signal for Mallards and Pintails to leave these dark waters and move to other marshlands. Paired drakes and hens in company with their kind rise from the bays and go directly into the northwest. I am impressed by their precision, for, although their numbers are scattered far and wide over the marsh, the departure is not along a solidly broad front. Instead, as the bands leave the bays, the flight resolves into well-defined lanes of travel. The movement over the lakeshore is not in a wide sweep. The crossings are at passes. From where I stand I can see a flight over the village of Delta; there is another over Dr. Cadham's garden, and still another not far to the east. It has been so for countless springs—the trails to the northwest cross the lake ridge at the same places year after year. Are these passes cues to orientation, each a step in the long journey from the wintering grounds to the breeding marshes far beyond?

The annual return of the Whistling Swan to their April rendezvous, the turning of the wavies at Slack's Bluff, the lakeshore crossings of the Mallard and Pintail are examples of the avian reaction to the pattern of landscape. These movements are not indiscriminate, nor are they directed primarily toward the final destination somewhere beyond. Here is an awareness of special plots of terrain along the way, responses to mere pinpoints on the map of total migratory movements. Here are the resting places and local crossings that are just as incidental, yet just as important, to the over-all journey as a Chicago transfer is to a transcontinental railway passenger. Clearly the Delta Marsh is a key point in the northward travels of a great number of waterfowl. Yet in Manitoba this is but one of many such stopping places. The Libau and Netley marshes at the south end of Lake Winnipeg are hosts to wildfowl each spring. Whitewater Lake, the marshes of Lake Dauphin and Lake Winnipegosis, and the delta of the Saskatchewan are all focal points where ducks, geese, and swans cross or stop for a while on their travels to the breeding grounds. These lakes and marshes are steps along the highway of migration.

There is a temptation to think of the journeys of waterfowl in terms of such steps. For instance, the Canvasback from Chesapeake Bay has a route marked by important stopping places at Lake Erie, Lake Winnebago in Wisconsin, Lake Christina in Minnesota, and Delta in Manitoba, to name but a few. The pattern is so broad, however, that any discussion would soon become lost in complexities should it begin with this wide aspect of migration. . . .

The Delta Marsh lies at the south end of Lake Manitoba, separated from the lake by a low, narrow, heavily-wooded sand ridge that skirts the shoreline. Behind the ridge, and protected by it from the lake, the marsh spreads south to reach the rich agricultural land of the Portage Plains. East and west the marshland stretches more than twenty miles, and at its deepest point there are five miles between the agricultural prairie and the lake ridge. From the air it is seen as a complex pattern of shallow bays, connecting channels, sloughs, and small potholes, all fringed with bulrush or cattail and set in a matrix of *Phragmites,* the tall "yellow cane."

Throughout the season, from spring break-up in April until freeze-up in November, the Delta Marsh has its own population of waterfowl. Early, this is made up mostly of breeding pairs, but soon bands of drakes that have abandoned their nesting hens come to the big marsh for their molting period. Here they don the drab eclipse plumage and become flightless, for ducks, like geese and swans, lose the flight feathers of the wing all at once and are unable to fly until new pinions are grown. Birds-of-the-year add to local numbers; and before summer is old, many youngsters raised elsewhere come to Delta. From early August until heavy frost there are constant arrivals and departures, comings and goings, some birds staying only a few days, others remaining weeks or months.

Not one of these wildfowl finds that a given part of the marsh serves all its needs. There may be a mile or more between the hen's nest and her territory. Most birds find their feeding, loafing, and graveling places at separate loca-

tions, often far apart; and each may have more than one locality for these activities. Some Mallards in late summer and autumn regularly travel ten to fifteen miles from their loafing bars to the stubble fields, such trips being made
twice daily. Except during the flightless period, each duck takes daily and often lengthy journeys within the realm of the marshland.

In the travel from marsh to lake, the local ducks cross the wooded ridge at
the same passes the transients used when they departed northward in migration. When a flock is flushed from the marsh, the birds seldom fly directly to
the lake by the shortest route. Instead they bend their flight east or west toward one of the passes where they cross over the trees to the lake. In August
and through autumn Mallards and Pintails that loaf on the lakeshore move
over these same passes in their journeys to the stubble fields. Many times I
have watched a flock of Lesser Scaup, Redhead, or Canvasback cruise along
the lakeshore for a mile or more, then suddenly swing south to cross over a
pass to the marsh. One July a band of pre-eclipse Redhead drakes fed daily in
a bay east of the village. A quarter-mile flight due north would have given
them a direct route; but instead of taking the short cut, they usually moved
west a mile to cross at a favored pass.

In general, the width of the lakeshore passes at Delta is 100 to 400 yards, although the core of a pass, through which goes the major flight line, often is
narrower than this. The main passage of birds through the pass may vary from
day to day, the travel within the boundaries apparently being dictated by the
wind's direction. It is not true that all trading is confined to passes; now and
then a flock makes a crossing well to one side or the other. On days of heavy
traffic, however, hundreds of ducks fly over the pass for every dozen going
elsewhere. So closely does the great majority hold to the crossings that these
lanes of travel are well-known to guides and hunters.

I have watched the flights over the lakeshore through sixteen years. The
pathways have been the same as long as the oldest guides can remember. Dr.
Fred Cadham, who has hunted the Delta Marsh since boyhood, tells me that
the pass over his cottage has been the same since 1898. For at least fifty-six
years—many generations in the life of waterfowl—ducks have moved between marsh and lake on this same path. I suspect the history of Cadham's
Pass is much older than this.

The gunner's eye detects little reason for this regularity as he watches from
marsh level. But a bird's-eye view from an aircraft reveals a sharp relation between the flight lines and the pattern of the terrain. Most passes are at narrows
where marsh water comes close to the lake ridge. Others are at channels
flowing near the ridge or cutting through to enter the lake. Some are at old

creek beds, long dry and overgrown, yet clearly defined from the air. In short, the pass is where there is the shortest distance between marsh and lake.

Such trailways are not confined to the lakeshore. These are doorways to the north, but the marsh itself is a pattern of aerial lanes as well marked by the flights of waterfowl as the roads on a highway map. In the marsh the travel follows the path of least resistance; that is to say, the trails take the easiest low-altitude routes over land, usually following the shortest path between two water areas. Where two water areas are connected by gap, channel, or creek, this is the passageway for waterfowl. In the absence of a waterway, the pass is at the narrowest neck of land separating two areas; or a flight may follow a dry channel bed that once linked two bodies of water. Where a creek meanders aimlessly, the more direct overland route may be favored.

The lakeshore passes are used regardless of wind and weather, but many marsh crossings serve only in certain winds. A given pass may be used regularly when the wind blows from the northwest or southeast, but may seldom or never be followed when the wind is from another direction, at which time travel is made by some more favorable course. Thus, in moving over the marsh, the duck has several trailways, from which one is selected according to the wind. Many a gunner has been disappointed when a shifting wind robbed him of a flight of ducks he had located the previous day. One afternoon Peter Ward and I stood at a narrow neck of land between two large bays. About 3 P.M. there began a flight of Canvasback that moved over us in an apparently endless stream until we departed at dusk. The wind was just south of west, and the birds came out of the northeast, alighting in the bay west of us to feed on the abundant beds of sago pondweed. It happened that we had but half a dozen shells apiece; hence it was with keen anticipation that Ward returned to the spot the following afternoon, well equipped for a fine shoot. But the wind had changed and, although he remained until dusk, no birds crossed the narrows. As he paddled home, Pete found the west bay again littered with Canvasback which apparently had arrived by some other route.

Some passes are very narrow. The crossing of ducks just mentioned was confined to a span hardly more than 30 yards wide. At one narrow gap the lane of flight is not more than 25 yards across, the width of the waterway. I know of several other passes that are similarly restricted. On the other hand, where a long thin strip of land separates two large lakes, the passes may be very wide.

Many of the passes are used by all species of ducks. Some, however, are followed frequently by one species and seldom used by others. I believe this is simply because different kinds move to different places to loaf and feed. Canvasbacks that rest daily on the open water of Cadham Bay fly east to their feeding waters over a route that is seldom followed by Mallards. Mallards crossing the marsh to stubble fields take flight lines rarely used by Canvas-backs. Several passes at Delta are used heavily only in late autumn, when Lesser Scaup crowd the marsh.

Since the marsh is a maze of scattered potholes, channels, bays, and sloughs, a flight of any distance must take a duck over a number of passes. The pass it-self is merely a step in the flight trail. In general, traffic from one pass to an-other follows well-defined routes. Where ducks cross large bodies of open water, the travel usually is straight and direct. But where the landscape has outstanding landmarks, the flight may be influenced by these. Where, for ex-ample, an open body of water is broken by an island, flight lines generally cut close to the isle. Where a bay has an undulating shoreline or clumps of islands, the trails digress according to these land patterns. Travel frequently follows the shoreline, usually swinging around rather than across points of land jutting into the bay. Where the shoreline is much broken, the trail moves from point to point. The main course of travel seldom swings over islands, more fre-quently following the waterways between them.

The height at which the bird moves greatly influences the course of travel. When flying low, a duck tends to obey land patterns in almost every detail; a shoreline or a creek is followed through all its meanderings. When moving high, the flight is more direct. The general course of a creek is followed, for in-stance, but the line of flight "cuts corners" and does not wind as the creek does.

On several recent occasions the establishment of new trails has come in re-sponse to changes in the pattern of the marsh. In the late autumn of 1945 a pond was dug at Station headquarters, located in a dry field where ducks sel-dom crossed. Next spring, waterfowl began using it, and in their approach ar-rived along regular flight paths never used before. In a south wind the line most frequently taken by Blue-winged Teal cuts over my yard, and we now see ducks flying past the kitchen window, where they seldom came before.

The tight adherence to trailways is well known to the hunter who sets out his rig of decoys where the ducks will cross. Gunners often refer to the path-ways as "leads," and the most successful native guides are those who are famil-iar with these in any wind. Some locations are "handed down" from father to son among the guides. Old Dan Ducharme once took me to a lead where the Duke of York had shot when he visited the marsh in 1901. This place is still a choice location for gunning Canvasback in a south wind. No doubt every marsh and lake across the land has its leads and passes, its "Narrows" or its "Hole-in-the-wall" where generations of gunners have shot. Wildfowlers, as a matter of fact, distinguish "pass shooting" from other types of gunning, and some of the most famous duck-hunting places are at passes. When a gunner travels to a new ground, he spends the first day of his visit studying the pattern of the flights to detect the flight lines. One old-time gunner visiting Delta for the first time spent a few minutes with a map of the marsh and then went directly to a narrows connecting two bays, where he found himself located on one of the best passes in the region.

At Buckeye Lake, Ohio, Trautman (1940:88) observed that in the diving ducks "the outstanding feature of arriving flocks was their pronounced tendency to approach the lake at or within a fourth of a mile of Sellers Point. During twelve years of observations at least 65 per cent of all arriving flocks came to the lake within a fourth of a mile of that point." In southern Oregon, Robert H. Smith (letter) noted that in local feeding flights out of Klamath Valley "both ducks and geese follow passes across the ridges to other parts of the basin and these passes are favorite shooting spots, particularly if it is windy. It is an odd sensation to hide among the sagebrush and junipers on a mountain pass and watch the birds beat their way up to you."

Geese and swans, like ducks, cross the lakeshore at the same places year after year. Some of these passes are the same as those used by ducks; others are at independent crossings which ducks seldom follow. Given the same wind, geese fly day after day along a line of flight from lake to stubble fields, often maintaining this regularity despite a daily barrage of gunfire met along the way. The geese seem more sensitive than ducks to changes in wind direction, however, and the slightest shift in the breeze will often prompt them to select a different flight-line. In a location I have watched for many years, the geese, I am confident, will come over in a southwest wind. In all other winds they cross elsewhere and, after many fruitless dawn experiences, I have learned that one may as well stay home as to go there when the wind is wrong.

Waterfowl are not the only birds that use regular lanes of travel. Reynaud (1899) noticed that other kinds follow "air roads invisible to our eyes, but which can be revealed by observation. The bird, like the quadruped, contracts the habit of always returning to the same point by the same route." In autumn the Black-bellied Plovers loaf on the lakeshore sandbars and, like Mallards (but not with them), they make twice-daily trips across the marsh to the prairie, where they feed on fallow fields rather than on stubble. In these feeding travels, plover move along the same flight lines day after day. When the Franklin's Gulls trade back and forth between lake and prairie, their travel shows a regularity similar to that of waterfowl. In the Herring Gull, Tinbergen (1952:5) found that the route of local travel in dune country "changes with changing wind." Black-crowned Night Herons follow established routes to the feeding shallows. A pair of crows I watched one year used the same route daily when traveling between lake ridge and the meadowland a mile south of the marsh. A robin almost always flies to the same fencepost in my yard before dropping to the lawn. When children frighten the Yellow Warbler from her nest by the hatchery door, she departs the same way every time. The Yellow-headed Blackbirds that steal grain from the duck pen generally use a routine approach. Day after day the Marsh Hawk that nests near the channel may be seen on its regular course down the north side of Cadham Bay.

Here is an orderly pattern of movement. The waterfowl of the Delta Marsh respond to the physical design of their environment in much the same way as elk or mice follow their earth-worn trails. But unlike the mammals, whose feet mark the paths for all to see, the bird leaves no record of its passing. These waterfowl must obey the natural shape of the land and water when moving from one area to another, responding to visual cues as these are presented by points and bays, channels and islands, reeds and willows.

Here is a rule of order, a design of habit. Free as the winds to fly when, where, and how they might choose, wildfowl hold almost as closely to lanes of passage as do earthbound mammals. Such habit, such conservation of energy, is probably a universal trait of animals. The game trails of larger mammals are well known to hunters; and who is there who has not seen the Meadow Mouse path in an old field? Our own lives we know to be influenced by habit. This permits us to accomplish complicated acts with the least expenditure of energy; it simplifies our world. Daily we take the same route to school or office, although many variations of the trail might be followed. We walk along the same streets, over regular short cuts to shop at the usual stores, and pick up the morning paper at the same corner because it is easier to follow an established pattern than to pioneer a new trail every day.

ROGER TORY PETERSON AND
JAMES FISHER

Sea Cliffs of Cape St. Mary 1955

ROGER TORY PETERSON (1908–1996) was born in Jamestown, New York, and studied painting at the Art Students' League in New York City. He began working on his now-famous *A Field Guide to the Birds* while in his twenties: published in 1934, it quickly became the most popular bird book in the world. As Merilyn Simonds Mohr writes in *Harrowsmith* magazine, "in handing the average American his own back-pocket expert, Peterson was laying the cornerstone of the modern environmental movement." In 1953, Peterson and the distinguished British ornithologist James Fisher spent fourteen weeks birding around the North American continent, starting in Newfoundland, down to the Dry Tortugas, across to California, and up to the Pribilof Islands—30,000 miles in 100 days. The result was *Wild America,* co-written and published in 1955, from which this excerpt is taken.

಴ • ಸಿ

WE ARRIVED at St. Bride's as it was getting dark. Kerosene lamps were being lit in the homes that outlined the cove, and a smell of fish hung about the wharves.

The day had been dank and cheerless, drizzling half the time. Although Newfoundland is noted for its fog and rain, this section of the Avalon Peninsula, jutting into the sea, gets far more than its share. I thought of the dogwood and redbud that was now in bloom around my home in Maryland. Here the vernal calendar had been put back a month—at least. Wet and shivering, we found the house we were looking for on the far side of the little town. Entering the wooden gate we were greeted by Mr. and Mrs. Thomas Conway, whose hospitality soon made us forget the bad weather.

The reason for our long trek over narrow roads through the spruce forest to the southern end of the Avalon Peninsula was to visit the gannet colony at

Cape St. Mary. James is a world authority on the gannet. His first love is the fulmar, that pearly gull-like relative of the albatross, but I suspect the gannet is his second. He plans to write a monograph on it soon, with his friend John Barlee. In 1939, with H. G. Vevers, he made a world census of the gannets; they and their correspondents visited nineteen out of twenty-two gannet colonies in existence. Of the 167,000 gannets breeding in the world at that time 109,000 were in Great Britain and Ireland. The New World came off a poor second with only 28,000 birds in six colonies (three in the Gulf of St. Lawrence and three off the shores of Newfoundland). Ten years later, in 1949, they repeated the census, finding twenty-nine colonies and about 200,000 birds. Gannets are on the increase.

The most spectacular New World colony, the one at Bonaventure Island off the Gaspé, is visited by scores of bird students every year. It has become a profitable thing for the innkeeper on the island to cater to—and even advertise to—an unending succession of summer gannet watchers. Kodachrome movies of this colony have been seen by hundreds of thousands of people in the Audubon Screen Tour audiences throughout the United States and Canada. On the other hand, the colony at Cape St. Mary sometimes goes for several years unvisited by any of the field-glass fraternity.

One of the main objectives of our Grand Tour of Wild America was to visit the nesting colonies of as many species of North American seabirds as possible. We had planned to collaborate on a field guide to the seabirds of the world, following the formula of my other Field Guides. Therefore I wanted James to see those seabirds which are not found on his side of the Atlantic— and particularly, the wealth of seabirds in the North Pacific.

But gannets are gannets. Those on the coast of Scotland are identical with those in Newfoundland. However, James wanted to see at least *one* New World gannetry. The one at Cape St. Mary was not very well documented even though its history goes back to about 1880. That is not old as gannetries go. The one on the Bird Rocks in the Gulf of St. Lawrence was recorded by Jacques Cartier in 1534. Several of the British colonies have histories that go back even farther than that, and James is quite sure that some have, in fact, been occupied for thousands of years. These are birds of ancient design; the gannet tribe goes back in the fossil record forty million years, at least.

After dreaming fitfully of gannets that night at the Conways' I was awakened by James, who reported that the weather was improving, the fog had gone.

April 15

This morning it looked rather better. I had a hard time getting Roger out of bed; it was about 9 A.M. when we started off for Cape St. Mary.

On the tip of the Cape there is a lighthouse, but this is served by sea, which this morning was too rough for small boats. To go overland from the village of St. Bride's to the lighthouse means ten miles out and ten miles back through a particularly sticky bog. Fortunately, we had a guide, Paddy Conway of St. Bride's, and he had a pack pony, and the pony carried out gear. At first the track was distinguished by deep mud ruts and telephone poles. Every now and then it went under water and we skirted round. After a bit we diverged toward the coast through a spruce bog in which fox sparrows were plaintively singing, reminding me very much of the Coigeach of Ross in the Highlands, with stunted spruce instead of heather. A juniper was growing prostrate, shaped by the winds, and there was much crowberry, *Empetrum nigrum,* and everywhere in the oozy sphagnum bogs was a new and unfamiliar plant, the plant of Newfoundland's old coins, the pitcher plant. Roger picked one to show me. It is said to be carnivorous. Its leaves, shaped like slender purplish pitchers, are usually half filled with water; the lip of the pitcher is covered with stiff downward-pointing hairs which make it impossible for any trapped insect to climb out.

We reached the sea bluffs and dry ground, to find, in rough water, under a bold 400-foot headland some hundreds of harlequin ducks. These fantastically patterned ducks, which the Newfoundlanders call "Lords and Ladies," had not yet departed for their breeding grounds on the white-water rivers of Labrador. Long-tailed ducks (or old-squaws) constantly flew past in little parties, and there were some red-breasted mergansers. There were many eiders, the males black with white backs, and a biggish flock of solid black ducks with yellow noses. The last proved to be the American race of the common scoter (which has much more yellow on its bill than our European form).

It was a slow journey. After about seven miles we descended to a westerly cove where there were two houses, two men repairing a fence, and a prodigious smell of drying fish. The fish racks were flat slatted shelves of split wood, giving good circulation of air; there were also drying houses for fish. Here our guide borrowed a cart. We crossed the river by a little slung bridge, while the horse took the cart through a ford. The rest of the track to the lighthouse was almost a "road," with dry footing. Tired, we ate lunch, reclining in a bed of prostrate matted spruce, while the sun came out fleetingly. Progressively the weather got better, so that by the time we had crossed an upland barren of juniper and crowberry and sighted the cart (which had gone ahead), it was full sun. Paddy was talking to two lighthouse keepers. As we approached the lighthouse (we had first seen its top about five miles away) we also heard, carried on the wind, the noise I associate with the finest remote Atlantic rocks, the noise of Eldey and St. Kilda, of the Bass and M″kines: the thrilling rattling of gannets, and the *taterat,* the angry sound of kittiwakes. The dear noises of the seabird colony, the great gannet noise. Only the fulmar was lacking.

By now the day had become really fine, though windy, and tired though we were from our ten-mile hike (it seemed like twenty) we all made haste to the noisy cliff. Round a cape east of the lighthouse the gannet rock suddenly appeared—just as I had remembered it from the photographs. We were on the top of a sloping 400-foot cliff; we went down this a bit to a vantage point out of the wind with one of the light keepers, another Conway (who had been in the British navy during the war). While Roger set up his cine camera, I counted the occupied gannet sites visible on the west side of their nesting rock.

Between us and the gannet rock was a great rock-bound cover with very steep slabby sides; the broader ledges were covered with guillemots, which looked rather like rows of erect white-breasted penguins, but mainly it was a kittiwakery, perhaps one of the greatest in the Atlantic New World, where there are not many. There were about 3000 occupied kittiwake sites here. Periodically, the birds would panic and swirl past the cliff face like a blizzard of snow. The locals call these small gulls *tickle-ace,* or something like that.

Circumventing the noisy kittiwake slab we finally reached the gannets, whose great stack (350 feet) is connected with the 400-foot mainland cliff only by a low impassable ridge.

What a wonderful show they put on for us! Thousands of birds, with a wingspread of six feet, covered the top and sides of the stack. Gleaming white with a golden wash on the backs of their heads and jet-black wing-ends, they were at the peak of nuptial beauty. Our glasses showed a bright green stripe along the top of each toe—clocks on their black socks. Paired birds faced each other, bowed, and lifting their heads high, crossed their bills. A constant succession of newcomers came in from the sea and made their awkward landings against the capricious wind; they back pedaled with their wings, threw their big feet forward, and trusted to luck. Others, tails depressed, took off from the slope with a curious retching groan, losing altitude at first as they pitched into space, before leveling off. Some joined those who were diving from a height, headfirst, like slender arrowheads into the deep blue water beyond the surf. But most of their fishing was probably done far from the home rock; gannets commonly fish fifty, or sometimes a hundred miles from their colonies. They must spend up to six hours on the wing on these ration runs, for they cruise at about forty miles an hour.

I estimated occupied sites on the top; and worked around and down to cover the east side of the colony. It seemed clear that, unlike most British colonies, the gannetry at Cape St. Mary was not fully tenanted in mid-April, and that the number of its occupied nests does not become stabilized until May. Our count, and estimate, gave 3476 occupied sites. This included about 13 sites occupied by birds on the rather inaccessible mainland ledges to the east of the stack. In 1939 Oliver Davies and R. D. Keynes, the last gannet counters to visit this place, had estimated 4394 occupied sites in the fullness of the season. Roger tells me that there are still many gannets passing northeastward along the New England coast in mid-April.

The attachment of the gannets to their nest sites at the time of our visit was not great. Some of them, even though separated from us by a hundred feet or more, would leave their nests entirely, although they had already built them up with much fresh grass. There were many fresh nests quite unattended. Had egg-laying been near, few would have taken the chance of losing nest material or even nest sites to their neighbors.

It was about four o'clock, with the long shadows, before we gave much attention to the guillemots on the kittiwake slab. Although guillemots (which in North America are called murres) are abundant off Canadian shores, most Americans do not have the opportunity to see them as readily as we do on the rocky shores of Britain.

For many years our knowledge of the guillemots of Newfoundland had been confused. The island is within the range of both the species, the common guillemot and the Brünnich's (which is an exceptionally rare visitor to Britain). At first it was thought that all the guillemots of Newfoundland were Brünnich's. But Peters and Burleigh (1951) state that all the breeding birds are common guillemots, and the Brünnich's, although abundant in winter, are "not known to nest in Newfoundland." Recently, however, Leslie Tuck has discovered a minority of Brünnich's guillemots breeding in two colonies off the east coast of Newfoundland. If we had not taken Roger's new 30 x Bausch and Lomb telescope with us, the situation at Cape St. Mary would have remained uncertain, for it was only when we put the powerful glass on the broad gray slab that we could detect among the crowded birds some which had shorter bills with a white mark at the base. Taking ledge by ledge I called out numbers while Roger jotted them down. A little over 10 per cent (actually 11.4) were Brünnich's guillemots, a substantial and hitherto unrecorded minority.

Another investigation we were able to carry out with the powerful glass was a count of the relative number of "bridled" birds in the population of common guillemots. North Americans usually refer to these individuals as the "ringed" phase. The bridle, spectacle, or ring—call it what you will—consists of a white ring round the eye with a white line running back from it. H. N. Southern, who meticulously examined the east Atlantic situation, discovered that the proportion of bridled guillemots mounts steadily from under 1 per cent in the southern parts of the bird's range to 50 percent in south Iceland and Bear Island. No such investigation has been made, however, on the west Atlantic population to see if there is a similar gradation, except that recently Dr. Harrison Lewis found that 17.7 per cent of the guillemots in the sanctuaries along the north (Labrador) shore of the Gulf of St. Lawrence were bridled. The interesting thing about our sample at this Newfoundland colony is that we got the same result—actually, 17.3 per cent.

We left the kittiwake slab when the light became too weak for photography and tracked to the lighthouse where Keeper Conway's pretty wife gave us a fine cup of tea. As there was only another hour of daylight we were offered beds, very kindly and quite seriously; but we said we really must push off (just as well in view of the next day's weather).

We got caught by night before we returned the cart to the cove. From there Paddy and the horse and a borrowed flashlight guided us back to St. Bride's. It was a tedious journey, though the way across gullies and bogs, often without any track at all, was found unerringly by Paddy and his horse (we were not sure which). A crescent moon descended into the sea before we were half way; it was quiet and still. There were faint shafts of aurora borealis, and the snipe were out, chippering and winnowing, much to Leslie's delight, as he counts these birds each spring.

Roger had bad luck earlier in the day when filming on a steep slope; he strained a muscle on the climb up. This played up seriously on the long way back and slowed him up a lot. He was very cheerful and good about it, but I knew he was in pain, particularly when we had to make the descent into each steep ravine which lay across our path and the equally steep climb out on the other side.

The route from the cove to within two miles of St. Bride's was really trackless; it was interesting how the necessity for concentration in the dark brought back unexpected memories of the outward journey through this very complicated terrain, including steppingstones in the river which we had to cross. Roger, with his limping leg, slipped and went into the icy water "by mistake on purpose" (to cool his wound?)—and had to change into a borrowed pair of heavy stockings. He said his leg felt better after that.

Paddy, I believe, thought once or twice that we'd never get there, though he was very skillful and patient. He knew the country perfectly. We at last picked up the telephone poles of the last two miles and splashed home— through puddles now, not round them. As we neared St. Bride's our footfalls on the stony roadway awakened people, who came out of the houses with flashlights and shone them at the strange cavalcade of horse, guide, and mud-spattered bird watchers. It was half past midnight; we were dog tired. Fourteen hours on the march—but what a day!

James was as reluctant as I to quit the comfort of his bed the following morning. We woke about 10 A.M. finding ourselves very stiff and out of training; it was blowing and snowy. Had we stayed at the lighthouse we would have had a far worse passage home, even with daylight, than on the quiet dark night.

It was a foul ride in the Chevy back to St. John's, though bravely we stopped now and then for a look at the sea. James added another bird to his lengthening list of oceanic acquaintances, the double-crested cormorant—an early arrival in these waters.

The softly falling flakes of snow had turned the spruce forest into a Christmas tree landscape. While we were crossing an open stretch of barrens, bleak in its white mantle, two willow ptarmigan flew across the road, alighted and walked about in the snow. But instead of their winter camouflage suits of white these two birds already had their spring plumage—brown with white wings—so they were very visible. I had, oddly enough, never seen this species, the commonest of the three ptarmigan, in North America (although I had seen it in Sweden—and we were to see many more in Alaska). These little sub-arctic chickens that grow feathery snowshoes for winter travel are circumpolar.

Although we had two or three more days in Newfoundland our trek to the gannetry marked the high point of our brief stay. It was still much too early for the wood warblers (a purely New World family), which enliven northern spruce forests from May to September. Not even the relatively early rusty blackbirds had arrived. We would meet these summer residents of Newfoundland en route.

But we seemed fated to have as much trouble getting out of this sea-girt province as we had when we came in. This time, when our plane was due to arrive, the weather at Gander, instead of being too bad, was too good. The aircraft, boosted by a following wind (east and southeast), still had plenty of fuel and had flown on without stopping to pick us up. However, we got space on a local flight to Halifax, Nova Scotia, where we would at least be able to find some way of getting to Boston.

That evening, James wrote in his diary: "Today I set foot for the first time in my life on the continental New World. Tomorrow it will be the fabulous United States of America. Roger seemed to be making all too little of this business, until I remembered that he belonged there."

RODERICK HAIG-BROWN

Place des Cygnes 1956

RODERICK HAIG-BROWN (1908–1976) was born in Sussex, England, and
moved to British Columbia in 1927 to work as a cougar hunter and fisherman. From 1942 on, he lived near Campbell River, British Columbia, where
he wrote most of his twenty-five books, including the fishing tetralogy for
which he is best known: *Fisherman's Spring* (1951), *Fisherman's Winter* (1954),
Fisherman's Summer (1959), and *Fisherman's Fall* (1964). He was a lifelong and
passionate conservationist, calling in 1966 for "a radical redefinition of economic values, a radical shift in North American purpose," and even a "radical
redirection of the individual North American character." After his death, his
daughter, Valerie Haig-Brown, collected his papers into three posthumous
volumes, the third of which, *Writings and Reflections*, includes the following
account of a rare encounter with a flock of trumpeter swans.

ঙ৹ • ৹ঙ

MY SON ALAN and I made a circle of the potholes on the last day of duck season. It was a windless day, almost mild, though there was snow on the northern
slopes of the ridges and every lake and pond for miles around had been frozen
for weeks past. We were at low elevation in logged-over country, but even here
there was open water only because the short, deep ravines of this little section
were fed by underground seepage from the big lakes, too warm to freeze in its
brief run. Few of the beaver ponds were frozen and the main stream, a good-
sized creek of constant flow, was not even iced along its edges.

Our search for ducks took us along a series of beaver dams, winding towards the steep head of a draw to the north of the main creek. We found only
a few buffleheads, but the likeliest place of all was still ahead. By swinging
southward, across two low ridges, we could come back to the main creek

where a well-placed beaver dam spread it into a dog-leg pool a hundred yards long by thirty or forty wide. The sandy bottom of the pool is weed-grown, even in winter, and its current is broken by several great water-logged tree trunks; the swampy edges grow strong grasses and weeds in black, peaty soil; if there were any ducks that had not forsaken fresh water for the tideflats, this was where they would be.

The pond is not an easy place to approach, especially on a windless day. We stopped at the crest of the second ridge to work out a plan. A hundred feet below us was a thicket of alders on a flat bench. Beyond them, I knew, the ground dropped away through another fifty feet or so to the edge of the pool. What little breeze there was came from downstream, so I decided to send Alan to wait at the bend below the dam while I made a wide circle to come out at the head of the pool. I had begun to explain the plan to him when a single, deep, musical *kronk* from beyond the alders made us both drop to our knees. "Geese," I whispered and my mind began to search furiously for some better way to approach them. But there were other sounds from the pool now, the splashings of heavy birds taking off from the water. They could not have seen us or winded us, and I felt they would not have heard us; the splashings were so heavy and so prolonged that I wondered if something else might have disturbed them—a deer starting ahead of us out of the alder thicket, perhaps even a cougar making an attack of his own on one of their number.

Then we saw the first flight; huge white birds in line on slow wings behind the bare tops of the alders, lifting steadily as they passed downstream, then swinging left to cross no more than fifty feet above the ridge we were crouched on. The sun was setting somewhere in the clouds behind us and there was a faint pink flush on the white feathers of the swans, repeated again on the distant white peaks of the mainland mountains just under their line of flight. There were six of them, two in line ahead, four others grouped in rough formation just behind the second; all were pure white adults, long-necked, great-bodied, with jet-black bills, jet-black legs, and feet held closely against their feathers. While they were still in sight, Alan's breathless whisper turned me to see the second flight, as it swung over the ridge to the west of us, no higher than the first and as close, so that the pattern of the feathers was visible on the white bodies and the sound of the sweeping wings was strong and clear.

We turned to each other, awed, yet laughing with joy at the tremendous thing we had seen and the way we had seen it. And it still was not over. A single swan, slow-winged and calm yet swifter in flight than the fastest duck or goose, came down the pool, lifted to the ridge, and passed right over our heads to join the others.

These were trumpeter swans, a scattering from the big band of a hundred or so that always winters somewhere in the valley, usually in the swamps at the head of the second big lake. But it was a much larger group than I had ever before seen away from the main band or in such a tiny pool. The temptation to go in there again was enormous, but I held off, for many reasons. The weather was bad, with frequent snowfalls and steady freezing, so I was fairly certain the birds would cling to the open creek. I did not want to disturb them too often and still less did I want to advertise their presence by beating a track in the snow that others might follow. But towards the end of February, I knew the time had come to look for them again. Within a few weeks, a month at most, they would leave the valley to travel north.

I chose a clear, sunny afternoon with a moderate, but steady, westerly breeze. There was snow on the ground, soft and rotten in the exposed places, but a foot deep in any sort of shade and on all the northern faces. Because the wind was westerly I decided to work up the creek, against it, towards the pool. I thought the swans would be feeding in the swampy edge on the crook of the dog-leg, and hoped I would be able to come close enough to get a good sight through glasses without disturbing them.

Cutting across the deep draws towards the creek—I had long ago decided never to go or come the same way twice—I wondered why I should believe they would still be there, in that tiny place, after a full month. There was the freezing weather, of course, but that was hardly enough; the big lakes along the main flow of the watershed were nearly always open where the larger streams came into them and the swans had wintered there safely for hundreds of years. This winter was no worse than a dozen others I remembered, not nearly so bad as some of them. But it was the winter that meant the first stages of destruction for the swans' old wintering grounds.

Ever since fall, men and machines had been moving in to clear the edges of the two upper lakes and build the dam that would flood them. There was a big camp at the edge of the great swamp on the second lake, the favorite wintering place of them all; logging machines clattered on the sides of the sloughs, cables slapped at the brush and tore away the trees that had been cut down. For the most part, the birds had accepted this calmly enough, after all, the open water, the grasses and seeds and roots they needed were still there and would be until the water came up behind the dam. But my birds, I felt sure, had not accepted it. They had been driven to the tiny beaver pond by the disturbance rather than by the freezing weather.

I chose to go into the pond against the wind, because it was impossible to move silently, or even quickly, on the half-rotten snow. But this brought me also squarely against the sun and I came in sight of the deep bend of the pool before I really expected to. I was still well back from the steep bank that dropped down to the lower end of the pond, among a scattering of young alders about a hundred yards from the bend. I stopped sharply and strained my eyes for sight of the swans, but the slant of the sun and the scattered snow patches made everything uncertain, so I began to search the grass clumps in the bend through the glasses. I found them. At first two birds, close together, feeding; then another single one beyond them. The distance was too great to see them as I really wanted to and the alders spoiled even the distant view I had. They had not seen me, but I was more afraid of their hearing than of their sight. I dropped to my knees and began to creep forward, cursing every rustle and crunch of the snow under my weight. I had covered perhaps thirty or forty feet when I heard the single warning *kronk* from somewhere much closer than the birds I was watching. I stopped and held my breath for as long as I could, but the warning note sounded again. Five swans came swimming upstream from under the high bank that still hid the tail of the pool from my sight.

Kneeling in the snow, I lifted the glasses carefully and focused on them. The glare of sun from the water made a bad light, but the swimming birds were a noble picture. Their necks were straight and high, white bodies floated well up on the water, glistening wakes streamed out behind them as they made way easily against the current. They were obviously alert, but not afraid or particularly disturbed and I hoped they might move up with the other three and settle to feeding. But their warning and movement had alerted the whole pond. A group of mallards talked nervously on the far side. I caught the movement of other ducks here and there while I watched the splendid procession move on, around the end of the first big log, into open water beyond that would bring them up to the other swans.

Then the nervous mallards took flight, a dozen of them clattering steeply up against the wind, followed at intervals by smaller groups. The swans seemed to be swimming more swiftly away from me. Suddenly the great white wings were spread, powerful black feet paddled once or twice against the surface of the water, the wings themselves touched water twice, perhaps three times, and the five were away, in clear flight, rising visibly on every wing thrust. I watched in admiration, expecting the other three to join them, but they did not, though the bugle notes of the flying birds seemed to call them. The two nearer ones had stopped their feeding and were standing straight among the tussocks of grass. The third, perhaps ten or fifteen yards beyond them, was floating in a little channel of water among the grass clumps, still feeding steadily. One of the nearer birds walked a few dignified steps and flapped its wings vigorously. The other walked towards it. Then, both were still except for little up and down movements of their heads and long, straight necks as they talked in short, soft musical sounds that barely reached me on the wind.

Again I hoped they would settle down. Again I was disappointed. Together they made two or three short, heavy steps, necks stretched forward, wings spread, and they were flying away into the wind after the others. But the lone bird made no move to follow.

I was afraid for it then, afraid it was sick or wounded. For a little while I watched as it fed, curving the long neck forward and down full length into the water, lifting it back to full straight stretch for a moment, plunging it down again. Then I began to move up. Soon I had to pass out of sight into the alder thicket. I worked through as quickly and silently as I could, but when I came in sight again the bird was swimming strongly up the middle of the pond, fifty or sixty yards away, turning its head and making soft, deep sounds that seemed nervous now that it was alone. I still supposed it must be hurt in some way, so I held on quite boldly and steadily towards it. It took off with the same astonishing ease as the others and flew after them.

As the swan passed out of sight around the curve of the high banks upstream, the pond seemed utterly desolate. I looked for ducks and saw only a single merganser towards the downstream end—but a tiny merganser, so small that I thought it couldn't be a merganser. I put the glasses on her and still couldn't believe what I saw. She was certainly a merganser and an American merganser at that, not even a redbreast. But a miniature bird; I felt puzzled, but really had no time for her.

The two swans that had flown together had swung back down the pool, passing within fifty or sixty yards of me, then turned away towards the north. But the first five and the last lone one had not reappeared and I felt they might have turned southward towards little Hidden Lake, which lay just over the ridge. The chance of another sight of them was too good to miss, so I crossed the creek and ploughed through the deep, soft snow of the north face until I topped the ridge and saw that Hidden Lake was solidly frozen. I turned back, coming to the creek again by the beaver dam at the downstream end of the long pool. The merganser was still there, the only bird on the pond. But she was a fine big bird now. Her russet head was bright, her pale breast smooth, the gray plumage of her wings and back shone in the sunlight. If anything, I thought, she was a little larger than normal size.

Ten days later I went into the pool again. This time I held well to the westward, aiming to come in from the upstream side. There was no wind and it was a dry, dull day; but it was much milder, and on the southerly slopes the snow lay only in scattered patches. I topped the last low ridge slowly and cautiously, keeping down and searching for clear, soft ground at every step. Again it seemed almost foolish to hope that the swans would still be there, but from the crest of the ridge I could see part of the grassy flat in the bend of the pool, through a screening of stumps and small trees. There was a small white patch, half-hidden by grass clumps. Even before I put up the glasses, I knew it was a swan.

The ground ahead sloped easily to a little bench that ran out to the steep bank just above the grass flat, within thirty or forty yards of where the swan was feeding. There was a big black stump there with a few small fir trees on either side of it—a perfect watching post, if I could reach it without being heard. So far as the one swan I had seen was concerned, I thought I might make it. But where were the others? Nearer or farther away? Upstream or down? One alarm note would destroy what I really wanted—the chance to watch them undisturbed in perfectly natural behavior.

The sixty or eighty yards ahead was far more difficult than it looked. I resolved to avoid every snow patch. But where there was no snow there were dry, rustling Oregon grape leaves or little willows. Big fire-blackened logs turned me or forced me to climb higher than I wanted, taller willow clumps blocked my chosen footing, the scattered snow patches seemed everywhere linked and unavoidable. But in the end I reached the stump and there had still been no alarm. Very slowly I eased my body over to one side, then raised my head. Two swans were down on the grass flat almost directly below me.

The swan I had first seen was in a little black pool of its own making, dug out in a soft place among the tussocks, feeding steadily. The other was standing several yards farther up on the flat, apparently fast asleep, neck curved back over body, the triangular base of the black bill just showing above a folded wing. The feeding swan was busy. His powerful neck plunged down, all the way in the water, driving the searching bill into the black ooze for roots and seeds. The head lifted, bill moving so that the red of the lower mandible was plainly visible. For a moment the neck, streaked with mud and dripping water, was held at full stretch while the proud head gazed sternly and alertly about. Then neck and head plunged forward again, the floating body drifting a little in recoil from the thrust and search. The movements were regular and unvarying: head down for three, perhaps four, seconds, then up and alert for exactly the same length of time, and down again.

Watching there, unseen, flooded by an excitement that satisfied every cell of mind and body, I felt an immense gratitude—to the swans, to their creator, to the little pool that had welcomed them in the frozen land and held them for me. But even as I felt these sensations I knew only too well the true source of both excitement and gratitude. These were not only the noblest and greatest of the world's wildfowl, they were also the rarest. A hundred years ago Audubon had watched "flocks after flocks" migrating along the frozen Mississippi, settling on the ice at night in hundreds, rising in the next day's dawn with a pattering of feet "that would come on the ear like the noise of great muffled drums, accompanied by the loud and clear sounds of their voice." I was watching just two, two of a few hundred remaining in the world. And I was watching these two only because the heedless, compulsive advance of men had invaded one more of their wintering sanctuaries.

The feeding swan continued his regular movements for another fifteen or twenty minutes, body and wing feathers gleaming in the clear light, their whiteness emphasized by occasional rolling drops of mud-blackened water thrown out from the raised head. Then the other swan awoke and raised its head. It stood for a moment, long neck curved gracefully over its body, then gently flapped half-open wings, and began walking slowly towards the other bird. As soon as it came close the first swan climbed easily out of his puddle and began walking ahead of his mate towards the main pool. Rather quickly they passed beyond my angle of vision, behind the stump.

I realized I was cramped and ready to move, so I straightened to my knees and worked over rather incautiously until I could see around the other side of the stump. The leading bird stopped, straightened his neck, then uttered his warning *kronk*. Now they were both alert, a little undecided but not panicky. They talked in soft, single notes, in the same key as the louder warning and always with a slight drawing down and sharp straightening of the neck. At the edge of the pool the lead bird uttered his warning again and I held the glasses on his breast and neck, trying to detect some stir from the great bugle windpipe; but I could see none—only the dip of head and neck as though to bring up the sound.

They went into the clear creek water then and at once began dipping their heads and necks to clear away the mud. The first swan was considerably the more vigorous in this, swimming strongly against the stream with neck extended just under the water until a small wave mounted over his back between his wings; then drifting slowly with the current, neck laid gracefully back over his body and swept from side to side against the feathers. It was not very successful cleaning. Both necks remained slightly streaked with the black mud or perhaps a permanent stain. But the birds seemed quickly satisfied and continued in straight-necked easy swimming with occasional gentle talk.

I had kept perfectly still, hoping they might forget about me or decide I was harmless. But they let themselves drift slowly back downstream to the first log. Here they held briefly, then turned for shore, waded out, and walked around it. They re-entered the water and drifted back to the second log, still talking a little, once or twice sounding the louder note. At the second log they waded out again, this time well up onto the grass flat. They kept on walking, rather aimlessly, so far as I could see, necks curved much of the time, but always straightening to produce the soft sounds that still reached me. One bird stretched its wings and flapped them, then both were almost still for several minutes. Quite suddenly both heads began to jerk up and down quite rapidly. A quick gabble of soft sound reached me. Then heads and necks stretched forward, wings spread, the great black feet made two or three running steps on the flat and both birds were in the air. They rose swiftly, with every strong wingbeat, climbed the steep banks of the pool, topped the alders, and swung away over the same ridge from which Alan and I had first seen them.

On the way out I followed the line of their flight and searched in the few likely places, but I did not really expect to find them again that day.

It was almost time for them to leave for the north. But these were two; a pair. The others had gone already, perhaps northward, perhaps to join the main band in the swamp at the head of the second lake. It was not too much to hope, I told myself, that these two had already chosen to stay and nest in the long pool on the open creek. It had treated them well through the winter and would treat them even better through the summer. And through the summer I would watch.

A week later I heard that the main band had disappeared from the second lake. Two or three days after that I made yet another cautious approach to the pool. It was empty. I searched the nearby beaver ponds and crossed to Hidden Lake, now free of ice. No swans. I came back to the pool, no longer cautiously. There were only the black swan holes among the tussocks of the grass flat and the fading, week-old tracks of huge webbed feet in mud or sand around them.

It is not yet April and I still hope I may find them again somewhere among the maze of swamps and beaver ponds that spring has opened. If not, perhaps it is just as well. There are too many people, too much is going on here now, for such great birds to nest in safety.

Geese 1957

MARGARET MURIE was born in Seattle, Washington, in 1902, and grew
up in Alaska, where her father was Assistant U. S. Attorney. She was the first
woman graduate of the University of Alaska, and later married Olaus J.
Murie, who became director and president of the Wilderness Society and
was the author of numerous books on wildlife, including *A Field Guide to
Animal Tracks* for the Peterson Field Guide series. Margaret travelled extensively with her husband throughout Alaska and Yukon Territory, where
Murie had gone to study caribou, waterfowl and the biology of the Alaska
Peninsula and the Aleutian Islands. Her account of these years was published
as *Two in the Far North* in 1957; in this chapter, "Geese," from that book, she
describes a goose-banding expedition she and her husband and their
year-old son took to the headwaters of the Old Crow River in Yukon
Territory.

⁊ • ⁊

"WILL YOU LOVE ME in December as you do in May?"

Jess was standing on the decked-over bow of the scow, poling and singing.
He had a very nice high tenor voice. I love to sing too. We both knew hundreds of songs, and I really believe this saved our sanity, our friendship, and the
success of the expedition. Down on the floor of the scow, just behind Jess, the
baby and I spent our days now in a four-by-four space under the light
muslin-and-netting tent a field naturalist friend in Washington had insisted
we take along. Life from June 29 on would have been fairly intolerable without it. Here in this space were the baby's box, beside it Olaus's collector's
trunk, and, piled on the trunk, all the baby paraphernalia and other small articles needed during the day. My stool was set in front of the chest, beside the

box. And that was all; this was our world. By leaning forward and putting my eyes close to the netting, I could catch glimpses of the outside world. It remained unvaried for five weeks: Jess's booted legs, the tip of the red-painted bow, a green blur of grass and willows on the shore, maybe a bit of sky. Sometimes I caught a view of Olaus, trudging along on shore, the line over his shoulder. He was "pulling her by the whiskers," as the trappers say; Jess, experienced with the pike pole, leaned his weight on every stroke in a steady rhythm, all day long.

So we slid along, and sang song after song, and estimated our progress, trying to pick out landmarks from the Geological Survey maps. But the Old Crow throughout its middle course has no landmarks; just high banks, brown stream, green shore.

Variation came when Olaus would signal frantically from shore. The song would stop in mid phrase. Then we would quickly haul up the canoe, and both men would get in and push off, after a flock of flightless young geese which by now would have taken fright and would be beating furiously through the water. By this time I would be out on the bow, pole in hand. "If we're gone too long, try to get to shore where you can hook a willow, and wait for us"—the parting shot as canoe, men, and geese disappeared around a bend upstream.

It was fortunate that the Old Crow *was* a sluggish stream. The scow drifted now toward one shore, now toward the other. I wound the bandanas tighter over my shirt cuffs to keep mosquitoes from crawling in, tied the strings of the head net tighter about my chest, leaned on the pole, and waited. If the slow current took us close to shore, I reached out and caught a branch with the hook. Then it was just sit there on the bow and hold it. If it were near Martin's mealtime and he began to call and fret, I could only pray that the bird banders would appear again sometime.

In ten minutes—or an hour—they would come, bringing a new story. "Hey, you should have seen your husband up there in the mud, trying to catch up with an old goose before he got over the bank." Or: "Jess should have been a football player; he made a peach of a flying tackle after two young ones. Well, that's six for us already today."

Sometimes the canoe would come in fast, sliding up to the scow, and Olaus would reach over and dump a gunny sack at my feet. "Don't worry; they won't hurt one another. We're going after another bunch up here."

The banders' advantage was that in these weeks the adult geese had shed their wing feathers and the young had not yet grown theirs, so that all were flightless.

One hot day the sack contained six full-grown but flightless geese. For forty interminable minutes I drifted, and poled, and watched the river in vain for the canoe, while those poor creatures never stopped squawking and wriggling. It was a big surprise for me when, after finally being banded, they all went down the stream again honking furiously, and unhurt.

Lunch was more ordeal than pleasure during these weeks. The men would try to build a fire for tea, but the willow, so much of it green, was poor fuel. Some days we merely went ashore with the tin grub box and ate a bowl of stewed fruit or tomatoes with pilot biscuits or cold sourdough pancakes and a bit of cheese. Bowl in hand, you loosened the string of the head net, poked the spoonful of food into your mouth, and quickly let the net down again. It was the same with all the bites. Even so, there'd be a few bugs to squash inside the net when lunch was over! This was merely taking in fuel for energy; it was no social hour.

Down in the tiny haven on the scow I heated mush or tomatoes or a bit of gravy on the Sterno outfit for Martin. He never came out of there until we camped at night. That is why we had to let him crawl about the tent as long as he liked in the evenings, and why Olaus romped and played with him every night. It was his only exercise during those five weeks.

Olaus has a biologist's scorn of allowing anything biological to disturb him. All creatures are a legitimate part of the great pattern he believes in and lives by. He ignored the mosquitoes with a saintly manner that made me furious at times. But one day he paid!

He and Jess had been chasing a lone white-fronted goose for a long time. As it was the first white-fronted goose of the season, it was worth a lot of time and effort. Olaus finally went ashore under a steep mud bank and waited for Jess to drive the goose to him with the canoe. From across the river, where I had hooked a willow, I watched the play. The goose swam upstream, Jess after it. Just as he came close enough to hope to turn its course, the goose dived. Jess waited and watched. As soon as the goose came up he paddled hard, trying to get ahead of it and force it to swim toward Olaus. The goose dived.

This went on for a half an hour. Every line of Jess's figure as he swung the paddle expressed determination; even under his head net I could see how his long jaw was set. The goose seemed fresh as a daisy. It rose each time with a quick sidewise glance at the canoe and a Bronx-cheer kind of honk.

Once she came up very near the scow. Jess came tearing past, talking to the goose. "God damn you, I'll get you if we have to go clear to the canyon together!"

Away they went around the bend; Olaus waved to me from across the stream, the kind of wave that said: "This is a funny life we're in, isn't it?"

Then the goose came swimming back again, paddling furiously, honking a little anxiously; right behind her Jess, also paddling furiously. And this time she decided shore was the place.

Olaus had lifted his net to watch the performance, and had also taken off his gloves—something Jess or I would never have done. Now he had to freeze into position, for the goose had begun to wade ashore at the spot where he was crouching. It padded determinedly up the bank. Suddenly it became aware of the figure there and hesitated. "Onk?" it questioned, and waited, watching Olaus. Then it put one web foot forward in the mud. "Onk?" again. Olaus didn't dare move an eyelid. Mosquitoes were setting in black clouds on his face and hands.

Out in the stream sat Jess, at ease in the canoe. Now it was his turn; he could make all the noise he wanted; he had forgotten his awful anger at that goose. "Heh, heh, heh," he said in his highpitched voice. "How you like the mosquitoes, eh? Nice comfortable position you're in, isn't it?"

Olaus kept silent; he was as determined to get this bird as Jess was. The bird took another very tentative step, looked at Olaus, and asked him again: "Onk?" No answer. From out on the river: "Boy, don't you wish you'd kept your net on! How long d'you think this will take? Watch her now!"

The goose took three steps; it was feeling the nearness of the overhung bank and safety above it. Like a fox drawing his legs up imperceptibly for a pounce, Olaus moved his feet, so carefully. "Onk?" Spring! Pounce! He had it round the body by both hands; they were sliding down the slippery mud together, and Jess was whooping: "Hang on, don't let her slip—I'm coming! How do your mosquito bites feel? Boy, don't anybody ever say anything to me about foolish as a goose; they're about the smartest damn critters you can find!"

They were slow, strenuous hours, chasing geese like this. Yet practically every goose we saw was caught and banded. Either the Old Crow had been much overrated as a nesting ground or something strange had happened in 1926, for we never found the "hundreds of thousands" someone had described to the powers in Washington. The days were hot and muggy, and we felt almost a claustrophobia down there between those steep banks of thawing Pleistocene mud, in a steaming, whining breathless world where insects were in full command. We human creatures were saved from insanity and death only by a few yards of cheesecloth and netting and leather. Sometimes the shield felt pretty thin. We longed for a breeze with passionate longing and welcomed a hard shower, because it downed the hordes for a while; and at least it substituted the sound of water for that other perpetual sound.

"Notice how much lower the banks are today? I think we're getting into different country." Olaus, always hopeful, always optimistic, was poling today.

Jess was on the line, over on the lower shore. His answer was prompt: "Can't be different country any too damn soon for me."

Five o'clock—the banks still lower, a clear sky. "Hey, Mardy, feel the breeze?"

I scrambled out from my "hole." What a feeling! Moving air! I looked up; the solid cloud of spiralling insects was gone; the wind had dispersed their formation, broken their absolute control of the land. "Can't I go ashore and walk a little? Martin's asleep."

I fell into step behind Jess, shoulder under the line. "Sure a lot more current here," he said. "Maybe we are getting into something different; even that old mud bank over there is pretty low. Looks as though it ends up ahead there. What's that?"

A dull boom, like a distant cannon shot, from upstream. "D'you hear that?" Olaus yelled. We threw our utmost into pulling, peering upstream. "Be a good joke if we found people up here after thinking we were the only ones in creation."

"I don't think it sounded like rifle fire exactly."

"Could some party have come over from the Arctic? You said it was only about eighty miles in a straight line now."

We rounded the next bend. "Boom!" Right there, near us. Then Olaus shouted, pointing; ripples were running out against the current in one place. In the mud bank on the opposite shore we saw a great lens of dirty brown ice. We watched. Crash! A big piece of ice suddenly dropped into the water, a rending, a crash, and a splash. Here was the exact northern shore of that ancient lake; the Pleistocene ice was being defeated by summer sun and the modern stream.

Suddenly Jess threw up his arm with a shout: "She's clear!"

I dropped the line and rushed to the very edge; there on our side was clear, shining beautiful water. As though sighting a new planet, we looked down into the bottom, into the beautiful yellow gravel. Then we looked across, and halfway over, there was the dark line in the stream where the Pleistocene mud was still falling off with the ice. "Come on," Olaus shouted. "Let's get above that mud. Look, it's flattening out up here. We *are* in different country."

A mile above the lens of ice we made camp, to the accompaniment of that cannonading; it exploded regularly, every two minutes by the watch. We had, in the space of a few moments, emerged into another world. The gravel bank was low to the stream, flat as a floor, dotted with all manner of brave arctic bushes and flowers. Better yet, there was a breeze blowing, and best of all, we were on top of the world; we had come up out of weeks in that Pleistocene hole.

We threw off our head nets, gloves, and heavy shirts, and stood with the breeze blowing through our hair, gazing all around. We could see, far out over miles of green tundra, blue hills in the distance, on the Arctic coast no doubt. This was the high point; we had reached the headwaters of the Old Crow. After we had lived with it in all its moods, been down in the depths with it for weeks, it was good to know that the river began in beauty and flowed through miles of clean gravel and airy open space.

Latitude 68 degrees, 30 minutes.

We had a paradise camp for a few days. The men went out in the canoe and explored the river upstream. It became shallow rapidly, and they satisfied themselves that there were no other goose grounds. Martin had a heavenly time, turned loose in the air and sunshine. He had long since learned that gravel hurt his knees; he did not crawl, but walked on all fours like a cub bear. Here on a long leash he explored, crawling right over the low bushes, playing peek-a-boo behind them, scuttling away like a laughing rabbit when someone "found" him.

Jess caught some eighteen-inch grayling the very first night in the clear pools just above camp. The baby stood at my knee and kept begging for another bite and another bite while Jess kept saying: "It can't hurt him; it's good for him," till we realized he had consumed a whole big grayling.

Jess is a real fisherman, and getting these beauties, our first fish in weeks, lifted his spirits a little. But he was experiencing a letdown of sorts. He was drawing away from us, into himself. After all, I don't know how one could expect a trip of this kind to be all sweetness and light unless the personnel were recruited in heaven. Plenty of things could have affected Jess. Olaus and I were together; we were content; his Clara was miles, weeks, months, away from him, and she was to bear their sixth child in August before he could be with her again. Then his motorboat had let him down. Every one of those slow miles up the river since June 29 must have reminded him of how easy it all would have been with that engine. And now after the tremendous effort was over and we had reached the headwaters—well, there had to be a letdown.

It was hard having Jess lost to us. He became a very polite stranger. At meals: "No thank you," instead of "Couldn't eat any more of the stuff!" "Yes, please," instead of "Hey, Mardy, you going to eat all the stew yourself?" He was even more polite to Olaus. They were really on the outs. Before, they had been two old pals on a trip together; now Jess was a stiffly polite employee; Olaus was the boss.

It was good that, while Olaus explored, Jess went fishing. I didn't blame him for needing to get away by himself.

Three days' respite from the mosquitoes; then it was time to turn south, back into the mud, and brown water, and clouds of insects. We all worked at sorting and reloading the outfit, in polite formality. The baby's little nook was placed amidships now, to make room up front for the rowing. The handmade oarlocks were put in place, then the two long oars, which had been made from two spruce trees. On that last evening, after the baby was asleep, Olaus and I slipped across the river in the canoe and climbed up onto the tundra. It was ten o'clock, July 26. The sun had just slipped below a distant blue ridge, but bright saffron light filled the northwest; the rest was pale blue. It was still daytime, but that very still, strange, exhilarating daytime of the arctic summer night, which can only be felt, not described. Here the flowing green-bronze tundra stretched as far as we could see—to the north, a few short ranges of hills; far to the south, rising pale blue off the flatness, the Old Crow Mountains again. In the morning we would be turning toward them.

We stood there for a long time, just looking. This might be our farthest north, ever. If we could only take a giant step and see the Arctic shore; we were so near.

Then our eyes came back to the near tundra, the velvety sphagnum hummocks, the myriad tiny arctic plants gleaming in the moss, in the golden light. The Labrador tea had gone to seed, but its sharp fragrance filled the air. In a tiny birch tree, a white-crowned sparrow, the voice of the arctic summer—"You will remember; you will remember," he sang.

PETER MATTHIESSEN

Fur Countries and Forest Lakes 1959

PETER MATTHIESSEN was born in New York City in 1927, the son of an architect who was also a trustee of the National Audubon Society. He was educated at Yale and the Sorbonne (while in Paris he co-founded the *Paris Review*). In 1956, in a green Ford convertible, he visited every wildlife refuge in the United States, and even travelled into Canada's Northwest Territories, to gather data for his monumental *Wildlife in America*, from which this excerpt is taken. The title is almost ironic: more than a scientific survey, the book is an outraged account of the decline in species and populations as a direct result of human greed and stupidity. His other fine books of natural history include *The Shorebirds of North America* (1967), *Oomingmak* (1967), and *Blue Meridian* (1971), but he is best known for two novels that have been made into films: *At Play in the Fields of the Lord* (1965) and *Far Tortuga* (1975).

⁊ • ⁊

THE GOVERNOR AND COMPANY of adventurers into Hudson Bay is known today as the Hudson's Bay Company, and its significance in the history of North American wildlife has been considerable. While it can scarcely be said that in the course of its long tenure the Company has proved a blessing to American wildlife, its policies have been far more constructive, in the main, than those of the lumber, mining, and other concerns which join it these days in a shrill effort to deny their part in the pillage of the continent's resources. In fact, the Hudson's Bay Company has made definite contributions, even from the beginning. Its field personnel has included men genuinely concerned with wildlife, and its comprehensive records have been most useful to naturalists for well over two centuries.

A typical contribution was the discovery, in 1861, of a rare new species of American goose by the company's chief factor, Bernard Ross. The Ross's goose winters in the Sacramento Valley region of California, with occasional individuals straying as far south as Bustilles Lake, Chihuahua, and its total numbers, more or less stable, have been estimated as low as two thousand, though five times that figure is probably more accurate. The birds are consistently shot as snow geese, which they closely resemble in miniature, and, though protected, are chronically imperiled. Confusion as to their actual number has been compounded by the fact that their breeding grounds, on the remote Perry River south of King William Sound, were not located until 1940, and research there is presently incomplete. The Perry River colony was found, fittingly enough, by Hudson's Bay Company personnel.

The Company's role in the history of another bird, while considerable, is less auspicious. Between 1853 and 1877 it handled 17,671 swan skins, a number which, while not staggering, represented an unhealthy proportion of the population of North America's largest waterfowl. The majority of these skins, then much in demand as items of female apparel, belonged originally to the trumpeter swan; the whistling swan, a smaller and more wary bird, had the added advantage of nesting farther north, out of harm's way.

The trumpeter was named for its voice: "I have heard them," wrote Samuel Hearne, a pioneer naturalist in Canada, "in serene evenings after sunset, make a noise not very unlike that of a French horn, but entirely divested of every note that constituted melody, and have often been sorry that it did not forbode their death." This statuesque bird, which attains a weight of thirty pounds and a wingspread of ten feet, bred formerly from western Alaska south to Indiana, and wintered from Chesapeake Bay and the Mississippi Valley west along the Gulf Coast, as well as in the lower Columbia River, and in the Sacramento Valley. It is now confined, in the United States, to the Red Rock Lakes district of Montana and to Yellowstone Park, with a few birds wintering on the Snake River in Idaho. There are also small breeding populations on the Copper River and on the wet spruce muskeg of the Kenai Peninsula in Alaska, which are presumed to winter with a resident population in southeast Alaska and British Columbia.

As civilization decreased their range, the swans became increasingly vulnerable to hunters, Indians, and trappers, who usually took them on their breeding grounds. In the 1920s, an estimated four hundred and fifty individuals remained of the flocks which had once carved the skies of a continent, and by 1935 only seventy-three remained in the United States. With complete protection, the bird has recovered very slowly, and its entire population now approximates fifteen hundred.

The varied and splendid waterfowl of North America have been decimated since early times, and, though we can attribute the original losses to such practices as market gunning and spring shooting, the fact is that bad land management, drought, and excessive drainage, in combination with the usual ravages of civilization, have since destroyed most of the waterfowl breeding and wintering habitat in the nation; in other words, the ducks, geese, and swans would be far reduced in number today even if never besieged by shot and shell. Protection has spared not the multitudes but the stragglers.

Curiously, however, the species imperiled have not been those most persecuted; only the redhead, of the popular market ducks, could ever be said to have approached the danger point. The Ross's goose and trumpeter swan were no more than incidental victims of the carnage, and the beautiful wood duck, which required full protection in the United States and Canada from 1918 to 1941, is a solitary woodland form. It declined by slow attrition, rather than on the grand scale of its swarming marshland relatives.

One obscure species, however, may well have succumbed to an earlier form of persecution. The Labrador duck is said to have been a strong and hardy bird, and the full reasons for its disappearance will probably remain mysterious. Nevertheless, though its nesting grounds were never discovered, it is assumed to have bred on the Labrador coast, once the favorite grounds of eider and other sea ducks pursued for their feathers and down. Between 1750 and 1760, a great many "feather voyages" were made to Labrador from the New England colonies, and, though these were abandoned shortly thereafter for want of victims, the native Indians and fishermen maintained a steady pressure on the remnant nests and eggs; it is possible, indeed likely, that the Labrador duck never recovered from this early onslaught.

In any case, this small, pretty black and white species flew south in winter at least as far as the Chesapeake Bay. The idea that the Labrador duck was "probably a mere straggler on the coast of the whole Atlantic, and chiefly inhabits the western side of the continent," was of course only wishful thinking. According to Audubon, "It also at times enters the Delaware River, in Pennsylvania, and ascends that stream at least as far as Philadelphia." The so-called "pied" or "sand-shoal" duck was already uncommon then, for Audubon himself never saw it alive; he based his description, as did other writers who came after, on a pair now owned by the Smithsonian Institution, shot originally off Martha's Vineyard by Daniel Webster. In 1872, the bird was called "extremely rare now, and apparently in a fair way to becoming extinct," a prophecy confirmed but three years later when, on the 12th of December, the last authenticated specimen was shot down by a gunner on Long Island.

Today, off Long Island's beaches, on a still day of winter, the great rafts of black and white pied sea ducks are a fine sight—the trim old-squaws and neat bufflehead, the mergansers and goldeneye and dark, heavy-bodied scoters.

The sharp air is clean, virtually odorless, and only the strange gabble of the old-squaws breaks the vague murmur of the tide along the shore. Alone on the beach, one can readily imagine that, momentarily, the loveliest pied duck of them all might surface, startled, near a sand spit, the white of it bright in the cold January sun, as it did winter after winter long ago.

The fur trade fast became the chief business of the colonies, exceeding in importance the commerce in timber and fish. The "fur countries," as they were called, were roughly that wilderness of forest lakes, of loons and geese, moose and bear, which we think of today, rather romantically, as the Great North Woods. In colonial times the term embraced the hardwood and evergreen backwoods of the Northeast as well as the spruce muskeg of eastern Canada, which stretches north from Quebec and the Great Lakes to Labrador and Hudson Bay; the western limits of the fur countries were then unknown. The region was bitter cold in winter and was composed largely of woodland tracts veined heavily with water. The cold encouraged a rich coat of fur, the wet habitat increased its luster, and the woodland shade protected the dark sheen from the bleaching effects of sunlight. These conditions were met to a certain extent quite far southward in the Appalachians and later in the Rockies, but furs taken elsewhere were generally inferior.

The most precious fur bearers were the various members of the weasel family—the winter short-tailed weasel in its white or "ermine" phase, as well as the otter, mink, pine marten, fisher, and wolverine. (Another weasel, the striped skunk, achieved a belated popularity with the decline of its less musky brethren.) Of these, only the aquatic mink and otter and the ubiquitous weasels remain widespread, at least in the United States, and the first two have been seriously reduced throughout their range. The marten, fisher, and wolverine, fierce, solitary carnivores dependent on deep, unbroken tracts of virgin forest, declined quickly. Probably the wolverine was never common south of Canada. A quick, powerful animal the size of a bear cub—and considered to be a bear, in fact, until the nineteenth century—it occurred formerly throughout the northern states from Maine to Washington, and south sparingly in the Adirondacks, the Rockies, and the Coast Range. Though an occasional wanderer is reported along the northwest border, the wolverine is now confined, in the United States, to a remnant population in the Rockies and in the Yosemite region of California.

The marten and fisher, however, were more widespread. Both species were found, in the Appalachians, as far south as Virginia, and the arboreal marten is still locally abundant in northern Maine and the Adirondacks, the wilder mountain areas of the Northwest, in Canada, and in Alaska. The fisher, a larger animal and individually, except for the rare strains of the red fox, the most valuable fur bearer among all North American land species, brought $345 in some years for an exceptional pelt. The price on its head contributed to its decline, but, like the marten, it has been most seriously diminished by lumbering, forest fires, and the elimination of pregnant females in winter trapping. It was disappearing in New York and New England by the nineteenth century, and has been called "alarmingly scarce" in the United States, although recently it made a good recovery in New Hampshire, Maine, and the Adirondacks. In Canada it decreased after 1870, and an estimated 10,500 are thought to remain in the Dominion. Unlike the wolverine and marten, the fisher is not a widespread Alaskan species, though it occurs in extreme southeast Alaska; it is still trapped wherever found, but its chief peril may lie in the destruction by lumbermen of the bark-eating porcupine, which is an important source of the fisher's food.

In the other families, the black bear and gray wolf were also taken whenever the chance presented itself (the muskrat, like the skunk, was a prize of a later, less glorious era), but the leading fur bearer, the creature of destiny the pursuit of which inspired much of the early exploration of North America, was not a wild carnivore at all but a sedentary, civic-minded rodent.

The beaver was once extremely abundant throughout the continent, the deserts of the Southwest and the tundra of the Arctic excepted. Exploited for its rich, dense fur from the outset, this largest of the American rodents commenced its decline as early as 1638, when to its misfortune the compulsory use of it in the manufacture of hats was decreed by King Charles II.

By this time the American beaver was already renowned in Europe—not surprisingly, since its virtues and attainments, as recorded by admirers well into the nineteenth century, have rarely been equalled by any animal before or since. The forepart of the beaver of yore, for example, was composed of meat, and the hindquarters, owing apparently to constant submersion, of fish, a circumstance of some comfort to religious Europeans, since it permitted the consumption of beaver even on fast days. The equipment of this marvellous creature included the forefeet of a dog and the hind feet of a swan, hooked teeth capable of capturing fish, and a tail of awe-inspiring versatility. Its mansion was an imposing edifice, several compartmented storeys of notched logs, the floors of which were carpeted with boughs of softest evergreen, "the window which looks out upon the water," observed the eighteenth-century naturalist Buffon, "serves them as a balcony for the enjoyment of the air, or to bathe during the greater part of the day."

Its physical endowments, however, were puny by comparison with the advanced evolution of its social mores, a vivid account of which was transcribed in 1825:

The beavers are divided into tribes, and sometimes into small bands only, of which each has its chief, and order and discipline reign there, much more, perhaps, than among the Indians, or even among civilized nations. . . .

Each tribe has its territory. If any stranger is caught trespassing, he is brought before the chief, who for the first offense punishes him *ad correctionem,* and for the second deprives him of his tail, which is the greatest misfortune that can happen to a beaver, for their tail is their cart, upon which they transport, wherever it is desired, mortar, stones, provisions, &c. and it is also the trowel, which it exactly resembles in shape, used by them in building. This infraction of the laws of nature is considered among them as so great an outrage, that the whole tribe of the mutilated beaver side with him, and set off immediately to take vengeance for it. . . .

The Indians have related to me in a positive manner another trait of these animals, but it is so extraordinary that I leave you at liberty to believe or reject it. They assert, and there are some who profess to have been ocular witnesses, that the two chiefs of two belligerent tribes sometimes terminate the quarrel by single combat, in the presence of the two hostile armies, like the people of *Medieve,* or three against three, like the Horatii and Curiatii of antiquity. Beavers marry, and death alone separates them. They punish infidelity in the females severely, even with death. . . .

The Great Hare at Red Lake wished to make me believe that, having come to the spot where two tribes of beaver had just been engaged in battle, he found about fifteen dead or dying on the field; and other Indians, Sioux and Chippeways, have also assured me that they have obtained valuable booty in similar circumstances. It is a fact that they sometimes take them without tails. I have seen such myself. In fine, these animals are so extraordinary, even in the eyes of the Indians themselves, that they suppose them men, become beavers by transmigration, and they think in killing them to do them a great service, for they say they estore them to their original state. . . . (from Beltrami, *La Découverte des sources du Mississippi*)

Whatever one's opinion of this service to the beaver, the high regard in which it was held in no way impeded its destruction, and since the animal is, in fact, rather stupid and defenseless, the progress of civilization was everywhere accompanied by its extirpation. The beaver hat went out of fashion in the beginning of the nineteenth century, but the beaver was virtually extinct east of the Mississippi shortly thereafter. John Godman, an early and articulate spokesman for animal protection, remarked in his *American Natural History*, published in 1831:

> It is a subject of regret that an animal so valuable and prolific should be hunted in a manner tending so evidently to the extermination of the species, when a little care and management on the part of those interested might prevent unnecessary destruction, and increase the sources of their revenue. . . . In a few years, comparatively speaking, the beaver has been exterminated in all the Atlantic and in the western states . . . and the race will eventually be extinguished throughout the whole continent. A few individuals may, for a time, elude the immediate violence of persecution, and like the degraded descendants of the aboriginals of our soil, be occasionally exhibited as melancholy mementos of tribes long previously whelmed in the fathomless gulf of avarice.

Godman's warning, while in advance of its time, was also tardy. A Hudson's Bay Company sale, in November 1743, disposed of 26,750 beaver pelts, as well as 14,730 martens and 1850 wolves; that these were by no means the only victims, even among their own kind, is indicated by the fact that 127,080 beaver, 30,325 martens, and 1267 wolves, as well as 12,428 otters and fishers, 110,000 raccoons, and a startling aggregation of 16,512 bears were received in the French port of Rochelle in the same year. People today who have no reasonable expectation of seeing even one of these creatures in the wild without considerable effort to do so might well look carefully at these figures. In the same year, too, for reasons which such harvests make all too evident, a French soldier and trader named Verendrye was seeking new sources farther west, where Cree Indians had informed him that the beaver were very numerous. Verendrye extended the canoe routes of the Great Lakes past Lake of the Woods and north to Lake Winnipeg, where he turned south into the prairies of the Dakotas and the Mandan country on the upper Missouri; probably he reached Montana and Wyoming, thus achieving the first recorded expedition to the virgin terrains of the American Northwest.

Meanwhile, English expansion westward had scarcely begun. Conrad Weiser's journey from William Penn's colony at Philadelphia to the Iroquois stronghold at Onondaga, near Lake Erie, 1729–1733, was a considerable undertaking, and Washington's expedition to the Ohio River country of western Pennsylvania, then contested by the French, was truly an expedition, even in 1753; the northern Alleghenies remained a barrier. Farther south, sporadic attempts to breach the Blue Ridge and the Appalachians were inconclusive until the era of the intrepid Daniel Boone. "It was on the first of May, in the year 1769," he recounted some years later, "that I resigned my domestic happiness for a time, and left my family and peaceable habitation on the Yadkin River, in North Carolina, to wander through the wilderness of America...." In Kentucky he "found everywhere abundance of wild beasts of all sorts, through the vast forest. The buffalo were more frequent than I have seen cattle in the settlements ... fearless, because ignorant of the violence of man." An Indian was to tell him, "We have given you a fine land, but I believe you will have much trouble in settling it." Settle it Boone did, losing a brother and two sons to the savages in the process. In 1776 he laid out for once and for all the Wilderness Road across the Cumberland Gap into Kentucky; the western horizon came in view across the rich heartland of the central continent in the same year American independence was declared.

"Notwithstanding America has withdrawn itself from us," Thomas Pennant wrote, just after the Revolution, "it is charity to point out the benefits they may enjoy, from the gifts of nature they possess." This sensible attitude was typical of Pennant, an Englishman whose *Arctic Zoology* is one of the foremost of all contributions to North American natural history. He was sensible, as well, in his observation that the Great Plains were once beneath the sea, that the red men had reached this continent by way of the Bering Strait, and that a sort of epilepsy was an affliction not uncommon among moose. In almost every respect, his text was superior to anything which appeared in the half-century after Catesby, including significant works by George Edwards (1743), John R. Forster (1771), and John Latham (1781).

Edwards, who never visited America, depended largely on Catesby and on the Hudson's Bay Company for his material, and was given to imprecise descriptions: the "quick hatch" or "wolverine," he reports, "was of the size of some wolves I have seen brought from Germany." Forster compiled what might be called the first American check list of wild creatures, including a list of 302 bird species, distinguished chiefly by its inaccuracy. Latham, like Edwards, was derivative and vague. It may well be that the most important pub-

lication of the period was the *Travels* (1753) of Peter Kalm, a Swedish corre-
spondent of Linnaeus who devoted considerable attention to American flora
and fauna. Another work of at least historic interest was the *Notes on the State
of Virginia,* first printed in Paris in 1781, by no less a person than Thomas
Jefferson, then a member of the United States Peace Commission seeking settlement of the war. The first of the few United States Presidents to concern
themselves with nature, Jefferson included in his treatise some accurate if
not very interesting information on wild species, and mentions the Carolina
parrot, passenger pigeon, and "white-billed woodpecker" among Virginian
birds.

The *Arctic Zoology,* then, could be called an epochal work, but it was com-
promised by Pennant's failure to adopt the binomial system, then coming into
general use, and a number of redundancies and outright errors mar the three-
volume work. He perpetuated Buffon's beaver legends, as well as the notions
that parrot guts were fatal to cats, that wolverines drop moss from tree limbs
to lure deer into ambush, and that wolves, when famished, dine on mud. For
the most part, however, he made the best of contemporary information. His
remarks on the growing scarcity of certain species were accurate, and it seems
fitting, in this regard, that a portrait of the ill-fated Labrador duck should have
been selected as his frontispiece. Of the elk, he reports a decrease in the face
of civilization, and says of the bison, "The Indians, by a very bad policy, prefer
the flesh of the Cows; which in time will destroy the species." (The idea that
the Indian was the sole culprit in the destruction of the bison was to gain in
popularity as its slaughter by white men increased.) The ivory-billed woodpecker he calls scarce, and though he refers to the "most amazing numbers" of
the passenger pigeon, he also quotes a letter he had from a Mr. Ashton
Blackburne, in 1770: "Sir William Johnson told me that he killed at one shot
with a blunderbuss, a hundred and twenty or thirty. Some years past they have
not been in such plenty as they used to be. This spring I saw them fly one
morning, as I thought in great abundance; but everybody was amazed how
few there were; and wondered at the reason."

Pennant refers also to a "strange animal seen by Mr. Phipps and others in
Newfoundland, of a shining black: bigger than a Fox; shaped like an *Italian*
greyhound; legs long; tail long and taper. One gentleman saw five sitting on a
rock with their young, at the mouth of a river; often leapt in and dived, and
brought up trouts, which they gave to their young. When he shewed himself,
they all leapt into the water and looked at him. An old furrier said, he remembered a skin of one sold for five guineas. The *French* often see them in *Hare
Bay.*" Since the otter was then a familiar animal and since Hare Bay is a coastal

habitat, the rest of the description leads one to suspect that the range of the now extinct sea mink may have been wider than is generally imagined. Little is known about this animal, which was first scientifically described in 1903 from bones discovered in Indian shell heaps near Brookline, Maine, but it has been called "fully twice as large as the mink from inland." "These sea mink," the same account says elsewhere, "used to bring considerably more than others on account of their great size." The usual range given for the sea mink is the coast of Maine, New Brunswick, and Nova Scotia; it is represented on earth by two poor skins and a number of bones.

HUGH MACLENNAN

The Mackenzie 1961

HUGH MACLENNAN (1907–1990), born in Glace Bay, Nova Scotia, attended Dalhousie University and later Oxford as a Rhodes Scholar. He returned to Canada to teach Classics at Lower Canada College in Montreal in 1935, and published his first novel, *Barometer Rising*, in 1941. When his second novel, *Two Solitudes*, won a Governor General's Award in 1945, he quit teaching and began writing full time. MacLennan was not only a nationalist, he was a regionalist: his novels and essays communicate a distinct sense of place and of the vastness of the landscape ("Space," he writes: "much of North American art and literature has been obsessed with it"). In *Seven Rivers of Canada* (1961), from which this description of his journey down the Mackenzie River is excerpted, his purpose was "to give a sense of the mystery, the beauty and the variety of our rivers, to indicate in passing how they link us with our past."

∾ • ∾

OF ALL THE places I have ever been in my life, I still remember the delta of the Slave—or rather, of the Peace—as the loneliest. Here is loneliness on a scale awe-inspiring, and increased by your knowledge of having seen no habitation for so long. Broad and flat, the marsh grass extends for miles, and there were more wild geese and duck than I had ever believed possible in a single place. We came out of the channel to the edge of the lake which stretched far away into the twilight looking cold and hostile, and in a strong wind it was kicking up a fast, ugly chop. The name they give to this place is Res Delta after Fort Resolution just around the bend of the lake from the river's mouth. (How tell-tale are the names of these Hudson's Bay Company posts in the Canadian North!) There were no ships on the lake, nothing here at all, apparently, but the geese, ducks, pelicans and the muskrats printing V-trails in the water as they swam away from the barges. I had the feeling that I was approaching nothing at all.

I was wrong: we were just about to meet the only known and identifiable human being between Bell Rock and Fort Providence.

He came sculling out to us in a rowboat and he looked like the French philosopher Jacques Maritain with a great shock of white hair, a strangely learned face and a still stranger expression in his eyes. He said only a few words and he did not come aboard. Provisions were handed down to him and he stowed them in his boat, then turned and sculled slowly back to the shore where I saw a pair of husky dogs sitting in front of a tiny shack, their mouths open and their tails bushed around their haunches. Somebody told me the man was employed here as watchman over the barges which often were moored nearby awaiting a change of tugs. I remember thinking he was no watchman of barges, but a watchman over eternity itself.

"You know," a deckhand told me, "that man's lived in Paris and Rome and all over the world. He knows about paintings and books. He told a friend of mine he knows about foreign women."

"What is he doing here?"

"I don't know, but it could be quite a story if anyone did know. He don't like talking. He never goes out. (By 'out' in these parts they mean 'out of the north'.) In the winter he has a job just as lonely as this somewhere else."

"Is he bushed?"

"No, I don't think he's bushed. Not by the bush, anyhow. A man can want to live alone, can't he?"

The remark may have been casual, or it may have been intended as a warning not to ask too many personal questions about people met in the North. I still don't know how it was intended.

Meanwhile there was a small conference in the wheelhouse because the captain had discovered we were entirely cut off from communication with anyone he wanted to talk to. In this country there are no phones except within the camps, no roads, no telegraphs. Radio is used for all messages and they are all sent in clear, with the Bell Rock sender servicing a district several times larger than Germany. The captain, a Japanese-Canadian called Albert Irey, was trying to reach Captain Brinki Sveinson of *Radium Yellowknife* whose ship he had expected to meet here at Res Delta. On Great Slave Lake it is impossible for any tug to push the barges: the heave of the deep water would break their hawsers. On the lake the barges have to be towed in line ahead secured by a heavy steel cable to the power winch at the tug's stern, and the maximum number of barges any tug can handle is four. *Radium King* would take the four smaller barges across; *Radium Yellowknife,* a more powerful ship, would take the four larger ones.

In the wheelhouse Albert was trying to raise the captain of *Radium Yellowknife,* but all he could hear out of the ship's radio was static and gibberish.

"It might be Russia, for all I know," he said and shrugged.

"Russia?"

"We often get Russia here when we can't get our own friends around a few bends of the river. Radio is a funny thing in these parts. There's been a local black-out for several days. Brinki could be within ten miles of us and I couldn't raise him. Anyhow, let's go."

Albert yanked the signal to the engine room, and for the next half hour he unscrambled the barges. Four were moored to the trunks of heavy trees, the other four were secured to the wire cable payed off astern, and in gathering dusk *Radium King* towed her barges out into the lake. Each barge was five hundred feet behind its leader, and the whole length of the tow was now longer than the *Queen Elizabeth.*

I didn't like the look of the lake at all. Those steep, rapid waves of inland seas have always seemed much nastier to me than the long roll of the Atlantic. The *King* was bucking in the head-sea throwing water and the water was very cold. Above the wheelhouse the radar fan revolved, but the screen was blank except for four dots astern, which were our barges, and the line of the lakeshore we were leaving. The wind drummed hard.

"How much water does she draw?" I asked Albert.

He flashed me a quick smile in the light of the binnacle: "About three and a half feet."

"She'll roll," I muttered, knowing how easily I get seasick.

"By the time the night's out maybe you'll think up another word for what she does."

The helm was put over, the *King* began a long, slow turn into the cross sea and the movement began.

"I think I'd better say good-night."

Clutching the guard rail I went down the ladder to the main deck, then I was nearly thrown down the next ladder into the cuddy where we slept. I swallowed a gravol, felt my head spinning and lay down on a cot with my clothes on.

I have been in a north Atlantic gale when the old *Empress of Britain*—the big one bombed to death in the war—shipped it green and solid over her sixty-foot-high fo'c'sle head. Once I spent five and a half hours on a ferry between Dover and Boulogne on a day when the weather was so bad that an English paper described it in a headline which later became famous: STORM OVER CHANNEL CONTINENT ISOLATED. On both those occasions I was deathly sick, but this night on Great Slave was worse. The *King* did not roll: balanced on the weight of her diesels, she flicked back and forth like a metronome trying to keep time to a czardas.

With eyes closed I reflected that Great Slave Lake, after all, is not a sea but a part of a river system. A little later with eyes open I remembered what had happened to the tug *Clearwater* the previous year on Lake Athabaska. Caught in a sudden storm, her captain had tried to shelter behind an island, but when he turned, the towing cable destroyed all his mechanical advantage in the water and the hammering waves capsized his ship. An air search found her the next day serving as anchor to her four barges, but all hands were lost. Then I remembered a story I had heard at Bell Rock about a war-time tow on Great Slave when the barges were carrying carbide and dynamite. The storm struck suddenly as storms do there, and as the water washed over the barges it ignited the carbide. The tugboat captain saw the flames in the night, cut his tow and ran for it. He was three miles away when the dynamite went up, but even at that distance the shock wave was strong enough to knock him off his feet.

Then I became so dizzy I didn't care what happened and somehow I dozed off. I woke with a crash, found myself on the deck half-standing against the side of the ship, thought she was going over and plunged for the ladder. I got on deck, seasickness forgotten, with a life-jacket in my hand, but there was no cause for alarm. The little *King* was flicking back and forth, the water was going over her scuppers, but I realized this was no storm. It was merely a dirty cross-sea working against a ship with only three and a half feet of draught. I went up to the wheelhouse and Albert was still there.

"We're getting along all right, but the wind's freshening. Still no sign of Brinki. It looks as if he's stayed on the other side. The wind may have been heavier over there. If he was out, we should have picked him up on the radar."

When I got back to the bunkhouse I found out what had thrown me out of my bed. The rolling had smashed one leg of my cot. It was impossible to repair it in this weather, so I lay down aslant and tried to get some sleep. It was a bad night and my back was in a partial spasm as a result of being thrown.

The next day the weather was easier, the dizziness wore off and we might must as well have been at sea, for no land was in sight. We moved steadily on at a speed of about four knots towing the barges, and then in a dead calm we approached land where, in a maze of islands, the lower Mackenzie issues from the Lake. The place is called Wrigley Harbour, but there is no habitation there, not even a shack so far as I can remember.

There was also no sign of *Radium Yellowknife* and our radio was still blacked out. Morris and I both knew the *King* was overdue at Yellowknife across the lake, and we took it for granted we would have to sleep in the open on the barges while we waited for our next tugboat.

"I guess Brinki must have gone over on a wider course," Albert said. "Otherwise we'd have caught him on our radar. He's probably coming back from Res Delta now. He should be here by 9:00 tomorrow morning."

I wondered if he would be, for in the North nothing ever seems to happen on schedule. Nor can anyone afford to mind. Storms on the lake are sudden, and so are frosts in the spring and fall. Last June *Radium King* had been frozen into the middle of the lake for ten days. Albert had the patience of the North which I lacked, as well as its valid optimism.

But we did not have to sleep in the open after all, for there was a dredger working in a swamp on the far side with a houseboat where the men slept. After securing his barges to trees, Albert sailed across and we glided up to a cluster of men waiting to welcome us in a haze of blackflies. Four of the men were big-muscled Indians and two of the white men had not shaved for days. The eyelids of one of them were red and swollen from fly bites and he did not even bother brushing the flies off his face when they settled. They took us aboard without question as people always take in strangers in the North. The Captain said there were two empty cots, one in the houseboat and the other in the wheelhouse of the dredger. Morris and I tossed; he won the houseboat and I the wheelhouse, and as both of us were tired we turned in. The last thing I saw that night was the riding light of the *Radium King* fading out as she sailed over the horizon of the Lake.

I woke at dawn wondering where I was, for a bright light was in my eyes. Never before or since have I seen such a sunrise. The sky over the river and land was a flat roof, livid and sinister, and it lay oppressively. In the east a blaze of orange had torn a jagged rent in the sky and the sunrise poured through between sky and water like a searchlight gone mad. It tore another rent in the west and travelled on into a sea of golden glory and the whole sky took fire all at once. A minute before it had been like the sky painted by El Greco over Toledo; now it was Turner's sky over the Thames estuary—but bigger, lonelier, more awe-inspiring. Then with savage and unnatural abruptness both holes in the sky closed, the fire died out and it was almost dark, and I saw the shadow—not the reality but the shadow—of an arrowhead of geese flash along the dim surface of the water.

For millions of years spectacles like these have occurred at this section of the river, watched by creatures no more sentient than mosquitoes, blackflies, bulldog flies, gulls, geese, ducks, ravens, pelicans, eagles, moose and bear.

What lay to the north-west I did not yet know, but I knew already that the nearest man behind me to the south was that white-haired hermit at Res Delta. In a moment of panic—the noun is accurately chosen—I wondered if human beings are necessary on this earth. Here was this colossal land, here this wild beauty, here this huge inland sea to the south feeding the great river that poured for twelve hundred miles through the wilderness to the world's most useless ocean above the Antarctic. What did the Creator want it all for?

I went back to my cot, shivered a little in my bed roll and woke half an hour later with the breakfast gong ringing.

After breakfast I smoked a cigarette with the machinist, an elderly man with a lined face, and asked him if he liked it here.

"You don't *like* it," he said. "The boat drops you and goes away, and the door is closed on you. We haven't been off this dredge for months. There's no place to go. But I keep coming back. For me it's a good life. For the fellows who've had trouble outside—I wouldn't say I was one of them—the north is a good place."

I asked him how many people lived along the river between Fort Smith and Aklavik in the Mackenzie delta.

"Maybe about five thousand Indians spread around. A few white men in Norman Wells stay the winters to keep the refinery up. A few more here and there at the posts."

The decks of the houseboat swarmed with flies. The dredger cut loose and went to work in the river and Morris and I sat in the bunkhouse and read. There was no sign of *Radium Yellowknife* and the chef told us the radio was still blacked out. It was the only thing he said all day. After the midday meal a breeze rose and took off the flies, so Morris and I borrowed fishing rods and walked a little distance along the shore and began casting. We saw many fish rising, but none rose to our spoons.

This is one of the most stirring sections along the whole system. Here, where the Mackenzie proper begins, the river slides cold and clean off the top of Great Slave Lake at a velocity of five knots with whorl-like eddies and rising fish, and at once it becomes absolutely fierce and masterful. All the sediment brought down by the Athabaska has been scattered to the bottom of Lake Athabaska; all brought down by the Peace to the bottom of Great Slave Lake. Here the system renews itself in a smooth, fast volume of water which aeons ago carved a great twisting trench down to the north. . . .

With a drop in the wind the flies swarmed back, and Morris and I went back inside the houseboat. Monotonously the afternoon wore on and I wondered if we would ever get out of this place. I was becoming wearier and wearier of these endless northern delays which always seemed inevitable. Once a bush plane flew overhead, but every time we scanned the horizon the lake was empty. Then, just after sunset, Morris rose quietly, looked out the porthole and said: "Cheer up! The tow is arriving."

Half an hour later we were aboard *Radium Yellowknife* talking to Captain Brinki Sveinson. While we had been tossing in the lake he had sheltered behind an island, not because he thought the lake dangerous for his ship, but because he had an empty vessel in tow which lacked ballast, and he was afraid she might capsize. He told us he would take us down river for two and a half days to his rendezvous with *Radium Charles,* which would in turn take us down to Norman Wells in another rendezvous with *Pelican Rapids.*

The next day our voyage down the Mackenzie began, and it took us longer to reach the Wells from Wrigley Harbour with our eight barges than it would take a modern liner to reach Southampton from New York. Hour after hour, day after day, night after night we passed down the curves and the islands into an ever-increasing sense of sheer immensity. The little posts lie from a hundred to a hundred and fifty miles apart, and nothing human is between them. The first post was Fort Providence where, in the year of Confederation, the sisters at the Catholic mission nearly starved to death. Then came Fort Simpson, Wrigley, Fort Norman, Norman Wells, Fort Good Hope, Arctic Red River, Fort McPherson, Aklavik, Reindeer Depot and Tuktoyaktuk (known on the river as Tuk or Tuk-Tuk) on the fringe of the Arctic Ocean. Because the river supplies all these posts with heavy freight, because there are no roads to supplement it, the Mackenzie system is the only one left on the continent which fulfills the old role all the great rivers once played. In one sense a Mackenzie voyage is like a journey into the past. This is the sole avenue of heavy traffic in a length of more than fifteen hundred miles, nor has the river changed in any important respect since the year when Alexander Mackenzie discovered it. Even the lignite beds he saw burning at Fort Norman burn there still.

Monotony, endless monotony and vast skies, but not a monotony which is depressing. Now the river thrusts fiercely along its trench and scoops great gouges out of the escarpments along the curves; now it flows silent and wide past swamps lined with willow trees; always it embraces islands. We sailed through the wide mirror of Mills Lake and the 3,000–foot-high whale-back of the Mackenzie Mountains emerged on the left, then the Franklin Mountains on the east. The mountains abruptly marshal the stream northward in the great curve now known as the Camsell Bend. I noticed the nights getting longer and cooler. On the first of September there was a frost in the night, fog in the morning and a great movement of wild geese flying south.

I cannot remember one day from the other, but I do remember that the radio was still blacked out when *Radium Yellowknife* was approaching its rendezvous with *Radium Charles*. A deckhand told me he could fetch Australia, but could not hear a thing from the *Charles;* he may have been kidding me about Australia, but I certainly know we picked up Russia one afternoon. Finally Captain Sveinson moored his barges and told Morris and me that he must return up river. The season was late and he could afford to waste no more time. He said he would be willing to keep us on board if we wished, but if he did so he would be unable to transfer us to a northbound vessel. However, he was sure *Radium Charles* would appear some time that day, and that it would be safe for us to wait for it on the barges.

So Morris and I stayed with the barges, *Radium Yellowknife* disappeared around the bend and we were alone on the river in total silence. I thought I saw a bear peering down at us from the top of the escarpment, but it turned out to be a broken, weather-worn tree stump. Then it began to rain and get cold. Wet, feeling what a psychologist would call a sense of insecurity, I walked about among the bales on the barges getting steadily colder. We pried open the door of one of the covered barges and looked for a place to sit. It was jammed to the walls with crates and boxes, but there were two boxes with barely room for both of us, so we sat down and I lit a cigarette. I was just beginning to enjoy it when Morris let out a chuckle and said: "Have you noticed what we're sitting on?" My box was labelled "Dynamite" and his "Dynamite Caps," so I tossed the cigarette over the edge of the barge and just sat. A little before dusk *Radium Charles* emerged around the bend pushing the remainder of our barges.

And so down the river to Norman Wells, the most substantial community of them all because it is not a Hudson's Bay Company trading-post but a little refinery town, the farthest north of any refinery in America. Here the Mackenzie swings out in a magnificent bight, the mountains afford a large plain on either side of the stream and the prospect is one of the finest on the continent. There are homes with gardens growing delphinium eight feet high, technicians and chemists and all the men necessary to keep a refinery in operation. The Wells lie just south of the Arctic Circle and have the last air strip in this part of the North. Below them down to Tuk all the planes are equipped with pontoons and land on the water.

Below the Wells the Mackenzie, having taken in many tributaries with a few more to come, carves almost directly down to the North. In summer the melting of the top layer of the permafrost turns the banks into a kind of slime and in winter the whole region would be locked in total darkness for a month were it not for the gleam of the stars on the snow and the light of the aurora. One old northern hand told me that he once was under a winter aurora so intense his dogs refused to work. The lights kept shifting first to one side then to the other, throwing the dogs' shadows as rapidly back and forth as the *Radium King* in a cross sea, so that the dogs whimpered, lay down and buried their heads in the snow. Below the Wells the contrasts along the Mackenzie are so extreme they can best be described in this sentence: the river enters a land of midnight sun in June and of midday night in December.

Finally this river enters one of the most enormous deltas in the western hemisphere, a fantastic region of submerged and emergent islands, of confused channels, of low banks slimy in summer from a permafrost several hundred feet deep out of which the occasional pingoe pops up, a wonderful country for muskrats and mosquitoes, and at the end of it the true arctic tundra at last. The delta extends north and south a distance of a hundred miles and its seaward spread is seventy miles, with the steep scarp of the Richardson Mountains rising abruptly out of the delta plain, while the easterly section is bounded by the low humped range of the Caribou Hills. Streams ramify here, and only from the air is it possible to visualize the complexity of the channels. The Peel, a sizable and partially navigable river, enters the delta in such a way that some of its lower stretches are easily confused with the master stream. Fort McPherson is located on the Peel, and on one of its channels stands Aklavik, or what remains of it after the community was shifted to Inuvik a few years ago. Here live Eskimos and a few white men. The permafrost is so near to the surface that when houses are built they use steam hoses in place of drills, and find glare ice at a depth of a few feet. Yet in prepared soil on top of the permafrost, cabbages the size of basket-balls have been grown under the perpetual sun of summer. Inuvik, the most northerly community in the hemisphere, has a latitude about the same as that of Norway's North Cape, but the sea it confronts is colder.

When winter comes to this region it does not come slowly; it strikes with a crack. I met a veteran of many years on the Mackenzie who told me that he once escaped having to spend an entire long winter in Aklavik by a matter of a minute. His was the last plane out, and as he stood on one of its pontoons filling his tank with gas, he suddenly noticed ice forming on the water. He threw the can away, jumped into the pilot's seat without even taking time to screw on the cap of the gas tank, gunned the plane and took off. The thin ice was crackling about the pontoons before he became airborne, and as he made his circle to head south he saw pack ice thrusting in and the lagoon from which he had risen turn opaque as though the frost had cast a wand over it.

SIGURD F. OLSON

Ile à la crosse 1961

SIGURD F. OLSON (1899–1982) was one of North America's best-known naturalists. Educated at Northland College, the University of Wisconsin and the University of Illinois, he was a teacher, writer and guide who also became president of the Wilderness Society and the National Parks Association. From his home in Ely, Minnesota, a few miles south of the Canadian border, he made regular canoe trips into the north country—where he was known as "le Bourgeois" in honor of his skill with a paddle and his love of the way of the voyageurs. *The Lonely Land* (1961), from which this chapter is excerpted, is an account of a 500-mile canoe trip along the great Churchill River in Saskatchewan, from Ile-à-la-Crosse to Cumberland House, following the route taken by the early explorers. Olson's other books include *The Singing Wilderness* (1956), *Listening Point* (1961), *Runes of the North* (1963), and *Open Horizons* (1969).

This lake and fort take their names from . . . the game of the cross which forms a principle amusement among the natives. The situation of this lake, the abundance of the finest fish in the world to be found in its waters, the richness of its surrounding banks and forests, in moose and fallow deer [probably Barren Ground caribou]*, with the vast numbers of the smaller tribes of animals, whose skins are precious, and the numerous flocks of wild fowl that frequent it in the spring and fall, make it a most desirable spot for the constant residence of some and the occasional rendezvous of others of the inhabitants of the country, particularly the Kniesteneaux.*

—*Alexander Mackenzie*

I WALKED to the end of the dock and looked over the canoes. Their bows were snubbed to the pilings and they floated freely, pulling gently at their moorings. The packs were stowed away and I counted them once more. Extra paddles, tracking lines, map cases tied to the thwarts, fishing rods, axes, all were there. The canoes rode well, not too high in the bows, but just enough. Peterborough Prospectors were made for the bush and for roaring rapids and waves. They embodied the best features of all canoes in the north. They were wide of beam with sufficient depth to take rough water, and their lines gave them maneuverability and grace. In them was the lore of centuries, of Indian craftsmen who had dreamed and perfected the beauty of the birchbark, and of French voyageurs who also loved the feel of a paddle and the smooth glide of a canoe through the water. All this was taken by modern craftsmen who—with glues, waterproof fillers and canvas, together with the accuracy of machine-tooled ribs and thwarts, planking and gunwales—made a canoe of which Northmen might well be proud. Our three lay there in the sunshine ready to go.

Back of the dock, the marsh grass was beaten down where the packs had been thrown. I went over, walked through the patch of sedge, and kicked around with my boots to see if some small item might have fallen out. A package of salt or pepper, the first-aid-kit, a compass, a reel, or a box of fishing lures, a hand of rope or twine, patching material for the canoes, the Carborundum stone for sharpening knives and axes—the loss of any one of these would cause trouble from the start. I walked back and forth, explored beneath a willow bush, and satisfied at last, returned to the canoes.

A number of Indians watched our final preparations. Corp. Albin Nelson of the Royal Canadian Mounted Police was there with his wife and Mr. and Mrs. Leonard Budgel of the Hudson's Bay Company. They had all been very kind, were used to expeditions starting off, understood how little time we had, and our need of getting swiftly underway.

Now everything was ready. Behind us was the luncheon at Prince Albert, the greetings and warnings, the photographs and interviews, the inevitable delays in getting all the gear and equipment together in one place, final messages and good-bys, the thousand-and-one necessary things that are time-consuming.

"The water is high," said Corporal Nelson, "possibly three feet above normal. You'll have to watch the rapids with the river over its banks."

"Camp on the sandspit," said Mr. Budgel. "It will be dry there."

We shook hands all around and got into the canoes—Tony and Omond in the first, Elliot and Eric in the second, Denis and I in the third. We would start that way and see how things worked out. The final decisions as to who would stay with whom was a matter of weight, strength, and endurance, something that could be determined only after several days of paddling. While the bow lines were being freed, I stood up in the stern for a final look around.

"Watch Drum Rapids," said one of the Indians. "Stay on the left after the fast water."

"Wolverine knows river," said another. "He live Patuanak."

I nodded, sat down and pushed hard against the dock. When safely out, we turned, waved good-by once more. We heard Corporal Nelson's motor and in a moment his boat swept past us and around for final pictures. We rolled in the swells, waved gaily again and then headed down the lake. We were alone on its placid surface. The Hudson's Bay Post with its scattered clusters of cabins and tents was to one side. On the dock was a black knot of figures. It was breaking up now. The Indians were going back to the village. Just back of the dock was the green airstrip carved out of the bush where we had landed only a few hours ago.

We headed for a long point a mile away, a promontory that would separate us from contact with the outside. That point was the door to the wilderness. When we rounded it, we would enter the world of Alexander Mackenzie, Peter Pond, and David Thompson, where nothing had really changed.

It felt good to be cruising again, good to feel the canoe responding to each stroke, to hear the ripple from the bow and the steady swish of our paddles. Our shirts came off and the sun beat on our backs.

Denis laughed out loud. "Bourgeois," he said, "we paddle well together, n'est-ce pas?"

His great shoulders bent to the work, and our canoe leaped forward. How easy to swing through a stroke without any encumbrance! Muscles were free again and so were our lungs. The air was clean with just enough coolness, and in it the smell of hundreds of square miles of spruce and waterways, muskeg and tundra, caribou moss and wet granite. Then suddenly the point was to our left and we were slipping by it into the open, with only distance and space to the north. Off to the left was Aubichon Arm reaching for Peter Pond Lake and Methye Portage on the great divide between the Churchill and the Mackenzie. Down that blue misty sweep had come the brigades of the past on their way to grand Portage to meet the men from Montreal.

Somewhere ten miles away was our camp site, but the distance meant nothing to us then. Ten, twenty, or forty miles at the moment, it was all the same, so good did it feel to be underway again. As the vistas took hold, all else was forgotten. The warm of the sun caressed us, and muscles that hadn't been used for a long time stretched themselves and tensed against the pull of our blades. We were seeing Ile à la Crosse as we wanted to, counting the miles and headlands as only canoemen do with time enough to absorb and study every detail of the shores. None of us said a word during those first hours. Now with the open horizons to the north all we wanted was to push ahead, soak up the first impressions of a great new waterway and feel those Peterboroughs move smoothly through the water.

Eric and Elliot were far to the right, Omond and Tony to the left, their paddles moving as rhythmically as ours. Their shirts were off too. The color of those backs would change from pink and white to brown. They were unscarred now—no scratches, no welts from black flies of the "bulldogs"—but all of that would come. The canoes rode high and their reflections shimmered in the light. They seemed very small on the vast surface of the lake and at times almost disappeared in the haze that hung above it. So small and fragile did they appear that it seemed almost presumptuous to expect them to reach their destination.

Once long ago I had written:

"The movement of a canoe is like a reed in the wind. Silence is part of it, and the sounds of lapping water, bird songs, and wind in the trees. It is part of the medium through which it floats, the sky, the water, and the shores. A man is part of his canoe and therefore part of all it knows. The instant he dips his paddle, he flows as it flows, the canoe yielding to his slightest touch and responsive to his every whim and thought . . . There is magic in the feel of a paddle and the movement of a canoe, a magic compounded of distance, adventure, solitude and peace. The way of a canoe is the way of the wilderness and of a freedom almost forgotten, the open door to waterways of ages past and a way of life with profound and abiding satisfactions."

We were in the groove again, and suddenly it seemed as though we had never been away from it. Strange how swiftly one moves into a wilderness way of life, how airplane terminals, crowds, cities, and jobs move into the background and seem unimportant compared to the fact that one is underway and on one's own. We had a camp site to find, tents to set up, gear to sort; the outfit must be whipped into shape before dark. Mr. Budgel had mentioned a sandspit somewhere down the lake, a beach off a point, and after an hour we saw it jutting out like a long brown finger from the west. We would find no rocks in the Ile à la Crosse country, no smooth shelves for landing and tent sites until we reached the Canadian Shield some days later. But a beach of any kind was better than a camp in the willows. With flood conditions on the Churchill, dry places would be scarce.

As we neared the sandspit, we had our first real glimpse of the lake's full sweep. "This is it," I kept saying to myself, "this is the Churchill country, Great Slave, Mackenzie," names that had haunted my dreams for years. "This," I said to myself, "is where you might have come half a lifetime ago had you not found the Quetico-Superior country north of Lake Superior."

The sandspit rose like a wall on the south side but leveled off toward the end of the point and on the north. Tent poles and drying racks for fish indicated an old Indian camp. The end of the spit was alive with pelicans, gulls, sandpipers, terns, and shorebirds of all kinds. Suddenly it seemed to rise, and the air was full of wings and the screaming of birds. It was our first encounter with the white pelicans; we watched them with delight as they soared in perfect wingtip formation down the lake. The smaller birds came back, reluctant to leave their feeding ground, and ran up and down close to the water's edge even when the canoes drew near. We circled the end of the point and found that on the far side where the waves came down the long sweep of the lake, the sand had been washed up level and smooth. We landed there and unloaded the canoes.

Back of the beach itself was a spot grown thickly enough with bear berry so that the sand would not get into our food and sleeping bags. I was glad to see it. A sandy camp at the beginning of an expedition can be a source of annoyance during the entire trip. No matter how careful one may be, sand always gets into everything. There was plenty of space, protection from the wind and a grand view down the lake. We would see both the sunset and the sunrise and out in the open, the birds, who were still protesting our presence.

Raspberry bushes grew in profusion. We quickly picked enough berries for supper, which would be an ample meal of fried ham, mashed potatoes, tea, and a loaf of fresh bread Mrs. Budgel had given us. There was plenty of driftwood for a fire and even before the tents were unpacked, a blaze was crackling under the old blackened pots. I sliced the ham and placed it in the frying pan, then laid out some tinned butter and jam. In half an hour supper would be ready.

The voyageurs were blowing up their air beds and laying out their sleeping bags. Once voyageurs slept on the ground under their canoes with only a single blanket to cover them. They had no mosquito bars, no real protection should it storm. Only the Bourgeois had a tent lined with spruce boughs, but still they slept soundly—as who would not after sixteen hours of paddling and portaging. Even the ground was soft to them and when they arouse what speed was theirs!

Thomas L. McKenney, according to Paul Provencher, recalled an instance from his expedition in 1826, "when his men took the canoe out of the water, mended a breach in it, reloaded, cooked breakfast, shaved, washed, ate and reembarked, all in fifty-seven minutes." We were not that fast because we had more equipment to pack. Usually it took a couple of hours to get underway in the morning, though camp was pitched in half the time at night.

The three-man seven-by-nine Baker tent went up for Elliot, Omond, and Denis. Shaped like a wedge with the entire front open and a broad protecting fly, it was our refuge when it rained during meal times. The low rear needed no supports and the front only one sturdy pole between two sets of crosses.

Tony and I had a seven-by-seven foot "A" tent which could be strung between two trees or, if none were available, supported by the conventional set of cross poles at each end.

Eric, who likes to sleep alone, had a small explorer's pup tent. Usually his pitch required no poles at all, merely a convenient branch to hold up the front end, and bushes or pegs for the side and rear ties.

All the tents were made of closely woven, waterproofed cotton cloth. They were fitted with good mosquito bars closed with zippers. Sod cloths all around the bottom were adequate enough so they could be firmly weighted down with stones, if necessary. We did not like sewed-in bottoms, so each ground sheet was separate and could be used as a tarpaulin in case of emergency. When the air beds and sleeping bags were laid down and the ground sheet carefully tucked over the sod cloth, no flies or mosquitoes could enter.

How swiftly a place becomes home when the tents are up and a fire burning. Our shelters looked cozy and almost permanent there above the beach, and the smoke from our fire made it seem as though we had been there a long time. It was almost as though we were still on the canoe trip of the year before when we covered the La Vérendrye route and camped on the beach at Grand Portage. Blair Fraser and John Endemann had been along then. Blair was now in the Near East for *Maclean's Magazine,* John at the South African Embassy in Rome. It was hard to believe a year had passed.

After supper we sorted the outfit, getting order out of confusion by checking items of personal gear, flashlights, knives, pencils, maps, and aerial photographs. Food was all important, so we sorted out mounds of muslin bags, breakfast, lunch, supper supplies, staples, and items for immediate consumption. The extra bags of flour, rice, peas, beans, sugar, reserves of bacon, salt pork, dried fruit went into a pack we would not have to touch for a week or more. Into the lunch pack went the various items we would need each noon, the condiments, the odds and ends of equipment in constant use. It would take several days for the outfit to shake down to the point where we knew the exact location of everything. The important thing now was to place the reserves in the bottoms of the packs, the items which might be used immediately on top where they could be found without trouble or lengthy searching. In time those food bags would become so familiar in appearance and feel that I could go through them in the dark and know by a touch exactly what was in each.

I looked over the foodstuffs. What a variety compared to that of the old-time voyageurs! All they had were dried peas or corn, possibly some fat or pemmican with whatever extra they could find. Day after day and week after week it was simply that. The cook had only one pot to worry about, though it was a big one. The flour soup went in the pot, and after it was nearly cooked, whatever meat or grease was available was added. A quart of peas or corn or flour per man was the usual daily ration.

According to the 1857 journal of Peter Jacobs, a native missionary, this was their standard food.

"The food that is generally prepared and eaten in these regions by voyageurs is what is called 'ahrubuhboo.' I do not know what the word itself means. I spell it as I hear it pronounced. All pork eaters from Canada do not know how to make it; I shall here tell my readers how I proceeded to make it; for it was this sort of food we had in the voyage. After I had got the wood in order, and made a good blazing fire, I took my kettle, went to the lake, and put in it about two quarts of water. While this was getting to boil over the fire, I took a two-quart hand dish half full of water, and put into it some flour, and stirred it till it looked like mush. The pan was now full. As the water in the kettle was now boiling, I took my pandish, and put all that was in it in the kettle, where it became thinner. I then took a stick and stirred. This, of course took some time to boil. When it boiled, I kept stirring it in order to prevent dregs of the flour soup from sinking and sticking to the bottom of the kettle and burning.

"If it burned, the dinner would be spoiled . . . When the flour soup was quite cooked, I removed the kettle from the fire; and while my soup was boiling hot, I jumped at my hatchet or tomahawk, and cut to pieces about a pound weight of pemmican, after which I threw this into the kettle. I stirred this quickly so that the grease of the pemmican might be dissolved in the hot flour soup. Thus ends the cooking. The time it takes to cook this is less than half an hour. It is very much like what is called in some countries burgoo. This 'ahrubuhboo' is first rate food for travelers in this country. At this time I poured it out in dishes for my men and myself, and made a good dinner out of it. Very often the men, when they are in a great hurry, instead of using dishes and spoons, pour out their 'ahrubuhboo' on the smooth and hollow rocks, where it becomes cooler in a short time, and eat it; those who have no spoons generally eat it in dog fashion, licking it up with their tongues."

What luxury was ours compared to theirs. For breakfasts we always had bacon or fish, Red River porridge, or oatmeal cooked with raisins and served with brown sugar, dehydrated milk and always a pot of strong, black coffee.

For lunches there was bread or bannock, with marmalade, cheese, corned beef or sausage and either a cold drink made of fruit crystals or tea; for supper, fish or dried meat with dehydrated vegetables and a pail of dried fruit. Any Bourgeois of two hundred years ago would have thought our supplies were a sign of softness and degeneracy. Actually the weight and the amount of bulk of our food, most of it dehydrated, was not much more than theirs, nor did it take any longer to prepare. We carried only enough food for two weeks. We could replenish our supplies at Stanley Post halfway down the Churchill. Approximately two pounds per man per day compared favorably with the weight of the standard ration of a quart of dried peas with some pork or fat for each voyageur in the days of the brigades.

After supper Tony and I went for a paddle. The water was already tinted by the sunset. It was too weedy and shallow for fishing, so we sat in the canoe a mile away from camp and listened. We had a tradition of after-supper paddles, he and I, and no matter if we had traveled all day and were dog-tired, if possible we pushed off for a final hour before rolling in. In a sense it was a luxury not to have any particular objective, and those last moments of idle drifting seemed a good way to end the day. We sat there in the glow and looked back toward the sandspit. The tents were very tiny and the smoke from our fire rose straight into the sky. There was no movement around camp, no lifting of wings, no sound of screaming birds.

"Bourgeois," said Tony, "it is good to be here, very good," and I knew what it meant for him to be away from the world of diplomatic functions, the endless whirl of social life in the capital, the delicate balancing of personalities and values, his ever-present responsibilities.

That night it seemed good to crawl into our sleeping bags, to lie there again and listen. Once I heard the howl of a husky dog from an Indian camp down the shore. At first I thought it might be a wolf, forgetting for the moment we were within ten miles of the post. I had seen tracks in the sand and had wondered. But the howl settled it. This was the land of the Crees and huskies and their music would be a part of every Indian camp we would pass. As we drifted off to sleep I could hear the wind rising behind us to the south, just a soft whispering over the sand, but enough to tell me that things were stirring. If it continued, by dawn we might have a gale behind us for the thirty-mile run to the end of the lake.

FARLEY MOWAT

Never Cry Wolf 1963

Born in 1921 in Belleville, Ontario, FARLEY MOWAT was introduced to the
Canadian Arctic by an ornithologist great-uncle in 1935. In 1947, Mowat returned to the Arctic, spending the two years there that resulted in his first
book, *People of the Deer* (1952), and its sequel, *The Desperate People* (1959),
both impassioned pleas for the Ihalmiut of the Keewatin Barrens, a people
that had been all but wiped out by government interference and the decline
of the caribou herds. Mowat's interest in caribou populations led to a study of
predator-prey relationships, and so he returned to the Barrens in 1960 as a
member of the Canadian Wildlife Service to make field observation on
wolves. His account of his investigations, *Never Cry Wolf* (1963), is one of the
most popular natural history books ever written; as this excerpt shows,
Mowat was one of the first biologists to recognize that wolves are not the
bloodthirsty predators that writers like Jack London had imagined
them to be.

AFTER SOME WEEKS of study I still seemed to be as far as ever from solving
the salient problem of how the wolves made a living. This was a vital problem,
since solving it in a way satisfactory to my employers was the reason for my
expedition.

Caribou are the only large herbivores to be found in any numbers in the arctic Barren Lands. Although once as numerous as the plains buffalo, they had
shown a catastrophic decrease during the three or four decades preceding my
trip to the Barrens. Evidence obtained by various Government agencies from
hunters, trappers and traders seemed to prove that the plunge of the caribou

toward extinction was primarily due to the depredations of the wolf. It therefore must have seemed a safe bet, to the politicians-cum-scientists who had employed me, that a research study of wolf-caribou relationships in the Barrens would uncover incontrovertible proof with which to damn the wolf wherever he might be found, and provide a more than sufficient excuse for the adoption of a general campaign for his extirpation.

I did my duty, but although I had searched diligently for evidence which would please my superiors, I had so far found none. Nor did it appear I was likely to.

Toward the end of June, the last of the migrating caribou herds had passed Wolf House Bay heading for the high Barrens some two or three hundred miles to the north, where they would spend the summer.

Whatever my wolves were going to eat during those long months, and whatever they were going to feed their hungry pups, it would not be caribou, for the caribou were gone. But if not caribou, what *was* it to be?

I canvassed all the other possibilities I could think of, but there seemed to be no source of food available which would be adequate to satisfy the appetites of three adult and four young wolves. Apart from myself (and the thought recurred several times) there was hardly an animal left in the country which could be considered suitable prey for a wolf. Arctic hares were present; but they were very scarce and so fleet of foot that a wolf could not hope to catch one unless he was extremely lucky. Ptarmigan and other birds were numerous; but they could fly, and the wolves could not. Lake trout, arctic grayling and whitefish filled the lakes and rivers; but wolves are not otters.

The days passed and the mystery deepened. To make the problem even more inscrutable, the wolves seemed reasonably well fed: and to baffle me to the point of near insanity, the two male wolves went off hunting every night and returned every morning, but never appeared to bring anything home.

As far as I could tell, the whole lot of them seemed to be existing on a diet of air and water. Once, moved by a growing concern for their well-being, I went back to the cabin and baked five loaves of bread, which I then took to Wolf House Bay and left beside one of the hunting paths. My gift was rejected. It was even scorned. Or perhaps Uncle Albert, who discovered them, simply thought the loaves were some new sort of boundary posts which I had erected, and that they were to be treated accordingly.

About this time I began having trouble with mice. The vast expanses of spongy sphagnum bog provided an ideal milieu for several species of small rodents who could burrow and nest-build to their hearts' content in the ready-made mattress of moss.

They did other things too, and they must have done them with great frequency, for as June waned into July the country seemed to become alive with little rodents. The most numerous species were the lemmings, which are famed in literature for their reputedly suicidal instincts, but which, instead, *ought* to be hymned for their unbelievable reproductive capabilities. Red-backed mice and meadow mice began invading Mike's cabin in such numbers that it looked is if *I* would soon be starving unless I could thwart their appetites for my supplies. *They* did not scorn my bread. They did not scorn my bed, either; and when I awoke one morning to find that a meadow mouse had given birth to eleven naked offspring inside the pillow of my sleeping bag, I began to know how Pharaoh must have felt when he antagonized the God of the Israelites.

I suppose it was only because my own wolf indoctrination had been so complete, and of such a staggeringly inaccurate nature, that it took me so long to account for the healthy state of the wolves in the apparent absence of any game worthy of their reputation and physical abilities. The idea of wolves not only eating, but actually thriving and raising their families on a diet of mice was so at odds with the character of the mythical wolf that it was really too ludicrous to consider. And yet, it was the answer to the problem of how my wolves were keeping the larder full.

Angeline tipped me off.

Late one afternoon, while the male wolves were still resting in preparation for the night's labors, she emerged from the den and nuzzled Uncle Albert until he yawned, stretched and got laboriously to his feet. Then she left the den site at a trot, heading directly for me across a broad expanse of grassy muskeg, and leaving Albert to entertain the pups as best he could.

There was nothing particularly new in this. I had several times seen her conscript Albert (and on rare occasions even George) to do duty as a babysitter while she went down to the bay for a drink or, as I mistakenly thought, simply went for a walk to stretch her legs. Usually her peregrinations took her to the point of the bay farthest from my tent where she was hidden from sight by a low gravel ridge; but this time she came my way in full view and so I swung my telescope to keep an eye on her.

She went directly to the rocky foreshore, waded out until the icy water was up to her shoulders, and had a long drink. As she was doing so, a small flock of Old Squaw ducks flew around the point of the Bay and pitched only a hundred yards or so away from her. She raised her head and eyed them speculatively for a moment, then waded back to shore, where she proceeded to act as if she had suddenly become demented.

Yipping like a puppy, she began to chase her tail; to roll over and over among the rocks; to lie on her back; to wave all four feet furiously in the air; and in general to behave as if she were clean out of her mind.

I swung the glasses back to where Albert was sitting amidst a gaggle of pups to see if he, too, had observed this mad display, and, if so, what his reaction to it was. He had seen it all right, in fact he was watching Angeline with keen interest but without the slightest indication of alarm.

By this time Angeline appeared to be in the throes of a manic paroxysm, leaping wildly into the air and snapping at nothing, the while uttering shrill squeals. It was an awe-inspiring sight, and I realized that Albert and I were not the only ones who were watching it with fascination. The ducks seemed hypnotized by curiosity. So interested were they that they swam in for a closer view of this apparition on the shore. Closer and closer they came, necks outstretched, and gabbling incredulously among themselves. And the closer they came, the crazier grew Angeline's behavior.

When the leading duck was not more than fifteen feet from shore, Angeline gave one gigantic leap towards it. There was a vast splash, a panic-stricken whacking of wings, and then all the ducks were up and away. Angeline had missed a dinner by no more than inches.

This incident was an eye-opener since it suggested a versatility at food-getting which I would hardly have credited to a human being, let alone to a mere wolf. However, Angeline soon demonstrated that the charming of ducks was a mere side line.

Having dried herself with a series of energetic shakes which momentarily hid her in a blue mist of water droplets, she padded back across the grassy swale. But now her movements were quite different from what they had been when she passed through the swale on the way to the bay.

Angeline was of a rangy build, anyway, but by stretching herself so that she literally seemed to be walking on tiptoe, and be elevating her neck like a camel, she seemed to gain several inches in height. She began to move infinitely slowly upwind across the swale, and I had the impression that both ears were cocked for the faintest sound, while I could see her nose wrinkling as she sifted the breeze for the most ephemeral scents.

Suddenly she pounced. Flinging herself up on her hind legs like a horse trying to throw its rider, she came down again with diving force, both forelegs held stiffly out in front of her. Instantly her head dropped; she snapped once, swallowed, and returned to her peculiar mincing ballet across the swale.

Six times in ten minutes she repeated the straight-armed pounce, and six times she swallowed—without my having caught a glimpse of what it was that she had eaten. The seventh time she missed her aim, spun around, and began snapping frenziedly in a tangle of cotton grasses. This time when she raised her head I saw, quite unmistakably, the tail and hind quarters of a mouse quivering in her jaws. One gulp, and it too was gone.

Although I was much entertained by the spectacle of one of this continent's most powerful carnivores hunting mice, I did not really take it seriously. I thought Angeline was only having fun; snacking, as it were. But when she had eaten some twenty-three mice I began to wonder. Mice are small, but twenty-three of them adds up to a fair-sized meal, even for a wolf.

It was only later, by putting two and two together, that I was able to bring myself to an acceptance of the obvious. The wolves of Wolf House Bay, and, by inference at least, all the Barren Land wolves who were raising families outside the summer caribou range, were living largely, if not almost entirely, on mice.

Only one point remained obscure, and that was how they transported the catch of mice (which in the course of an entire night must have amounted to a formidable number of individuals) back to the dens to feed the pups. I never did solve this problem until I met some of Mike's relations. One of them, a charming fellow named Ootek, who became a close friend (and who was a first-rate, if untrained, naturalist), explained the mystery.

Since it was impossible for the wolves to carry the mice home externally, they did the next best thing and brought them home in their bellies. I had already noticed that when either George or Albert returned from a hunt they went straight to the den and crawled into it. Though I did not suspect it at the time, they were regurgitating the day's rations, already partially digested.

Later in the summer, when the pups had abandoned the den in the esker, I several times saw one of the adult wolves regurgitating a meal for them. However, if I had not known what they were doing I probably would have misconstrued the action and still been no whit the wiser as to how the wolves carried home their spoils.

The discovery that mice constituted the major item in the wolves' diet gave me a new interest in the mice themselves. I at once began a mouse-survey. The preliminary operation consisted of setting some hundred and fifty mousetraps in a nearby bog in order to obtain a representative sample of the mouse population in terms of sex, age, density and species. I chose an area of bog not far from my tent, on the theory that it would be typical of one of the bogs hunted over by the wolves, and also because it was close at hand and would therefore allow me to tend my traps frequently. This choice was a mistake. The second day my trap line was set, George happened in that direction.

I saw him coming and was undecided what to do. Since we were still scrupulously observing our mutual boundaries, I did not feel like dashing outside my enclave in an effort to head him off. On the other hand, I had no idea how he would react when he discovered that I had been poaching on his preserves.

When he reached the edge of the bog he snuffed about for a while, then cast a suspicious glance in my direction. Obviously he knew I had been trespassing but was at a loss to understand why. Making no attempt to hunt, he began walking through the cotton grass on the edge of the bog and I saw, to my horror, that he was heading straight for a cluster of ten traps set near the burrows of a lemming colony.

I had an instant flash of foreknowledge of what was going to happen, and without thought I leaped to me feet and yelled at the top of my voice:

"George! For God's sake HOLD IT!"

It was too late. My shout only startled him and he broke into a trot. He went about ten paces on the level and then he began climbing an unseen ladder to the skies.

When, sometime later, I went over to examine the site, I found he had scored six traps out of the possible ten. They could have done him no real harm, of course, but the shock and pain of having a number of his toes nipped simultaneously by an unknown antagonist must have been considerable. For the first and only time that I knew him, George lost his dignity. Yipping like a dog who has caught his tail in a door, he streaked for home, shedding mousetraps like confetti as he went.

I felt very badly about the incident. It might easily have resulted in a serious rupture in our relations. That it did not do so I can only attribute to the fact that George's sense of humor, which was well developed, led him to accept the affair as a crude practical joke—of the kind to be expected from a human being.

The realization that the wolves' summer diet consisted chiefly of mice did not conclude my work in the field of dietetics. I knew that the mouse-wolf relationship was a revolutionary one to science and would be treated with suspicion, and possibly with ridicule, unless it could be so thoroughly substantiated that there would be no room to doubt its validity.

I had already established two major points:

1. That wolves caught and ate mice.
2. That the small rodents were sufficiently numerous to support the wolf population.

There remained, however, a third point vital to the proof of my contention. This concerned the nutritional value of mice. It was imperative for me to prove that a diet of small rodents would suffice to maintain a large carnivore in good condition.

I recognized that this was not going to be an easy task. Only a controlled experiment would do, and since I could not exert the necessary control over the wolves, I was at a loss how to proceed. Had Mike still been in the vicinity I might have borrowed two of his Huskies and, by feeding one of them on mice alone and the other on caribou meat (if and when this became obtainable), and then subjecting both dogs to similar tests, I would have been able to adduce the proof for or against the validity of the mouse-wolf concept. But Mike was gone, and I had no idea when he might return.

For some days I pondered the problem, and then one morning, while I was preparing some lemmings and meadow mice as specimens, inspiration struck me. Despite the fact that man is not wholly carnivorous, I could see no valid reason why I should not use myself as a test subject. It was true that there was only one of me; but the difficulty this posed could be met by setting up two timed intervals, during one of which I would confine myself to mouse diet while during the second period of equal length I would eat canned meat and fresh fish. At the end of each period I would run a series of physiological tests upon myself and finally compare the two sets of results. While not absolutely conclusive as far as wolves were concerned, evidence that *my* metabolic functions remained unimpaired under a mouse regimen would strongly indicate that wolves, too, could survive and function normally on the same diet.

There being no time like the present, I resolved to begin the experiment at once. Having cleaned the basinful of small corpses which remained from my morning session of mouse skinning, I placed them in a pot and hung it over my primus stove. The pot gave off a most delicate and delicious odor as the water boiled and I was in excellent appetite by the time the stew was done.

Eating these small mammals presented something of a problem at first because of the numerous minute bones; however, I found that the bones could be chewed and swallowed without much difficulty. The taste of mice—a purely subjective factor and not in the least relevant to the experiment—was pleasing, if rather bland. As the experiment progressed, this blandness led to a degree of boredom and a consequent loss of appetite and I was forced to seek variety in my methods of preparation.

Of the several recipes which I developed, the finest by far was Creamed Mouse, and in the event that any of my readers may be interested in personally exploiting this hitherto overlooked source of excellent animal protein, I give the recipe in full.

SOURIS À LA CRÈME

INGREDIENTS:

One dozen fat mice   Salt and pepper
One cup white flour   Cloves
One piece sowbelly   Ethyl alcohol

[I should perhaps note that sowbelly is normally only available in the arctic, but ordinary salt pork can be substituted.]

Skin and gut the mice, but do not remove the heads; wash, then place in a pot with enough alcohol to cover the carcasses. Allow to marinate for about two hours. Cut sowbelly into small cubes and fry slowly until most of the fat has been rendered. Now remove the carcasses from the alcohol and roll them in a mixture of salt, pepper and flour; then place in frying pan and sauté for about five minutes (being careful not to allow the pan to get too hot, or the delicate meat will dry out and become tough and stringy). Now add a cup of alcohol and six or eight cloves. Cover the pan and allow to simmer slowly for fifteen minutes. The cream sauce can be made according to any standard recipe. When the sauce is ready, drench the carcasses with it, cover and allow to rest in a warm place for ten minutes before serving.

During the first week of the mouse diet I found that my vigor remained unimpaired, and that I suffered no apparent ill effects. However, I did begin to develop a craving for fats. It was this which made me realize that my experiment, up to this point, had been rendered partly invalid by an oversight—and one, moreover, which did my scientific training no credit. The wolves, as I should have remembered, *ate the whole mouse;* and my dissections had shown that these small rodents stored most of their fat in the abdominal cavity, adhering to the intestinal mesenteries, rather than subcutaneously or in the muscular tissue. It was an inexcusable error I had made, and I hastened to rectify it. From this time to the end of the experimental period I, too, ate the whole mouse, without the skin of course, and I found that my fat craving was considerably eased.

FRANKLIN RUSSELL

The Island of Auks 1965

FRANKLIN RUSSELL was born in Christchurch, New Zealand, in 1926, and moved to Canada in 1954. While in Canada, he wrote many of the books that established his reputation as a naturalist, including *Watchers at the Pond* (1962), an account of a year's life in, around and under a natural pond. Moving to the U.S. in 1963, he wrote *Searchers at the Gulf* (1970), which started out as "a comprehensive natural history of the Gulf of St. Lawrence," but ended up as a brilliant portrayal of any gulf—perhaps including that between modern humankind and nature. "Either Gulf," he writes, "may yield whatever a searcher chooses to find in it." In the 1960s, he made many forays to islands in the Gulf of St. Lawrence and the Bay of Fundy which resulted in *The Secret Islands* (1965), and the chapter describing his trip to Funk Island, off the east coast of Newfoundland, is reprinted here.

&· ֎

ARTHUR STURGE was caught in an immortal moment, straining back on his oar as he moved the heavy dory toward Funk Island. This was the last lunge of the journey; the longliner heaved behind us; Uncle Jacob had bellowed his final exhortation of good luck.

I saw the island close up as I glanced over Sturge's shoulder, and I knew I was duplicating the experience of a thousand men before me. From the boat it seemed incredible that such a stream of humanity—explorers, Indians, sealers, whalers, codfishermen—had ever reached this lonely place. Yet the island, and its auks, had drawn them as it was drawing me.

The island was a blank wall of rock, thirty feet high, suave and bland, and topped by a thin, fast-moving frieze of murres who, presumably, were anxiously watching our boat. I have read about a moment of truth, even written about it, but not until I was in this dory, in this place, did I really understand what it meant. It was the final throw of the dice. Would we be able to land? "Hard to say. Them waves is risin' high . . . "

I looked toward the island and saw the water pitching, silent and ominous, up the blank rock. I had come this far, but now I could think only of being capsized—dashed against the rocks or maimed under the boat's keel. I had already talked to a dozen men who had traveled thousands of miles only to be turned back at this point.

I sat in the back of the dory, carried forward by the momentum of a determination long sustained. In a moment, the boat was rising and falling against the rock face on six-foot waves. "Get up front," Arthur Sturge said.

He eased the boat toward the rock. Willie hunched in the bows. At the peak of a wave, he jumped, grabbed at the rock face, and clung. I could see that the rock was gouged with handholds into which my fingers must fit as I jumped. "Arl roight!" Arthur shouted.

Willie now had his back to the rock; he was facing me so that he might try to seize me if I fell. The boat rose and wobbled at its peak; I jumped, hit the rocks and felt my fingers slip into the grooves. As I clung there, I realized the grooves were man-made. Of course. Other men had met the same problem. Of course they had done something about it. These grooves into which my fingers fitted so neatly might have been cut in Drake's time, or before, when the Beothuk Indians came to plunder the island; or had they been cut by Eskimos, a thousand years before Christ?

Muscles knotted, and I strained upward. The problems of landing on Funk Island have remained unchanged. Rockets to the moon and the splitting of the atom mean nothing when it comes to landing on Funk Island. The equation for success is constant: an open boat with a skillful oarsman and a man willing to jump.

Willie had disappeared over the top of the rock while I was still absorbed in finding hand- and footholds in rock slippery with algae and bird excrement. I mounted the crest of the rock and Funk Island spread out, an explosion of sight, sound, and smell. I saw, but I did not see; I saw dark masses of murres in the distance; I saw curtains of buzzing kittiwakes interposing themselves like thousands of pretty white butterflies; I saw rolling hummocks of bare rock. But it was the sound that came to me first. We walked forward over intransigent, bare granite, and the sound swelled like thunder. A literate biologist has described it as "a rushing of waters," but that description does not satisfy poet or artist. It is orchestral, if a million players can be imagined: rich, sensuous, hypnotic.

When we came to the edge of the first great concourse of birds, perhaps two hundred thousand of them staining the rock densely black and white, the orchestral analogy became even more vivid because I could hear, among those thousands of voices, rippling spasms of pathos and melancholy— Brahmsian. The adult birds cried *ehr-ehr-ehr,* crescendo, diminuendo, gushes of emotion. The cries of the flying birds—and there were thousands in the air— swelled and faded in haunting harmony as they passed low overhead. Buried in this amalgam of voices were the piping screams of the young murres, sounds so piercing they hurt the ear.

We moved around the periphery of the murres. With every step, I was conscious of new expansions in the scope of sound. A sibilant undertone to the massive main theme was faintly discernible, the sound of innumerable wings beating: *flacka-flacka-flacka-flacka.* Wings struck each other—*clack, clack, clack*— as birds, flying in thick layers, collided in mid-air. Then another buried sound, a submelody, a counterpoint: *gaggla-gaggla-gaggla.* The gannets were hidden somewhere among the murre hordes. Other sounds were reduced to minutiae in the uproar: the thin cries of herring gulls, the rasping moans of kittiwakes hovering high overhead.

I had been on the island an hour and only now was I really registering the sound of it.

Next, overwhelmingly, came real vision. The murres were massed so thickly they obscured the ground. The birds stood shoulder to shoulder, eyeball to eyeball. In places, they were so densely packed that if one bird stretched or flapped her wings, she sent a sympathetic spasm rippling away from her on all sides.

All life was in constant, riotous motion. Murre heads wavered and darted; wings beat; birds landed clumsily among the upraised heads of their comrades; birds took off and thrashed passageways through the birds ahead of them, knocking them down. Chicks ran from adult to adult; eggs rolled across bare rock, displaced by kicking feet.

The murres heeded me, yet they did not. I approached them and a rising roar of protest sounded, a concentration of the general uproar, which seemed not directed at me at all but at the outrage of intrusion. I walked away from them and the roar died instantly.

The sun was well up, a brilliant star in an azure sky, and I walked to the quiet shore, away from the main masses of murres. Willie had disappeared into a gully. Perhaps I needed time to assimilate. But there was no time. The multiple dimensions of the sight came pouring in. The air streamed with birds coming at me. I threw up my hands, shouted at them, but the shout was lost, ineffectual, not causing a single bird to swerve or otherwise acknowledge me.

At least a hundred thousand birds were aloft at once. They circled the island endlessly, like fighter bombers making strafing runs on a target, flying the full length of the island, then turning out to sea and sweeping back offshore to begin another run. They came on relentlessly and the sky danced with them.

This was not, I realized, the hostile reaction of individual birds who saw their nests threatened. Instead, the murres were a tribe of animals resisting a threat to their island. Individually, they intimidated nothing. Collectively, they emanated power and strength. I looked into a thousand cold eyes and felt chill, impersonal hostility in the air.

I climbed to the top of a ridge and looked down the length of the island, looked into the masses of birds hurtling toward me, looked down to the grounded hordes, a living, writhing backbone of murres, murres, murres. Then, after the visual shock came the olfactory impact.

The smell of Funk Island is the smell of death. It is probably the source of the island's name, which in various languages means "to steam," "to create a great stench," "to smoke"; it may also mean "fear." The island certainly smells ghastly. No battlefield could ever concentrate such a coalition of dead and dying.

A change of wind brought the smell to us, choking, sickening. As I walked down a slope and out of the force of the wind, the air clotted with the smell. In a hollow at the bottom of the slope, it had collected in such concentration that I gagged and my throat constricted. The fishermen knew the smell was poisonous. Uncle Jacob Sturge had told me how one fisherman who tried to run through the concentration of birds was nearly gassed unconscious.

The smell of Funk Island comes from a combination of corruption. There are no scavengers, except bacteria, so dead bodies lie where they have fallen. The debris of a million creatures has nowhere to go. Eggs by the scores of thousands lie everywhere, so that I could not see which were being brooded, which were rotten. In one small gully, unwanted or untended eggs had been kicked together in a one hundred foot driftline by the constantly moving feet of the birds.

The smell of the island came in diminishing waves as the sea breeze died and the heat rose from the rocks. A ripple of explosions fled away among a nearby concentration of birds. I listened; the sound was manlike. It reminded me of a popgun I had used when I was a boy. From a nearby hill packed with murres, another flurry of explosions, then single shots haphazardly firing all around me. If the smell of the island needed an exemplifying sound, this was it. The explosions were the sound of rotten eggs bursting in the growing heat.

I walked, while the smell gathered in my nostrils and took on various identities. It was the thin, sour smell of bird excrement: acidic, astringent, more than a hundred tons of it splashed on the island every day. Underlying that smell was the stench of the rotting fish which lay everywhere after being vomited up by the parent murres but not eaten by the nestlings. The smell was of putrescence, of oil, of fish, and of an indescribable other thing: the stench of a million creatures packed together in a small place.

I walked halfway down the length of the island, a distance of perhaps five hundred feet, but my progress was slow because of the difficulty I had in assimilating everything I saw.

In my mind were scraps of history. I was thinking, for instance, of how Newfoundland's ancient Indians, the Beothuks, camped in a gulch when they were on bird- and egg-hunting expeditions; of how, until recently, the gulch was an archaeological repository of old knives, spoons, belaying pins, and broken pots, testifying to more than two hundred years of exploitation of the island by hunters of meat, oil, eggs, and feathers.

Willie appeared on a far ridge. He was standing at the edge of Indian Gulch. I walked toward him along the rim of a concourse of murres. A feeble spring flowed into the gulch and created a small pond, which was also fed by the sea during heavy swells. Sea water belched up into it through a narrow crack in the rock. Into this pond poured a ceaseless flow of excrement, coughed-up fish, bodies, rotten eggs, and live nestlings. By midsummer, the water was mucid, pea-green, fermenting, almost bubbling with corruption.

The murres were not distressed by this putrid mess; as Willie walked along the top of the gulch, hundreds of them dropped down to the water and floated. Suddenly, the pond was roiled into green foam as a group of birds took off. Their departure triggered another flight, which because murres fly poorly, was a failure. The birds crashed on top of each other or piled into heaps along the steep banks. This drew a sympathetic flight from murres perched precariously on the cliffs and a cloud of birds took off. Their departure sent eggs and nestlings spilling off the cliffs into the water.

But on Funk Island, nothing matters. Death is nothing. Life is nothing. Chaos is order. Order is a mystery. Time is meaningless. The deep-throated roar of the colony cries out to a heedless sky. The human observer, cowed by its primitive energy, by its suggestion of the unnameable, stumbles on blindly.

As I walked, I examined my growing sense of reality and sought a guidepost to what it all meant. I had thought (an hour before? two hours? it was nearer to four hours) that a sweep of Brahmsian rhetoric could describe the island. Already, the image was obsolete. Now, I felt a mechanistic sense, Prokofievian, an imperative monotone, the sound of Mars. The struggling, homuncular forms piled together in such utter, inhuman chaos denied any ordered view of the universe.

I had to wonder whether a poet had preceded me to the island; or did the island have a counterpart elsewhere? De la Mare's disgust at the massacre?

> And silence fell: the rushing sun
> Stood still in paths of heat,
> Gazing in waves of horror on
> The dead about my feet.

It was nearly noon, and sun flames reached for the island and scorched it. I was enervated, but I was also recovering normal sensibility, which brought me *details* of the life of the murre colony. Everywhere I looked now, young murres looked back. In places, they were packed thirty and forty together among the adults. There is only one word to describe them and it is not in any dictionary. They are murrelings: tiny, rotund, dusky balls of fluff with the most piercing voices ever given a young bird. Their piping screams must be essential for them to assert themselves above the roar of the adults. How else could they identify themselves to their parents? Yet, bafflement grew as I watched them. One murreling in that featureless mass of birds was infinitely smaller than one needle in a stack of hay. How contact is kept with the parent birds remains a mystery of biology.

Warned by the scope of destruction in the colony, I was not surprised to find that the murrelings were expendable. Life moves to and from the colony at high speed. A murreling fell from a rock, bounced into an evil puddle, and was trampled by a throng of adults. Hearing screams from a rock I disengaged a murreling jammed in a crevice, looked down, saw a mass of fluffy bodies wedged deeper in the crevice. Murrelings fell from cliffs into the sea, rose and floated in foam, screaming. Murrelings lay dead among pustular eggs; they lay in heaps and windrows in olivaceous puddles.

I knew from murre literature that the murrelings often became shocked by prolonged rain and died by the thousands. That in the context of this island, was not surprising. An *individual* death was shocking. Willie had walked back up the other side of the island and we met at the edge of a group of murres. Willie groaned.

"I don't feel well," he said, rolling his eyes in mock nausea.

As he spoke, I looked over his shoulder in horror. In the middle of the murre mass, standing on slightly higher ground, was a group of gannets. These birds, though inferior in number, occupied the best territory. Though dominant, they seemed to have an amicable relationship with the murres. In places, murres and gannets were mixed together; murrelings gathered around gannets as though they were murres.

A gannet on a nest had reached down casually for one of these nearby murrelings, and as I watched, upended it and swallowed the struggling youngster. It was not the sight of such casual destruction that was shocking; it was the sound of the murreling dying.

It screamed when it was seized by the gannet's beak, which was bigger than the murreling's entire body. It screamed as it was hoisted into the air. Horrifyingly, it screamed loudest as it was being swallowed. The gannet, though a big, powerful bird, had to swallow hard to get the murreling down. Its neck writhed and its beak gaped and all the time the awful screams of the murreling came up out of the gannet's throat. The cries became fainter and fainter.

"Horrible," Willie said. "Oi never gets used to it." The roar of the birds became a lamentation, a collusion of agony and sorrow. The flying creatures seemed to be in streaming retreat. Why that murreling and not any of the others still around at the feet of the gannet? If gannets really relished murre flesh, surely they would quickly wipe out all the murrelings near them. But they do not.

It was now afternoon and the sun plashed white and pitiless light on rock. For some time, I had been aware of a growing disorientation. I took a picture to the east, seventy thousand birds; to the west, one hundred thousand; in the air, twenty thousand. The noise, the smell, the screams, the corpses, the green puddles, pushed bonily into my chest. I fumbled with film but could not decide how to reload the camera or, indeed, remember what setting to use, or how to release the shutter.

"Oi t'ink oi'll go and sit behind dat rock," Willie said. "Oi goes funny in de head after a while here."

Uncle Jacob had mentioned that the island could drive a man mad. I was being sickened by the pressure of it. Once, in Australia, I watched men systematically kill several hundred thousand rabbits they had penned against a fence. The steady thocking of cudgels hammering rabbit skulls continued hour after hour, eventually dulling the eye and diminishing the hearing. On Funk Island, my observing sense was losing its ability to see and to record.

I sought release in reverie and walked, half-conscious of what I was doing, toward an incongruous green field that lay alone in the middle of the island. Its bareness suggested another place of personal memory, and an association of ideas. My ancestors were Scottish and fought the English at Culloden. When I went to Culloden, two hundred years after the battle, I was overwhelmed by those long, sinister mounds of mass burial of the clans.

This Funk Island field was also a midden of slain creatures. It was a great natural-history site, as significant to an ornithologist as Ashurbanipal's palace would be to an archaeologist. Here, generations of flightless great auks had flocked to breed after eight months of oceanic wandering. Their occupancy built up soil. Here, also, they were slain throughout the eighteenth century until they became extinct, probably early in the nineteenth.

A puffin bolted out of the ground ahead and flipped a bone from her burrow entrance as she left. I knelt and clawed a handful of bones out of the burrow. I saw other burrows, bones spilling out of them as though they were entrances to a disorderly catacomb.

This was not fantasy. These were great-auk bones, still oozing out of the earth nearly a hundred and fifty years after the last bird had gone. The bones permeated the ground under my feet; puffins dug among them and kicked them aside to find graveyard sanctuary. Life in the midst of death.

All at once, walking across bare rock, the murres well distant, I felt a release. Willie was not in sight; the longliner was off fishing somewhere. The granite underfoot changed texture, became a desert I had walked, then a heath, a moor I had tramped, and eventually, all the bare and empty places of earth I had ever known. I felt the presence of friends and heard their voices. But something was wrong. Some were still friends but others had closed, deceitful faces. Inhibition and self-deception fell away; flushes of hate and love passed as the faces moved back and forth. Forgotten incidents came to mind. What was happening?

Uncle Jacob's voice: "A man could go mad on the Funks."

This was enough. I turned toward the shore, to the *Doris and Lydia,* which had appeared from nowhere. Willie leaped eagerly from his place of refuge behind a rock. The roar of the murres receded. I imagined the island empty during much of the long year, naked as a statue against the silent hiss of mist coming out of the Labrador Current, or the thunder of an Atlantic gale piling thirty-foot waves up the sides of the island.

"She be a sight to see in the winter," Uncle Benny had said.

The seasons of millennia switched back and forth. The island suffocated in the original gases of earth: argon, radon, krypton, xenon, neon. The island disappeared in yellow fog, and water slid down its sides. The island was a corpse, dead a million years, its surface liquefied, with rot running into its granite intestines. The island festered, and rivulets of pus coursed down its sides. The island was death. The island was life.

Only in retrospect could the island become real. Later, I was to return to the island and actually live on it in order to turn my disbelief into lasting memory. Willie moved parallel to me, jumping from rock to rock and displacing a fluttering canopy of kittiwakes. He was a different man now as he met me at the landing site, beaming and lighthearted.

"So dat's de Funks, eh?" he said, and he was proud that I had seen it.

In the boat below us, Arthur and Cyril smiled. Arthur was relaxed now, in contrast to his silent, absorbed intensity when he was trying to get me to the island, and on it. Both men, and Willie, poised at the top of the cliff, were caught for a moment by the camera, like toreros who have survived a bloody afternoon and will hear the bugles again tomorrow.

With a final look over my shoulder at the silently fleeing birds, I slid down the cliff to the boat and Funk Island became a part of the history of my life.

Banks Island 1986

American naturalist BARRY LOPEZ (1945) took to visiting the north while studying wolf-caribou relationships for his book *Of Wolves and Men*, which won the John Burroughs Medal in 1978. As a contributing editor for *Harper's* magazine, he travelled for five years in Alaska and the Canadian Arctic, fascinated by its "sublime innocence" and by the degree to which "people's desires and aspirations were as much a part of the land as the wind, solitary animals, and the bright fields of stone and tundra." The result was *Arctic Dreams* (1986), a monumental survey of the Arctic's many facets. This excerpt from the chapter on Banks Island is a weaving of natural history and human mythology that presents a total portrait of one of the North's most magical animals, the muskox. His other books include *Desert Notes* (1978), *Giving Birth to Thunder* (1978), *Sleeping with His Daughter* (1978) and *Winter Count* (1981).

IT IS THE MIDDLE of June, so it is apparent, as it would never be on a dark and frozen day in December, that the Thomsen River is actually a river. It rises among unnamed creeks in east-central Banks Island and flows black and sparkling under the summer light, north to Castel Bay on M'Clure Strait. It is a highway of nutrients, and northwest Banks Island is an arctic oasis because of it, a kind of refuge for plants and animals.

The verdant, fertile valley of the Thomsen River is striking country in part because so much of the rest of the island is a desert of gravel, of bare soils and single, far-flung plants—a patch of yellow cinquefoil blooms, say, or a bright green cushion of moss campion. On the west bank of the Thomsen, where I am camped between Able and Baker creeks, the landscape is stark: gully erosion has cut deeply into a high-rising plateau to the west. But even here is a suggestion of the refugelike character of the Thomsen River Valley, for these desert-colored shores were never touched by Pleistocene glaciers. Like most of western and interior Alaska, much of Banks Island went unscathed during the glacial epoch. These, in fact, might have been the shores of an ice-free Arctic Ocean 20,000 years ago.

I have come here to watch muskoxen. The muskox, along with the American bison, is one of the few large animals to have survived the ice ages in North America. Most all of its companions—the mammoth, the dire wolf, the North American camel, the short-faced bear—are extinct. The muskox abides, conspicuously alone and entirely at ease on the tundra, completely adapted to a polar existence.

I am sitting at the edge of a precipitous bluff, several hundred feet above the Thomsen, with a pair of high-powered binoculars. At this point the river curves across a broad plain of seepage meadows and tundra in a sweeping oxbow to my left; on my right Baker Creek has cut a steep-banked gash into the badlands to the west. Far to the south, in front of me, are clusters of black dots; at a distance of more than two miles they arrest even the naked eye with a strange, faint reflection. The mind knows by that slow drift of dark points over a field of tan grasses on an open hillside that there is life out there. But an older, deeper mind is also alerted by the flash of light from those distant, long-haired flanks. The predatory eye is riveted.

The broad valley in which the muskoxen graze has the color and line of a valley in Tibet. I raise my field glasses to draw it nearer. Beyond the resolution of the ground glass the animals look darker, the tans of the hills more deeply pigmented, and the sky at the end of the distant valley is a denser blue. The light shimmers on them. I recall the observation of a Canadian muskox biologist: "They are so crisp in the landscape. They stand out like no other animal, against the whites of winter or the colors of the summer tundra."

I put the glasses back on my lap. A timeless afternoon. Off to my left, in that vast bowl of stillness that contains the meandering river, tens of square miles of tundra browns and sedge meadow greens seem to snap before me, as immediate as the pages of my notebook, because of unscattered light in the dustless air. The land seems guileless. Creatures down there take a few steps, then pause and gaze about. Two sandhill cranes stand still by the river. Three Peary caribou, slightly built and the silver color of the moon, browse a cutbank in that restive way of deer. Tundra melt ponds, their bright dark blue waters oblique to the sun, stand out boldly on the plain. In the centre of the large ponds, beneath the surface of the water, gleam cores of aquamarine ice, like the constricted heart of winter.

On the far side of the Thomsen other herds of muskoxen graze below a range of hills in clusters of three or four. In groups of ten and twelve. I sketch the arrangements in my notebook. Most remarkable to me, and clear even at a distance of two or three miles because of the contrast between their spirited, bucking gambols and the placid ambling of the others, is the number of calves. Among forty-nine animals, I count twelve calves. The mind doesn't easily register the sustenance of the sedge meadows, not against the broad testimony of the barren hills and eroded plateaus. It balks at the evidence of fecundity, and romping calves. The muskoxen on the far side of the river graze, nevertheless, on sweet coltsfoot, on mountain sorrel, lousewort, and pendant grass, on water sedge. The sun gleams on them. On the melt ponds. The indifferent sky towers. There is something of the original creation here.

I bring my glasses up to study again the muskoxen in the far valley to the south. Among fifty or sixty animals are ten or fifteen calves. I regard them for a while, until I hear the clattering alarm call of a sandhill crane. To the southwest an arctic hare rises up immediately, smartly alert. To the southeast a snowy owl sitting on a tussock, as conspicuous in its whiteness as the hare, pivots its head far around, right then left. The hare, as intent as if someone had whistled, has found me and fixed me with his stare. In that moment I feel the earth bent like a bow and sense the volume of space between us, as though the hare, the owl, and I stood on a dry lakebed. The moment lasts until the hare drops, becomes absorbed again in the leaves of a willow. The owl returns its gaze to the river valley below.

The indictment of the sandhill cranes continues; I shift my perch so they cannot see me, and their calls cease.

Behind me to the north my four companions, dressed in patterns of color unmistakably human, are at work on a hillside: archaeologists, meticulously mapping the placement of debris at a nineteenth-century Copper Eskimo campsite called PjRa-18, or, informally, the Kuptana site. Like others in the region, this campsite sits near the top of a windswept hill and looks down on well-developed sedge meadows, exceptional muskox pasturage. Scattered over 20,000 square yards at the campsite are more than 27,000 pieces of bone, representing the skeletal debris of about 250 muskoxen. The archaeologists call it a "death assemblage." There are also rings of river stones there, which once anchored caribou-skin tents against wind and rain; and the remnants of meat caches built of shale and ironstone slabs, and of charcoal fires of willow twigs and arctic white heather. The lower jaw of an arctic char, eaten a hundred years ago, still glistens with fish oil. A sense of timelessness is encouraged by this primordial evidence of human hunger.

The muskoxen grazing so placidly in the hills to the south and in the sedge meadows to the east, so resplendent with life, are perhaps descendants of those, whose white, dark-horned skulls now lie awry on the land.

The story of this camp begins in the previous century.

In September 1951, Captain Robert M'Clure was guiding HMS *Investigator* along the north coast of Banks Island, desperate for relief from the press of heavy ice in the strait later named for him. Toward the island's eastern cape M'Clure found a shallow, protected embayment, which he called the Bay of God's Mercy. He and his men overwintered there. The following summer the ice did not go out of the bay, and they were forced to overwinter again in the same spot. In the spring of 1853 a rescue party reached them from HMS *Resolute,* a sister ship in winter quarters at Melville Island. (Both ships were part of a British search force looking for the lost Franklin Expedition.) M'Clure, reluctantly accepting the fact that *Investigator* was inextricably trapped, abandoned the 450–ton, copper-sheathed vessel and followed the rescue party back to Melville Island.

Copper Eskimos living more than 200 miles away on Victoria Island some-how learned of the abandoned ship. (These Kanghiryuakmiut and Kanghi-ryuachiakmiut people, from around Minto Inlet and Prince Albert Sound, had never seen white people. They would not be contacted by whites until American whalers visited them in 1906. Shortly thereafter they would be named Copper Eskimos, identifying them with the tools they made from lo-cal copper deposits.) When the Victoria Island people first crossed over the spring ice of Prince of Wales Strait to Banks Island is not known, but they left a clear trail up the Thomsen River Valley to Mercy Bay.

It was ironic that such wealth should fall into the hands of the Victoria Is-land people. Until that moment they had found themselves at the far end of not one but two arctic trade routes. The first came from the west, from Sibe-ria across the north coast of Alaska; the other came from the south up the Mackenzie River from the interior of Canada. Now they could reverse the flow of trade goods.★ Rarely had they seen the likes of the materials they found at Mercy Bay, and never in such abundance. The shore cache and the ship itself were as marvelous to them as the discovery of a well-provisioned vehicle from space.

The Eskimos likely traveled lightly on their annual excursions to Mercy

---

★ The reversal in the flow of trade goods initially confused anthropologists trying to figure out the de-velopment of trading patterns in the Far North. Others, unaware of the effect the *Investigator* had had on the lives of Victoria Island Eskimos, mistakenly assumed for years that these tribal groups were part of a pristine aboriginal culture.

Bay, saving space on their small sleds and inside dog panniers for salvaged materials. Most prized were strips of iron and sheets of canvas, and softwood boards, which were easier to carve than caribou antler. Also copper sheathing, woven cloth, hemp lines, wool yarn, and leather boots (for the leather alone—they were completely unsuitable as arctic footwear, a point the British were slow to learn).

On their journeys north, except for small amounts of seal meat and blubber carried with them from Victoria Island, the Eskimos ate what they killed en route—an occasional caribou, molting geese (which, flightless, could not escape), fish, and a great many muskoxen. They drove the muskoxen out of the sedge meadows along the river and up onto hilltops where, predictably, they turned to make a stand and Eskimo dogs held them at bay. The hunters shot them with copper- and iron-tipped arrows, the shafts carefully assembled from willow twigs bound together with bits of sinew. (Today, shoulder blade after shoulder blade bears the small, round arrow hole, at an angle that would have carried the arrow straight to the heart. Their knowledge of the animal's anatomy was precise.)

The muskoxen were butchered where they fell, and a camp was set up. From such camps, presumably, small parties traveled back and forth to the *Investigator* and its cache all summer. In early fall, when the first snows provided a traveling surface for the sleds, the people returned south to country where seal hunting would hold them in good stead through the coming winter. The same camps were used year after year, apparently, and the skeletons of hundreds of muskoxen piled up at some of them, like PjRa-18. By 1981, scientists had found 150 such campsites, large and small, along the Thomsen River, along with the dismembered skeletons of abut 3000 muskoxen.

The muskox population, some think, collapsed under this heavy hunting pressure before the ship and its cache were fully exploited. (Remnants of the cache remain. The ship either sank in the bay or floated away—it has never been found.) After about 1890, no people from Victoria Island traveled the route anymore.

Between 1914 and 1918 the explorer Vilhjalmur Stefansson crossed Banks Island several times, but he never once saw muskoxen. None, in fact, was seen thereafter anywhere on the island until the summer of 1952, when a Canadian biologist spotted a lone bull in the Thomsen River drainage. The bull could have been part of a small, remnant population, previously undetected, or from a group that crossed over from Victoria Island and followed the same route the Eskimo had taken to the north. During the 1950s and 1960s muskoxen were seen sporadically on northern Banks Island, and surveys conducted in the early 1970s confirmed the presence of between 1200 and 1800 animals. A 1975 survey indicated further increases, and surveys in the early 1980s revealed the population had reached an astonishing size—16,000 to 18,000 animals.

The phenomenal recovery of muskoxen on Banks Island is something biologists cannot adequately explain. They do not have enough information about muskox reproductive biology and nutrition or about the play of other factors, such as prolonged periods of favorable weather or the absence of caribou competing for some of the same food. Informally, however, there is agreement that the lush sedge meadows and grasslands of the Thomsen River Valley have played a critical role in the recovery at the northern end of the island, and in the extension of the animals' range toward the south.

A modern visitor to the Thomsen River district feels the resilience of the country right away, in the rich and diverse bird life, the numbers of arctic fox, the many lemming burrows, and in the aggregations of arctic hare and caribou grazing on the hillsides. And in seeing how many calves there are in the muskoxen herds. The valley is robust and serene with its life.

To leave the story here, with the herds recovered and the hunting excesses of the Copper Eskimo a part of the past, would serve a sense of restitution. We could imagine that the muskoxen had been killed out by rough and thoughtless people, preoccupied with retrieving the wealth at Mercy Bay. An isolated incident. But a parallel with incidents at Pond's Bay suggests itself; and something else about man and nature and extinction, much older, flows here.

Fatal human involvement with wild animals is biologically and economically complicated. In the 1940s and 1950s, Banks Island Eskimos all but wiped out the wolf population at the southern end of the island in an effort to protect their arctic fox trap lines from scavenging. In 1981 and 1982, they brought heavy hunting pressure to bear against muskoxen in the southern portion of the island, to protect the caribou herds upon which they are dependent for food, which, in their view, compete poorly with muskoxen for the same forage. (The northeastern end of the island, the Thomsen River country, the Eskimos regard as an oasis, an endlessly productive landscape from which animals pour forth to satisfy the many needs of mankind for flesh and hides, bones, sinews, and furs. They neither hunt nor trap there.)

Hunting wild animals to the point of extinction is a very old story. Aleut hunters, for example, apparently wiped out populations of sea otter in the vicinity of Amchitka Island in the Aleutians 2500 years ago. New Zealand's moas were killed off by Maori hunters about 800 years ago. And zoogeographers working in the Hawaiian Islands discovered recently that more than half of the indigenous bird life there was killed off by native residents before the arrival of the first Europeans in 1778. (The motivations of the hunters involved are unknown to us. Nor do we know whether they understood the consequences of their acts. Nor, if they did, whether they would have behaved differently. Some anthropologists caution, too, that the apparent incidents of slaughter of bison at buffalo jumps in North America and of caribou at river crossings in historic and prehistoric times were ethical in context and consistent with a native understanding of natural history and principles of conservation.)

Man's ability to destroy whole wildlife populations goes back even farther than this, however. Arthur Jelinek, a vertebrate paleontologist, has referred to early man in North America in very harsh terms, calling him a predator "against whom no [naturally] evolved defense systems were available" and "a source of profound changes" in the ecosystems of North America at the beginning of the Holocene. This was "an extremely efficient and rapidly expanding predator group," Jelinek writes, with "a formidable potential for disruption."

The specific events on which Jelinek bases these judgements are the catastrophic die-offs of large mammals that began about 18,000 years ago in North America and in which he believes man played the crucial role. Collectively the events are known as the Pleistocene extinction.

We are used to thinking of the North American plains as a place that teemed with life before the arrival of Europeans—60 million buffalo and millions of pronghorn antelope, elk, and deer, and grizzly bears and wolves. Oddly, however, this was only the remnant of an aggregation of animals the likes and numbers of which were truly staggering. By comparison with the late Pleistocene, eighteenth-century North America was an impoverished world, one "from which all the hugest, the fiercest, and the strangest forms had recently disappeared." Giant armadillo, ground sloths that stood as tall on their hind legs as modern giraffes, the North American cheetah, saber-toothed cats, mammoths, fleet horses and camels, and close relatives of the muskox as well—all were gone, both species and populations. And the land itself had changed radically. Where the eighteenth-century traveler saw deserts there had once been lush grasslands, and great herds of browsers and grazers and their attendant predators and scavengers.

There are sharply differing explanations of why all these animals died out at or near the end of the Pleistocene, but there is some general agreement that it was for one of two reasons. Either the climate changed swiftly and radically and the animals couldn't adapt, or they were hunted to extinction by man. Some scientists are quick to discount human hunting as a factor. They find the idea that this "intelligent" predator was a waster of meat untenable (though evidence to the contrary is overwhelming in early as well as modern times). And they are skeptical about the killing efficiency of the weapons and hunting techniques involved. They also believe there were too few human beings by far to account for the sheer numbers of animals killed. A climatic explanation alone, they suggest, might suffice. The land, according to this argument, dried up, and the composition and distribution of plant life changed radically. The large herbivorous mammals most dependent on these plants died out, along with their predators and scavengers. In this model the predatory efficiency of man is sometimes regarded as the final blow to the ecosystem at a time of extreme environmental stress.

Intricate, cogent, and forceful arguments have been made in support of both explanations. That man played a significant, if not decisive, role, however, seems inescapable. His capacity to do so is clear and, to judge from the fate of the plains buffalo, the passenger pigeon, the great auk, and the bowhead whale, he can be lethally and extensively efficient. The pattern, some would argue, is still with us, and the extinctions are about to increase again, because of the exponential destruction of natural habitat attendant upon the expansion of human numbers.

We lament the passing of the Eskimo curlew, the sea mink, the Labrador duck, Pallas' cormorant, and Steller's sea cow. Their lives are now beyond our inquiry. Our reluctance to accept direct responsibility for these losses, however, is sound if somewhat complicated biological thinking, rooted in a belief that there is nothing innately wrong with us as a species and in our belief that we are not solely responsible for every extinction. (The California condor, for example, is perhaps doomed on its own ecological account.) Our recent biological heritage has been exactly this, to sharply reduce the populations of other species or eliminate them entirely and occupy their niches in the food web whenever we had need or desire. It is not denigrating, not even criticizing from a certain point of view, to so understand ourselves. The cold view to take of our future is that we are therefore headed for extinction in a universe of impersonal chemical, physical, and biological laws. A more productive, certainly more engaging view, is that we have the intelligence to grasp what is happening, the composure not to be intimidated by its complexity, and the courage to take steps that may bear no fruit in our lifetimes.

Squatting over the detritus at the Kuptana site on a June evening, picking at the earth between two willow runners with a muskox rib, one cannot blame the Copper Eskimo who killed the muskoxen here. Perhaps they even understood, at some level in the human makeup now irretrievable to us, that the muskoxen would come back, even if it seemed they had killed them all. Nor can one blame the modern Eskimo hunters on the island for wanting to get rid of wolves to protect the cash income from their trap lines, or to get rid of muskoxen to ensure a good supply of caribou meat. They are trying to adapt to an unorthodox, for them, economics. But we could help each other. Their traditional philosophy is insistent on the issue of ethical behavior toward animals. Within the spirit of this tradition and within the European concept of compassionate regard may lie the threads of a modern realignment with animals. We need an attitude of enlightened respect which will make both races feel more ethically at ease with animals, more certain of following a dignified course in the years ahead, when the animals will still be without a defense against us.

Here in the dirt, pushing past the desiccated winter pellets of muskoxen with my rib bone, past the fresher pellets of arctic hare, past windblown tufts of shed caribou hair, and a layer of dry, curled leaves from willows and saxifrage, I find a damp and precious mud. A foundation. Whatever their moral predilections may have been, the Kanghiryuakmiut and Kanghiryuachiakmiut ate the flesh of the muskoxen who browsed these willows. They made ladles from their horns, tools from their bones, and slept through the first, freezing storms of autumn on the thick insulation of their hides. And they survived. In the long history of man, before and after the coming of the glaciers, this counts for more than one can properly say.

When I stand up and look out over the valley I can feel the tremendous depth of time: myself at this 100-year-old campsite, before a valley the scientists say was never touched by glacial ice, and which the modern Eskimo say is and has been a sacred precinct. The muskoxen graze out there as though I were of no more importance than a stone. The skulls of their ancestors lie in the sun at my feet, and cool winds come down the Kuptana slope and ride up over my bare head.

R. D. LAWRENCE

In Praise of Wolves 1986

RONALD DOUGLAS LAWRENCE was born in England in 1921 and, with a degree in mammalogy but already something of "an academic maverick," came to Canada in 1955 "to study the nation's wild environment, a task that in my naïveté I thought would take three or four years." It was eleven years before he wrote his first book, *Wild Life in Canada* (1966), and he has gone on to write nineteen others, including *Cry Wild* (1970), the story of a timber wolf; *The Ghost Walker* (1983), about pumas; and, in 1988, his definitive *The Natural History of Canada*. *In Praise of Wolves* (1986), from which this excerpt is taken, is his account of raising two orphaned British Columbia wolf cubs, Tundra and Taiga, on his property in southern Ontario.

Through nature, through the evolutionary continuum and ecological relatedness and interdependence of all things, we are as much a part of the wolf as the wolf is a part of us. And as we destroy or demean nature, wolves, or any other creature, great or small, we do no less to ourselves.

—Michael W. Fox, *The Soul of the Wolf*

THE WINTER of 1984–85 was long and severe in our part of Ontario. Temperatures fell in December to thirty-five degrees below zero, and the snows piled higher and higher as the nights lengthened; but although the business of splitting stove wood and clearing pathways through the white blanket that insulated the land considerably increased my workload, the beauty of our forests and the high glee with which Tundra and Taiga greeted the hibernal changes more than made up for the additional tasks that were imposed on me.

I remember the way that the wolves reacted to the first really heavy fall of snow during a morning in early December. There was no wind. The flakes, each as large as a fingernail, descended lazily, fluttering like small and aimless butterflies and landing as gently as thistledown, every one individually noticeable, all of them together forming a white screen that softened the outlines of the entire landscape.

The moment we left the house, carrying their morning snack, Tundra and Taiga rushed to the fence, their fur covered in snow that flew off in small clouds as they danced excitedly while waiting for us to arrive.

Entering the enclosure after we had fed them, we were greeted briefly but exuberantly before the cubs began running and leaping aimlessly, pausing now and again to nose into the snow, then rolling in it, all four legs in the air and kicking frantically, only to jump up and start the whole process all over again, as exuberantly as before. Presently, Tundra stopped dashing about and began to catch snowflakes, snapping to left and right with head slightly raised, evidently surprised when each snow-star that he caught disappeared the instant his jaws closed on it. Taiga immediately copied his actions; but whereas Tundra became thoughtfully puzzled when the flakes vanished, Taiga showed herself to be completely exasperated by her inability to *bite* a single one of those elusive targets. Impatient as she is, she quickly gave vent to her frustrations, leaping upward frantically, snapping rapidly, and yapping, her voice shrill and discordant.

Meanwhile, Tundra appeared to realize that the flakes were related to the snow upon which he and his sister had been quenching their thirst. Having formed this conclusion, he came trotting toward us, now and then catching a flake or two as he traveled and demonstrating that he was tasting each droplet of melt by the way he moved his mouth and licked his lips. Upon arriving at my side, he flopped down, lifting a back leg and soliciting my attention. This caused Taiga to abandon her fruitless assaults on the snowflakes in favor of dashing up to Sharon so as to leap at her affectionately; she did this with far too much abandon, in the process scratching my wife with her sharp claws.

Seeing that Sharon's face had been rather badly scraped and that blood was flowing from her bottom lip, I grabbed Taiga by the scruff and forced her to lie on her side, whereupon the over-enthusiastic young wolf became instantly contrite; but because I wanted her to understand that she had taken too much of a liberty with the Alpha female of our pack, I shook her scruff and scolded her sternly. Taiga whined pitifully, wet herself, and sought to lick me; but before I could release her so that we all might "kiss and make up," Tundra rushed over and fastened his jaws on her neck, his great fangs brushing my fingers as he sought to reinforce my authority by pinning her head to the snowy ground while emitting a low growl.

When Sharon noticed what was going on, she forgot her pain and interceded on Taiga's behalf, scolding Tundra and me and telling us that Taiga had not meant to be so rough, a fact of which I was well aware. In any event, having disciplined the recalcitrant young wolf, I forgave her. So did Tundra. The four of us then had a "love-in" during which Taiga, perforce, had to lick Sharon's face in her inimitable style. While his sister was thus engaged, Tundra positioned himself behind Sharon's crouching form, raised himself slowly and carefully on his back legs, and settled both his great paws on her shoulders, holding that stance as he dab-licked my wife's forehead. A few minutes later, the young wolves ran off to play in the snow and we left the enclosure. Sharon watched the cubs as I closed the gate, then turned to me.

"They look as if they are in their element," my wife remarked.

"They *are* in their element," I replied. Walking toward the house, I reminded Sharon that wolves thrive in winter, provided they can get enough to eat. Indeed, they actually enjoy the cold and play in it even when fully adult.

In the early autumn, wolves begin to grow their thick, woolly underfur, and their long, rather coarse guard hairs become glossy. Soon afterward, they are garbed in coats so thick that they add about a third to their bulk, raiment that makes them impervious to the cold and keeps them dry even when they must enter water, for the underfur is made impermeable by natural oils.

Our cubs were no exception. By October they had started to grow their new finery, and they appeared deceptively large in it. Tundra showed areas of coppery brown on his back and sides; Taiga lost most of the attractive russet tones that had decorated her face, flanks, and legs; she was now light fawn, almost white in places. But because young wolves do not get their permanent colors until they begin to molt in May and June of the following spring, the tones they acquire during their first winter make it impossible to determine what their adult coloration is going to be. Despite the browns that showed up in Tundra's coat, I felt fairly sure that he would revert to black during the spring molt, for this is usual in pups that are born black. In Taiga's case, however, although I thought that she might return to at least some of the colors that she had exhibited as a pup, I was far less certain.

The heavy snowfall that had so delighted the cubs was the harbinger of true winter, ushering in temperatures that caused the thermometer to plunge well below zero two days after the skies had cleared and allowed the sun to shine again upon the wilderness. During daylight, the differences between sun and shade temperatures were enormous. On one occasion, at noon, while the thermometer on the north side of our log house registered ten degrees below zero, I hung a spare thermometer in the direct sunlight striking the south side of the barn. The mercury climbed to sixty-seven degrees *above* zero within three minutes.

At night, of course, it was a different story. Under clear skies, the temperature dived as soon as the sun fell behind the trees; it continued to drop until it reached its lowest point at about 3:00 or 4:00 A.M. Between times, the blue-black heavens were filled with numberless stars, the constant sparkling of which was periodically complemented by the phosphorescent displays of the northern lights.

During those nights, I would often go outside, enter the enclosure, and squat in the snow, flanked by the wolves. Silently, communicating through body contact, we would watch the red–green stars and the coruscating aurora borealis and we would become as one under the blazing heavens. Sometimes I would be compelled to howl; and even as I prepared to do so, Tundra and Taiga would be equally urged, their ululating songs rising above my puny voice and echoing throughout the wilderness.

Regardless of the cold, the wolves slept in the open, disdaining the barn and the brush shelter that Murray Palmer had made for them; their bedding places were easy for us to find when we entered the enclosure every morning, because their body heat always melted the snow and ice, creating saucer-like depressions about three feet in diameter. The pups never slept in the same place twice in succession, although when an old depression had been properly covered by new snow, it would be used again, the reason being that by the time they awakened in the morning the melted area had turned to ice, its hard surface preventing the wolves from settling themselves comfortably on it again the following night. Like dogs, wolves trample down a sleep area by circling over it a few times, then they lie down and shuffle themselves into position, their hips and shoulders pressing on the snow or ground and creating slight indentations that fit the contours of these bony parts. Curled up, their noses covered by their bushy tails, they then sleep comfortably.

Tundra and Taiga often slept so close together that the two saucers they melted took the shape of a figure eight; but even when their bodies were not actually touching, no more than a foot separated their bedding places. Usually, the presence of only two saucers made it evident that the cubs had slept undisturbed in the same location, but some mornings we would find four depressions, two in one part of the enclosure and two in another. Such evidence told us that the wolves had been awakened and had evidently investigated the cause of their disturbance.

On Christmas day, Sharon prepared a special meal for Tundra and Taiga, arranging the food so artistically in their bowls that I was prompted to ask if it was for us or for the cubs. This reminded us of an evening in September during Alison's visit when we had eaten the meat intended for the wolves and they had dined on our freshly ground sirloin of beef that was supposed to have been made into hamburgers and grilled outside. The error was not discovered until after we had enjoyed the "wolf burgers," when Sharon remarked that she had been surprised to notice that the ground beef bought that day for our use had turned very dark by late afternoon. My daughter then realized that she had unwittingly taken the wolf meat out of the refrigerator and handed it to my wife, who had used it to prepare the hamburgers. None of us experienced any bad aftereffects, however. In fact, Tundra and Taiga most often eat the same meats that we ourselves consume, the only difference being that they usually ate theirs raw.

In February, the cubs showed signs of restlessness and howled frequently at night, which suggested that although they were not yet sexually mature, they were experiencing some preadolescent hormonal changes in concert with the breeding season. Then, too, wild wolves and coyotes often howled from within the surrounding forests, and their cries, no matter how faint, invariably elicited replies from our wards.

During February's full moon and under clear skies, the cubs became especially restless, at first playing excitedly while uttering high-pitched barks that were punctuated by companionable growls, but soon after midnight they began to howl repeatedly. We were in bed, but I got up, dressed, and went outside, using the side door of our house, which is not visible from the enclosure. I wanted to watch and listen, if possible, undetected by the cubs.

The moonlight was considerably enhanced by the snow, offering excellent visibility as I walked quietly to stand in the shadow of the garage, from there watching through field glasses. Tundra and Taiga were sitting side by side at the far end of the open part of the enclosure. They were staring intently toward the northwest, their bodies rigid, their ears pricked forward. At first the night was utterly silent, but after a few moments the howl of a wolf rose above the forest. In near unison, our wolves responded, their calls harmonizing with the more distant song of their wild relative. I timed the performance. It lasted one minute and forty-seven seconds and ended as abruptly as it had begun, the three wolves becoming silent almost simultaneously, as though by prearrangement, although our two lagged fractionally behind the forest-dweller.

I had thought that the cubs were completely unaware of my presence, for they had not even glanced briefly in my direction when I stationed myself close to one corner of the garage. But now they both turned and trotted toward the gate; upon reaching it, they stood and stared directly at me, or at least into the shadows in which I stood. Then they whined and began to dance expectantly, so I left my shelter and walked down to them, entering the enclosure and squatting between them, stroking them and being licked in turn. Ten minutes later I returned home, glad to be back in the warmth. The temperature outside had fallen to thirty-two degrees below zero. Back in bed, I read for a time before turning out the light, but as I began to doze, the wolves howled again. If there was a better way to go to sleep, I don't know it.

Spring was late arriving in 1985. And it was a wet season, a period during which temperatures rose and fell repeatedly at first, one day showing the promise of melting snow and new plant growth, the next bringing fresh avalanches of white. But if the humans started to get a bit fed up when April was ushered in with a snowstorm, Tundra and Taiga welcomed the changeable weather. They especially enjoyed the new, wet snow, rolling in it, play-fighting, and generally having a wonderful time, quite oblivious of the fact that they greeted us every morning soaking wet and shockingly covered in mud, much of which they shook on us as we squatted outside the fence while giving them their morning snack. After such encounters, we would return to the house spattered by nearly black mire and soaked to the skin, although the pleasure we derived from being with the yearling wolves and watching the enthusiasm with which they greeted the change in seasons could not be dispelled by dirt or moisture.

On April 27, the cubs were one year old. Sharon prepared them each a birthday dish consisting of such delicacies as slices of boiled ham, salami, liver pâté, and freshly ground hamburger, the whole enhanced by tastefully arrayed raw chicken wings and decorated by sprigs of parsley! As though wishing to celebrate the birth of two such wonderful beings, the day dawned sunny and warm and two robins appeared on the lawn. Then the ravens came, six of them settling in the trees within the enclosure, there to whistle and coo and croak with great abandon. I accused Sharon of being overly imaginative when she maintained that the birds were singing "Happy Birthday" to our wolves.

The weather continued to improve. When May arrived, new buds showed on the trees; wildflowers started to appear. So did *hordes* of blackflies. Fortunately, the birds had also arrived by this time: tree and barn swallows, warblers, sparrows, and flycatchers, all of them feasting on the bloodsuckers; but they left more than enough to pester the wolves and their human companions.

Now Tundra and Taiga spent most of the day inside the barn, having soon learned that blackflies infrequently bite in semidarkness. At night, when the pestiferous gnats quelled their bloodthirsty desires in favor of sheltering on plants and grasses, the cubs busied themselves outside, playing, digging, chewing up old logs, and frequently interrupting their activities in order to howl.

Toward the middle of the month, Taiga began to molt, her thick underfur coming out in handfuls when Sharon brushed her, a task that my wife performed with dedication because she saved the woolly fur, which she intended to spin and to weave on her floor loom so that it would eventually become a part of some mysterious garment, the design of which was not to be divulged to me.

Taiga greatly enjoyed the grooming. She would lie on her side, eyes closed, while Sharon plied the wire brush assiduously, clearing the fur off after four or five strokes and stuffing each little bundle into a pocket. Tundra, whose coat was still tight, would often try to eat the brush, or would otherwise interfere by biting Taiga, who, not unnaturally, would become annoyed and snarl at her brother. I don't know just how much wool Sharon got from Taiga, except that it gradually filled two shopping bags while the wolf became sleeker and looked appreciably smaller. In due course, she emerged wearing a coat that was the color of butterscotch on the back, sides, and flanks, and russet behind the ears, forehead, and legs. Most attractive.

Tundra began to molt three weeks after his sister. He, too, was brushed by Sharon, although much of his wool was rejected because, being a male, his guard hairs were more numerous, longer, and coarser and they became inextricably mixed with the wool. Guard hairs, I am told, have to be removed from the fur if this is to be spun; this intelligence may have gladdened Tundra's heart, for he appeared to think that being brushed was beneath his dignity; he demonstrated this by seeking to bite the brush.

At this time we again began to get visitors. Some were repeaters and known to Tundra and Taiga, who always remembered them and greeted them profusely. Others were strangers. Most of these were also given enthusiastic welcomes. But one afternoon the arrival of a married couple elicited a surprising reaction from Taiga.

At first, both wolves rushed up to the fence, demonstrating their usual eagerness to greet the newcomers, but when we arrived at the wire and Tundra leaped up to greet the female visitor, Taiga began to growl at him. As the male wolf persisted, his sister became more and more aggressive, biting him, pushing him down with her front paws, and even causing him to flop on his side and whine submissively while seeking to lick her. Unlike the two men whose stress had caused Tundra to react aggressively, Taiga clearly objected to the attention that her brother was trying to lavish on the woman. Although the wolf was directing her aggression at her brother, I thought it best to bring the visit to an end. Thinking about Taiga's behavior, I could only conclude that for some reason she had become jealous of the visitor.

Two weeks later, another couple arrived. They, too, were strangers to the wolves. On this occasion, it was Tundra who reacted aggressively toward Taiga when she sought to greet the man. Once again I had to interrupt the visit.

To date, the wolves have reacted in this way toward six visitors whom they have never seen before. Tundra has become aggressive toward Taiga on four occasions when she has sought to jump up and lick a male's extended hand; Taiga has twice been aggressive toward Tundra when he has tried to greet a female visitor.

I hold to my initial conclusion: the wolves become jealous and direct their aggression toward each other rather than toward the object of their jealousy. But why is it that only certain individuals produce this reaction? If the wolves continue to demonstrate such selective jealousy, I hope that it will be possible to question the visitors without causing them embarrassment, for I am convinced that individual hormonal metabolism *during the time of contact* is responsible for the negative behavior that both wolves had demonstrated. Meanwhile, I am encouraging those visitors who have already been made welcome by Tundra and Taiga to return periodically so that we may see if the behavior of the wolves changes at any particular time. In this regard, talking with Mike Collins about the matter, we decided that since his wife, Lou, had not seen the wolves since they were two months old, he would bring her to visit them so that we might monitor their behavior.

When Mike and Lou arrived, they walked down to the enclosure, but although almost a full year had elapsed since the cubs had seen Lou—and then on one occasion only—they immediately remembered her and made a great fuss over her. There the matter rests.

I have no doubt that jealousy is responsible for the other reactions and I feel confident that an individual's hormonal activity at the time of arrival furnishes the scent that causes the jealousy, but there is much yet to be investigated. Beth Duman's experience with Nahani supports the jealousy theory.

To this writing, Tundra and Taiga have received 109 visitors; only eight of them have produced negative behavior. Significantly, when Tundra reacted aggressively upon detecting stress in the two male visitors mentioned earlier, Taiga retreated from them, ears back and tail between her legs, leaving Tundra to deal with them on his own. Furthermore, both wolves become mildly jealous of each other when Sharon and I are with them and we stop to caress one or the other. This is a twice-daily occurrence that has been taking place since they were only two months old; it demonstrates sibling rivalry. Usually, as soon as one of us bends to pat one wolf, the other wolf rushes up and seeks our attention, at the same time growling at its sibling and biting it in a controlled fashion. But if only one of us is in the enclosure, there is no rivalry between them; they are then quite likely to station themselves on either side of Sharon or me so as to be petted simultaneously. Often under such circumstances, after the initial greeting, one wolf will go and lie down, perhaps ten feet away, content to rest while the other is getting attention. This is something that neither of them will do when we are both in the enclosure. Yet, at feeding times, neither is the least bit jealous of the other. In the morning, they still maintain their positions, Taiga in front of me and Tundra in front of Sharon. During the afternoon feed, they continue to trade bowls, or to feed out of the same one. At this time also, if one comes to us to be caressed, the other doesn't seem to object. And during the frequent play periods that we enjoy daily, neither of them exhibits rivalry and will often take turns at chasing and being chased.

Our wolves are now fourteen months old, and although each has strengthened the early characteristics that we observed in them, their individual personalities remain the same. There are occasions when both are stimulated at the same time regardless of weather, hour of the day, or any other influence that we can detect. In such a mood, they leap joyfully at us, nose into our clothing, lick us, and play-bite our fingers, but do so softly. Then they dash away, chasing one another, only to return to us, smiling and exuberant. On other occasions, especially after they have been particularly active during the night, they are sleepy and very loving, inviting caresses and refraining from competing with each other. Then there are the times when they are seriously preoccupied with their own affairs. It may be that a squirrel has perched itself high up in a tree within their enclosure and sits there shrieking at the wolves while eating spruce-cone seeds; or they may have found a fresh mole tunnel and are attempting to capture the animal. They become very interested when ducks land on our stream, or when they see one of our beavers swimming on the surface. Once, last spring, a large beaver surfaced within ten feet of the enclosure while we were walking with the cubs, and although the big rodent submerged quickly, Tundra and Taiga remained near the spot, waiting for it to reappear with the kind of patience that only a predator demonstrates. The beaver wisely kept away.

Apart from those occasions when they are so stimulated that nothing seems able to dampen their enthusiasm, I have noticed that they are as much affected by the weather as we are. On high-pressure days when the sun is strong and a cool breeze is present, they become extremely active and playful.

Conversely, during periods of low pressure they are quiet, gentle, and seemingly lazy, and they yawn a lot, gaping wide and stretching their bodies at the same time. On really hot days they sleep a good deal, seeking out shady locations or retreating into the barn. The heat also depresses their appetites and they are more inclined to be solitary.

Daily, the wolves demonstrate some new behavioral trait, the reason for which is often impossible to determine even though I have been studying the species for so long; and although I am always intrigued *and* frustrated when I can't understand their motives, I am not surprised. In fact, at those times when we cannot detect the underlying motives that prompt a particular kind of behavior, I do not consider that we have failed, but rather that we have once again established that wolves are as individualistic as humans and that it is folly to ascribe to all members of the species those personal traits observed only in some of them. It is not so much the ways in which wolves act, but the reasons for their actions. It is easy to tell when a wolf is content, happy, excited, afraid, or aggressive, for they all demonstrate these emotions in more or less similar ways. The challenge is to be able to know why they are so motivated. Many behaviorists have all too readily formed hard-and-fast conclusions that purport to explain fully the behavioral motives of all wolves, but if it is borne in mind that sociologists and psychologists are still unable to understand all personal motivations that prompt behavior in humans, the reason for our failure to properly understand wolves (or any other species of animals) soon becomes apparent. Western man has for too long thought of himself as a super-being who is in no way to be compared with the "brute beasts" with whom he must share the world environment. As a result, he has persistently denied that animals think, have emotions, and are capable of making individual decisions.

Such egotistic bias has caused many biologists and especially behaviorists to think of animals as purely mechanical creatures to be studied and described in clinical ways. These people consider as odious any attempt to compare the habits and behavior of their "subjects" with those of humans, an attitude manifested in the contempt in which they hold those who dare to make such comparisons, accusing them of anthropomorphism. The term is borrowed from two Greek words, *anthropos,* meaning "man," and *morphos,* meaning "shape." Translated into plain language, anthropomorphism ascribes human form or attributes to a being or thing that is not human, especially to a deity; it is therefore largely misused when it is applied to those of us who discuss animals in proper English.

When an investigator painstakingly avoids using human terms in order to describe the deportment of animals, such a person most often produces scientific papers that are almost incomprehensible to laymen and can only partially be understood by a colleague, even after several readings. At the same time, the champions of abstract description frequently confuse the perceptual abilities of humans with the perceptual capabilities of animals, which are much greater than our own. Thus they find it impossible to measure the total reality of life.

We cannot smell the world of the wolf, we cannot hear it, we certainly do not see it in its proper perspective, we cannot taste it, and we do not know how to come to terms with it. Instead, we blunder through it, believing that we are the masters of creation and refusing to accept that the "lower animals" are constantly in touch with the realities of the universe. If such an approach persists, humankind will continue to defy nature and will surely fail to secure the peace that it so desperately needs. But the wolf can teach us. With its uncanny perceptions and a social system that closely resembles our own, this much-persecuted animal can put us back in touch with our own realities, once we begin to understand and respect it.

Sharon and I live with Tundra and Taiga in this awareness. We know that in teaching us about themselves, they are also teaching us about ourselves and about our own kind. We share life with them in full trust. We love them, and we know that they love us; we *try* to understand them, and they most definitely understand us.

Sometimes we are asked, "What are you going to do with your wolves?"

We reply that we do not intend to *do* anything with them. We are simply going to live with them. And we hope that they will continue to teach us about the realities of life.

HAROLD HORWOOD

Fire Dance 1987

HAROLD HORWOOD was born in St. John's, Newfoundland, in 1923. A Liberal Member of Parliament in 1949, he left politics in 1951 and wrote books of fiction, travel and biography, including *Only the Gods Speak* (1979), *White Eskimo* (1973), and *Bartlett* (1977), a biography of the Canadian explorer Captain Bob Bartlett. "I wrote three novels and a book of short stories," he says, "before I realized I would rather have written *Walden* than all the novels published in English in the nineteenth century." His first book of natural history, *The Foxes of Beachy Cove* (1967), was a quiet, introspective description of Newfoundland's Beachy Cove Valley. After moving to Nova Scotia's Annapolis Valley, he wrote *Dancing on the Shore* (1987), from which "Fire Dance" is taken. Horwood has been hailed by Farley Mowat as "incontestably one of the best nature writers of our times."

* • *

I HAVE SEEN the willets dancing in the springtime on the shore, dancing not only on the short salt grass that is covered monthly by the tide, but dancing in air, like butterflies, or salamanders wrapped in flame. This three-dimensional dance, a spiral reaching toward the sky, expands and replicates the helix that is at the core of life: the double spiral of the chromosome, the protean spirals of the albuminoids, the simplicity and perfection of the circle with the added dimensions of motion and time, the elements that make of all perfection a transience, a flowering, and a becoming.

Such is the dance of these feathered spirits; they move in rhythmic measures through the radiance that glimmers from the waves, as twin planets might move, each orbiting the other about their common centre, then rise like twirling smoke, still orbiting, and quiver at perihelion before returning to the earth to complete the dance with intertwined circles once more, a quadrilateral symmetry, adorned at both ends with simple but decorative motifs, like a minuet or a scherzo.

Arthur Cleveland Bent, who devoted himself to writing the *Life Histories of the Birds of North America* (and actually completed a good deal of it before he died), took part in many a mass shooting of shorebirds, chopped up many a carcass, and poked around in the half-digested mess of many a willet's last meal to study its "food habits." But he never saw willets dancing, as I have seen them, or knew them in the way I know them, not as "things" to be described and reported, but as companions in life's adventure. I have seen a willet at little more than arm's length sitting on her four mottled eggs knowing full well that I was not an agent of death, but an ambassador from one of life's neighboring countries. By walking humbly in the world, and treating its living inhabitants with respect, you can learn far more about their true nature than Bent and Audubon and other disciples of Newton ever imagined.

For a long time this boldly patterned shorebird, slightly bigger than a pigeon, was almost extinct. The wealthy gunners of the nineteenth century, the clubmen of the Atlantic coastal resorts, some of whom killed thousands of shorebirds in a single day for sport, came close to destroying the willet. They succeeded in destroying the Eskimo curlew. Mass slaughter for sport ceased to be respectable just in time to save the willet, which in recent years has been slowly reoccupying its former range, and spreading northward through Nova Scotia. Today it nests all along the shores of Annapolis Basin, as it did in early Acadian times, each pair the tenants of a patch of salt marsh or of a clearing in the nearby woods. They feed on the mud flats, pulling marine worms from their burrows, and snapping up the so-called beach fleas, the *Orchestia,* which look more like tiny shrimps than fleas, and the larval flies that live by the millions under ropes of rotting seaweed cast up by the Fundy tides.

The willets nest in a little clearing in our ravine, as well as on the salt marsh near our beach, and often perch on our roof-tree, calling loudly to one another: "Kiddily-dee! Kiddily-dee!" a call that they repeat as they circle overhead protesting human intrusion on their nesting territory. I have to stretch my imagination pretty far to imagine one of them calling "Pill-will-willet," as they are said to do along the American shores in migration. Perhaps they speak a different language in the south. They arrive here in April and immediately advertise their presence with conspicuous territorial flights and loud musical calls. Much more than the quiet robins (some of whom may be here all winter), the willets are the true criers of the spring.

Because I live in the middle of a colony of nesting willets, I have been privileged to see their courtship dance as Audubon and Bent never did. Indeed, up to the time Bent published his *Life Histories* no one had ever reported seeing this fanciful dance, surely one of the most remarkable among all the dances of wild creatures.

The willet is a striking bird, with wing stripes that flash like flags, white on black, all the more brilliant because it is seen most often against the sombre background of the sand flat or the salt marsh. The bird engages in frequent display, holding the wings straight up as it stands erect (somewhat in the pose of a gilded archangel by Giovanni) showing off its bold design like a costume in a pageant. Such displays are thought to be a part of courtship, and they may often be just that, the bird, at a distance, signalling: "Look at me! See how beautiful I am!" But the display is not a part of the dance. Once the birds are close together they no longer need display. Their interest already aroused, they concentrate on the symmetry of the dance without distraction.

As for the display, there need not be another willet around to see it. A bird that wants to show off its fine feathers will display in front of just about anything. A willet will show off to a flock of sandpipers, or to its own reflection in a pool of water. A yellow-shafted flicker will sit on a branch and display the golden lining of its wings to a chickadee or a redpoll. The most extreme example of inappropriate display I ever saw was a peacock displaying to a sparrow. Obviously there are motives other than courtship at work here. They could be territorial, warning off poachers. They could be nationalistic, drawing the group together. Or they could be simple self-delight, the kind of unstudied posing you see in a child displaying for the camera. Fashion models are taught to do this in eye-catching clothes, but even ten-year-olds will do it instinctively; I've seen the same pose again and again in nude children facing the camera, hands locked behind the head, smiling with self-delight: "Look at me! See how beautiful I am!"

Willets nest on the ground, either in dry patches of the salt marshes along our shore, or in the adjoining woodland glades. They usually hatch four chicks, which promptly leave the nest and follow their parents about, cheeping to be fed on worms, slugs, or insects from the beaches. The chicks are not often seen by casual visitors to the shore, for they are very secretive until ready to fly, and very inconspicuous in their mottled camouflage. In danger or alarm an adult will pick up a chick, and fly off to safety with the youngster clamped between its legs, returning for others until the whole brood is removed. By late summer, when fully fledged and grown, young willets become quite bold, flying in small flocks, often five to ten birds together, along the tide line, or wheeling overhead to inspect intruders walking through their favorite feeding ground.

In late summer or early autumn many small flocks of willets from other nesting colonies appear along our shore, fattening themselves for their overseas flight to the southern Atlantic coast or the West Indies. From my canoe around Goat Island or Porter's Point I have seen assembled flocks of perhaps a hundred and fifty of them at one time. They pass on southward to St. Mary's Bay, and finally depart from Cape St. Mary's, Yarmouth, or Cape Sable, flying perhaps a thousand miles over the ocean before they touch land again. My neighbor Bill Percy sees them on the Florida beaches in early spring, and I in March on the beaches of South Carolina, each of us wondering if they are the same birds we see at home.

How do they navigate? Apparently by the sun and the stars. They have a grid at the back of the eye that is supposed to act as a star chart, though nobody can explain exactly how it works; it isn't the kind of thing you can discover by cutting up a willet and looking at the scraps under a microscope. But though their flight is direct and true in clear weather, they become lost in fog. If the weather remains "thick" for a long time they will collect in a flock, alight on the sea, and wait for the weather to clear. This seems to rule out magnetic navigation (suspected in some other birds) and to suggest that they orient themselves by the sky. Perhaps they cannot fly above the clouds, as some migrants can do, but they are well able to rest on the water like a flock of phalaropes, and, with semi-webbed feet, are fairly well equipped for swimming.

A hundred years ago many thousands of Eskimo curlews used to gather here, just as the willets gather today, feeding on the ripe berries and the burgeoning insect life of late summer, working southward until they reached the islands around Shelburne and Barrington Passage, where they began a flight of epic proportions; they would cross the open ocean in a great sweep of five thousand miles to South America and then fly over the jungles and the pampas to the high plateau of Patagonia at the distant tip of South America, returning through central Canada to the Arctic in the spring. In those days there may have been a hundred thousand curlews over Annapolis Basin at one time.

Gunners here and in Labrador found them an easy target. Like passenger pigeons, they were killed for market; the Hudson's Bay Company bought them and canned them for export. The teal-sized birds were so tame and easy to shoot that gunners quickly exterminated them. A favorite trick was to capture a wounded curlew and keep it alive as long as possible, making it scream its distress call. Instead of warning away its companions, as would happen with so many other birds, this attracted them. They came flying to the aid of the wounded bird, and were destroyed in their turn. The biggest slaughters of all took place in the American Midwest during the spring migration, when Eskimo curlews were hauled away by the cartload.

By 1900 the once-plentiful curlews had become rare. By 1910 they were no longer worth pursuing for meat, but had achieved great value as museum specimens. Then, as now, there were "scientists" who believed that no bird had achieved its highest destiny until it was stuffed and labelled and stored in the drawer of a museum. So, as happened with other rare birds, skin-hunters exterminated the last Eskimo curlews in order to sell them to the taxonomists. The last birds ever certainly seen alive were shot in Argentina in 1924 and 1925 for a museum in Buenos Aires. There have been doubtful reports of survivors from time to time ever since.

The curlews always flew in mixed flocks with golden plovers, which were also hunted to what seemed like extinction. John James Audubon was with a party of gunners near New Orleans in March 1821 when they exterminated an estimated forty-eight thousand golden plovers in a single day. But a few golden plovers survived and increased when at last such massacres were outlawed. By the 1950s I was seeing golden plovers quite frequently on the Newfoundland tidal flats. By the 1980s they were still uncommon, but by no means rare during autumnal migration in Nova Scotia. I saw them on the rim of the basin in 1985 with mixed flocks of sandpipers and smaller plovers.

Meanwhile, that other curlew of the east, the Hudsonian, also a companion of the golden plover, seems to have survived fairly well. Unlike the similar Eskimo curlew, it is a wild bird, difficult to approach, found often on barrens far from tidal flats, feasting on blueberries and partridgeberries with its smaller companions until it is ready to leave on its flight across the ocean. This curlew still forms mixed flocks with golden plovers. No one has ever explained the symbiosis between curlews and plovers, but it must exist. Perhaps one species is a more efficient navigator, and the other a more efficient sentry. Something like that. For it is only during migration that the birds show this strange need for companionship between totally different species.

The dancing willets helped to reconcile me to an idea that I spent most of my lifetime rejecting—the fundamental place of dance in nature. I grew up in a world where human dancing was "dry fucking," a Hollywood perversion in a class with the "French kiss," and that may be why I rejected it out of hand. Neither Nietzsche nor Havelock Ellis, with their meditations on the dance, reconciled me to its fundamental nature, but nature herself eventually

did. If shorebirds and chimpanzees and honey bees all dance, and if fundamental particles dance in the cloud chamber, who am I to deny the cosmic
connection?

The mesons dance like a swarm of bees, living and dying in the flickering
cloud. They appear like sparks and vanish, but, unlike sparks, dying they re-
store the balance, return their parent to the state she enjoyed before their
birth. It is as though they might be a small burst of exuberance, a signal only,
like the honking of geese, proclaiming the passage through eternity of a living
body.

Rhythm begins far down in nature, perhaps as far down as the resonance
of fundamental particles—which may, after all, be not quite so fundamental as
once was supposed; it paces the universal dance of the molecules; it is inher-
ent in the quartz crystals that keep our watches running on time. The earth
dances with the sun and the moon, creating the regular rhythm of day and
night, of summer and winter, of spring tide and neap tide. All those rhythms
in turn are transmitted to living creatures: we see them most notably in the
slow dance of the sea anemones in a tidal pool, in the rising and falling of the
worms on a clam flat. Even in the darkness of a laboratory tank, shut away
from the daylight and the outside world, such creatures will continue the
rhythms that their ancestors learned on the shores of some vanished ocean,
taught to them by the dance of the solar system, in the years when life was
young.

Dance is rhythm in four dimensions: the three dimensions of space, and
the fourth that we call time. It seems to be fundamental in the world. My
children danced without ever being instructed, without even having a suggestion made to them. When the rhythms of music stirred them (as I played a
mouth organ) they got out on the floor and began dancing.

Birds of many species dance—crows, partridge, herons—some a grave
minuet, others a wild tarantella. More mammals than hares dance in more
months than March. I have seen a wolf dancing with his shadow, and have
heard that even elephants, those eight-ton mammoths with legs like the
trunks of trees, solemnly dance in their jungle glades, as well as in human
circuses.

Rhythm may well be as fundamental in the universe as order. Just as we see
the crystals of copper sulphate fashioning themselves into blue-green fronds
like prophecies of trees billions of years before the first trees were imagined,
so we see the particles in the meson cloud living out their lives in a perfectly
regular dance at a level of organization so primitive that even matter, as we
know it, does not yet exist, not to mention the life and the social orders and

the flow of history that will emerge from this meson dance ten billion years later.

Order, pattern, symmetry, rhythm—all may seem to be abstract qualities, not to be considered in a class with matter and energy. And yet, when we think about the question, we may conclude that these abstract qualities could be just as fundamental to the universe as the "forces" that bind the elemental particles into atoms, and are now pictured as still other particles with such fanciful names as "gluons." Order, pattern, symmetry, and rhythm operate at the highest and lowest levels of perception. The binary stars dance, and so do the Cepheid variables, those flashing stars that measure out the spaces between galaxies. The galaxies rotate about their cores, and perhaps even the galactic clusters, moved by the same principle as the mesons a million orders of magnitude away, move about one another in a pattern so slow that only the Ancient of Days could perceive it.

But the meson who lives only a few billionths of a second is also a partner in the divine dance. And the willet, who lives in the half-way house between the meson and the galaxy, dances before god like David the king, saying yea and amen to the great flow and rhythm of life.

DON GAYTON

The Grass and the Buffalo 1990

DON GAYTON was born in 1946 in the western United States, where he earned a degree in agronomy from Washington State University. He moved to Canada in 1974, studied plant ecology at the University of Saskatchewan, and now works as a range manager in Nelson, British Columbia. His first book, *The Wheatgrass Mechanism* (1990), subtitled *Science and Imagination in the West-ern Canadian Landscape*, is a holistic study of prairie ecosystems, incorporating pure science, natural and human history, which he does not separate: "To me," he writes, "prairie is a thin membrane of grass, stretched tightly over secret horizons of soil, and shaped by drought, geography, and solitude." The essay excerpted here explores the interplay between prairie tallgrass and buffalo migration patterns, as well as between grass and soil, people and nature, and our outer and inner selves.

❧ • ☙

BISON, BISON. He is the ur-creature of Western North America: his flesh and blood are mingled with the very flesh and blood of this continent. Land, water, and flora were bent and shaped by him. He was the lord of the open western frontier. When that frontier closed, the living buffalo became a dying symbol. His time was from the last of the glaciers until the first of the white men. That era is like a distant symphony for us; we hear a phrase here, a chord there. When that music is finally reconstructed, buffalo is sure to be the coda.

Physical traces of his massive presence can still be seen.

Buffalo have a great need to rub, and on treeless prairie, the only objects tall and rigid enough for them were the rare boulder erratics, huge stones that somehow missed being pulverized by glaciers. Rubbing stones on rangeland became sacred sites, and paths converged on them from all points of the buffalo compass. (No one knows from how far they came.) The stones sit in deep, rounded depressions, the result of generations of animals working their way around them.

Geologists in the Dakotas puzzled for decades over some anomalous transverse slashes seen along ridges and river valleys. The slashes were gradually disappearing through cultivation, but aerial photographs of natural areas showed them extending over long distances. Explanations for the slashes ranged from glacial compression to seismic fault lines. Their very size and depth made it difficult to accept animal origin. But in the end, they were seen to be buffalo trails, braided heartlines across the palm of the land.

The size of the population at full flower will never be known. Frank Gilbert Roe, whose 1000–page book on the buffalo is a monument of obsessive scholarship, refuses to speculate. He does quote Ernest Thompson Seton's estimate of 50,000,000, a comfortable number. Roe also cites another observer, a Kansan from the mid 1800s, whose description puts the size of the buffalo population in perspective. The Kansan tells of a westward train trip that was held up for *three days* while a single migrating herd crossed the tracks.

Our buffalo were a conscious sacrifice. The entire history and ethos of North American settlement would have to be rewritten to accommodate their survival as wild animals. All that remains now are a few ranch herds, plus animal-park specimens in places like Moose Jaw and Calgary, where once the animal moved in imperial herds of 10,000. We keep the buffalo's image though, and it has powerful cultural overtones of wildness and independence. Buffalo is the ultimate doomed rebel.

Ranchers in the west have experimented with commercial buffalo herds over the years. The animal has a good feed conversion ratio, needs little care, and produces very lean meat. But 10,000 years loose on the prairies have left their stamp. Corrals and holding pens must be made from telephone poles and two-by-tens. Calves that are tied up frequently kill themselves trying to get free. The genes for this wildness run deep: it takes two and three crosses with domestic cattle before the offspring—beefalo—are tractable.

Near the very end of the buffalo era, in the 1870s, prairie settlers collected buffalo bones for sale. One major shipping depot was just southeast of present day Regina, on the banks of Wascana Creek, at a place that became known as Pile o' Bones. Periodically the collected bones were loaded on freight cars and shipped east to be ground into fertilizer. Fuzzy photographs of this bone depot still exist. The neatly stacked bone piles stand out stark white alongside the dark freight cars and loading docks. The scene is strongly reminiscent of Dachau.

The pace of buffalo killing picked up dramatically at the end. Hunters, European tourists, fur traders, even Indians seemed desperately anxious to be rid of the great staggering buffalo enterprise, to put it out of its misery, perhaps. Many animals were shot for sport, their carcasses left untouched or with just the tongue removed.

During Sitting Bull's stay in southwestern Saskatchewan, it was U.S. military policy to intercept any northward-migrating herds and turn them back before they crossed into Canada, thus ensuring fatal separation of the Sioux from their sustaining buffalo.

The last Canadian buffalo herd was dispatched in 1878, but the American herds hung on a few years longer. The final curtain fell about 1891, in central Montana, when the last free-ranging herd was destroyed.

Individual animals remained—prairie rogues and small boreal forest groups. At their lowest ebb a few decades ago, the North American population stood at around 30,000. We have since pulled back from the brink to a captive population of roughly 100,000.

Buffalo grazed and rolled and trampled and dunged their way over this land for 10,000 years, and would have had a profound effect on our vegetation. The native grasses of buffalo range should be well adapted to these grazing animals, since we know that buffalo eat grass almost exclusively. Curiously though, many of our native grasses seem exquisitely sensitive to grazing of any kind.

If these grass species—the fescues, stipas, and wheatgrasses—evolved hand in hand with the shaggy buffalo, why then are they so fragile? Why do they decline so quickly under modern cattle grazing, to be replaced by other, less desirable vegetation?

The question forms a classic triangular problem, one of grazing, range grass physiology, and prehistoric buffalo herd movements. There are good intellectual dimensions to this question, from the practical all the way to the subcellular, and finally down the long sightline of paleontology. Some tentative answers are beginning to emerge.

Suppose there were four great regional buffalo herds. In late fall, horizons of midcontinental prairie turn pastel pink and blue, sloughs freeze hard, and the northern distances inspire melancholy. Forage is now mere wisps of dry grass, beaten by the wind. Individual bands of the first herd, the northern prairie herd, slowly rendezvous, reluctant to leave their chosen grassland. But finally they do leave, heading *north* to Canadian boreal forests or *west* to the sheltering foothills of the Rockies. Once in the forests, buffalo have shaken the cutting winds of winter prairie, and they can bed in insulating snow.

Good forage—fescue and pinegrass—has grown there undisturbed all summer, and can be nosed out from under the snow. In the foothills, herds can
water in streams that run all winter, instead of breaking ice or eating snow.

When spring calves come, herds move short distances, and melting snow
uncovers more unused forage. The edge of the forest becomes a favored zone,
providing the best of both worlds. The bugs are not bad yet, and the herds lin-
ger on in the forest. Finally, in full summer, prairie calls, and herds rumble past
the Red Deers, Havres and Nipawins of the future, heading back to the center of the continent.

When they arrive, the cool-season stipas and wheatgrasses have already
finished their period of rapid spring growth. Grazing would have little impact
on them now, as they coast toward maturity and senescence. Meanwhile, the
fescue grasses back in the foothills and parkland wintering areas have a chance
to regrow undisturbed.

Suppose a second herd, this one summering in modern-day Montana and
the Dakotas. As winter approaches, they move *southward* to the tall grasses and
mild winters of the central plains. Here, in Kansas and Missouri, was the one
part of the prairie that may have experienced season-long grazing. The tallgrass prairie of this area contained a large percentage of warm-season, C_4
grasses. This was the Eurasia of the north American continent, the one place
where summer and winter grazing may have overlapped, as various herds
shifted in and out of the area.

A third regional herd might summer on the high plains along the eastern
flanks of the Rockies, moving west into the foothills for winter.

Like geese in their flyways, these herds seem to have moved separately,
each in its own broad and looping pattern of season and geography. Variations
in a year's weather might cause the pattern to shift and rearrange, so no two
migrations would be exactly alike. Still more variation would be introduced
by the exact route a herd followed, and its selection of particular grazing and
wintering places. Unfenced Western North America was ideal terrain for ran-
dom behavior. Herds may at times have simply flowed, the erstwhile leaders
following their noses to the most immediate grass, shelter or sunlight.

Buffalo are very mobile. Wildlife biologists proved this by tracking a small
captive herd in Yellowstone National Park. A technician would follow the
herd quietly during the day and then make camp near them when they bed-
ded down for the night. Time and again the technician would wake up at
dawn to find the herd long gone, several miles away and moving fast.

When a big herd did stop to graze, chaos would reign. Grazing pressure
was incredible; new leaves, old leaves, dead stems and seed heads were all

either eaten or mashed into the ground. Shrubs were broken off and trampled. Vast quantities of manure and urine were laid down and the surface soil was thoroughly stirred up. In a very few days nothing edible would remain and the herd would leave. Then, because of the massiveness of the western space, three, five, even ten years might elapse before another herd would return to that same site.

How do we know this grazing pattern? We don't really. There is no ancestral evidence, no blurry photographs to study. Explorers' accounts from the middle and late 1800s described buffalo whose migrations were already profoundly disturbed. What conclusions we do have are the result of imaginative hypotheses and real conceptual daring. Scientists are uncomfortable with this kind of speculation, and use it only when confronted with deep complexity, as in the functioning of plant phloem, or in the case of minimal evidence. Historical buffalo migration is a classic case with no direct empirical evidence. The problem tweaked the interest of two archaeologists from Simon Fraser University in British Columbia. They confronted the migrations using a plant biochemistry tool called carbon dioxide isotope discrimination.

The carbon of atmospheric carbon dioxide has a normal atomic weight of 12. In the course of natural and cosmic events, a slightly different stable isotope is created, and there is a small, constant fraction of CO_2 in the atmosphere whose carbon has a weight of 13 instead of the normal 12. This is the mundane basis for what has become a wonderfully sensitive bioassay. Conventional cool-season grasses, with a C_3 metabolic organization, recognize and discriminate between the two isotopes of carbon, and fix them into their tissues in a specific ratio to one another. Warm season, C_4–metabolism grasses maintain a very different, but also constant, carbon isotope ratio. So constant are these ratios that they can be used as a chemical benchmark to distinguish between C_3 and C_4–type plant tissues.

The two SFU archaeologists saw that by using isotope discrimination analysis they could track the stable isotope carbon 13 as it wended its way through buffalo metabolism. The carbons fixed into the leaves of grasses are converted to the tissue and bone of grazing animals, still maintaining their appropriate isotopic ratio. Thus bone tissue of grazers living in C_4–dominated southern prairie would have a very different carbon 13/carbon 12 ratio than bone from more northern grazing animals that lived on a strict C_3 diet.

The researchers collected ancestral bison bone from various sites in the Alberta foothills. Their hypothesis was that these bones should have a ratio typical of cool season C_3 grasses, since those types are dominant in the foothills and the northern prairies. Sure enough, the opposite, null hypothesis was proven: the bone carbon ratio was intermediate between C_4 and C_3 diets. So the buffalo cycled, the scientists concluded, between northern C_3 forest and southern C_4 prairie.

North American rangeland needs a consumer, we know that much. Protect a site from use for 15 years or so and it gets rank with dead material. Grass growth is restricted, snow mold becomes a problem, and soils stay cold far into the spring. We know the indigenous consumers were buffalo, grasshoppers, and fire, but we don't know how to replace them.

Ten thousand years allowed the grass and the buffalo time to develop a subtle biogeographical transaction. The grasses arranged their geographical locations and their life cycles in a way that minimized use during growth and maximized it during dormancy. The buffalo, for their part, guaranteed that when they did graze a site they would do it aggressively, indiscriminately, briefly, and rarely. All of the manure and urine generated at that site was returned to it and churned into the soil, along with seeds and litter. There was no hundred percent guarantee to the grazing transaction, but it was just consistent enough for both grazed and grazer to shape their lives and gene pools to it.

Seasonal grazing was unique to the New World; the Old World ranges in the Altai, the Caucasus, and Turkestan were used year around, and domestic herding started there thousands of years sooner than in North America. The grasses of those regions—brome, crested wheatgrass, cheatgrass, among others—could not escape their grazers, and were forced to perform growth and reproduction in their presence. Thus the annual cycles of many Old World grasses are brief explosions of vegetative growth in early spring, followed by a race to flowering and senescence. Seeds are programmed to germinate quickly; life cycles are compressed from months down into weeks, and their engines of growth run on a very lean mixture of water and nutrients. Genes are programmed for maximum leaf and minimum root.

Cunning Canadian botanists of the early 1900s traveled to these places and recognized their unique grazing environments. When they returned home, battered suitcases disgorged packets of seed they had collected. The performance of these introduced grasses on the prairie research stations—Swift Current, Manyberries, Lethbridge—was stunning. The crested wheat grasses and Russian wild ryes could germinate, grow, and hold down soil in the harsh dustbowl. Prairie Farm Rehabilitation agronomists, real heroes of the dirty thirties, traveled to hundreds of farmer meetings, one driving while the other one slept, to spread the gospel of these grasses. Thousands and thousands of eroding wheat fields were planted with crested wheatgrass and saved from further destruction.

But the season of crested will never suit the ghosts of departed buffalo, and thus it remains an alien on North American range. The ground in between crested plants gradually becomes bare and sterile. No other vegetation develops. The tough and wiry crested seed stalks begin to accumulate, leaving no room for new leaf growth. Roots break down quickly, leaving little stable organic matter in the soil.

Crested does fit the needs of our domestic cattle, in one special instance. In early spring they can be turned onto crested pasture to feed on its prodigious early growth, while leaving the native pasture to the spring rest it is accustomed to.

What about the fourth great north American buffalo herd, the one that would have grazed on the vast resources of intermountain bluebunch wheatgrass west of the Rockies? It simply did not exist. Historical evidence speaks only of small and very occasional groups of buffalo in the entire intermountain region. The Cascade rain shadow apparently held the level of grass growth and drinking water to below the needs of the buffalo, and perhaps the mountain ranges made the spaces too confining. So the Pacific Northwest Grasslands coevolved with aridity, solitude, and the occasional deer, antelope, and elk, but no buffalo. Therein may lie the exquisite sensitivity of bluebunch wheatgrass to grazing.

For a few decades, this bluebunch grass carried a good portion of the early western cattle industry and the quirky subculture that went with it. But the bluebunch has given way, gradually but profoundly, to the invading cheatgrass, another Eurasian alien. Now bluebunch is a pathetic remnant, and cheatgrass dominates some 40,000,000 acres of its original range. Knapweed, a thistle-like European broadleaf, commands another 2,000,000.

The old trails and rubbing stones mark one of the world's great migration cycles. The buffalo niche remains, tenanted awkwardly by our grain and cattle, but the living presence of the wild animal is no longer with us. There is a residue of its spirit though. When I get far enough away from the grid roads and wheat fields, I sense a buffalo-energy in this land, running from calving ground, through trail and salt lick, to buffalo pound and rubbing stone. As long as we retain some native prairie, that energy will remain.

MERILYN SIMONDS MOHR

Stubborn Particulars of Place 1991

MERILYN SIMONDS MOHR was born in 1949 in Winnipeg, Manitoba, and moved at the age of eight to Campinas, Brazil. In 1961, she returned to Canada and later studied drama and English at the University of Western Ontario, then moved to a small rural property near North Bay, Ontario, where she lived until 1987. A regular contributor to *Harrowsmith* and *Equinox* magazines from 1978 to 1991, her many articles and books, including *Canoe Craft* (1983) and *Sunwings* (1985), display a strong commitment to the environment in the fields of energy and resource conservation. She has received the Greg Clark Award for Outdoor Writing and a Science Writers of Canada Award. In the following essay (which first appeared in *Harrowsmith*), she embarks on a more personal exploration of the effects of the human presence on the natural landscape.

ध • ஜ

AT THE BEGINNING of the last century, my great-great-grandmother, Margaret Cornfoot, left her home in Aberdeen, Scotland, sailed to Canada and walked north with her grown children from the end of the rail line in Orillia, Ontario, to a scrap of land she had purchased, sight unseen, near what is now the town of Gravenhurst. If her husband came with her, there is no record of him. Nor do I know what she thought when she saw the foreboding rocks and trees that greeted her. What I do know is that they felled the maples and pines, cleared the land, made the landscape their own. For all their hard work, it remained, after all, a stone farm, yielding crop after crop of granite and little else. Only the stone piles grew. They stayed on, for a while. There are streets in Gravenhurst named for her grandson: George Street, Elder Street. The log house, added to and shored up by someone else's forebears, and

Margaret's gravestone—an obelisk of gray granite—are still there, but the family eventually dispersed, and by the time I was born our connection with that part of the province was largely mythological.

So when I moved to North Bay with my husband in 1977, my immediate affection for the north caught me unawares. I had lived all my life in the south, in the flamboyant, overbearing tropics of Brazil and the fertile farmland of southwestern Ontario. By comparison, the spare boreal forest and recalcitrant rock seemed a restrained and exacting landscape indeed. Our first spring on Stonehill Acres, 50 acres of second-growth conifers interrupted here and there by shoulders of rock that shrugged out of the ground, I often thought of Margaret. Was she, like me, drawn by its indifference?

Every day, I walked in the bush, ostensibly to pull the skeletons of decomposing wrecks to the road so they could be carted off to the dump—every northern property, it seems, has a few derelict cars buried on its back forty. I returned with a steering wheel one day, a door the next, then a fender, and once, a windshield, intact, that I positioned in front of the hay bales, facing south, to give the bunching onions an early start.

As I parted the undergrowth to reveal yet another chassis and dragged hood after hood by its corroded ornament to the road, I became familiar with more than the anatomy of automobiles. Inside the rotted hulk of a 1940s Dodge, coils of filligreed green poked through the back seat. Near the edge of the clearing where our house stood, a twining plant with maple-like leaves and spiny gourds embroidered a bumper. The forest floor was cushioned with stiff little clutches of dark, glossy leaves; the red berries, when I crushed them between my fingers, smelled faintly of mint. There were loftier plants, too, with slender, May-green leaves waving over shorter stalks of berries. Soon, I was carrying Peterson in my parka pocket, and learning from him the names of these plants that were my new neighbors: the fiddleheads and wild cucumbers, the wintergreens and sarsaparilla.

Eventually, there came an end to the scraps of rusted metal that I could haul to the road, but the walks continued. I no longer needed an alibi. Unabashedly, I commiserated with the bladder campion on its name, gave the ironwood tree a friendly tap, congratulated the black cherry on the profusion of its blooms and did what I could to relieve the hazelnut bushes and pin cherry trees of the shrouds spun by voracious caterpillars. In the winter, when the snow was thigh deep, I made my rounds on snowshoes and skis, translating the hieroglyphics of hoofprint and spoor, occasionally sighting the moose or wolf that had made them. Birdsong remained, for the most part, an undifferentiated concerto, but I did learn to recognize by sight the jays and owls and four kinds of grosbeak that lived in our woods, the buntings and warblers I glimpsed as they passed through to warmer wintering grounds. I never felt the urge to follow. Every year, the landscape was becoming more mine; every year, more distinctly itself.

At one end of the property, just west of the clearing, was a massive upheaval of granite that rose abruptly from a stream. Early one June, I crossed the water, swollen by spring run-off, on a bridge made of two poles, then climbed The Big Rock, levering myself up the mossy slope by crooking my arms around the saplings that seemed to poke straight out of barren stone. The top of the granite outcropping was almost perfectly flat, the edges fringed with alders and balsam fir, weed trees that somehow got a foothold in the first folds of the uplifted rock. On the north edge, in an indentation so shallow that it might have been made by the heel of my palm, a solitary pink lady's slipper grew in a patch of moss. Until now there had been only the dangling chartreuse bells of Solomon's Seal and the pale umbrels of wild leek. The lady's slipper was the first flower of color. It held its head high in the forest, drooping its leaves so that its sensuous lower lip would be more prominently displayed.

Back at the house, I pulled from the kitchen shelf a turn-of-the-century household guide given to me by my great-aunt Mabel. Sure enough, *Mother's Remedies* listed Lady's Slipper in the "Herb Department," right after Juniper and before Life Root. The flower was a Valerian, a member of the orchid family that grows, uncharacteristically, in cool climates. "Taken for delirium," the book said.

I remembered orchids from my youth, clusters of pale yellow flowers staring down at me from between the lianas in the Bosque, a bit of preserved jungle that passed for a park in the Brazilian city where I grew up. Worm-like roots clutched at the tree trunk; splayed, crimson tongues thrust from between the puckered white lips of the waxy blooms. Their petals spattered with speckles the color of dried blood. Their little animal faces terrified me. Could this elegant bloom rising from the granite floor really be a distant relative?

Lady's Slipper. It was not a name I would have chosen for it. I looked it up in *The Private Lives of Orchids,* hoping for a more appropriate nickname. No such luck. Lady's Slippers grow in temperate climates around the world and though the connotation shifts from practical to religious to fanciful, cultures are apparently unanimous in their choice of central image: in German, *Frauenschuh,* woman's shoe; in Russian, *Mariin Bashnachock,* Mary's Slipper; in French, *Sabot de Vénus* or *Sabot de la vièrge,* Venus' shoe or shoe of the virgin;

in Ojibway, *Neemidi moccasin,* Dancing Slipper. To the settlers of this country, they were moccasin flowers, squirrel shoes. Even the Greek name of the genus—*Cypripedium*—means Aphrodite's little shoe. Stubbornly, I held to my contention that there was little that was pediform in the Lady Slipper's translucent pink, swollen sac. Lady's Purse, perhaps, or Pouting Plant or Pregnant Polly. Despite the fact that "orchid" derives from the Greek work for testicle—some orchids have a pair of tuberous roots that look remarkably like male genitalia—there was something undeniably female about this particular flower.

Every spring for ten years, May was punctuated with trips to the rock to look for signs of her arrival. I fussed over that patch of moss, straining for a glimpse of a pale green sprout, hardly able to keep myself from poking in the soil to see if she was stirring. The anticipation made me delirious. It was like waiting for a favorite aunt to appear for her annual visit: you haven't heard from her all year, you don't know if she's still alive, you aren't sure if you've come to the train station on the right day, or even if this is the right station. All the indentations in the rock began to look familiar; other patches of moss tried to trick me with sprouts of painted trillium and Canada mayflower. It had been a year, I thought in despair when she still had not appeared by the end of May, and a lot can happen in a year.

But the lady's slipper never failed me. One day late in the second spring, beside the dry, broken twig that I recognized as last year's flower stalk, a spike pushed through the ground, its tightly furled leaves gradually unfolding to reveal, inside the second, innermost leaf, a stem. Well, not a stem really, because the Latin name for this species—*acaule*—means stemless. It was a flower stalk that grew directly from the base of the plant, between the two leaves. And on top of this tall stalk eventually uncurled the most exquisite flower I have ever known.

It was always worth the wait. Four wisps of brownish tissue—two sepals and two petals, virtually indistinguishable and already parchment crisp— spread their arms like a cross. From the center dropped a pendulous pink sac formed by two opposing petals folding themselves together, like the sleeves of a silk kimono. When, a few days after the bloom first emerged, I took a break from gathering wild strawberries in the field beside the house, I noticed a bee disappear inside the bulging lower lip of the lady's slipper. Could this beauty be carnivorous? I got down on my hands and knees. At the bottom of the sac, I saw a cleft in the petals. The pink flesh was so translucent that I could see the shadow of the bee buzzing about inside. I was reminded of something I once read—that prisons have "pink rooms" where violent offenders are taken to calm themselves—and I wondered if the bee was relaxing in its rosy room. Within a few seconds, the insect emerged from a small hole on the right side of the top of the sac. What had it been doing in there?

I could not bring myself to pick the flower to probe the intimacies of its structure. Others had. The vibrant pink color and sweet fragrance of the lady's slipper, it seemed, attracted bees to enter the slit in the front of the sac. But it was a one-way door: the petals folded inward. At the top of the pink lip were two exits; inside they were light-colored and flagged with nectar-coated hairs to attract the bee, who had probably tippled a little before it crawled out. As the bee exited, it brushed past a little round green knob—the male parts of the lady's slipper—that left pollen stuck to its back. On the front of the flower, between the two exits, was a bright green pad that the bee also brushed against—the female part of the flower. As it moved from lady's slipper to lady's slipper, the bee was collecting and depositing pollen. For its trouble, it got a few sips of nectar in the pinkest of salons. Not a bad deal.

Over the next few years, most of the plants and birds I came to know I associated with a certain season. Spring began with the return of the tree sparrows with their rusty caps and little stickpin breasts. Tiny blue violets bloomed in the ditch and, for a brief time, the woods at the edge of the field were carpeted with trilliums, only rarely white, more often their ominous blood-red relatives, the Death Flower, and occasionally, petals edged in navy blue and streaked with deep purple. Blue flags bloomed, whether planted by some previous owner or wild, I could not tell. As the days warmed, the wild calla down by the stream would unfold its white spathe to reveal a stiff little spadix covered with tiny yellow flowers. And in the woods, from the center of a whorl of bright green leaves, the brilliant white starflower would emerge. By midsummer, the clearing was daubed with black-eyed Susans, daisies, Devil's paintbrush and purple vetch, the ditches thick with bouncing Bet, St. Johnswort and milkweed. Chokecherries dripped from the hedgerows. Then, the Indian hemp bloomed with its waxy pink bells and the pokeberries began to darken. Before long, the vireos were gorging themselves on bunchberries and it was time to pick the pearly everlastings.

But through it all there was the lady's slipper, a constant warp thread in my developing fabric of colors and textures and sounds. It outlasted the summer. When it first bloomed in early June, the flower sepals and petals were guarded over by one slender green leafy bract. As the flower faded, the shaft between the bract and the sepals began to grow. By August, the bloom had shrivelled to a brownish-pink rag and the fruit swelled, lifting itself up until the inch-long seed casing poked brazenly into the wind. Sometime late in the summer, the ribs split and through the narrow slits, thousands of seeds, like black saw-dust, sifted out into the breeze. The empty seed pod gamely held its head above the snow until, by early December, it had disappeared beneath the weight of winter.

As hard as I looked, I never found another pink lady's slipper on our land. I am not surprised, really. Orchids are the largest family of flowering plants in the world: there are 25,000 species, two dozen of them native to northern Ontario. But the *Cypripedium,* the Lady's Slippers, are the most primitive. Re-production is a delicate matter for them.

An orchid seed does not develop like other plant seeds. It is too tiny to carry much nutritional baggage. When it lands on moist soil and germinates, it swells to a minuscule corm. And that is as far as it goes. The protocorm does not grow into a lady's slipper unless the germinated seed is joined by a soil fungus in the genus *Rhizoctonsia.* It isn't in a hurry—it can wait for up to two years—but without fungus, there is no offspring.

The fungus and the seed live in symbiosis, but like many marriages, it is a precarious partnership, right from the start. The fungus originally seeks out the orchid seed to feed on its pathetically limited reserves of oil and protein. The orchid embryo, for its part, counterattacks, and starts to digest the fungus. Sometimes the fungus destroys the seed and sometimes the seed devours the fungus, but when conditions are right, the adversaries establish a delicate, mu-tually beneficial relationship, the fungus living off the outer tissues of the em-bryo while the orchid feeds off the parts of the fungus that penetrate deeper inside. Even after the seed and fungus set up housekeeping together, however, several seasons may pass before an orchid flowers. The *Cypripedium* apparently holds the record: it can take up to seventeen years to bring forth its first bloom.

Because of its delicate living arrangements—the fungi continue to help mature orchids absorb food from the soil—the lady's slipper cannot be trans-planted. So, when I left Stonehill Acres, and my marriage of seventeen years, I left the lady's slipper behind. It has been four springs and still, during the first day of May, I am driven to look for the tender green shoots of my orchid. I never stop yearning for the cold gray granite that never flinches under my foot, as the limestone in this new place does. And I always think with longing of the weedy balsam firs and their tentative toehold in that indifferent place. But it is the lady's slipper I miss the most. I think now that I liked her so well because she survived on so little.

Before I left the north, I walked with my husband to the little hollow in the granite and pointed out to him the exact patch of moss where the lady's slipper would make her appearance. I recently heard that he has raised a building on that flat rock, that a car drives across that uplifted stone shoulder. Perhaps he forgot about the pink lady's slipper. Or perhaps he has learned other ways of making the landscape his own.

SEÁN VIRGO

The Falcon 1991

SEÁN VIRGO was born in Malta in 1940, lived in South Africa and England, and moved to Canada in 1966. "My mother gave me Grey Owl's 'The Tree' and Charles G. D. Roberts's *Kindred of the Wild* when I was very young," he says, "and the myths stuck." He taught at the University of Victoria and has lived in some of Canada's wildest places, including the Queen Charlotte Islands and a Newfoundland outport. An intense relationship with physical nature has informed all his writing. His first collection of short stories, *White Lies and Other Fictions,* appeared in 1980, and a novel set in the Solomon Islands, *Selakhi,* was published in 1987. In *Waking in Eden* (1991), from which "The Falcon" is taken, Virgo returns to the myths that have stuck with him since reading Roberts's animal stories.

⁂

THE FALCON came down upon a dead branch and looked out towards the sea. It ordered its breast feathers, raked each wing in turn with a hind claw, and fell into a dream.

It sat for five hours, into late afternoon, without moving, except that the eyelids crept up and down a few times each hour, and the nostrils occasionally flared.

A person watching the bird might have guessed (an attempt to unriddle—which is to reduce—the monstrous, tormenting stillness on that branch) that the creature's blood had returned to the flow of the universe. That guess would be partly true.

But the bird is both there and not there. Like a singular child in a brown study.

Its waking nostrils felt a whisper of juniper smoke. Its waking eyes stared unfocussed at the horizon till the sky became its eyelid, and it entered the dream.

It dreamed, as all animals do and as we, at the heart of a reverie, might also dream, of its making. Not the conception of the bird itself, but of its kind. And the makers in that dream are so close to human in their form and movement, that the animals are confused in their dealings with us. Translucent, transtemporal, the living perpetual walls of *thuja* and *gingko* wood. Never consumed, the knucklebone juniper coals in the braziers. The murmur of voices, soft laughter, the measure of bells. The hesitant, careful footsteps of a certain apprentice.

There's no word in our language which means *"He or She"*. No word for *"He/She"*. And *"It"*, being neutral, is too far removed, for this story, from both Human and Angel.

I brought in a natural thing this morning—an aspen leaf from the beaver-pond—and have let it fall, to decide.

Black/He, Silver/She.

It dips and spins, and is tumbled over by the heat of the woodstove. It lies on the hearth like a black penny. He.

He walked, walks, shall sometime walk with special care.

He dreamed that the form he was carrying out to the drying racks might be the masterpiece.

Dreamed that his part in its making might elevate him.

That even, unthinkably, his Master might step aside . . .

Already the surface of the bird was drying, white patches upon the gray clay. He moved carefully, head bent over his burden, hands cradled under the linen shawl on which the creation lay.

He had passed, has passed, shall have passed this way, it seemed, an infinite number of times. Grown not weary, but charged with desire. He believed that he saw things a heartbeat before his Master. He could always predict now what the Master would do. He could, he felt, do it all himself. But there was, is, shall be no end to apprenticeship.

If by a miracle the Master upheld this piece. If it were glazed and fired (with his hand's part in each stage) and then brought from the kiln and approved. If it were given breath and released into Time, would he also be chosen? Be given Masterhood, his own space to be filled in the Fabric, his own atelier?

He crossed the courtyard, where water played and the light danced over the form he carried. Other apprentices heard him crooning to himself. He was sure it was perfect. As nearly perfect as could be allowed.

He longed for change. His footfalls echoed as he passed again into the cloisters' covered walkway. That his potential be realized, that he be given power. An eternity of discipline, patience, obedience. The inflexible system. Dreaming was his only exercise of freedom, and without freedom how could there be creation?

But he loved the work more than himself. He knew that his dreams might tarnish its perfection, and even as he reproved himself he realized that the Master had forgotten—yes, forgotten to mar the piece; had omitted the last, vital, minute stroke of damage (an elbow-nudge, thumb-smear, or nail-stroke), the refusal of perfection that was Life's hallmark.

The inner exultation was so great that his limbs went cold. He turned his face from the others who watched him pass. The Master had faltered. He carried a perfect creature, and only he knew it, and his own ambition was the vital flaw in it. It *would* be chosen.

Trembling, he hurried inside, and at the drying-hall's threshold he tripped, trips, shall forever be tripping, clutching the doorway and swivelling inwards as the precious cargo flew out upon the floor into ruin.

The sound of an egg at the end of its fall from the nest. The aroma of kneaded clay.

He fell on his knees. The apprentices of the place came hurrying over, the hall rippled with their laughter, the laughter that heals by commending inexperience. He was laughing too.

But the bird was cracked open, misshapen, smudged. The intricate mass that packed its interior was split into many fragments. Just one of the eggs rolled away in a wide, unsteady circle, and a new apprentice retrieved it and handed it back, solemn-eyed.

He wrapped it in the linen shawl and left the hall, while they swept up the broken clay. For them, just another small accident.

He stood in an empty corridor, refusing to accept the loss, his failure, the merciful eyes of his Master. The egg was intact. The linen shawl held the imprint of the bird's wing.

He passed through the walls into nothingness and at once began to conjure the landscape: that part of the Fabric—multiform, manifold—which was their province.

Around him, out of a mist, grew a scattering of birch trees. Stones jutted, moss-cloaked, from the sparse earth. Bracken ferns rustled, flies boomed, there was thyme and mint in the air, and a hill-stream rushed through.

Beyond the trees there was open moorland and low cliffs, with heather and lonely thorntrees, quaking cotton-grasses, a wide sky. A hare limped past, a family of chickadees went overhead, fawn-breasted, flying and calling in bouncing flurries. A larksong cascaded high overhead, a raven's cry echoed across the cliffs.

He breathed in the essence of the waiting land. The color, light, perfume—the colors most of all, blended and cherished by the evening sun: wet rocks, a wavering plume of water, late snowpatches on the fells, the haze of whin, heather, stone. And in all this a vacancy: a longed-for cry, energy, talons, a whistle of wings.

He closed his eyes, and passed back through the living walls. The bells were silent, the atelier dreamed with the Master, and the wheelhouse was empty.

But when the clay was wedged and centered a terrible doubt possessed him. The place was haunted by himself and his Master. He stood empty; self-consciousness chilled the room. The knowledge, he knew, was there in his hands and his heart, but he felt like a novice.

He moved through the room, rehearsing the very first lessons, so long absorbed that they seemed a forgotten language.

The snake foundation, the spinal ridge. The left hand right hand blueprint of symmetry laid down for all animals. The harmonic balances (the high-left heart, the low-right liver). The skin. The seam. Transpiration.

He remembered the yearning moorlands. Imaged his hands as a bird's beak, weaving a nest of heather-stems, bents and sheepswool in the lee of a granite boulder. He heard the whistling cry that would knit the sky's fabric together. Felt the wings in the back of his mind. He bent over the wheel.

When the bells started in again, softly, to the fountain's dance, he was back in the drying-hall, greeting the new apprentices with the bird in his hands.

The Falcon shifted on its branch. A pair of crows swooped round the tree, mocking, but it ignored them. Even when they perched beside it, bobbing and scolding. They saw themselves mirrored in the abstracted eyes and grumbled uneasily, abandoning their sport to drop down the hillside, in long slow glides towards the valley floor.

The Master stood to the right of the table, his assistant to the left. The bird lay between them. On the surface all was symmetry: the apprentice's brush mirrored the Master's exactly. Their shadings blended over the seam. They finished the wings, painting so exactly in unison that the Master laughed in delight. There was singing out in the halls. Sometimes the apprentice seemed almost to anticipate; the Master might have been following his pupil.

The bird came through the fire unflawed. "It is perfect" said the Master "Isn't it?" For a moment his eyes looked teasingly into his pupil's, and then he held up the creation for the gathered apprentices. "It is finished" he said quietly, smiling, and turned to unlock the window on Time.

He held the bird out. It shuddered upon his hand. Its eyes opened and it stared back in for a moment, black brilliant mirrors.

Its tail quivered, and it slipped from the Master's hand, flying fast through the element, its wingtips shaping a tunnel of light. The wingbeats came echoing back like the laughter of children, and filled the atelier.

The Falcon woke, looked out and, in a flickering instant, was gone round the hillside into the hunter's light.

The Master stepped back from the window and held up his hands. And he laughed, laughs, shall always be laughing at the way of it.

GRETEL EHRLICH

Time on Ice 1992

GRETEL EHRLICH (b. 1946) was born in California, educated at UCLA
Film School, went to Wyoming in the mid-1970s to write a film, and ended
up staying; there, she and her husband took up cattle-ranching near Shell, in
the north-central part of the state. The transition from urban film-writer to
rancher is brilliantly delineated in *The Solace of Open Spaces* (1985): "Living
with animals," she writes, "makes us redefine our ideas about intelligence."
As this essay shows, traveling in the Canadian Arctic has more or less the
same effect. Ehrlich is also the author of two books of poetry—*Geode/Rock
Body* (1970) and *To Touch the Water* (1981)—the novel *Heart Mountain* (1988),
and a second collection of stories, *Islands, the Universe Home* (1991). "Time
on Ice" first appeared in *Harper's* magazine.

ᏋᎧ • ᎧᏋ

THE READING we just took says the wind has stiffened to twenty knots. Fog
comes and goes. It was a hole in the fog through which my plane descended
this afternoon; now, at midnight, I'm looking up from seven-foot-thick ice
and see sun circling like a necklace, a halo, a draw-string that pulls tight entrances to the body of sky and earth.

Later, I press my face into an *aglu,* which is what the Inuit call a seal's
breathing hole. I peer down past the lair—a snow cave where a seal bears her
pups in spring—and past empires of turquoise ice into black, into the 500-
foot-deep universe of the Arctic Ocean.

I'm in the north Canadian Arctic, ten miles from Cornwallis Island on the
frozen waters of Barrow Strait—1,000 miles from the North Pole—at the
camp of my friend Brendan Kelly, an American research biologist affiliated
with the University of Alaska. Brendan is completing a doctorate at Purdue

University, studying and writing about the evolution and behavior of ringed seals, the most common type of seal found in the Arctic. When Brendan came here in March, on a National Science Foundation grant, the nights were forty, fifty below zero. Now, in May, it's balmy at ten above, and when snow comes it's so icy it sounds like sugar scouring the 16' x 20' Parcoll tent Brendan shares with his assistant, William Stortz—a carpenter in Alaska when he's not pursuing ringed seals—and two black labradors Brendan has trained to sniff out seals under the snow.

Here, at the top of the world, clouds sweep down so low the landscape appears flattened, as if Earth were clamped by a vise. I sleep on water, walk on water, dream on water—albeit frozen. The top seven or eight feet of Barrow Strait freeze each September and stay frozen until mid-June. To the north of us are the numerous Queen Elizabeth Islands—brown, rocky outcrops in a world of ephemeral ice.

In the Arctic, one day is six months long followed by one night. Time as we know it—divided into darkness and light, sleep and wakefulness—does not exist here. Rather, it keeps stretching from brightness to brightness, shuttered out only by occasional, arbitrary human sleep.

At 2:00 A.M. we eat dinner: steaks. Brie, pilot bread, and mushy potatoes that have frozen, thawed, and refrozen several times. Our dinner music, courtesy of numerous microphones on the ice, is the sound of seals breathing as they come up from the cold Arctic waters to rest in their lairs. Near us as we eat, one of the five laptop computers powered by a photovoltaic panel calculates and diagrams the depth and frequency of seals' dives—ultrasonic pulses transmitted from seal to laptop via "pingers" (acoustic transmitters) that Brendan has attached to their fur and hydrophones he has set in the water.

Outside, fog is followed by frost fall. At 6:00 A.M. the sun is in the northwest. Clouds come from the west, then the south. Planes of light break ice into dazzling white lines, gray troughs, blue mirages in which distant island cliffs rise double-decked.

After breakfast William and Brendan start working on a new net design. The idea is to live-catch seals in their lairs, bring them to the tent, attach pingers to them, and release them into the water where they were found. Tall, big-boned, with a curly head of hair and deep-set Arctic blue eyes, Brendan is one of the few researches who retrieve seals this way.

But all week, Brendan tells me, the seals have been coming up into the nets and escaping. Back to the drawing board: Brendan designs, William executes. Two new nets with hoop-skirts hang from the ceiling and, needle and thread in hand, William sews an intricate, revised set of pulleys and alarms into the white folds.

Brendan has studied ice-breeding seals in the Bering Sea, in the Beaufort Sea, and in Barrow Strait, as well as walruses in the Chukchi Sea. Fifteen years ago he began coming to the Arctic in the spring to study ringed seals. "So little is known about them because they spend most of their lives under the ice," he says.

Late one afternoon we leave the tent to set one of the new nets, packing it gently in a komatik—a long sled—pulled behind a snowmobile. The black labs race ahead of our machines, veering off suddenly whenever the whiff of seal lures them but coming back to show us the way.

The entrance to this *aglu* is vagina-shaped; we squeeze the net in, careful not to set off any triggers that would cause the purse string at the bottom to draw tight. A hydrophone is lowered down, and we head back to the tent to wait until the seal swims in.

Before reaching camp, somewhere out on the expanse of ice, we stop and walk: clear sky, rising temperature, blocks of rough ice sticking up like great blue crystals or teeth that have been knocked out and left behind. Snow under our feet glitters in cold sun. Griffith Island is a lean arm of white against miles of powder blue. Brendan tells me that this blue is the result of the Tyndall effect: short wave-lengths of light that have been scattered by air bubbles or particles.

Another midnight dinner listening to seals' deep breathing. If a seal swims up into the net, she'll set off an alarm that we'll hear. Nothing yet. Only the intimate sounds of a mother seal, then her baby, and the sound of scratching as they abrade the ice at the edge of the breathing hole to keep it open. All night in sleep there is the white noise of receivers and the sounds of seals mixing with our human sounds; all night the sun shines.

On my fourth day in camp Brendan and William cut a large hole in the ice with chain saws, pulling blocks out with giant tongs. Eighty-four inches down through ice, then the black Arctic sea. A tent goes over it. "This is the poolside suite," Brendan announces, hoping a seal will use it as a breathing hole and visit us while we're in bed. Then we lay sleeping bags around the hole. A jellyfish rises to the surface. Looking down, I can see where ice ends and darkness begins: It's like looking past the edge of our universe, and I wonder what kind of seeing this is. We sleep lightly, but no seal comes.

In the morning it is so warm the meat in the food cache is in danger of thawing. William and I build an icebox using blocks lifted from the seal hole.

It's an arduous task, like building an igloo, mortaring ice with snow. Around us surface ice begins to melt: all the blue of the world is here, even if there isn't any such thing as blue.

From time to time I stop in the middle of a small task and glass the horizon with binoculars. North of here a big chunk of ice calved off Ellesmere Island floats in a southwestern arc; it is big enough to be inhabited by a research team that simply goes with the flow and reports back where that current takes them. In this way, too, I follow the wayward arc my thoughts make and see how easily they are lost—ephemeral on ephemeral ice.

Sleep again, then an alarm sewn into one of the nets is triggered by a seal. We leap up, fumbling our clothes; put on overalls, caps, gloves; jump onto snowmobiles; and race to the lair. (There are at this time four nets set—four lairs among hundreds being monitored.) "It would kill me if I drown a seal in one of my nets," Brendan says. (It happened one time.) He probes the *aglu* with a blunt, long-handled pole: no seal. Blocking the hole with his face, he peers in: the bottom of the net is open. The seal has come and gone; the purse line didn't close.

The temperature plummets. Our fingers and feet are numb. Back at camp, we eat bacon, potatoes, and cheese biscuits, drink coffee, and redesign the net. Brendan's silences—perhaps born of so many years on the ice—seem sad. I read Chukchi shaman tales (beautifully translated by Howard Norman) about ghost-laden kayaks, seal hunts that go badly, caribou skins that talk in the night. As the wind picks up everything talks, everything is alive. The walls of our tent talk over our talking, everything living talks to everything dead, and polar-bear skins walk at night on red ice where they hunted seals.

The next day Brendan and I set out for the Inuit village of Resolute, on Cornwallis Island. Scooting fast across ice, we come to a three-foot crack—a flaw or lead where shore-fast ice has broken from ice that moves with the tides. I get off and Brendan "jumps" the snowmobile over the opening, but when I jump, one leg slides in and there is that terrible moment when I know I've done something stupid. As Brendan turns to see what's wrong, I claw my way to safety. He merely grins and we ride on.

I spot sled dogs—huskies—chained to posts and gnawing on seal and dog carcasses. We weave through them, Brendan's labs peering bashfully from the komatik. Up through the boneyard into the village: maybe fifty houses newly sided with bright vinyl. It's late afternoon and the young men are packing up their sleds to go seal hunting: caribou skins for warmth, food, gasoline for the snowmobiles, and rifles which replace the harpoons they once used.

In 1953 seventeen Inuit—mostly caribou hunters from Baffin Island and Inoucdjouac in northern Quebec—were brought to Cornwallis Island to plant the Canadian flag and live on its barren slopes and frozen seas. They were the first inhabitants of the island since the Thule people had been driven out by the Little Ice Age 500 years before. It is not a hospitable place: Almost nothing grows except for the lichen that grinds away at sedimentary rock. The new settlers were 1,000 miles north of their previous home, and while they had volunteered to move some later asked to be sent home. Now 770,000 square miles of the Northwest Territories, including Cornwallis, have been given over to the Inuit, who are calling the area Nunavut, meaning "our land." It is theirs, except they will hold mineral rights to only 14,000 square miles.

We drive through rows of small clapboard houses. In one yard polar-bear skins are stretched from wooden frames, and in another two whale-bone jaws rest against a wall. There's a clinic, a school, a general store. Two children, their faces hidden behind their dog-ruff hoods, want to ride in the komatic with the dogs, and we let them. Women in long dresses pass, carrying babies on their backs, flashing their beautiful ear-to-ear smiles. Looking back at Resolute from the top of a hill, I'm astonished that any people have survived at all in this realm.

Prevailing winds circle with the sun. I feel gusts in my face, then behind me, and the clouds take the sky from all sides like a flower closing at the end of the day; snowflakes drift, sun makes long shadows lean out of ice floes. Brendan locks his legs around me as we fly across the landscape, then we stop at a sizable chunk of multi-year ice (ice that formed two or more winters ago, ice that has not melted seasonally) and chip blocks to take home and melt for drinking water. I look for polar bears. Three weeks before, Brendan tells me, one strolled by with her cub and took a bite out of his tent. Now three eider ducks fly by, low to the ground, and far out where our tent is but a tiny orange speck, the mirage of a blue lagoon shimmers.

Wash dishes, empty slop bucket, melt ice, heat water for tea, bake cookies in our tiny, unevenly heated propane oven, feed the beloved dogs. Brendan logs in data: the time and duration of a seal coming into a lair, its position under the ice, the length and duration of dives. But what does this tell us about a seal's life? What is the seal thinking, dreaming? "How to understand what we know, how to find the patterns that connect, that's a question too infrequently asked—especially by scientists," Brendan says ruefully. "We're so backward. Some of my colleagues are still arguing over whether animals even have a consciousness."

Late one night, after a dinner of roast lamb, rice tinted yellow with bottled lemon juice, and watery wine out of a cardboard box, the weather changes. Low clouds to the south undulate over Somerset Island, thickly amassed, like the notation of some unearthly music. Heat waves shiver upward from the ice. Where cracks have appeared, the sky darkens, reflecting water. "Water sky" it is called, used by the Inuit to find leads in ice where seals will be basking.

The wind comes while we are asleep: toolboxes and books falling off shelves wake us. The whole tent shudders, the windward side collapsing into the room. Brendan runs outside in underwear to pee and jumps back in quickly, blasted white with snow. "Life in 'the attic,' ain't it grand!" he says gleefully. The laces that pull the tent panels together begin to stretch apart. Wind intensifies, snow drifts against us. We put on more layers of clothes and huddle around mugs of coffee.

The alarm goes off; seal in hole number 3. Brendan and William dig out a snowmobile while I gather equipment, and we race into the wind. Snow has turned to ice; it cuts our faces as we fly.

A small seal, which Brendan identifies as a male yearling, sticks his nose into the air, greeting us. "Hi, sweetheart," Brendan coos, picking him up under the pectoral flippers and laying him on the snow. "How about a little ride in the komatik?" The seal is frightened. Brendan and William struggle to lift him into the box on the sled.

A seals' nose is shaped like a Y; the nostrils close watertight after intakes of breath. His whiskers are translucent and beaded. Puffy cheeks, wet gray rings around soft eyes—no tear ducts. As his coat dries, he is silvery with black rings spotting the fur. A pungent smell fills the tent. "He's been eating cod," Brendan says.

When we try to attach the pinger by dabbing a small circle of fur with glue, the yearling seal gets scrappy. Brendan gets bitten on the thighs. William and I stop everything to clean the wound—seal bites are known to cause infections.

"What do their mothers do to calm them?" I ask.

"They scratch the baby's back with their claws," Brendan says, so I rake my fingernails across his back; he flips over and I scratch his chest too. His eyes close; he shoves his head into one corner of the box and sleeps, front flippers twitching once in a while like a sleeping baby's hands.

By 6:00 P.M. the young seal is back in the water, pinger attached. The storm has worsened. To get back from the lair to the tent I walk in front of the snowmobile following what I think are the tracks, though I'm not sure.

"That's where dogs come in handy," Brendan says. "They leave their mark along the trail and it shows up even in blizzards."

Now our reading tells us that the wind is at forty-five knots and gusting to sixty. The nylon lacings that hold the tent panels together are tearing. We draw them tighter. All the shelves—with tools, five laptop computers, receivers, transmitters, charged batteries, books, charts, and maps—have to be pulled into the center of the room. And the tall antenna toe-nailed to the tent's wooden floor and sticking up through the ceiling is listing perilously. It could bring the whole tent down if it goes, William says, so Brendan climbs the curved outside wall of the tent and lowers the metal pole.

The noise makes sleep impossible. "What will happen if the wind gets worse?" I ask as we lie side by side on the floor—dogs and humans, all in sleeping bags. "The tent will blow away and we might die of exposure," Brendan says, then smiles. "But we probably won't."

Then we sleep. In the morning the landscape is totally changed. Snow has buried all traces of life and topography: snowmobiles, komatiks, food caches, skis, ice floes—all gone. Snow drifts in wide fans like sand dunes. The wind ebbs, then gusts to sixty-five knots again. The plane I was supposed to take to Montreal does not land. Our two-way radio goes dead. Contact with Jerry McEachern, who calls faithfully every evening from Shelf—shorthand for the Polar Continental Shelf Project, a research base set up by the Canadian government—is lost. I can't see Cornwallis or the buildings at Shelf when I go out to pee. Turning away from the wind, my backside is sandblasted by flying ice crystals.

Three days go by. The tent breathes in and out. It is like living in someone else's lung. Finally the wind subsides. I walk far away from the tent to see what I can see. Snow has drifted in steep, smooth walls streaming back from rough ice, and where ice is blown clear of snow, it is pale blue. We poke in drifted snow to find things, then digging begins. The engines and cowlings of snowmobiles we unearth have to be thoroughly cleaned.

Brendan drives me to Shelf to see about getting a plane out. It is so warm suddenly that we don't bother with jackets. The skis of the snowmobile splash through meltwater. Jerry has arranged for me to get on the first flight that can get up here. I'm shocked, when I look at the calendar, to see we are well into the first week of June. After a much-cherished shower we start back to camp. Looking out over Barrow Strait past Cape Martyr, around Sheringham Point toward Allen Bay, I see the floor of the world has turned blue; only the islands are white.

By afternoon many small cracks have appeared in the ice beneath us, some straight, some zigzagging. The dogs approach cautiously, then leap wide. The white massifs of grounded ice floes, which from a distance look like tall masted schooners, shelter cerulean ponds. Blue earth merges with blue sky, every hue pale and delicate. We pass two kill sites where polar bears not long ago feasted on seals: circles of blood and fur and a bashed-in lair. Bear scats are topped off with Arctic fox scats. The glory of ice becoming sea again fills my eyes: it is like skating over the blue iris of an eye.

Two days later, at the tiny, crowded airport, Brendan and I sit wordlessly. Inuit women wait with their babies encircled by fur. They are going to other islands to visit relatives and once again live among caribou. Brendan's eyes blaze blue as ice. He will stay on until the meltwater reaches his knees and life from the frozen sea becomes impossible. "It seems as if I just get to know my way around when it all melts again," he says, and the old sadness comes back into his voice. There is nothing else to say. Then the plane, half cargo, half people, takes me away.

Two weeks later I hear from him. It has been raining in Resolute. Magnetic storms on the sun have disturbed radio contacts, and the planes are unable to land because their instruments don't work. The ice is going fast, he says. He's had to move onto the island. When I ask him what the landscape looks like now, there is a pause, then he says: "Yesterday a ship passed through the middle of the strait pushing ice with its bow. I watched it demolish what was left of the ice; it went right through where our tent used to be; where we lived is gone."

Acknowledgments

JOHN JAMES AUDUBON: from *Audubon and His Journals,* Volume I, by Maria R. Audubon, Dover Publications Inc., New York, and General Publishing, Toronto, 1960 and 1986, used by permission of the publisher. HENRY BESTON: from *The St. Lawrence,* Farrar & Rinehart Inc., New York and Toronto, © 1942 by Henry Beston. FRED BODSWORTH: from *The Last of the Curlews,* Dodd Mead & Co., New York, 1954, and McClelland & Stewart (New Canadian Library), Toronto, 1963, used by permission of the author. JOHN BURROUGHS: from *Works of John Burroughs IV: Locusts and Wild Honey,* Houghton Mifflin Company, Boston and New York, © 1979, 1895, 1904, and 1907 by John Burroughs. GRETEL EHRLICH: "Time On Ice," from *Harper's Magazine,* March 1992. DON GAYTON: from *The Wheatgrass Mechanism: Science and Imagination in the Western Canadian Landscape,* Fifth House Publishers, Saskatoon, 1990, used by permission of the author and publisher. GREY OWL: from *Tales of an Empty Cabin,* Macmillan of Canada, 1936 and 1975, used by permission of the publisher. FREDERICK PHILIP GROVE: from *Over Prairie Trails,* McClelland & Stewart, Toronto, 1957, used by permission of A. Leonard Grove. RODERICK HAIG-BROWN: from *Writings and Reflections,* © 1982 by Ann Haig-Brown, McClelland & Stewart, Toronto, used by permission of the publisher and Harold Ober Associates, New York. SAMUEL HEARNE: from *A Journey to the Northern Ocean,* edited by Richard Glover, Macmillan of Canada, Toronto, 1958, used by permission of the publisher. H. ALBERT HOCHBAUM: from *Travels and Traditions of Waterfowl,* University of Minnesota Press, Minneapolis, 1955, used by permission of the publisher. HAROLD HORWOOD: from *Dancing on the Shore: A Celebration of Life at Annapolis Basin,* © Harold Horwood 1987, McClelland & Stewart, Toronto, and E. P. Dutton, New York, reprinted by arrangement with Bella Pomer Agency Inc. FLORENCE PAGE JAQUES: from *Canadian Spring,* Harper and Brothers, Publishers, New York and London, © 1947 by Francis Lee Jaques and Florence Lee Jaques. E. PAULINE JOHNSON: from *Legends of Vancouver,* Saturday Sunset Presses, Vancouver, 1913. PEHR KALM: from *Peter Kalm's Travels in North America: The English Version of 1770,* revised from the original Swedish by Adolph B. Benson, © 1934 and 1964 by Hannah N. Benson, Dover Publications Inc., New York, and General Publishing, Toronto, used by permission of the publisher. LOUISE DE KIRILINE LAWRENCE: from *To Whom the Wilderness Speaks,* Natural Heritage/Natural History Inc., 1989, used by permission of the publisher. R. D. LAWRENCE: from *In Praise of Wolves,* © 1986 by R. D. Lawrence, used by permission of Harper-Collins Publishers Ltd. in Canada and Henry Holt & Co. Inc. in the United States of America. ALDO LEOPOLD: from *Round River: From the Journals of Aldo Leopold,* Luna B. Leopold, ed., Oxford University Press, Oxford and New York, © 1993. BARRY LOPEZ: from *Arctic Dreams: Imagination and Desire in a Northern Landscape,* © 1986 by Barry Lopez, used by permission of Charles Scribner's Sons, an imprint of Macmillan Publishing Co. HUGH MACLENNAN: from *Seven Rivers of Canada,* Macmillan of Canada, 1961, Laurentian Library edition, 1977, used by permission of the estate of the late Hugh MacLennan. PETER MATTHIESSEN: from *Wildlife in America,* copyright © 1959, renewed 1987 by Peter Matthiessen, used by permission of Viking Penguin, a division of Penguin Books U.S.A. Inc. MERILYN SIMONDS MOHR: from *Harrowsmith* magazine, May 1991, used by permission of the author. FARLEY MOWAT: from *Never Cry Wolf,* McClelland & Stewart, Toronto, 1963, used by permission of the author. JOHN MUIR: from *Travels in Alaska,* Houghton Mifflin Company, Boston and New York, 1915. MARGARET MURIE: from *Two in the Far North,* Alfred A. Knopf, New York, 1962, used by permission of the author. SIGURD F. OLSON: from *The Lonely Land,* McClelland & Stewart Ltd., Toronto and Montreal, 1961. ROGER TORY PETERSON AND JAMES FISHER: from *Wild America: The Record of a 30,000-Mile Journey Around the Continent by a Distinguished Naturalist and His British Colleague,* Houghton Mifflin Company, Boston, © 1955 by Roger T. Peterson and James M. McConnell Fisher.

About the Editor

A former editor of *Harrowsmith* magazine, WAYNE GRADY has edited several previous anthologies, including *From the Country: About Rural Canada*, *The Penguin Book of Canadian Short Stories*, and *The Penguin Book of Modern Canadian Short Stories*.

Bright Stars, Dark Trees, Clear Water

was set in Bembo, a typeface based on the fine Venetian "old face" designs used throughout the sixteenth century. This version is based on the types first used by the Venetian scholar-publisher Aldus Manutius in the printing of *De Aetna*, written by Pietro Bembo and published in 1495. The original characters were cut in 1490 by Francesco Griffo, who, at Aldus's request, later cut the first italic book types. Originally adapted by the English Monotype Company, Bembo is one of the most elegant, readable, and widely used of all contemporary book faces.

The book was designed and composed by The Typeworks, Point Roberts, WA.